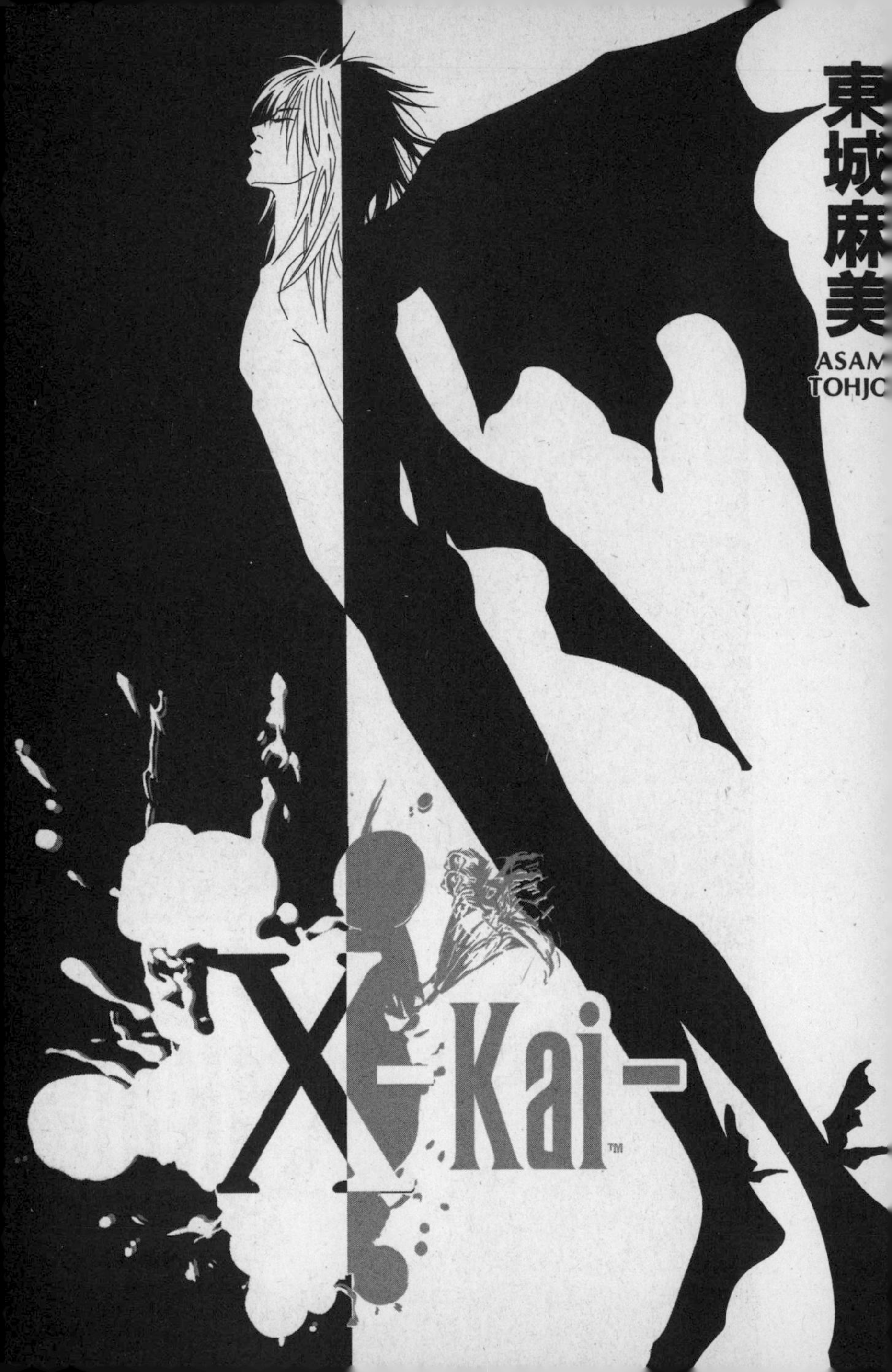
東城麻美
ASAM
TOHJO
X-Kai-™

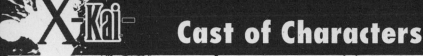

X-Kai- Cast of Characters

Kaito Yagami
Florist by day and assassin-for-hire by night, this quiet man seems to harbor deep secrets.

Sugaru
A mysterious beauty who brings top-secret assignments to Kaito.

Renge
A young boy who was rescued from the streets by Kaito and now lives with him.

The story so far:

Kaito lives two very different lives. During the day he runs a flower shop, but at night he is a cold-blooded mercenary killer. When the mysterious beauty Sugaru visits the flower shop with a secret assignment, Kaito carries out the assassination. As his signature he leaves a Casablanca lily, a flower for the dead.

One day, a serial murder case mimicking Kaito's methods makes the news. As Kaito seeks the real killer, he meets an innocent young boy named Renge, who has information that helps Kaito find the real killer. However, one of the killings still remains unsolved. Kaito discovers that Renge actually committed the murder, imitating Kaito's techniques. Kaito, who sees his younger self in the lonely Renge, swears to protect the boy so that he will never again have to stain his hands with blood. Kaito takes Renge under his wing and into his home.

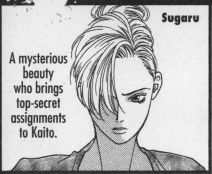

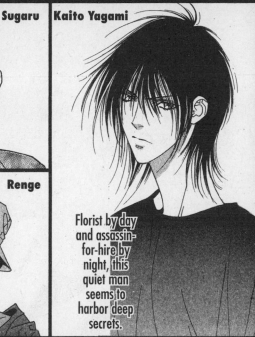

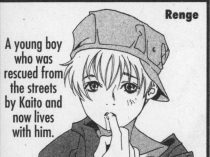

Secret 4

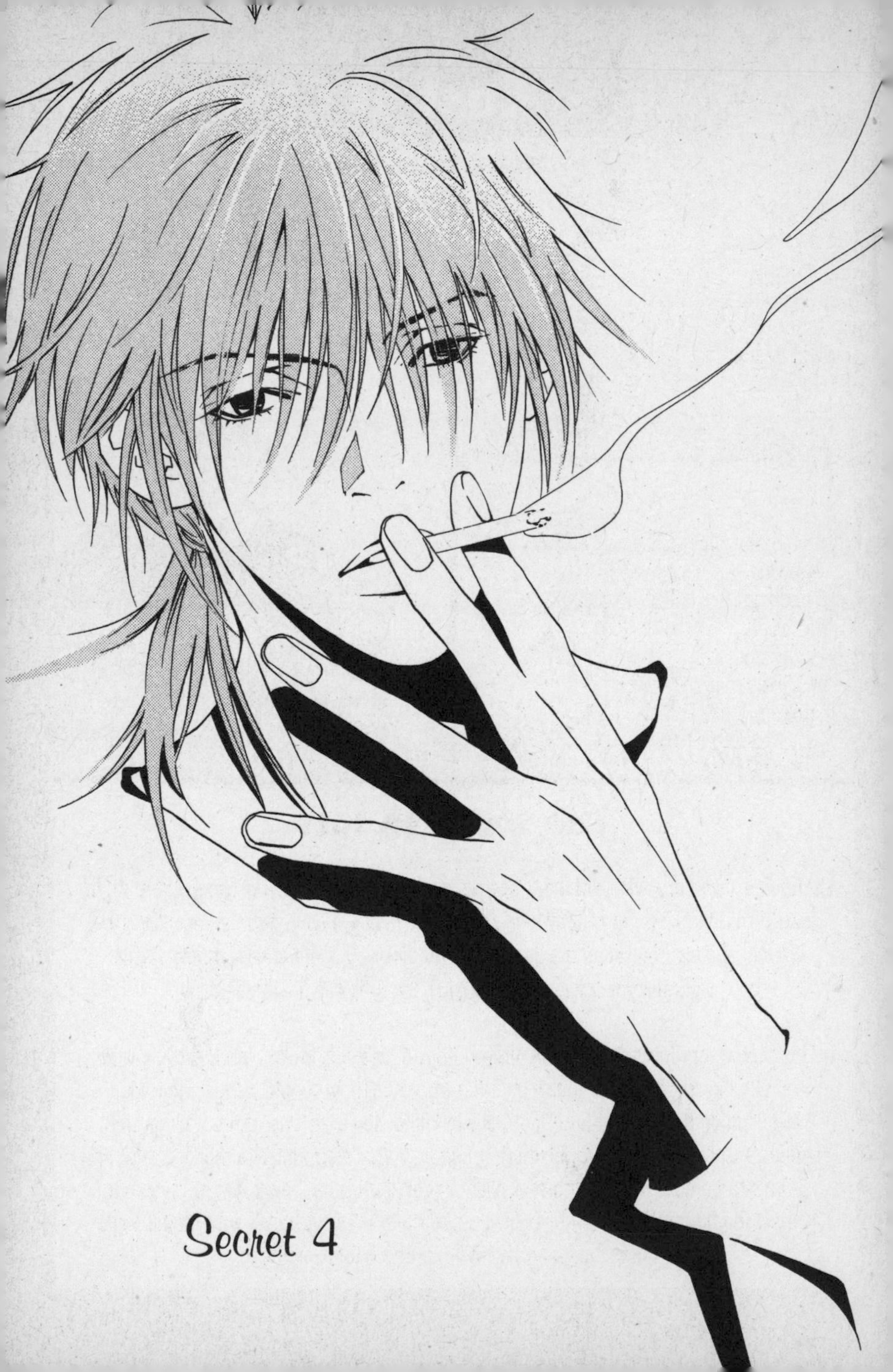

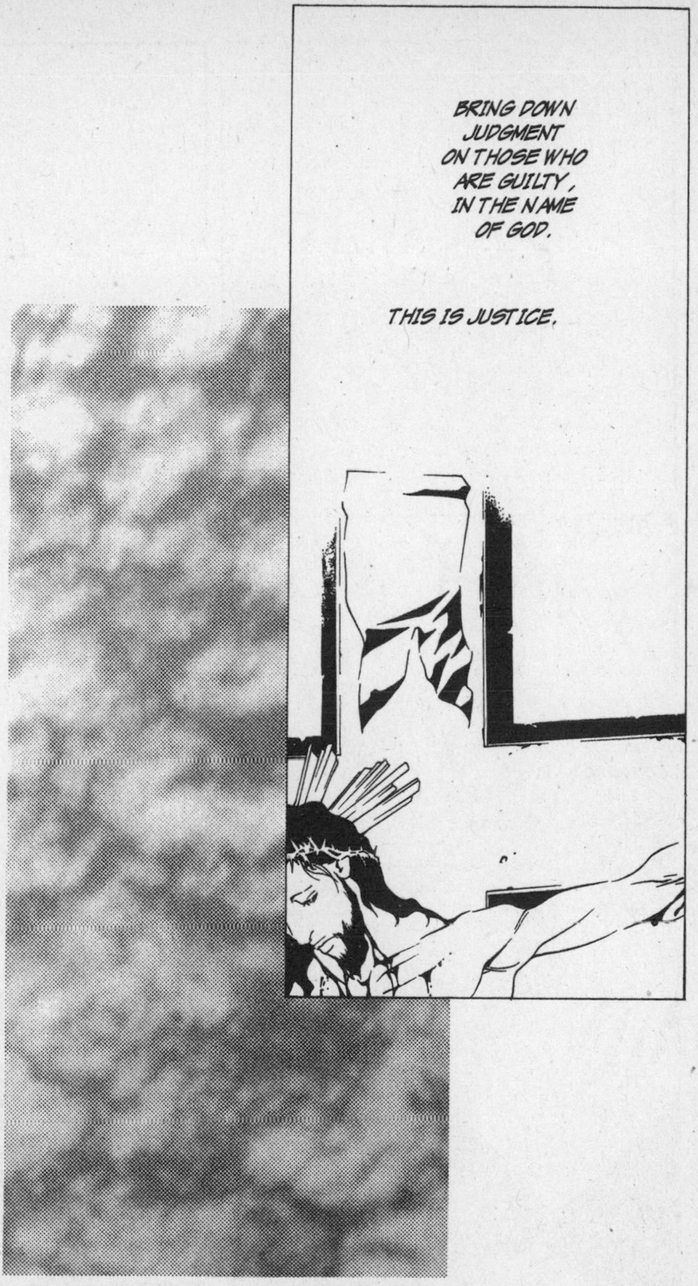
BRING DOWN JUDGMENT ON THOSE WHO ARE GUILTY, IN THE NAME OF GOD.
THIS IS JUSTICE.

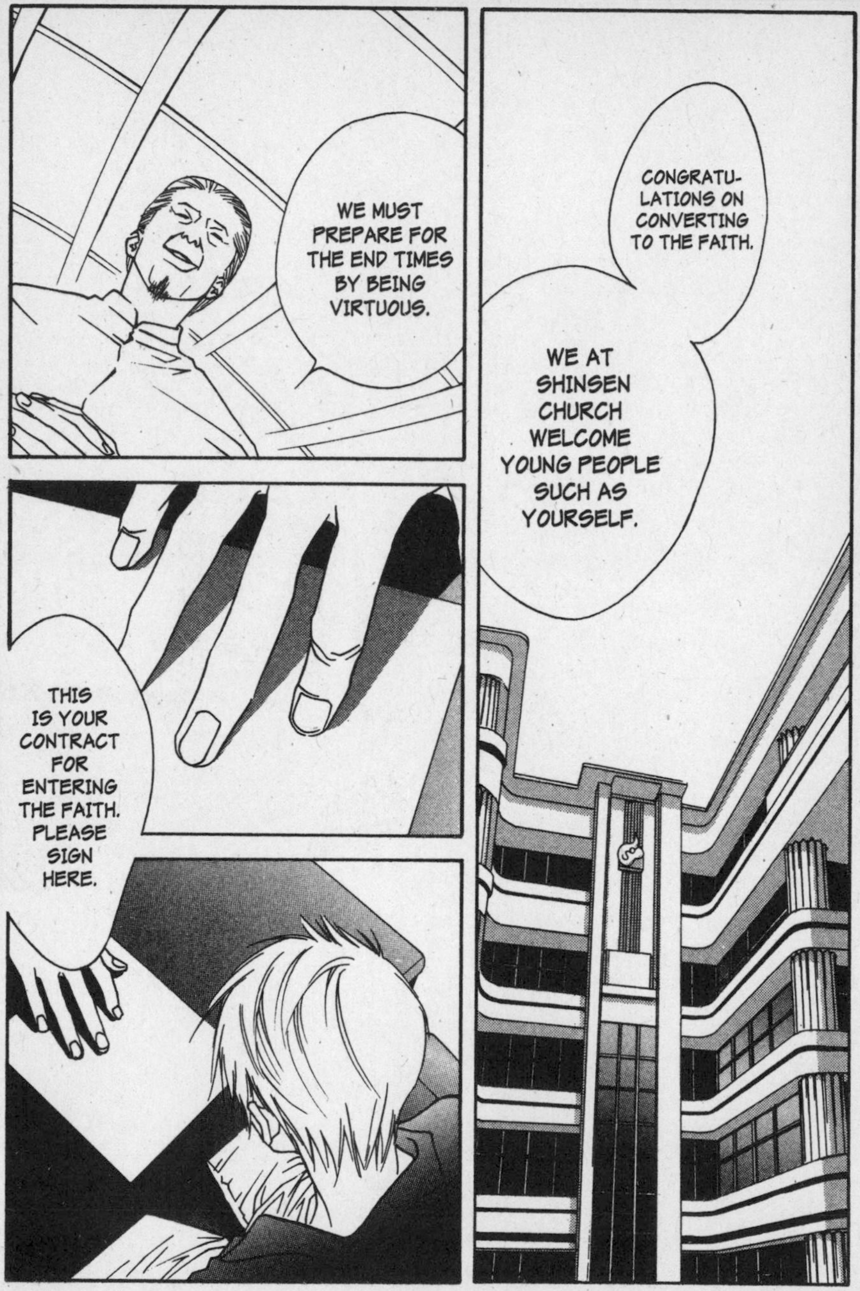
CONGRATU-LATIONS ON CONVERTING TO THE FAITH.
WE AT SHINSEN CHURCH WELCOME YOUNG PEOPLE SUCH AS YOURSELF.
WE MUST PREPARE FOR THE END TIMES BY BEING VIRTUOUS.
THIS IS YOUR CONTRACT FOR ENTERING THE FAITH. PLEASE SIGN HERE.

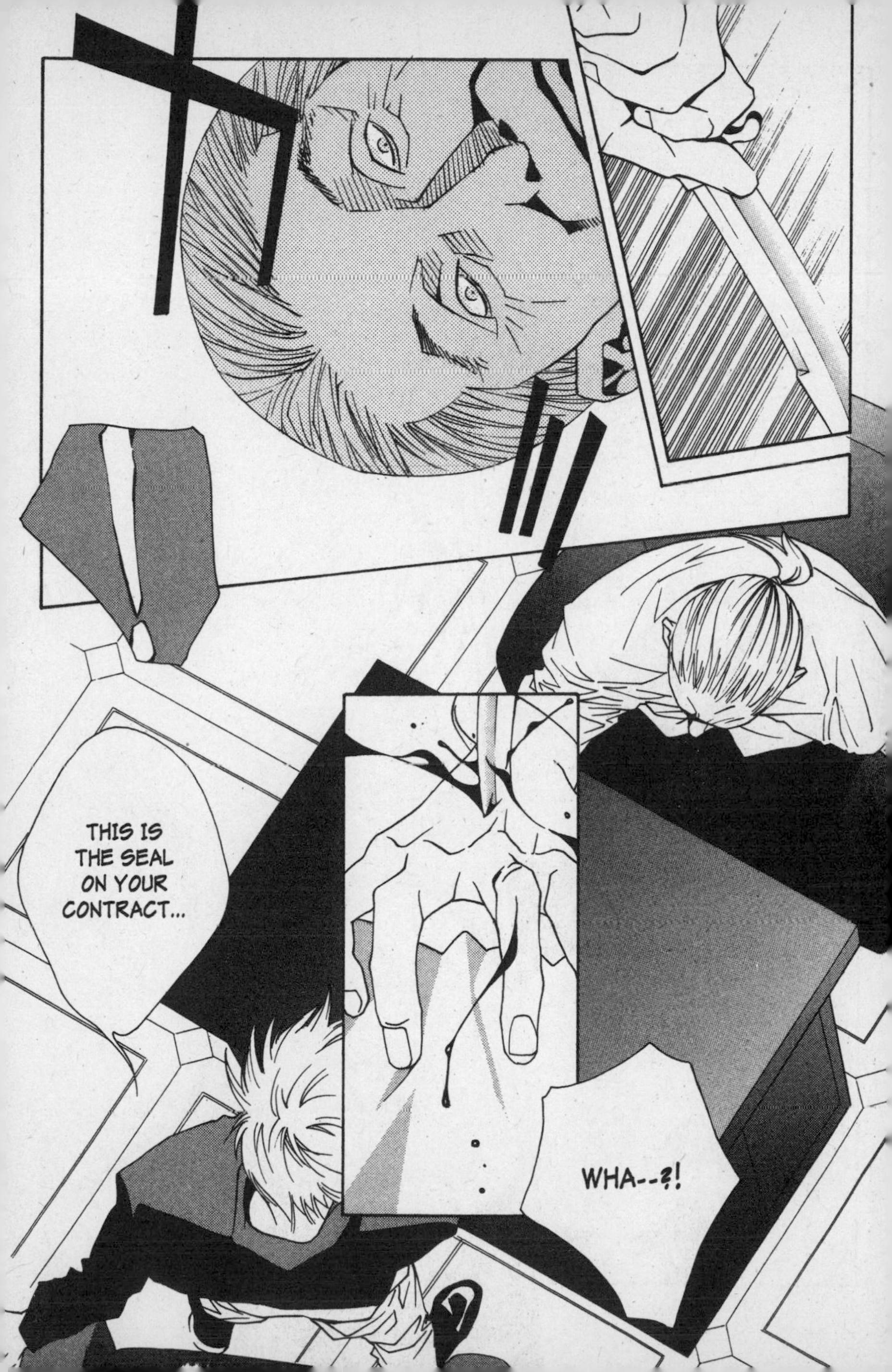
THIS IS THE SEAL ON YOUR CONTRACT...
WHA--?!

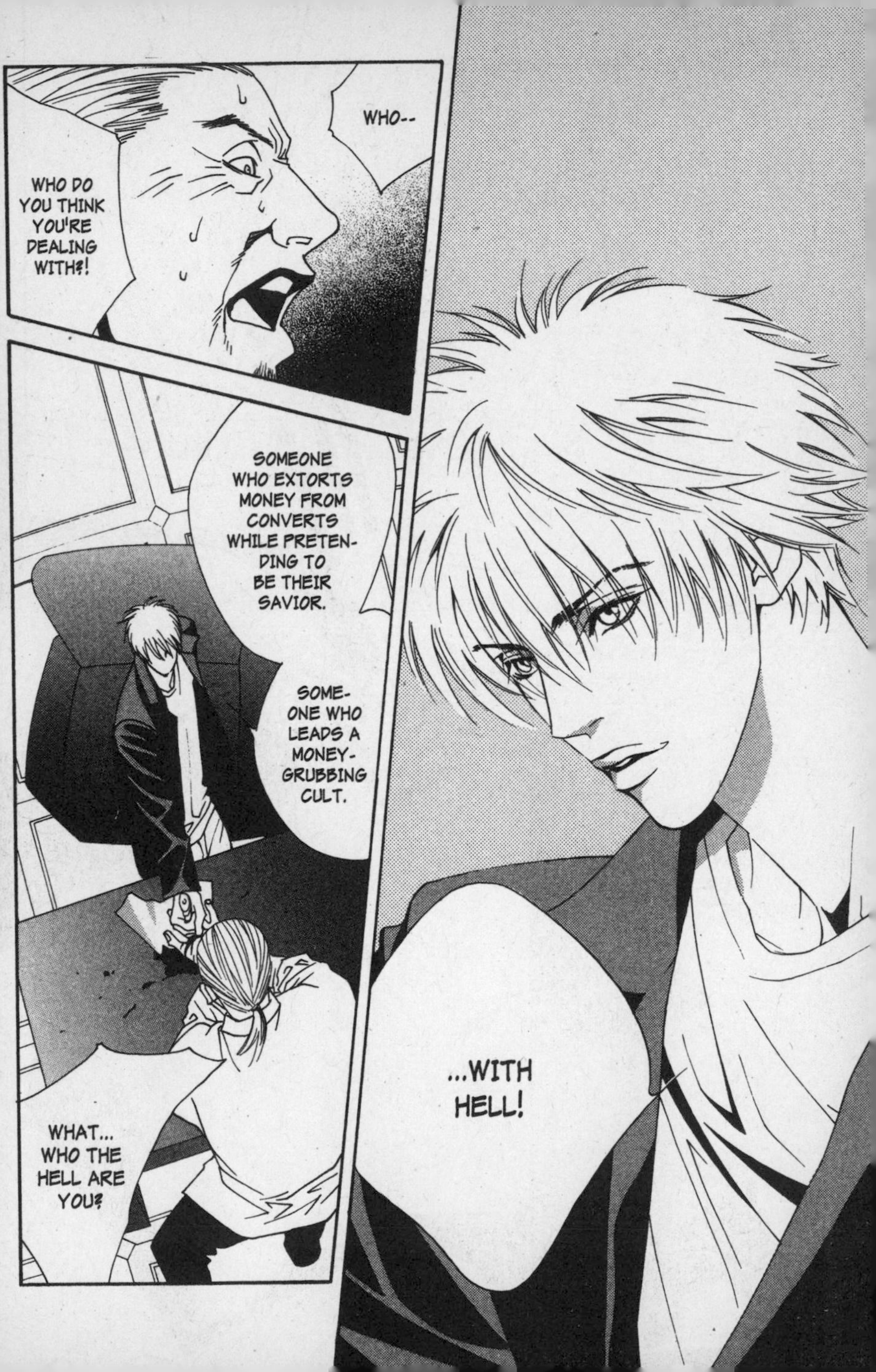
WHO--
WHO DO YOU THINK YOU'RE DEALING WITH?!
SOMEONE WHO EXTORTS MONEY FROM CONVERTS WHILE PRETEN-DING TO BE THEIR SAVIOR.
SOME-ONE WHO LEADS A MONEY-GRUBBING CULT.
WHAT... WHO THE HELL ARE YOU?
...WITH HELL!

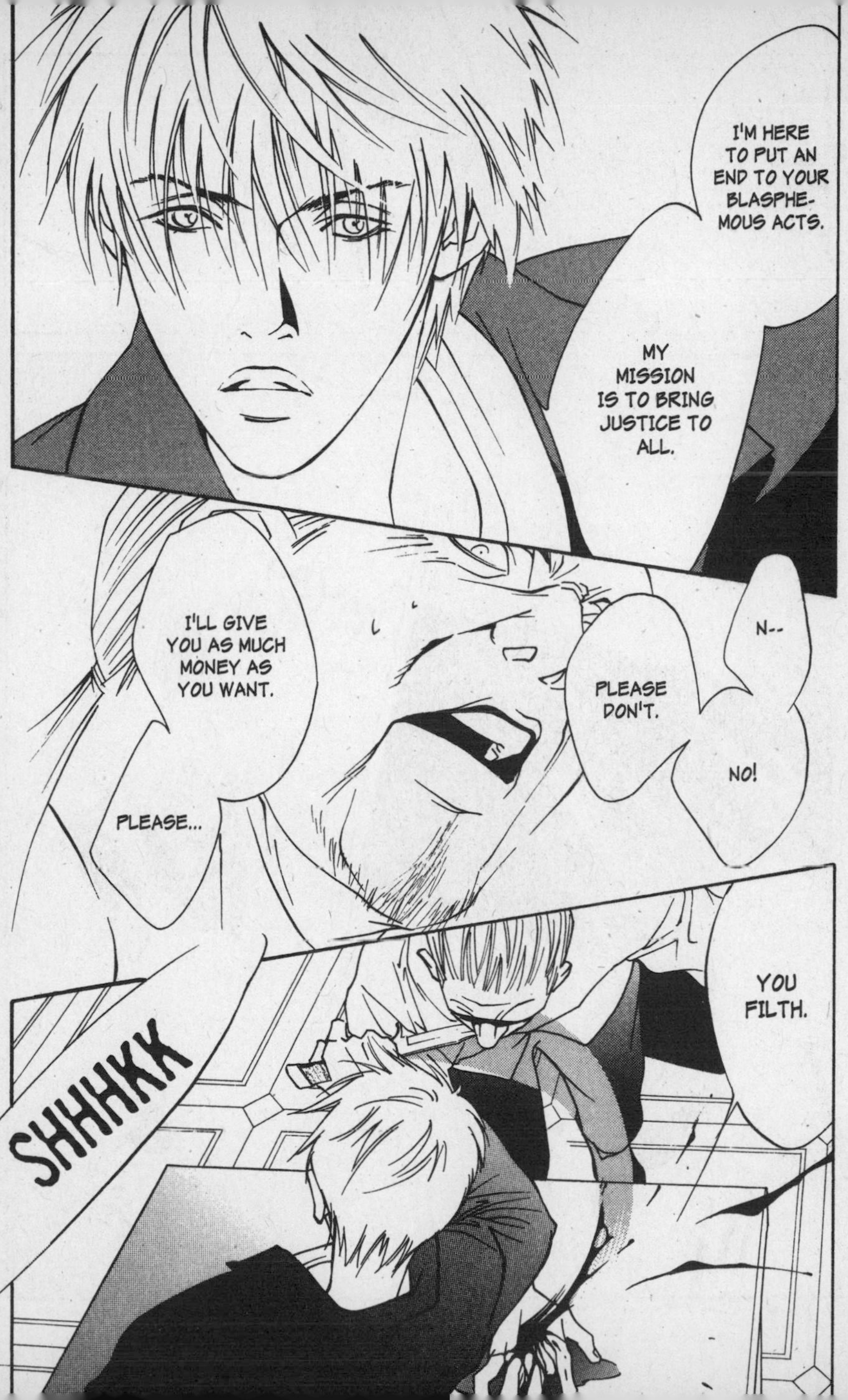
I'M HERE TO PUT AN END TO YOUR BLASPHE-MOUS ACTS.
MY MISSION IS TO BRING JUSTICE TO ALL.
N--
PLEASE DON'T.
NO!
I'LL GIVE YOU AS MUCH MONEY AS YOU WANT.
PLEASE...
YOU FILTH.
SHHHKK

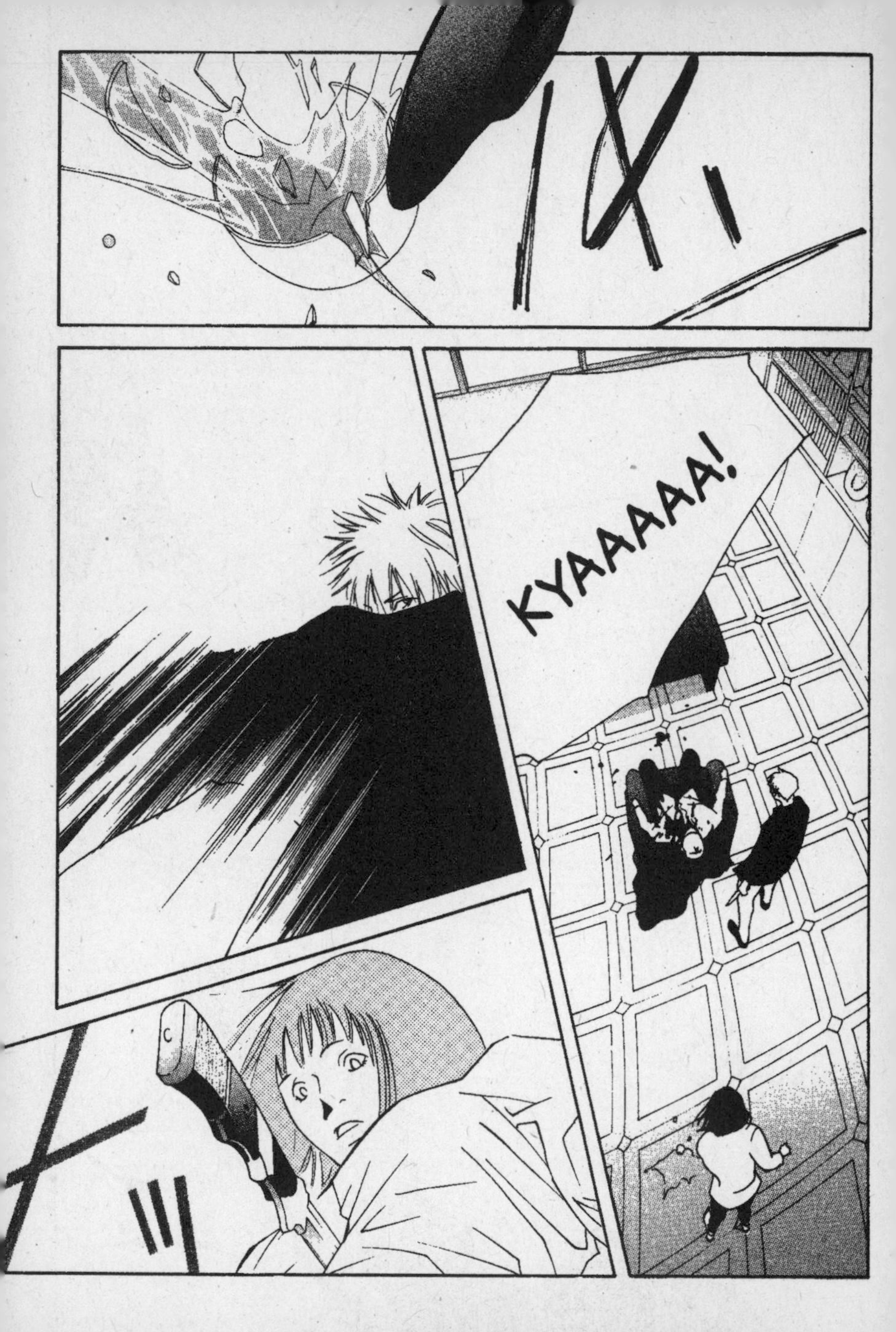
KYAAAAA!

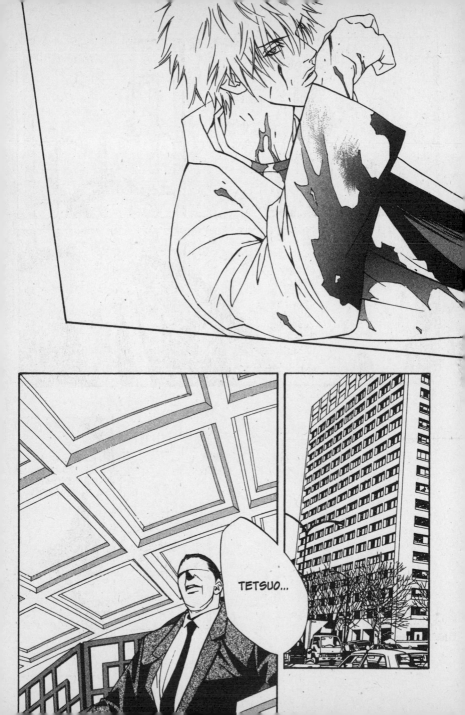

TETSUO...

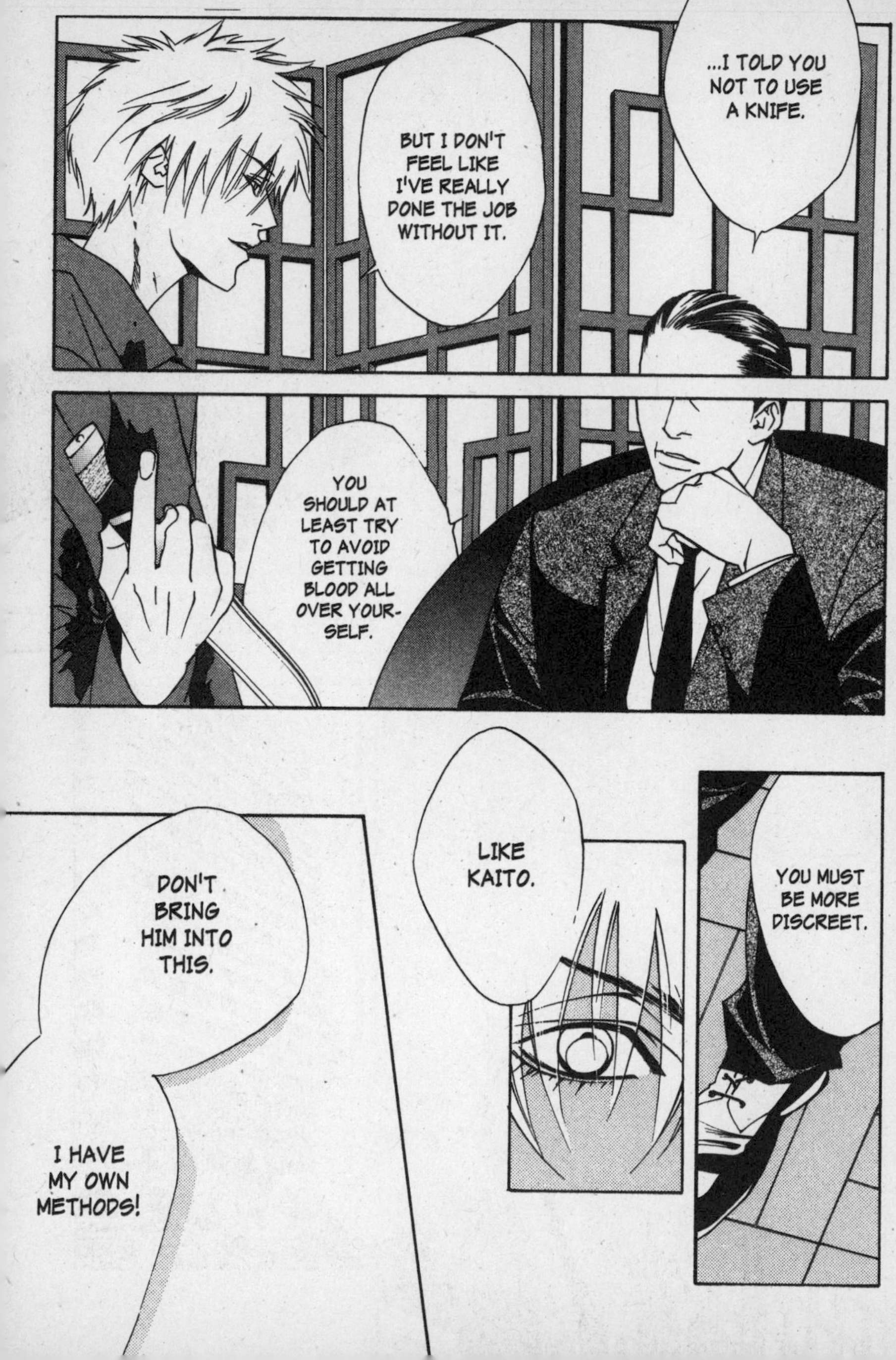
...I TOLD YOU NOT TO USE A KNIFE.
BUT I DON'T FEEL LIKE I'VE REALLY DONE THE JOB WITHOUT IT.
YOU SHOULD AT LEAST TRY TO AVOID GETTING BLOOD ALL OVER YOUR-SELF.
YOU MUST BE MORE DISCREET.
LIKE KAITO.
DON'T BRING HIM INTO THIS.
I HAVE MY OWN METHODS!

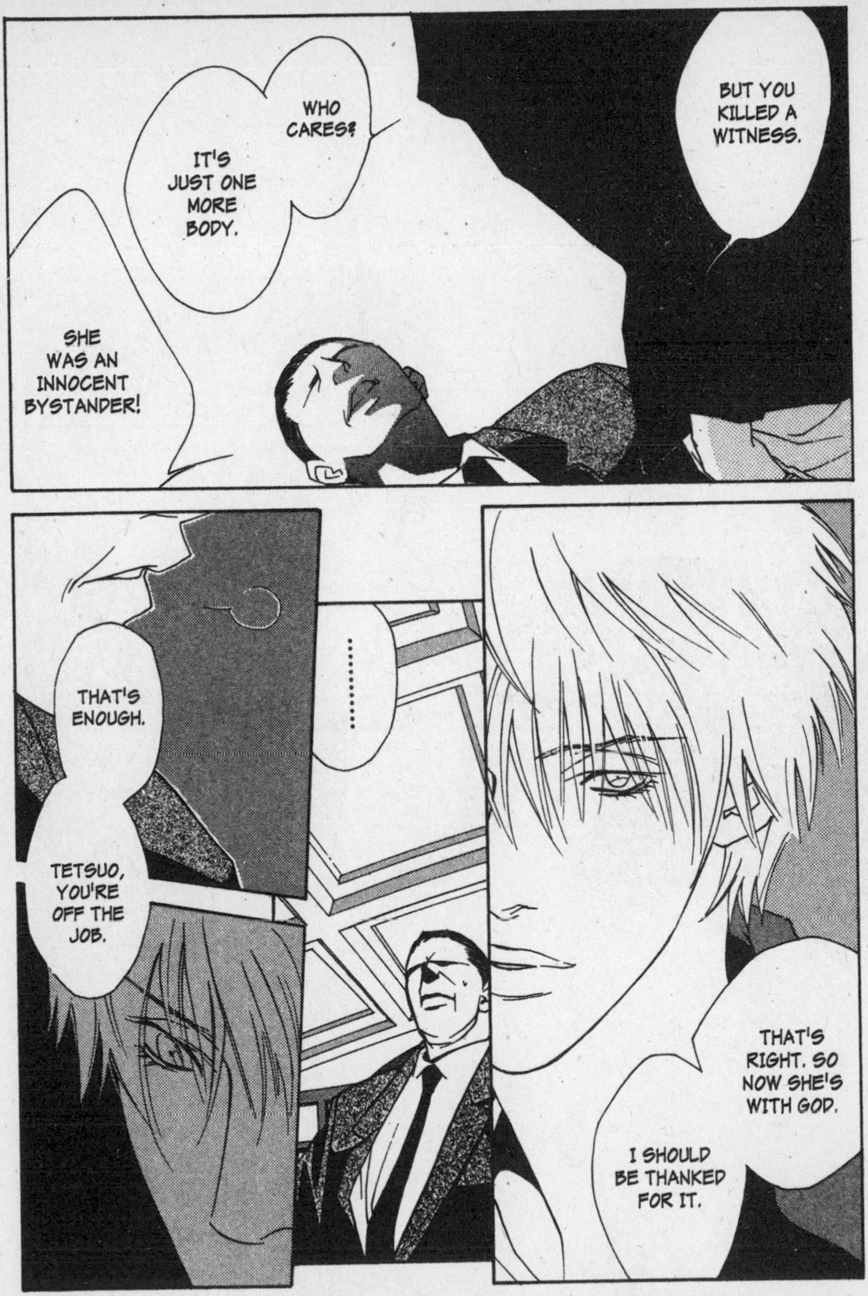
BUT YOU KILLED A WITNESS.
WHO CARES?
IT'S JUST ONE MORE BODY.
SHE WAS AN INNOCENT BYSTANDER!
THAT'S RIGHT. SO NOW SHE'S WITH GOD.
I SHOULD BE THANKED FOR IT.
....
THAT'S ENOUGH.
TETSUO, YOU'RE OFF THE JOB.

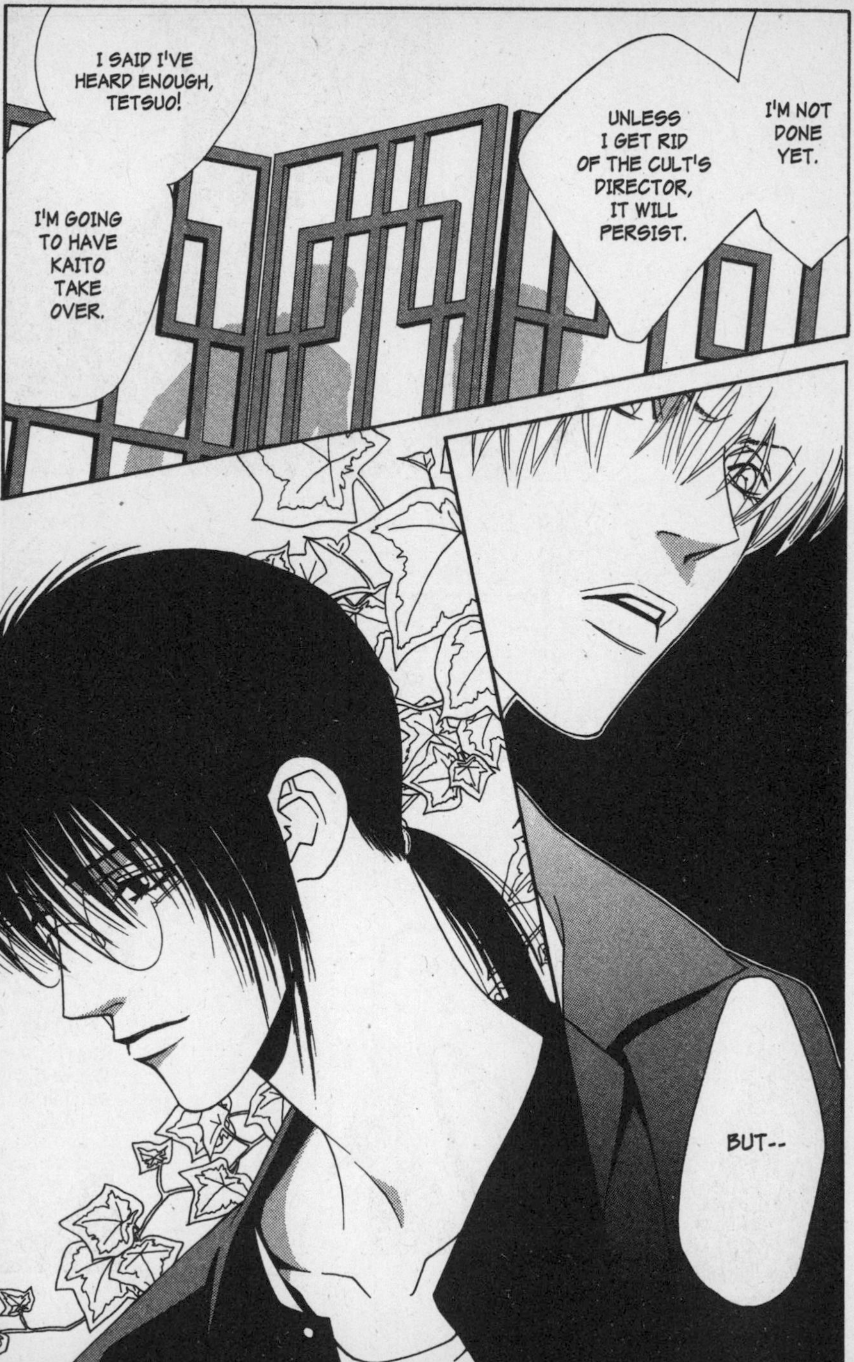
I'M NOT DONE YET.
UNLESS I GET RID OF THE CULT'S DIRECTOR, IT WILL PERSIST.
I SAID I'VE HEARD ENOUGH, TETSUO!
I'M GOING TO HAVE KAITO TAKE OVER.
BUT--

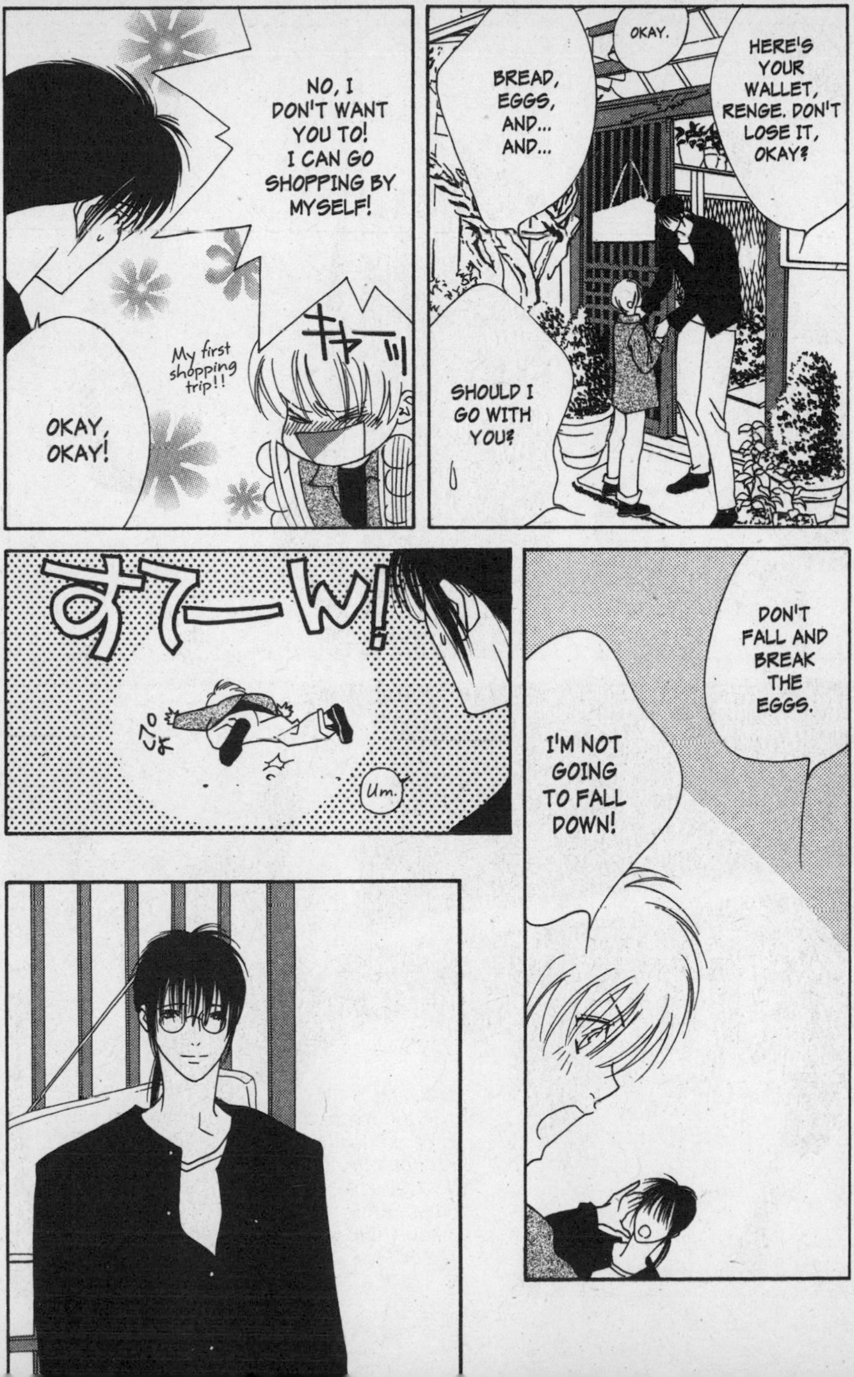
HERE'S YOUR WALLET, RENGE. DON'T LOSE IT, OKAY?
OKAY.
BREAD, EGGS, AND... AND...
SHOULD I GO WITH YOU?
NO, I DON'T WANT YOU TO! I CAN GO SHOPPING BY MYSELF!
キャーッ
My first shopping trip!!
OKAY, OKAY!
DON'T FALL AND BREAK THE EGGS.
I'M NOT GOING TO FALL DOWN!
すてーん!
Um.

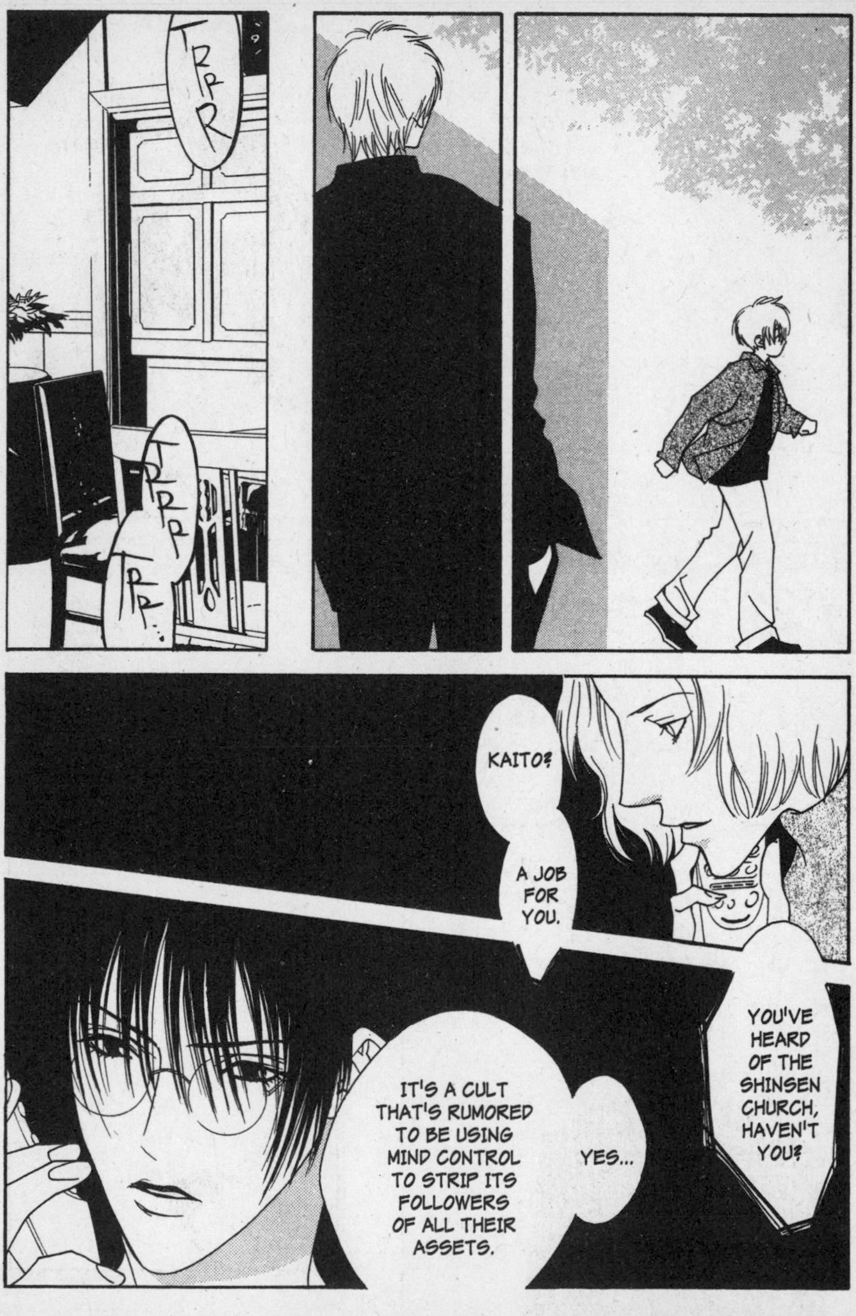
TRRR
TRRR
TRR...
KAITO?
A JOB FOR YOU.
YOU'VE HEARD OF THE SHINSEN CHURCH, HAVEN'T YOU?
YES...
IT'S A CULT THAT'S RUMORED TO BE USING MIND CONTROL TO STRIP ITS FOLLOWERS OF ALL THEIR ASSETS.

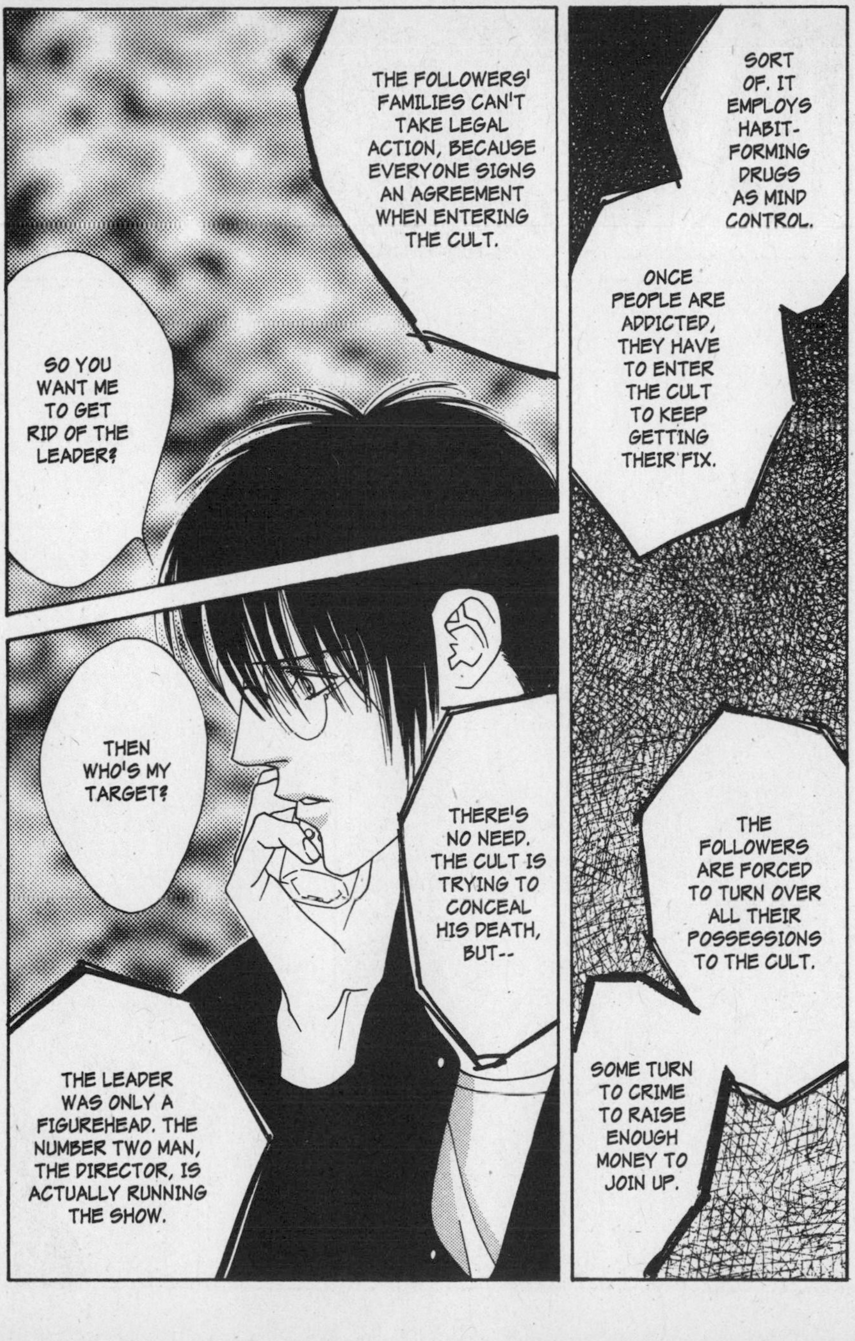
SORT OF. IT EMPLOYS HABIT-FORMING DRUGS AS MIND CONTROL.
ONCE PEOPLE ARE ADDICTED, THEY HAVE TO ENTER THE CULT TO KEEP GETTING THEIR FIX.
THE FOLLOWERS ARE FORCED TO TURN OVER ALL THEIR POSSESSIONS TO THE CULT.
SOME TURN TO CRIME TO RAISE ENOUGH MONEY TO JOIN UP.
THE FOLLOWERS' FAMILIES CAN'T TAKE LEGAL ACTION, BECAUSE EVERYONE SIGNS AN AGREEMENT WHEN ENTERING THE CULT.
SO YOU WANT ME TO GET RID OF THE LEADER?
THERE'S NO NEED. THE CULT IS TRYING TO CONCEAL HIS DEATH, BUT--
THEN WHO'S MY TARGET?
THE LEADER WAS ONLY A FIGUREHEAD. THE NUMBER TWO MAN, THE DIRECTOR, IS ACTUALLY RUNNING THE SHOW.

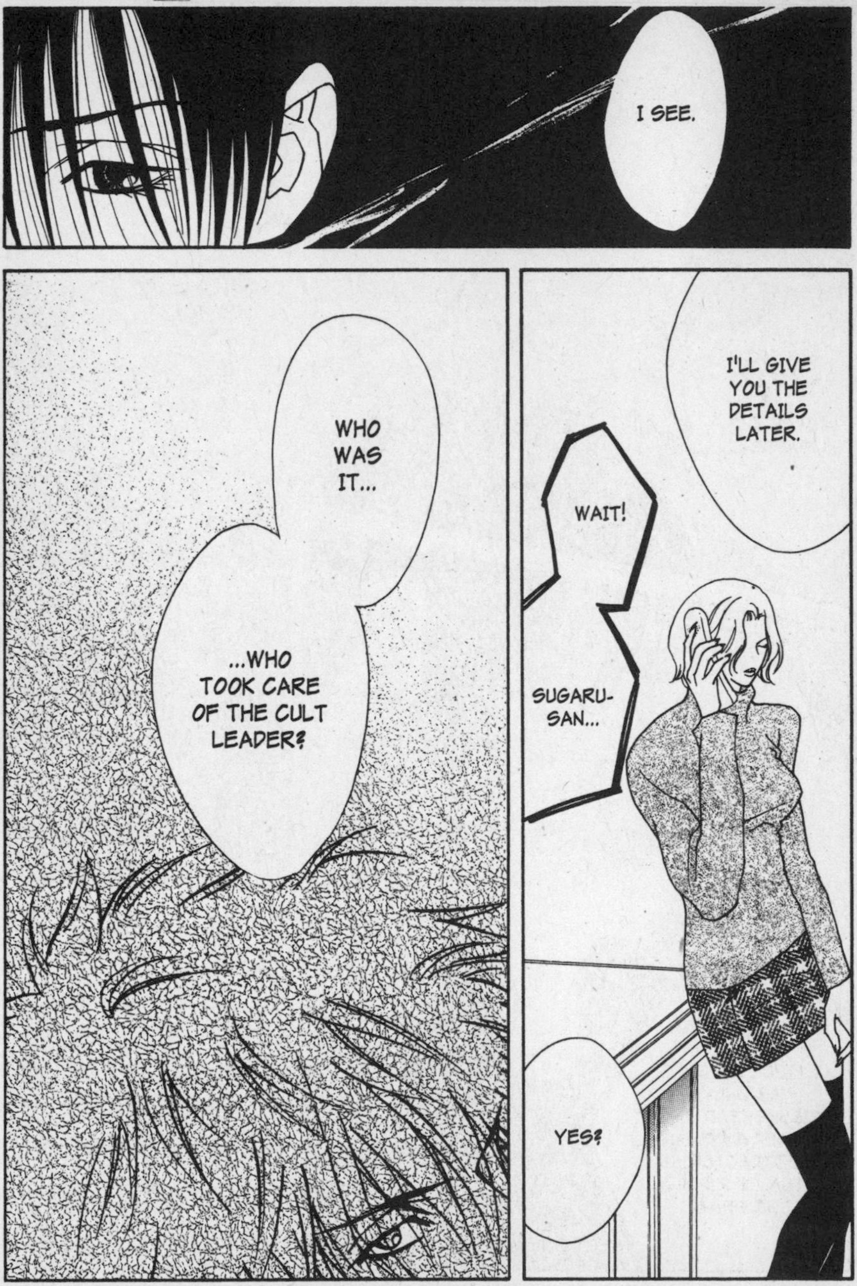
I SEE.
I'LL GIVE YOU THE DETAILS LATER.
WAIT! SUGARU-SAN...
YES?
WHO WAS IT...
...WHO TOOK CARE OF THE CULT LEADER?

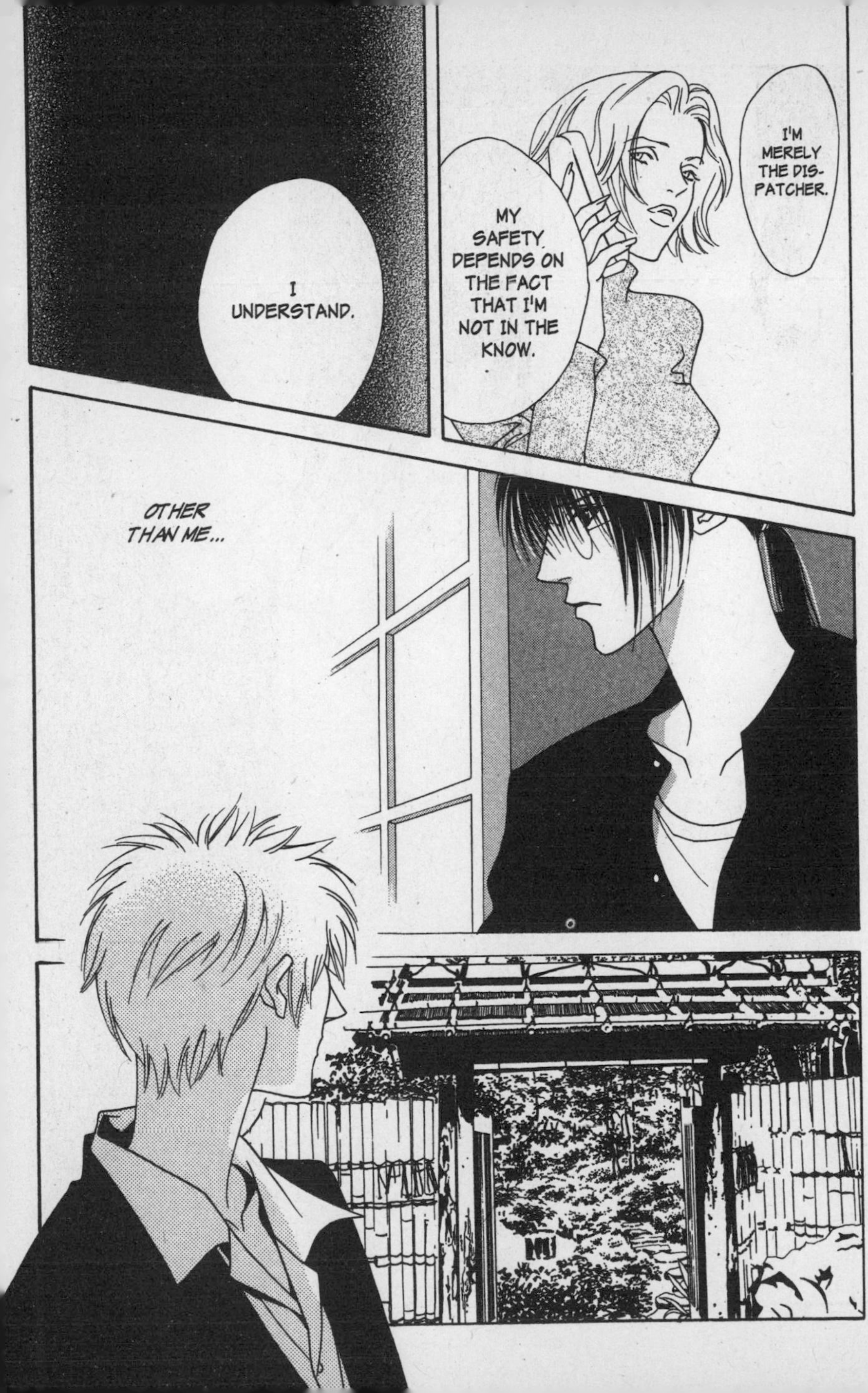
I'M MERELY THE DIS-PATCHER.
MY SAFETY DEPENDS ON THE FACT THAT I'M NOT IN THE KNOW.
I UNDERSTAND.
OTHER THAN ME...

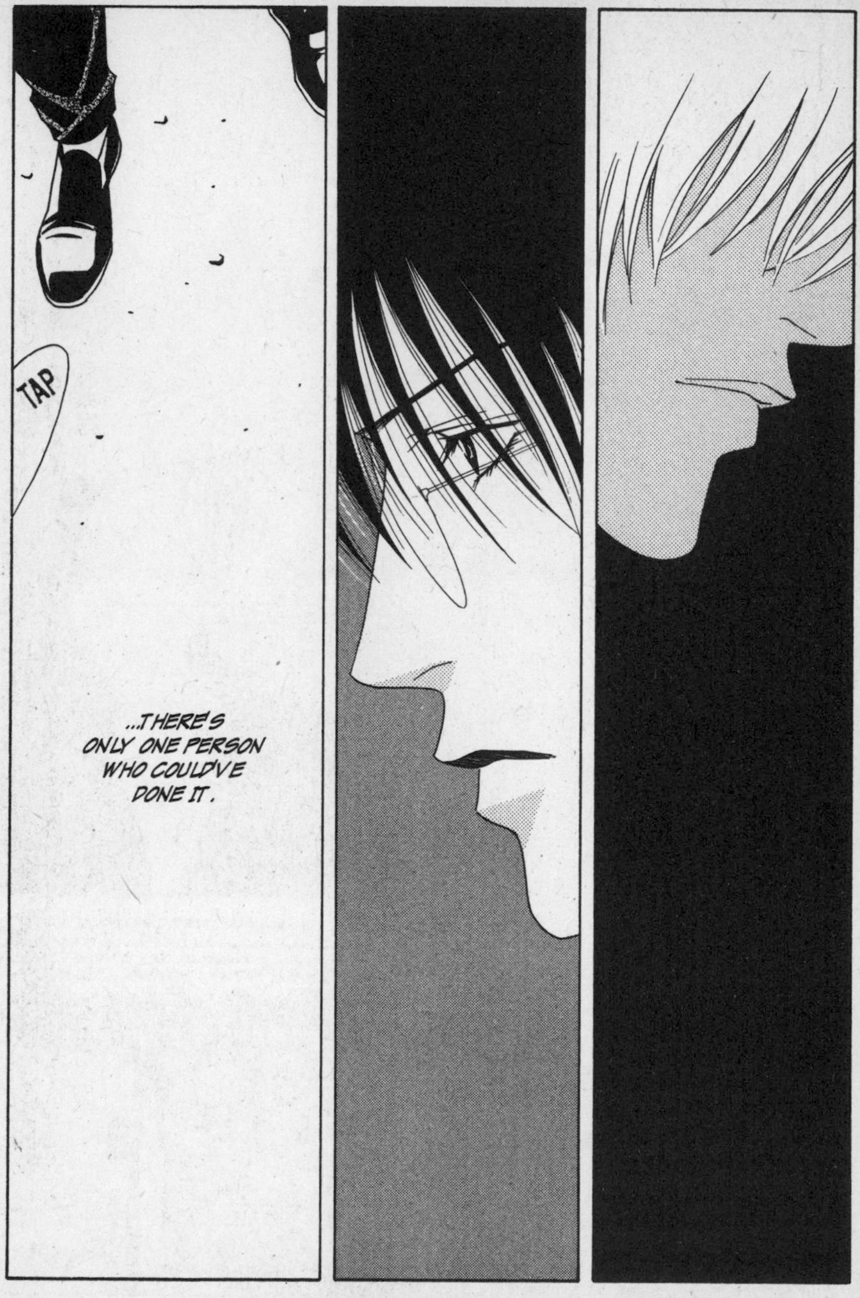
TAP
...THERE'S ONLY ONE PERSON WHO COULD'VE DONE IT.

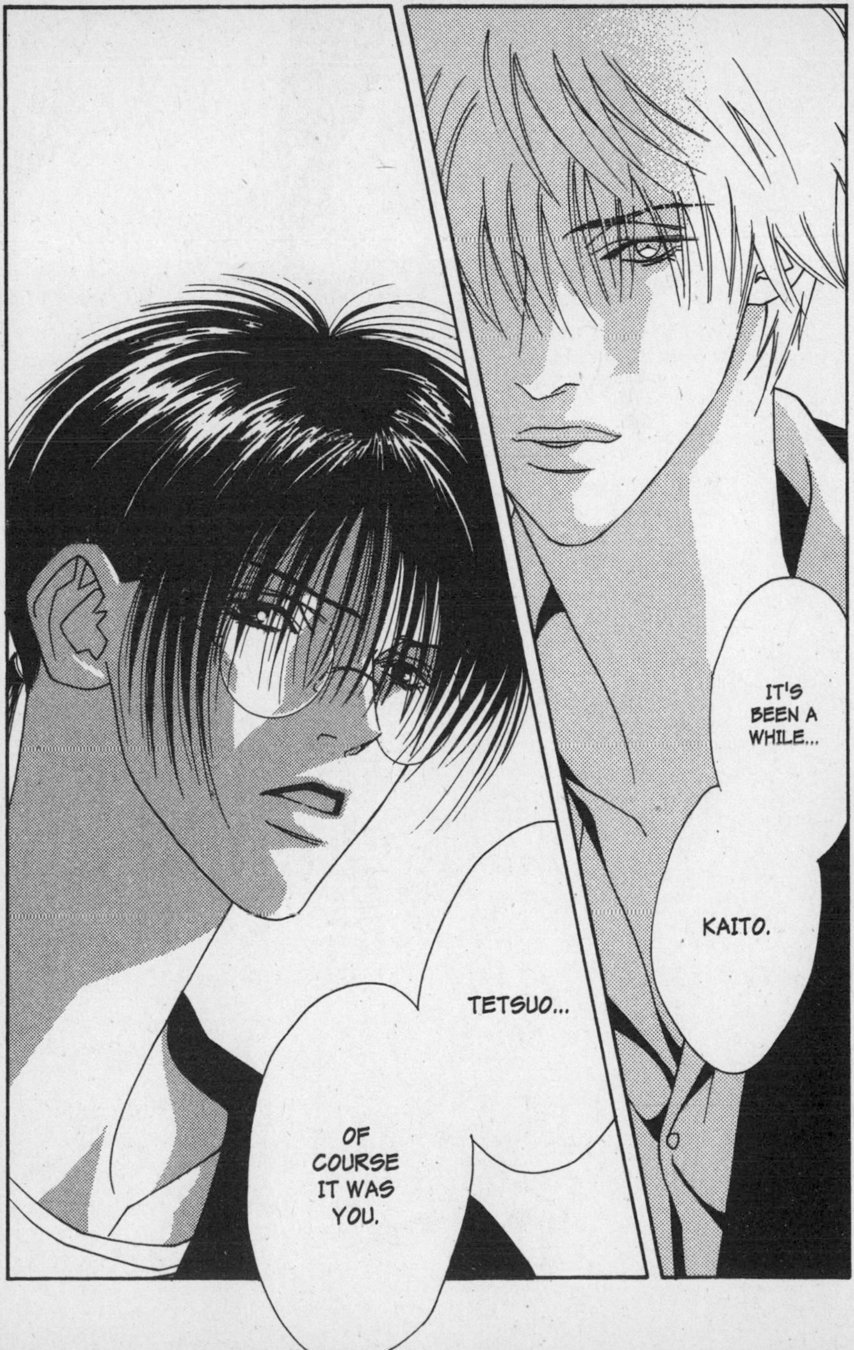
IT'S BEEN A WHILE...
KAITO.
TETSUO...
OF COURSE IT WAS YOU.

HOW LONG HAS IT BEEN...
...SINCE WE LEFT THE ORPHANAGE?
EH, KAITO?

WE GREW UP IN A SMALL ORPHANAGE ATTACHED TO A MONASTERY ON A LITTLE ISLAND.

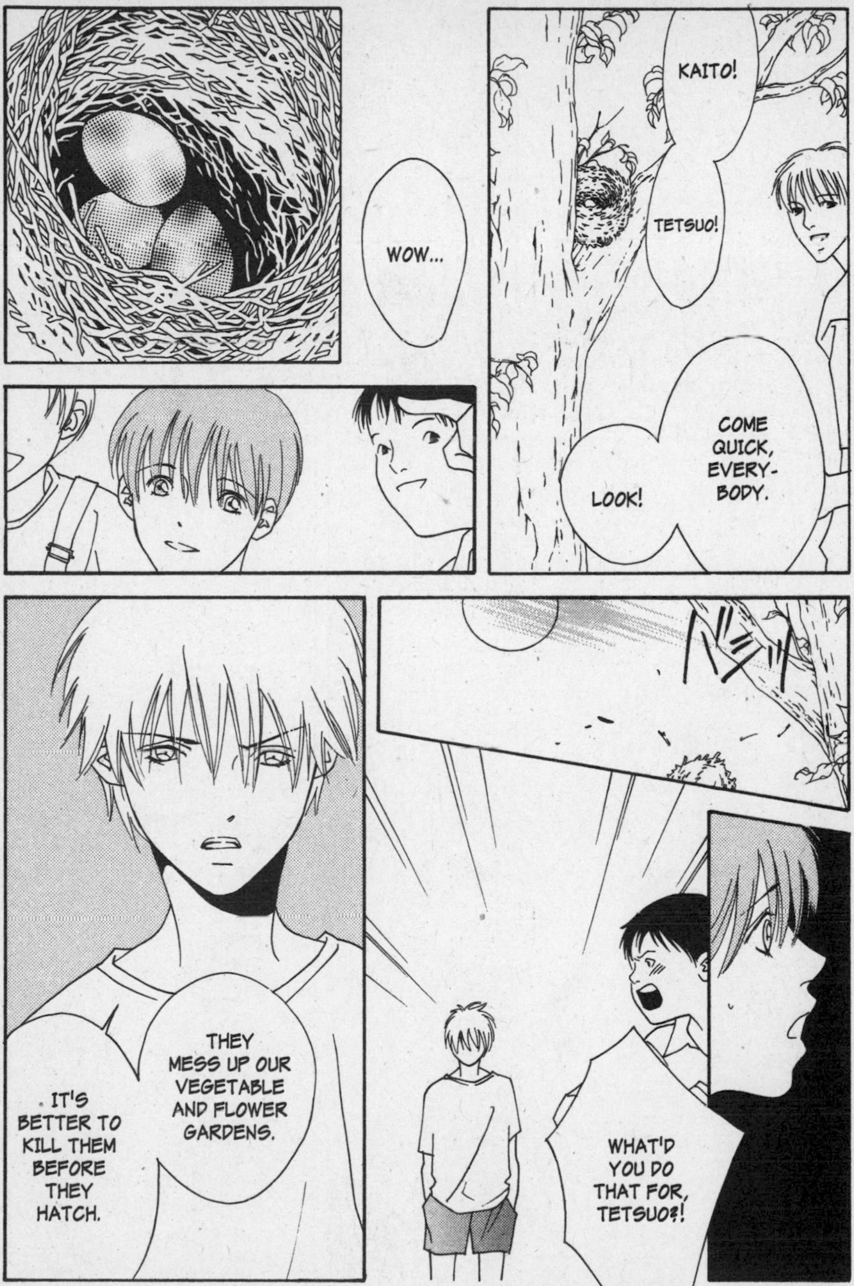
KAITO!
TETSUO!
COME QUICK, EVERY-BODY.
LOOK!
WOW...
WHAT'D YOU DO THAT FOR, TETSUO?!
THEY MESS UP OUR VEGETABLE AND FLOWER GARDENS.
IT'S BETTER TO KILL THEM BEFORE THEY HATCH.

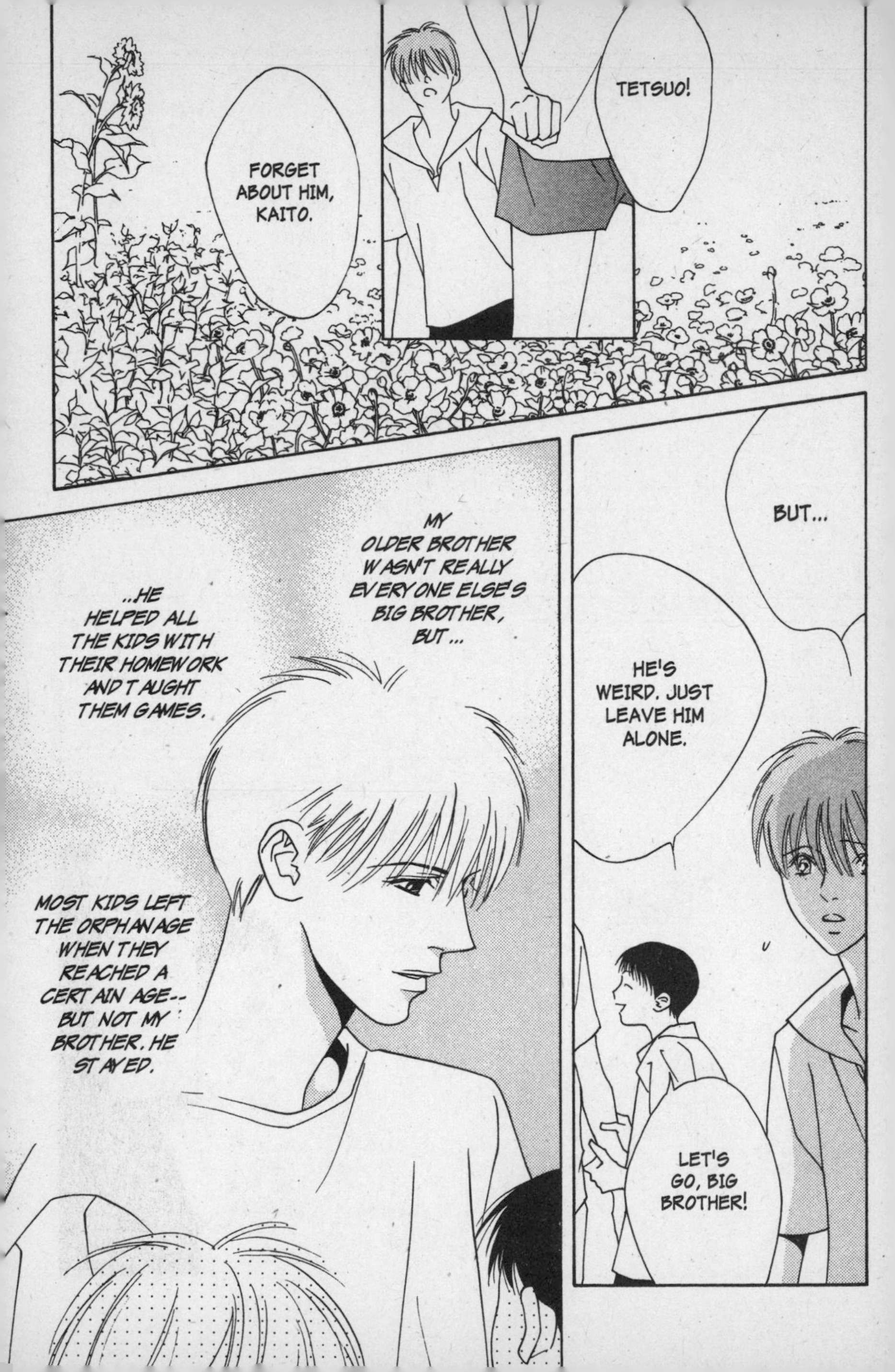
TETSUO!
FORGET ABOUT HIM, KAITO.
BUT...
HE'S WEIRD. JUST LEAVE HIM ALONE.
LET'S GO, BIG BROTHER!
MY OLDER BROTHER WASN'T REALLY EVERYONE ELSE'S BIG BROTHER, BUT...
...HE HELPED ALL THE KIDS WITH THEIR HOMEWORK AND TAUGHT THEM GAMES.
MOST KIDS LEFT THE ORPHANAGE WHEN THEY REACHED A CERTAIN AGE--BUT NOT MY BROTHER. HE STAYED.

EVERYONE LIKED MY BROTHER, BECAUSE HE WAS SO KIND.

EVERYONE EXCEPT TETSUO.

TETSUO WAS A LONER...

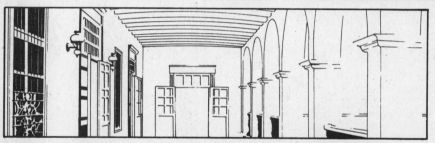

TETSUO.

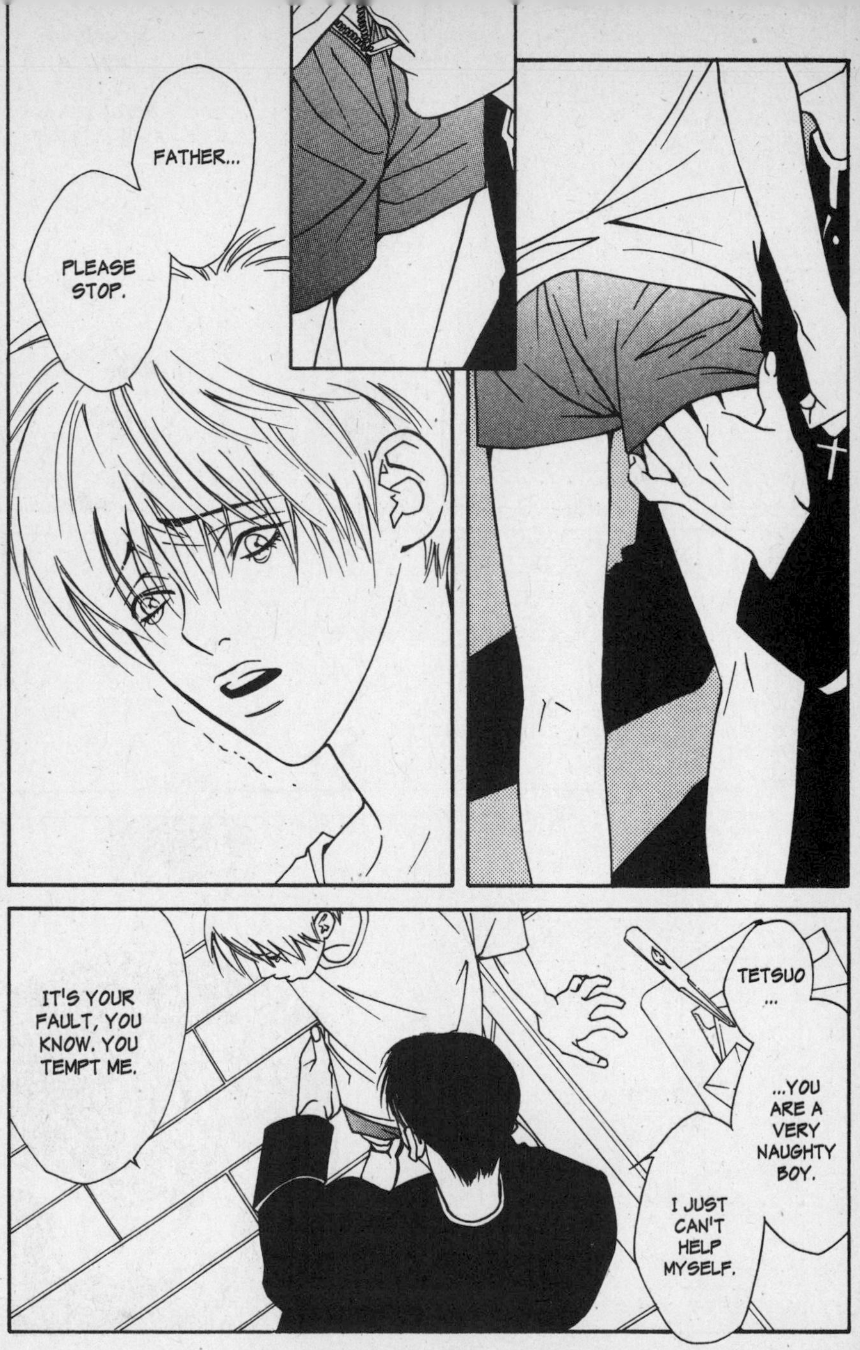
FATHER...
PLEASE STOP.
TETSUO ...
...YOU ARE A VERY NAUGHTY BOY.
I JUST CAN'T HELP MYSELF.
IT'S YOUR FAULT, YOU KNOW. YOU TEMPT ME.

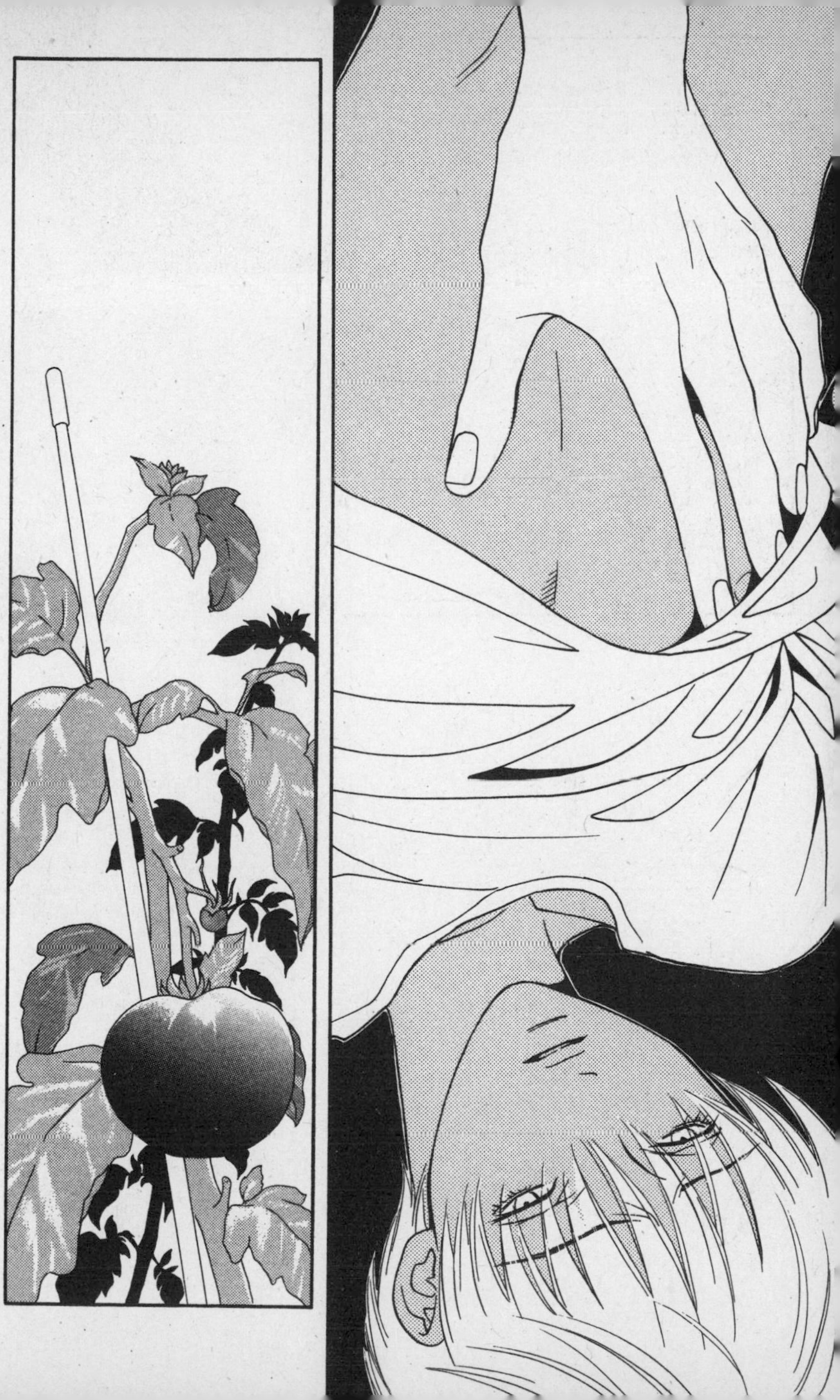

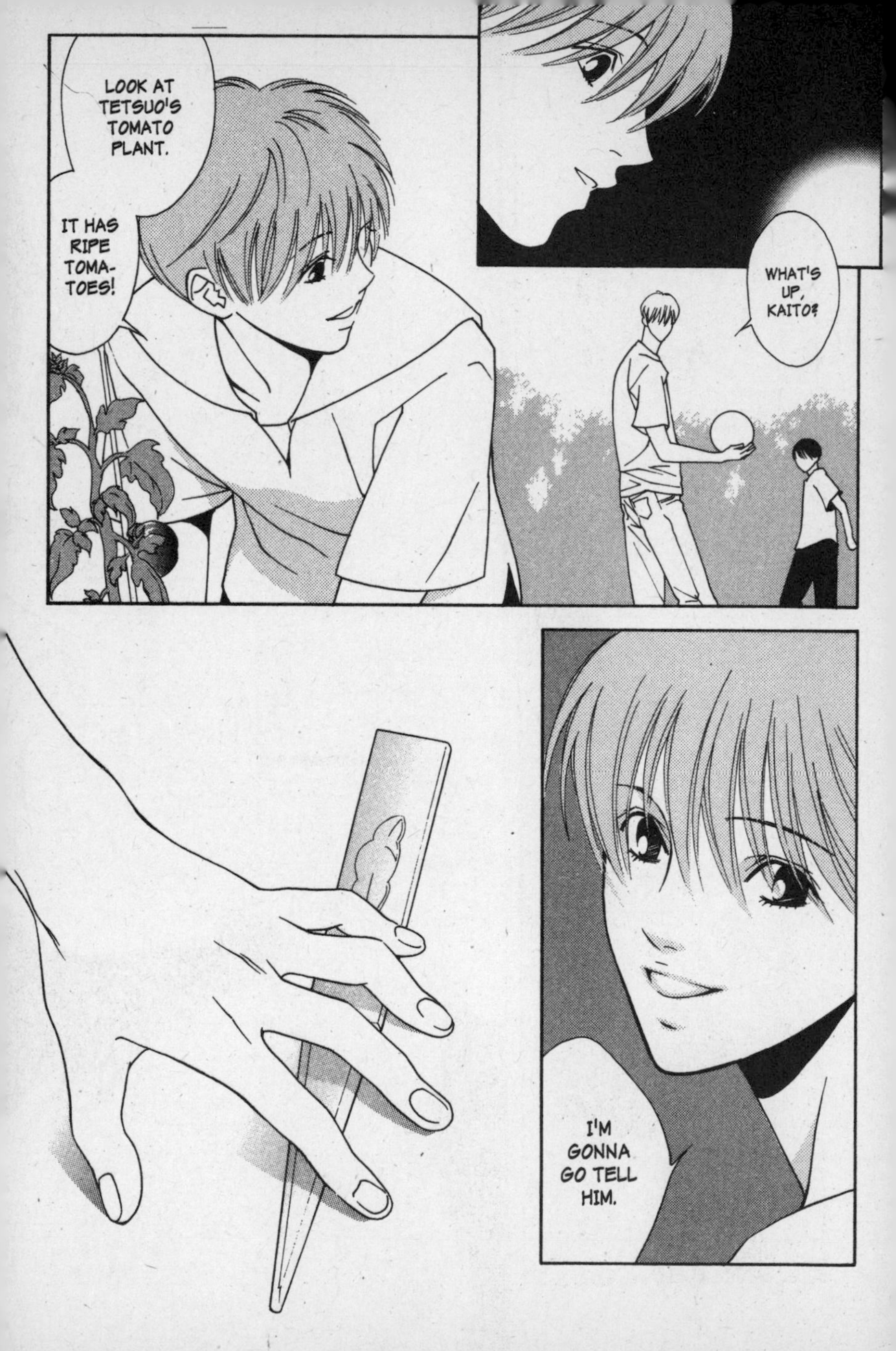
WHAT'S UP, KAITO?
LOOK AT TETSUO'S TOMATO PLANT.
IT HAS RIPE TOMA-TOES!
I'M GONNA GO TELL HIM.

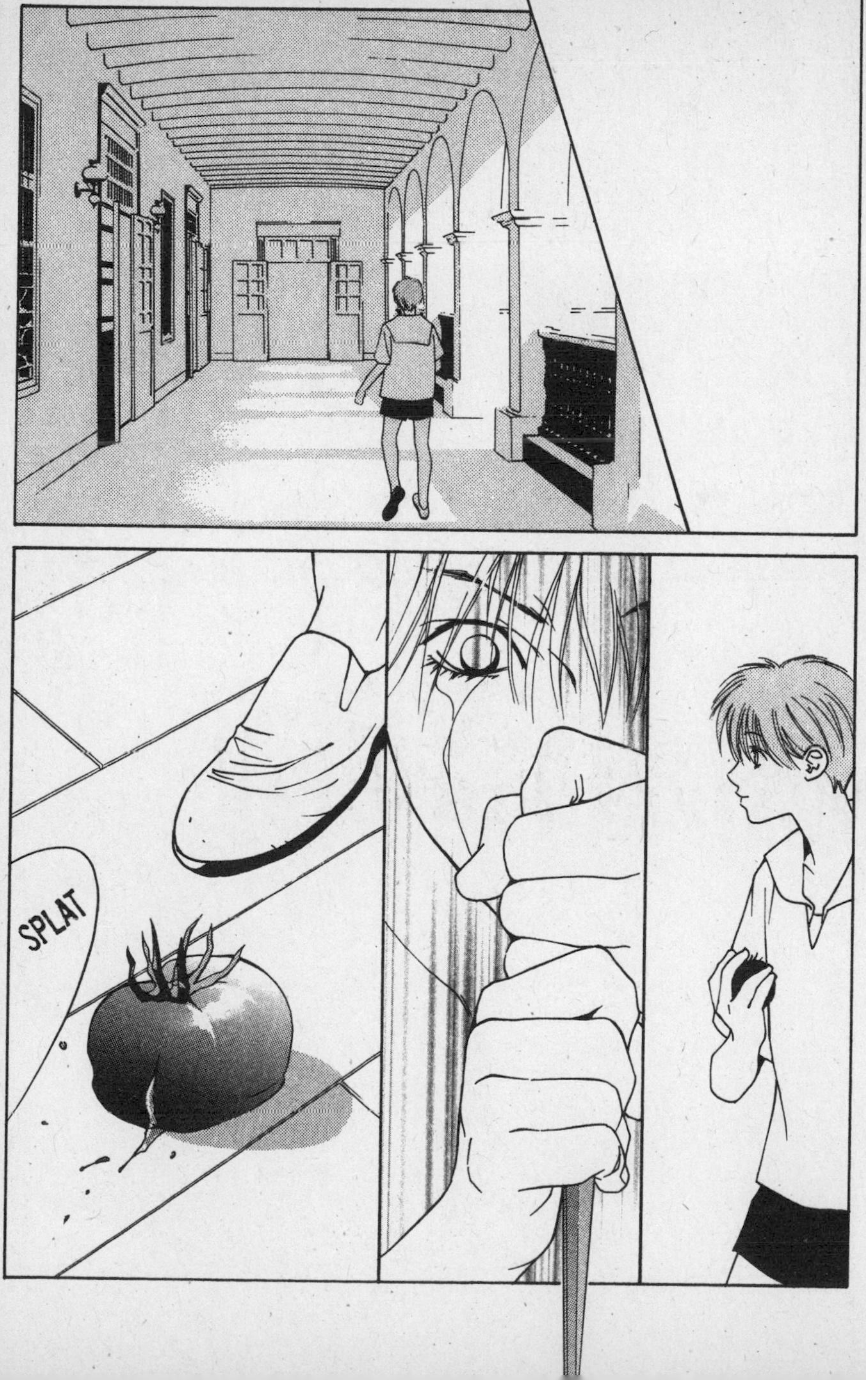
SPLAT

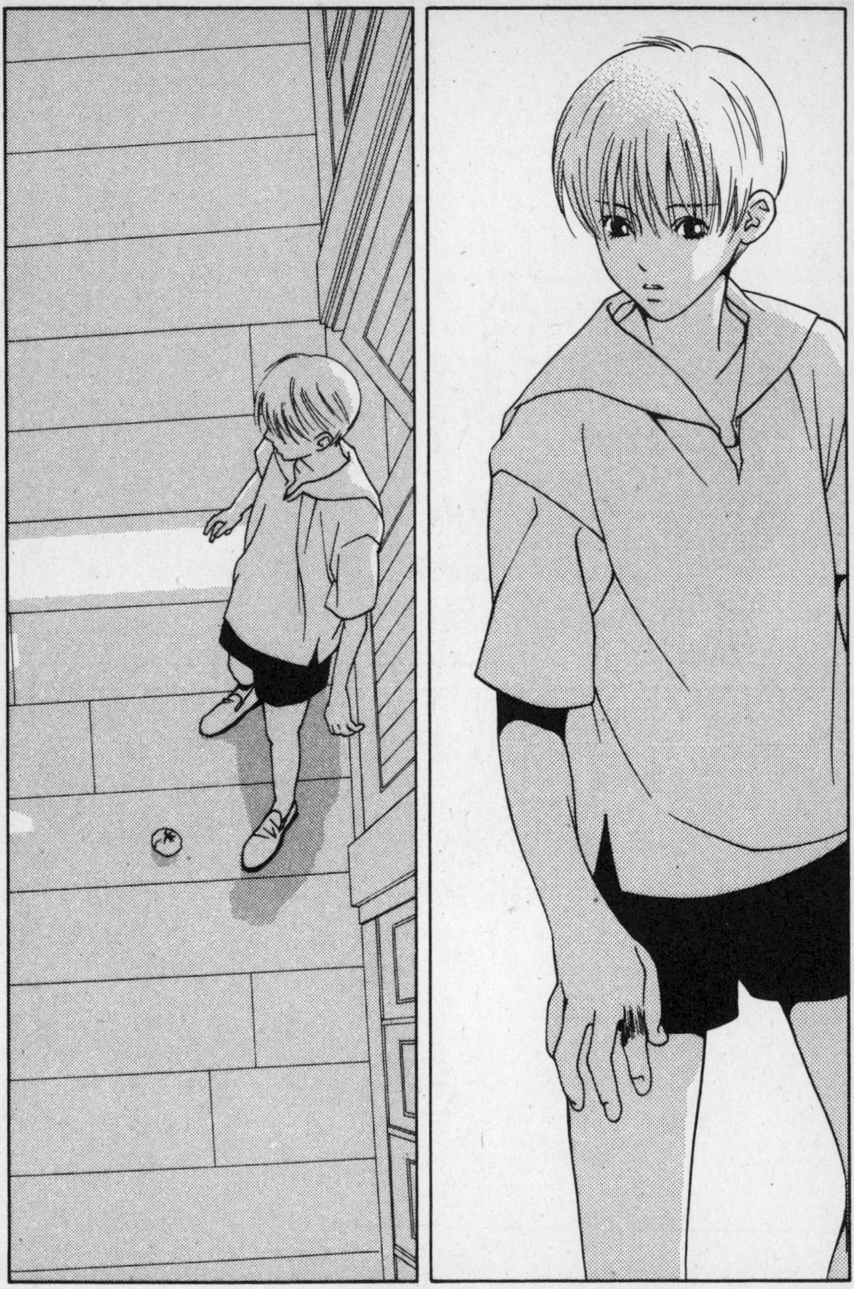

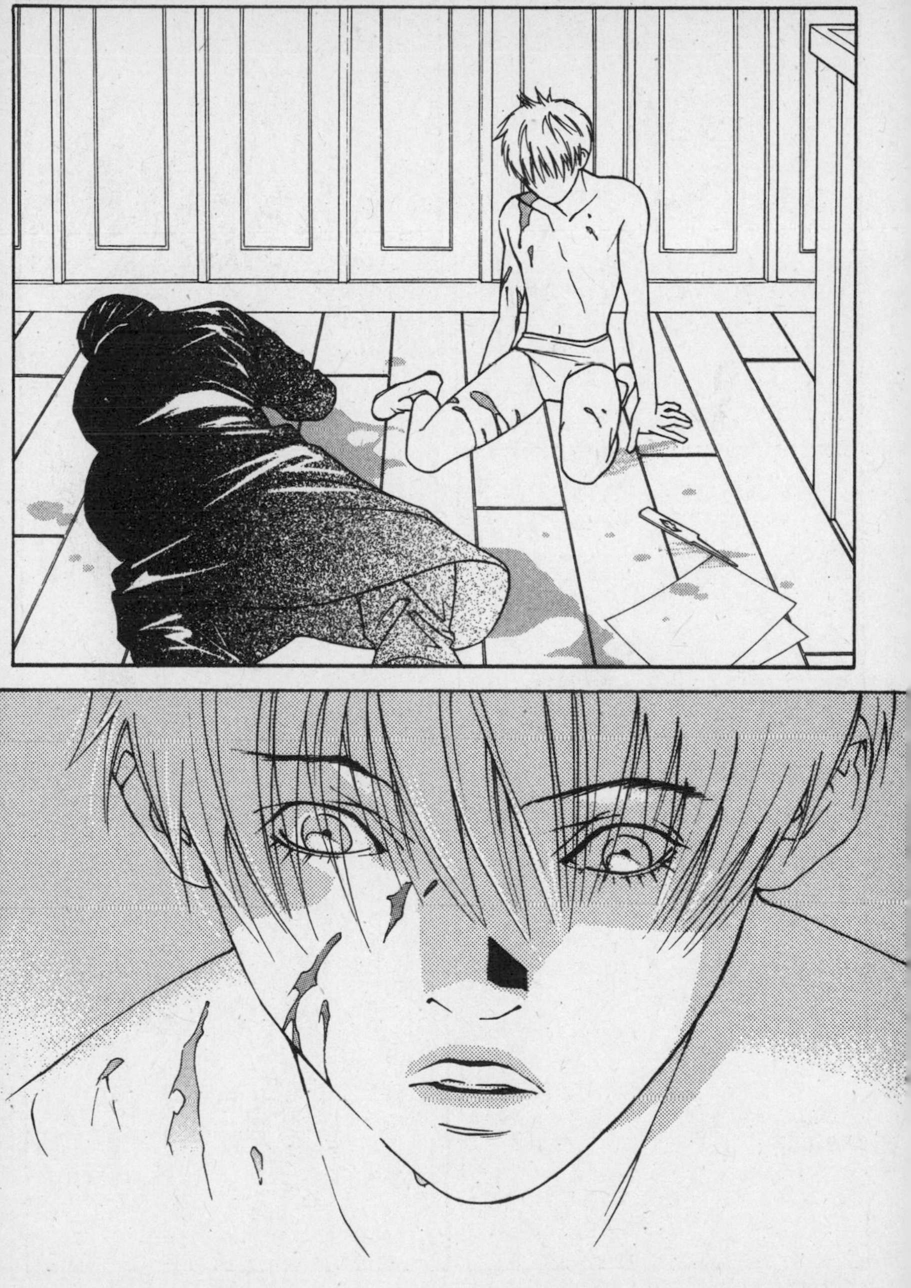

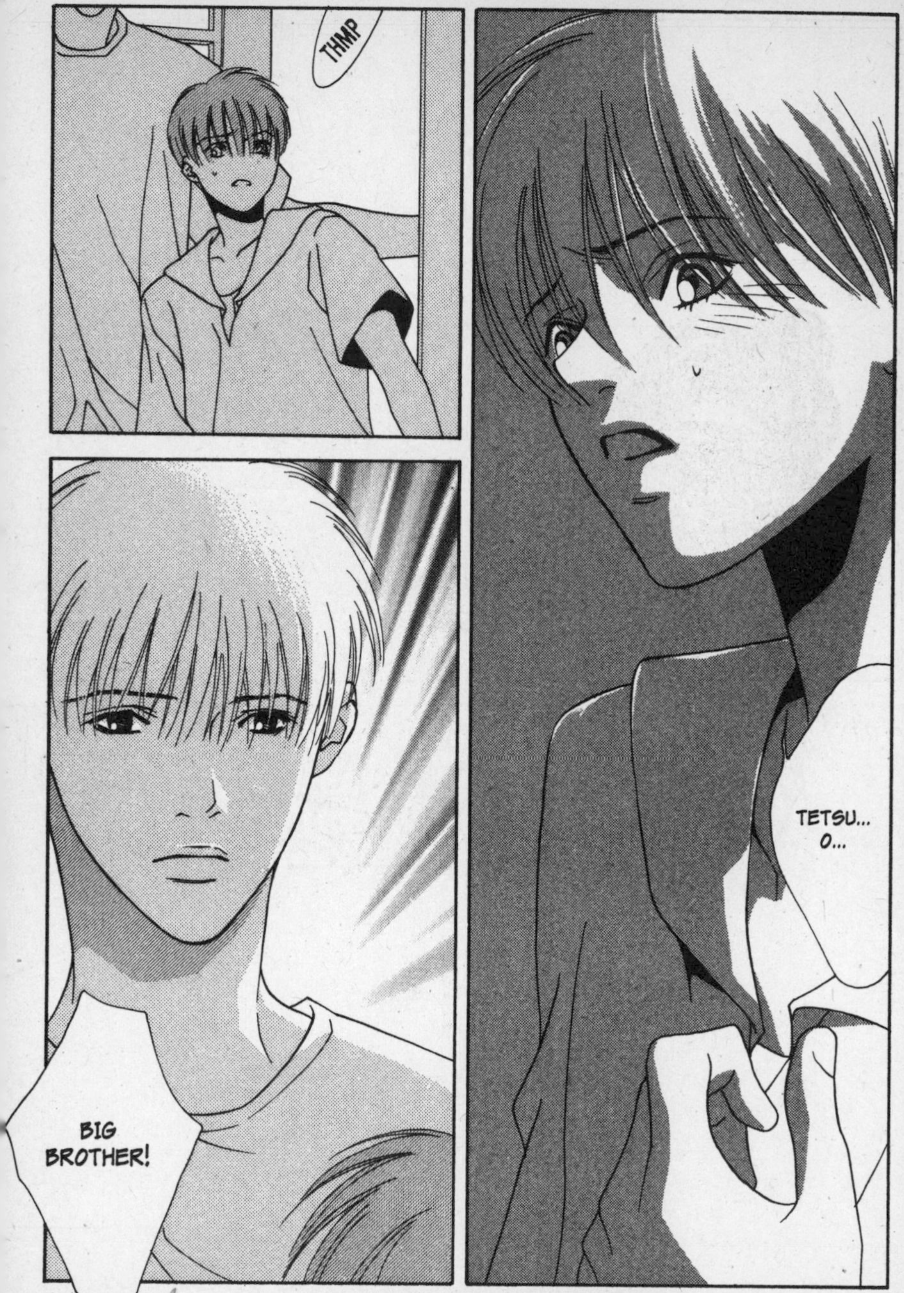
TETSU... O...
THMP
BIG BROTHER!

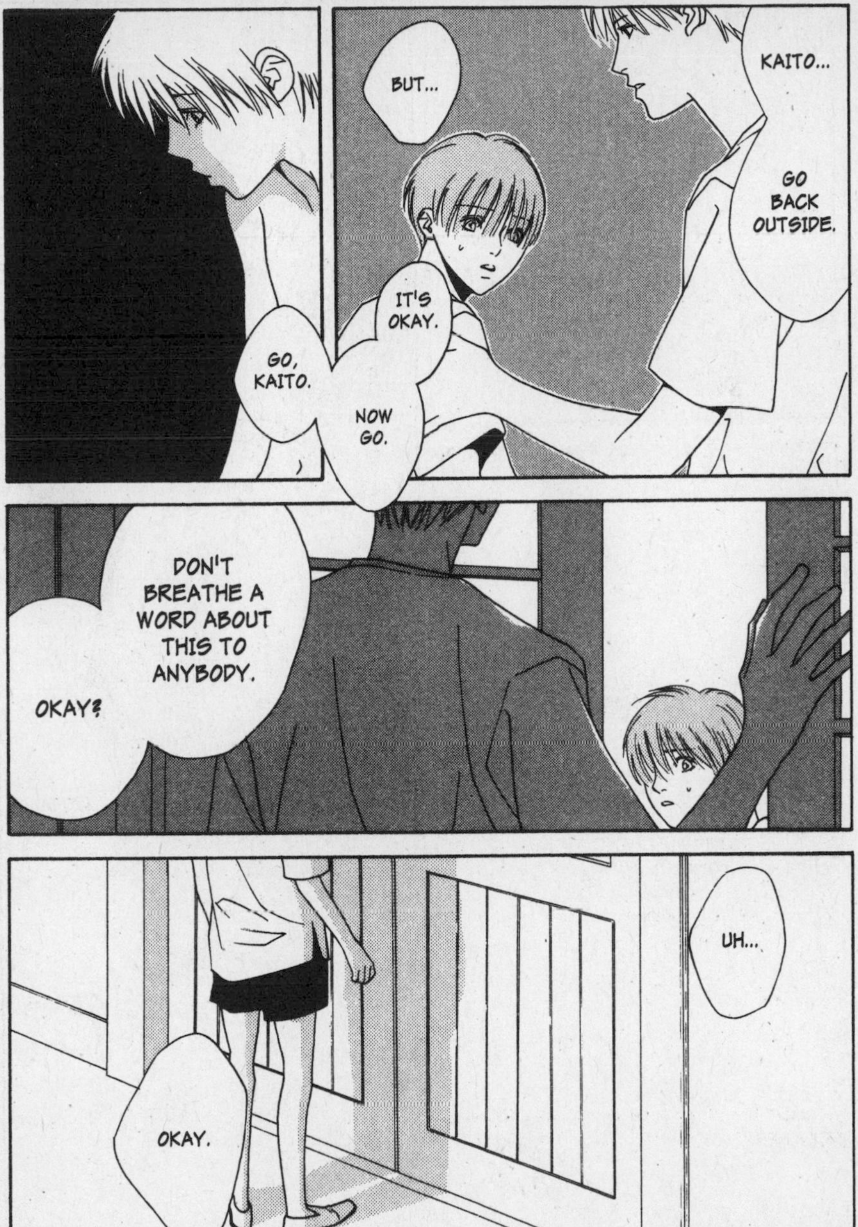
KAITO...
GO BACK OUTSIDE.
BUT...
IT'S OKAY.
GO, KAITO.
NOW GO.
DON'T BREATHE A WORD ABOUT THIS TO ANYBODY.
OKAY?
UH...
OKAY.

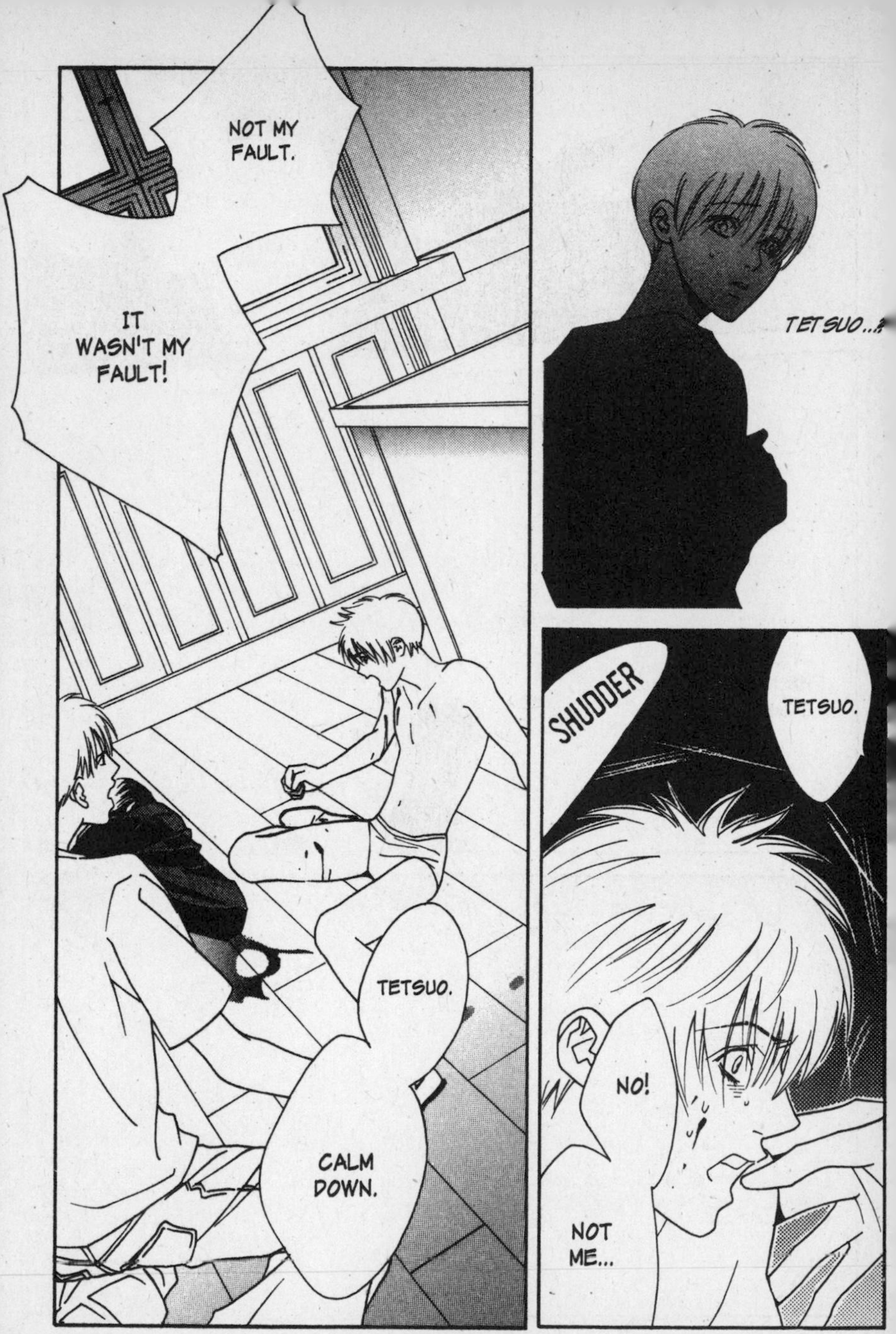
TETSUO...?!
SHUDDER
TETSUO.
NO!
NOT ME...
NOT MY FAULT.
IT WASN'T MY FAULT!
TETSUO.
CALM DOWN.

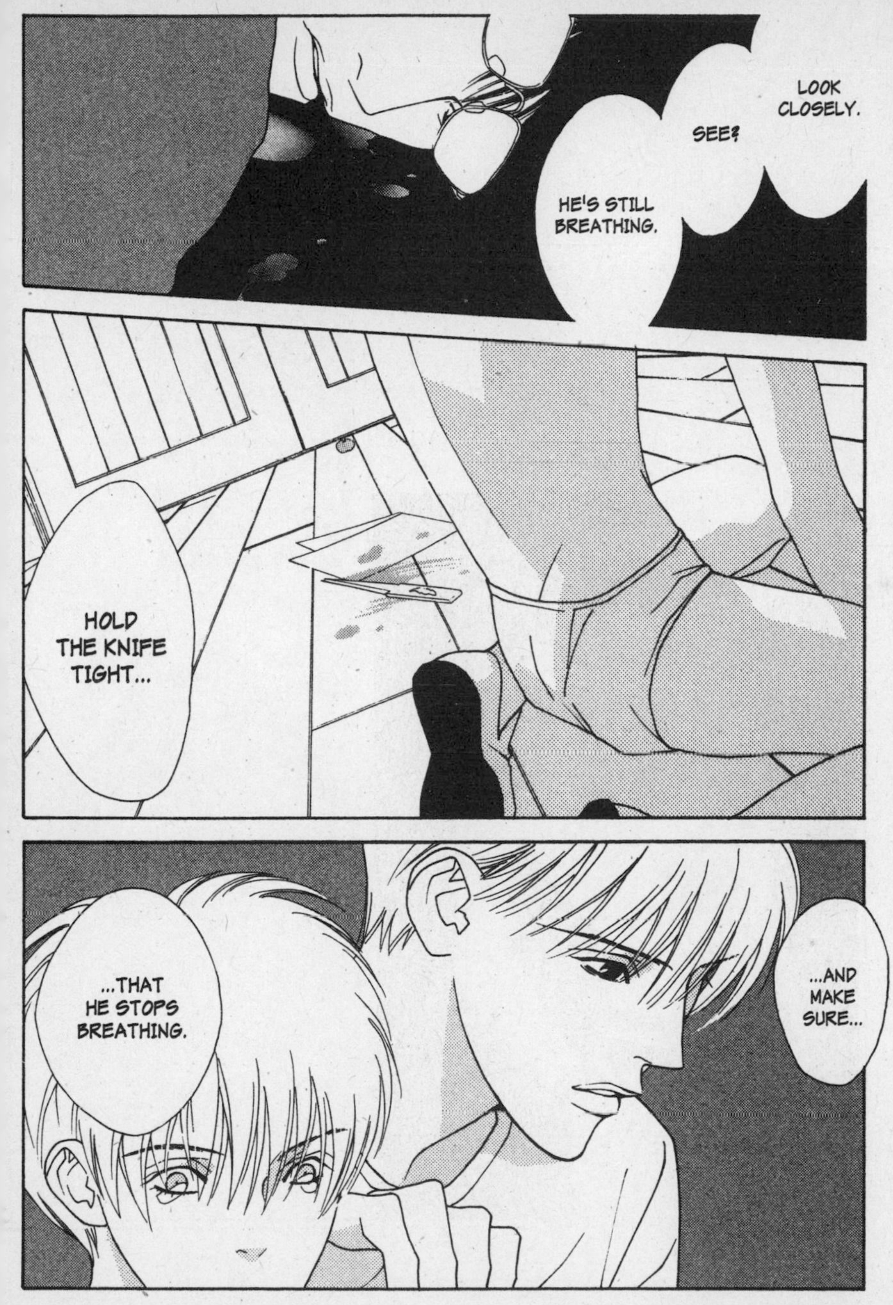
LOOK CLOSELY.
SEE?
HE'S STILL BREATHING.
HOLD THE KNIFE TIGHT...
...AND MAKE SURE...
...THAT HE STOPS BREATHING.

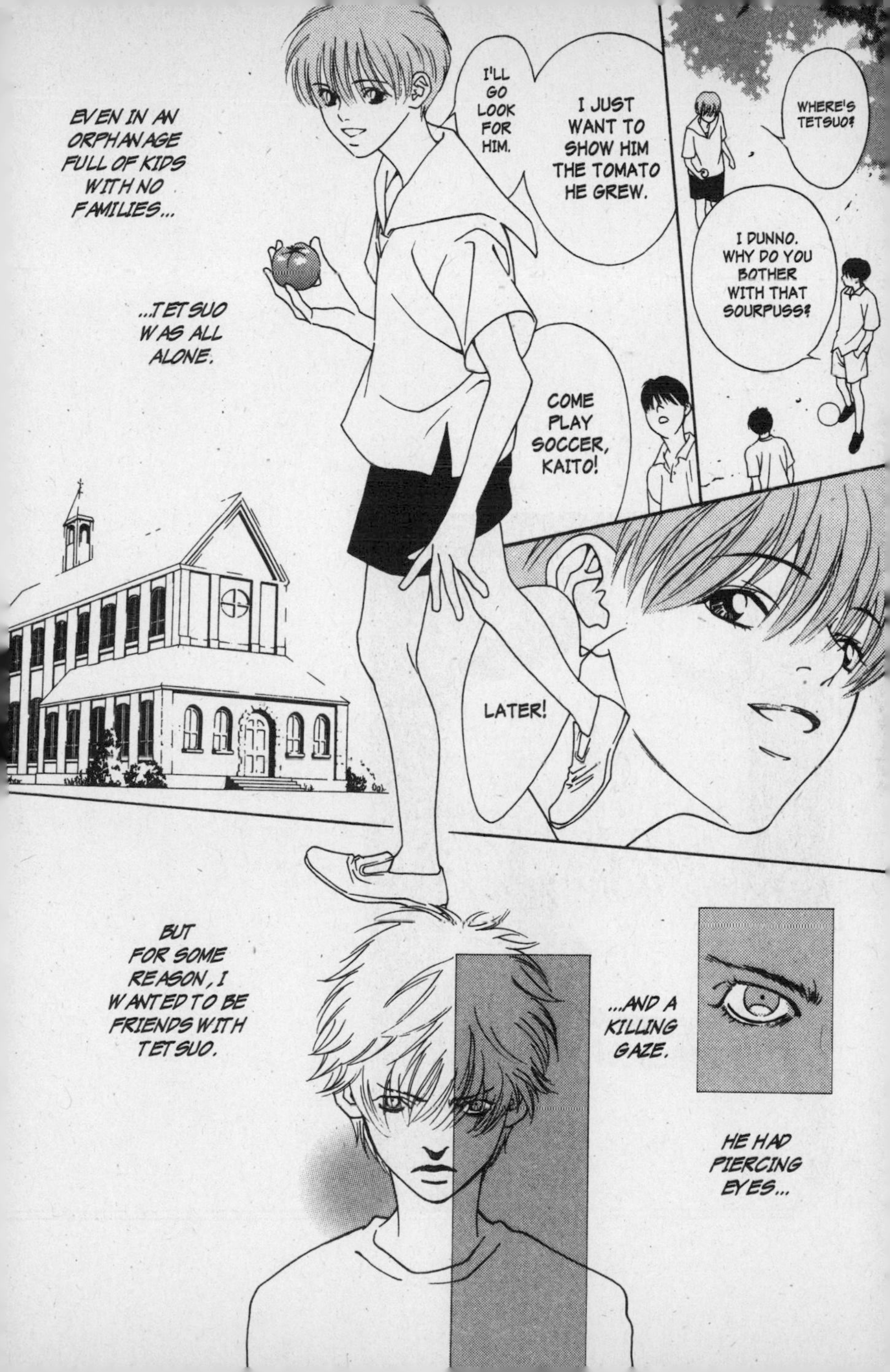
WHERE'S TETSUO?
I DUNNO. WHY DO YOU BOTHER WITH THAT SOURPUSS?
COME PLAY SOCCER, KAITO!
I JUST WANT TO SHOW HIM THE TOMATO HE GREW.
I'LL GO LOOK FOR HIM.
LATER!
EVEN IN AN ORPHANAGE FULL OF KIDS WITH NO FAMILIES...
...TETSUO WAS ALL ALONE.
HE HAD PIERCING EYES...
...AND A KILLING GAZE.
BUT FOR SOME REASON, I WANTED TO BE FRIENDS WITH TETSUO.

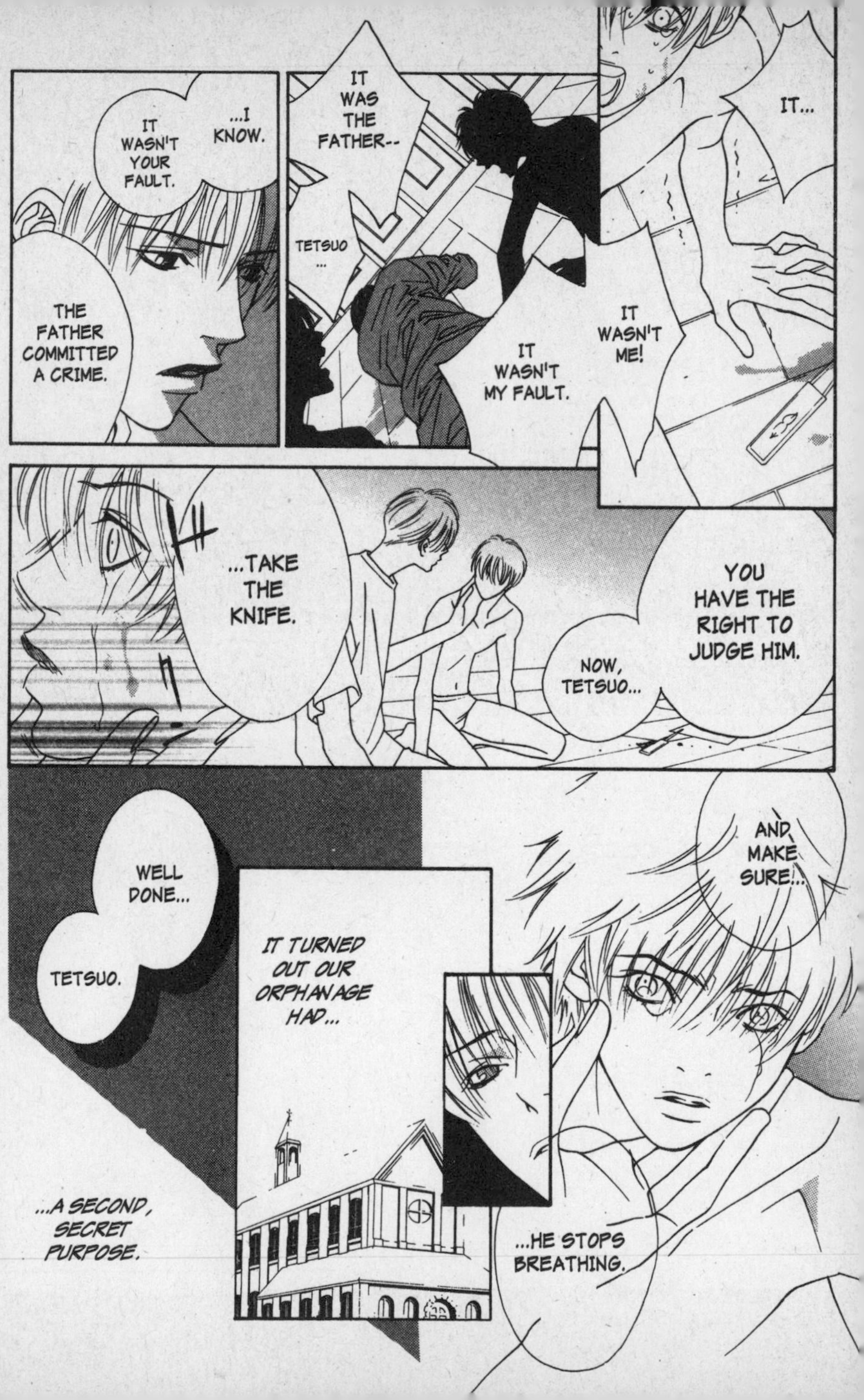
IT...
IT WASN'T ME!
IT WASN'T MY FAULT.
IT WAS THE FATHER--
TETSUO...
...I KNOW.
IT WASN'T YOUR FAULT.
THE FATHER COMMITTED A CRIME.
YOU HAVE THE RIGHT TO JUDGE HIM.
NOW, TETSUO...
...TAKE THE KNIFE.
AND MAKE SURE...
...HE STOPS BREATHING.
WELL DONE...
TETSUO.
IT TURNED OUT OUR ORPHANAGE HAD...
...A SECOND, SECRET PURPOSE.

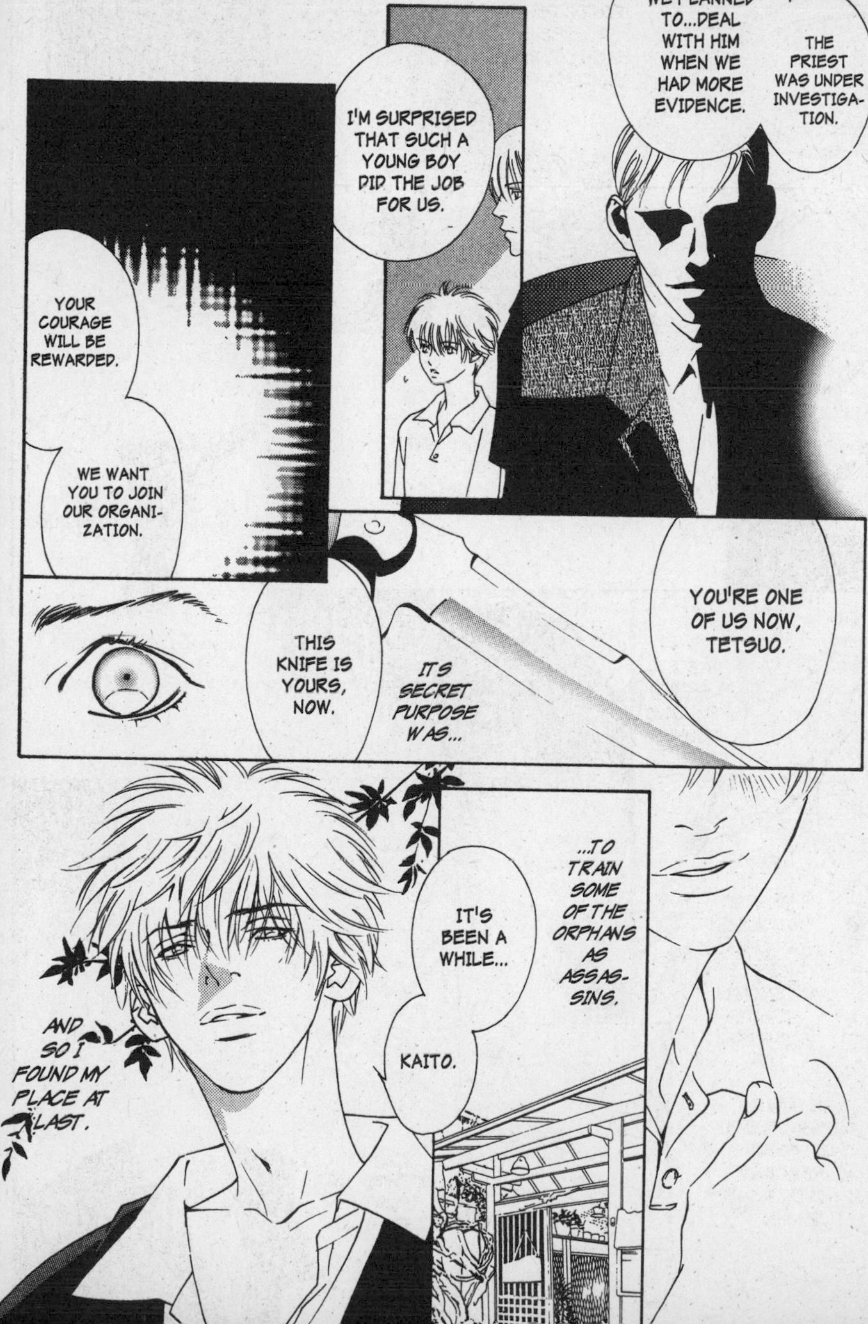
THE PRIEST WAS UNDER INVESTIGATION.
WE PLANNED TO...DEAL WITH HIM WHEN WE HAD MORE EVIDENCE.
I'M SURPRISED THAT SUCH A YOUNG BOY DID THE JOB FOR US.
YOUR COURAGE WILL BE REWARDED.
WE WANT YOU TO JOIN OUR ORGANIZATION.
YOU'RE ONE OF US NOW, TETSUO.
ITS SECRET PURPOSE WAS...
THIS KNIFE IS YOURS, NOW.
...TO TRAIN SOME OF THE ORPHANS AS ASSASSINS.
IT'S BEEN A WHILE...
KAITO.
AND SO I FOUND MY PLACE AT LAST.

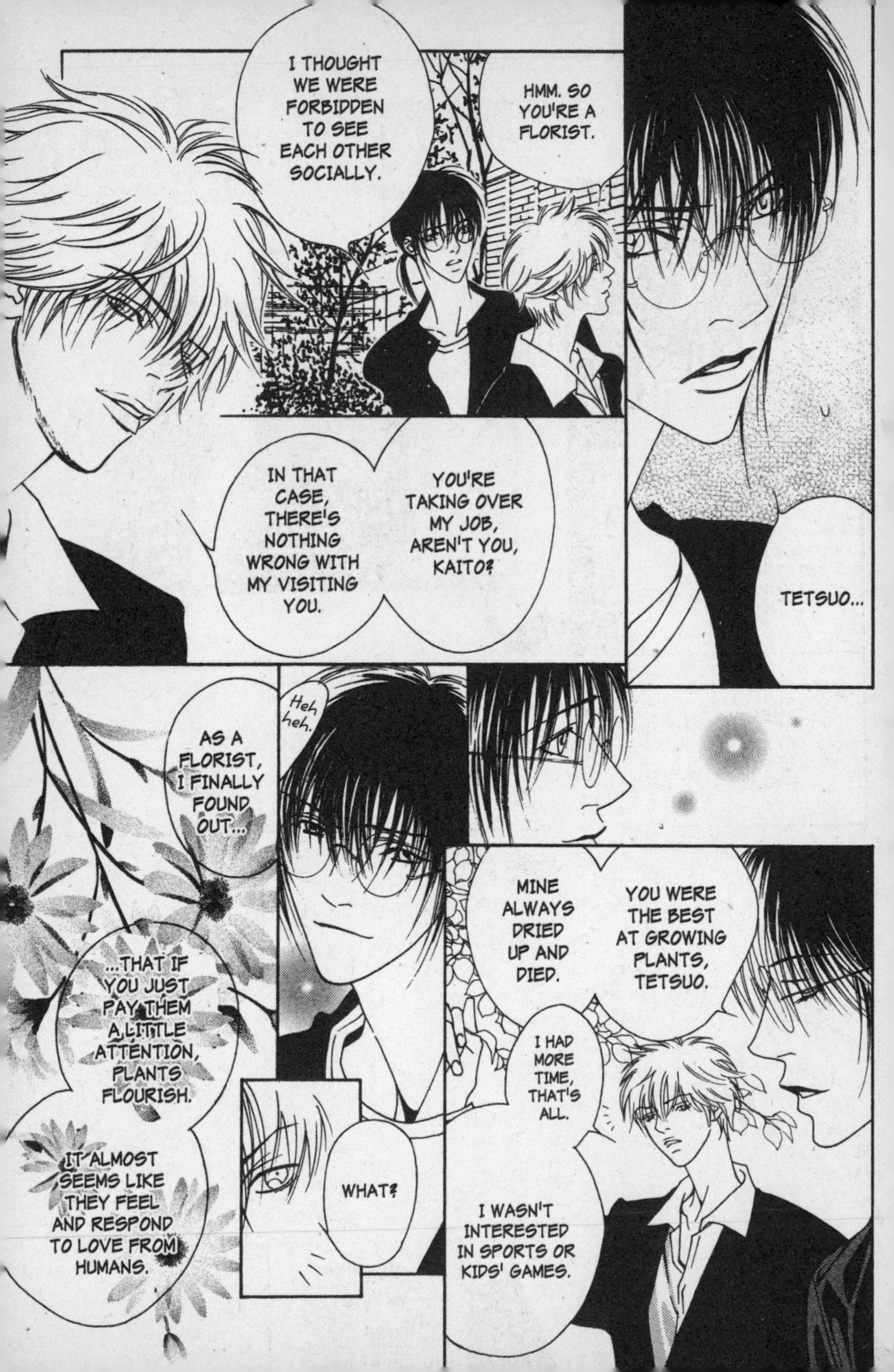
TETSUO...
HMM. SO YOU'RE A FLORIST.
I THOUGHT WE WERE FORBIDDEN TO SEE EACH OTHER SOCIALLY.
YOU'RE TAKING OVER MY JOB, AREN'T YOU, KAITO?
IN THAT CASE, THERE'S NOTHING WRONG WITH MY VISITING YOU.
Heh heh.
AS A FLORIST, I FINALLY FOUND OUT...
...THAT IF YOU JUST PAY THEM A LITTLE ATTENTION, PLANTS FLOURISH.
IT ALMOST SEEMS LIKE THEY FEEL AND RESPOND TO LOVE FROM HUMANS.
WHAT?
YOU WERE THE BEST AT GROWING PLANTS, TETSUO.
MINE ALWAYS DRIED UP AND DIED.
I HAD MORE TIME, THAT'S ALL.
I WASN'T INTERESTED IN SPORTS OR KIDS' GAMES.

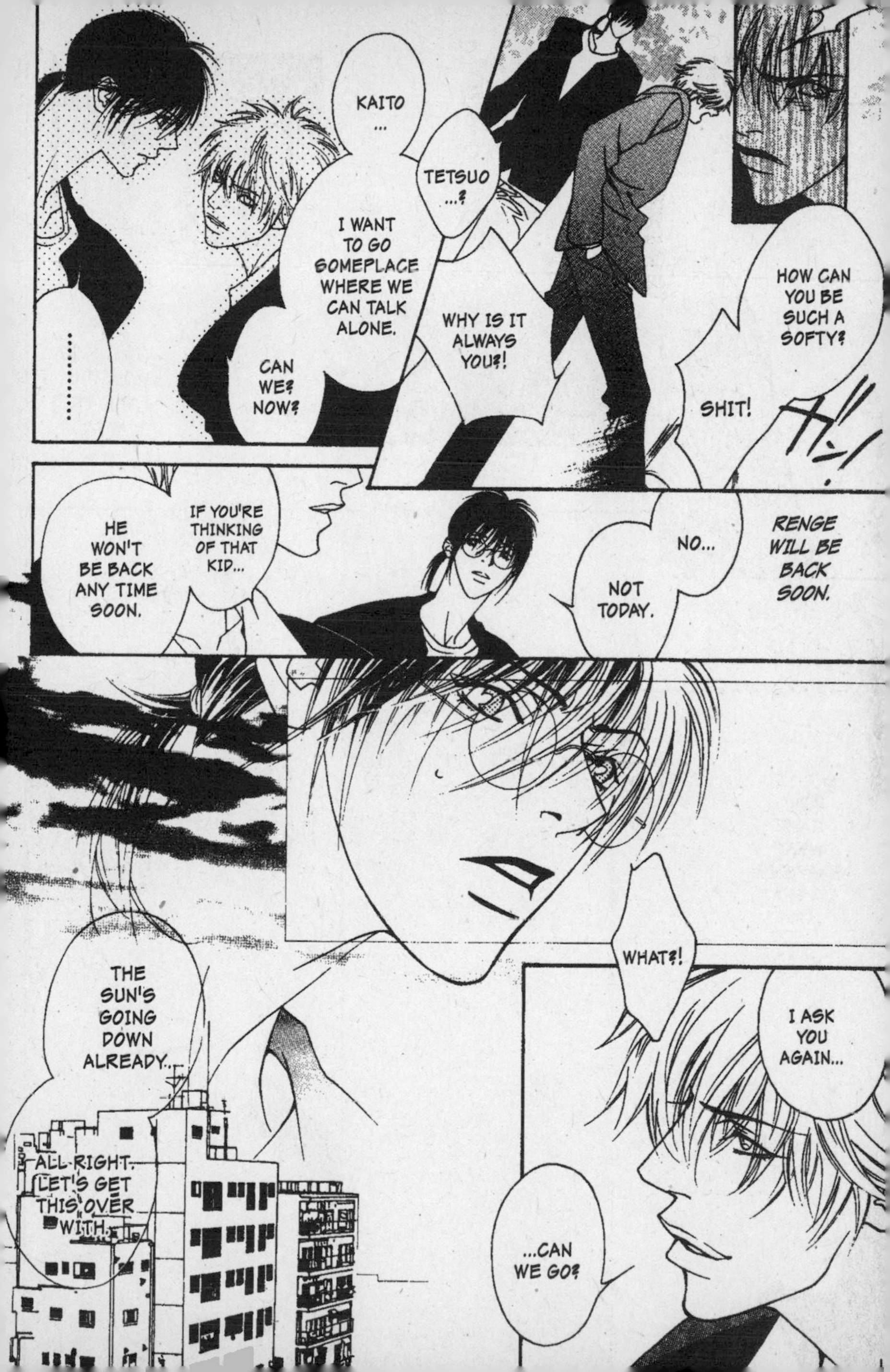
HOW CAN YOU BE SUCH A SOFTY?
SHIT!
TETSUO ...?
WHY IS IT ALWAYS YOU?!
KAITO ...
I WANT TO GO SOMEPLACE WHERE WE CAN TALK ALONE.
CAN WE? NOW?
....
RENGE WILL BE BACK SOON.
NO...
NOT TODAY.
IF YOU'RE THINKING OF THAT KID...
HE WON'T BE BACK ANY TIME SOON.
WHAT?!
I ASK YOU AGAIN...
...CAN WE GO?
THE SUN'S GOING DOWN ALREADY...
ALL RIGHT. LET'S GET THIS OVER WITH.

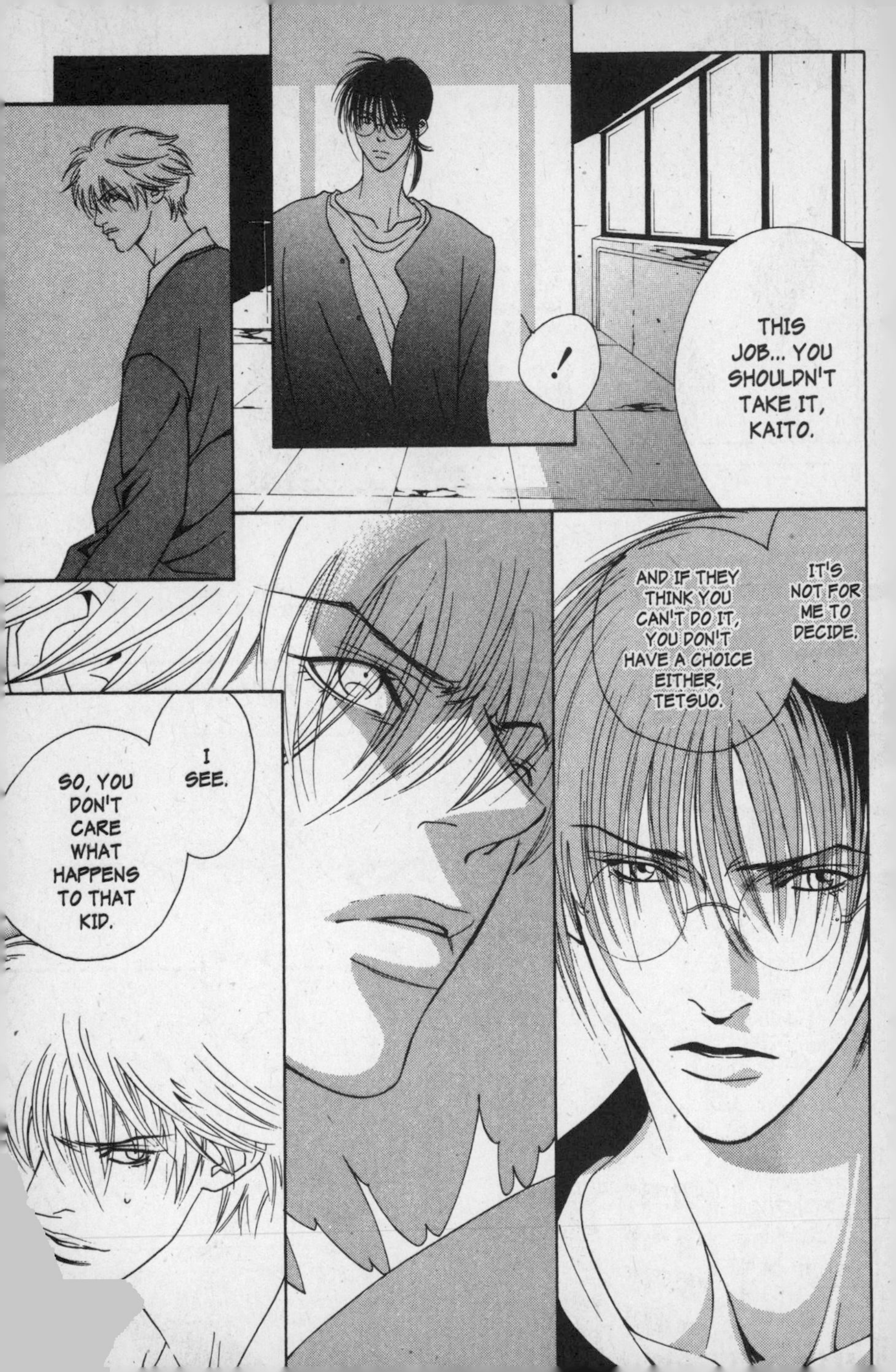
THIS JOB... YOU SHOULDN'T TAKE IT, KAITO.
!
IT'S NOT FOR ME TO DECIDE.
AND IF THEY THINK YOU CAN'T DO IT, YOU DON'T HAVE A CHOICE EITHER, TETSUO.
I SEE.
SO, YOU DON'T CARE WHAT HAPPENS TO THAT KID.

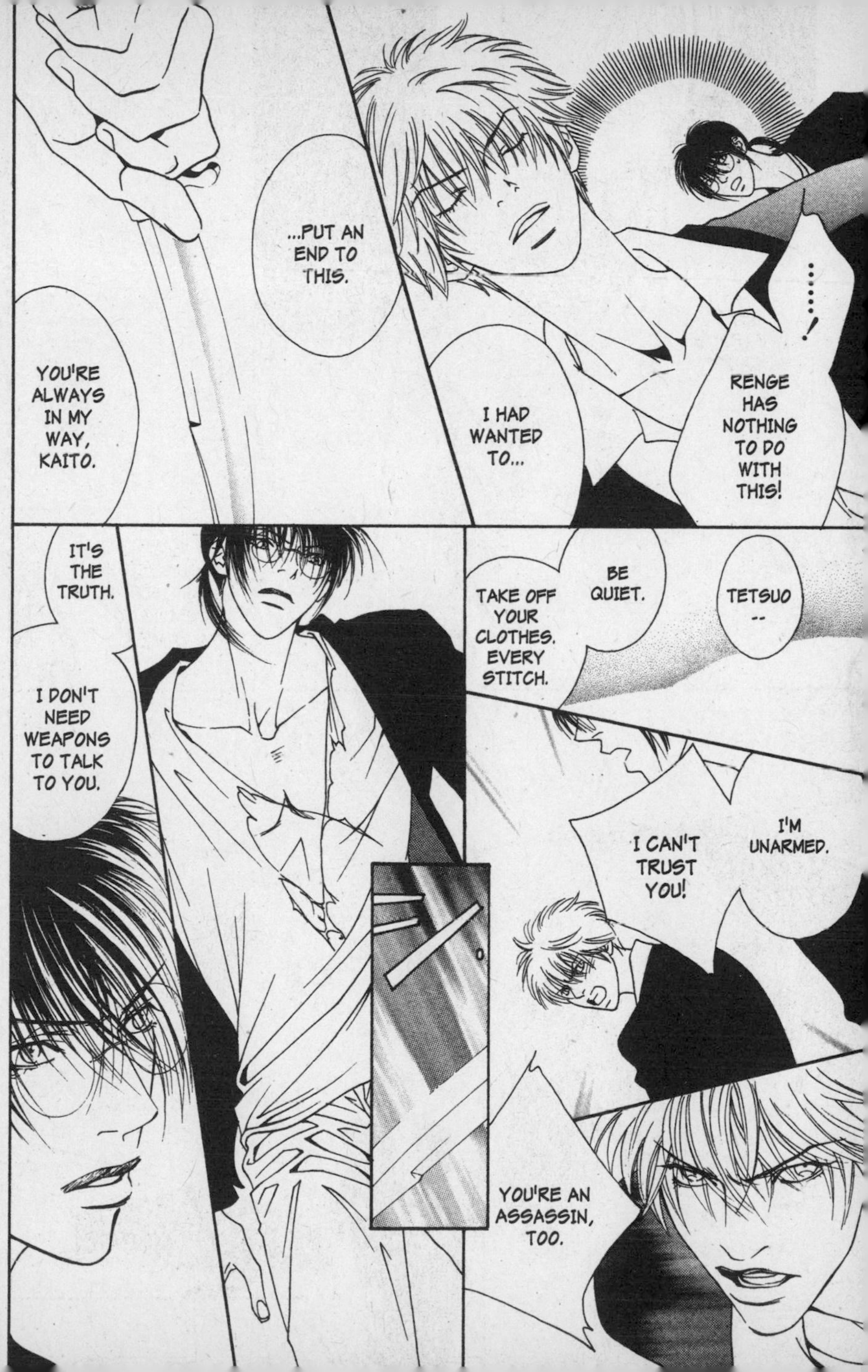
......!
RENGE HAS NOTHING TO DO WITH THIS!
I HAD WANTED TO...
...PUT AN END TO THIS.
YOU'RE ALWAYS IN MY WAY, KAITO.
TETSUO --
BE QUIET.
TAKE OFF YOUR CLOTHES. EVERY STITCH.
I'M UNARMED.
I CAN'T TRUST YOU!
YOU'RE AN ASSASSIN, TOO.
IT'S THE TRUTH.
I DON'T NEED WEAPONS TO TALK TO YOU.

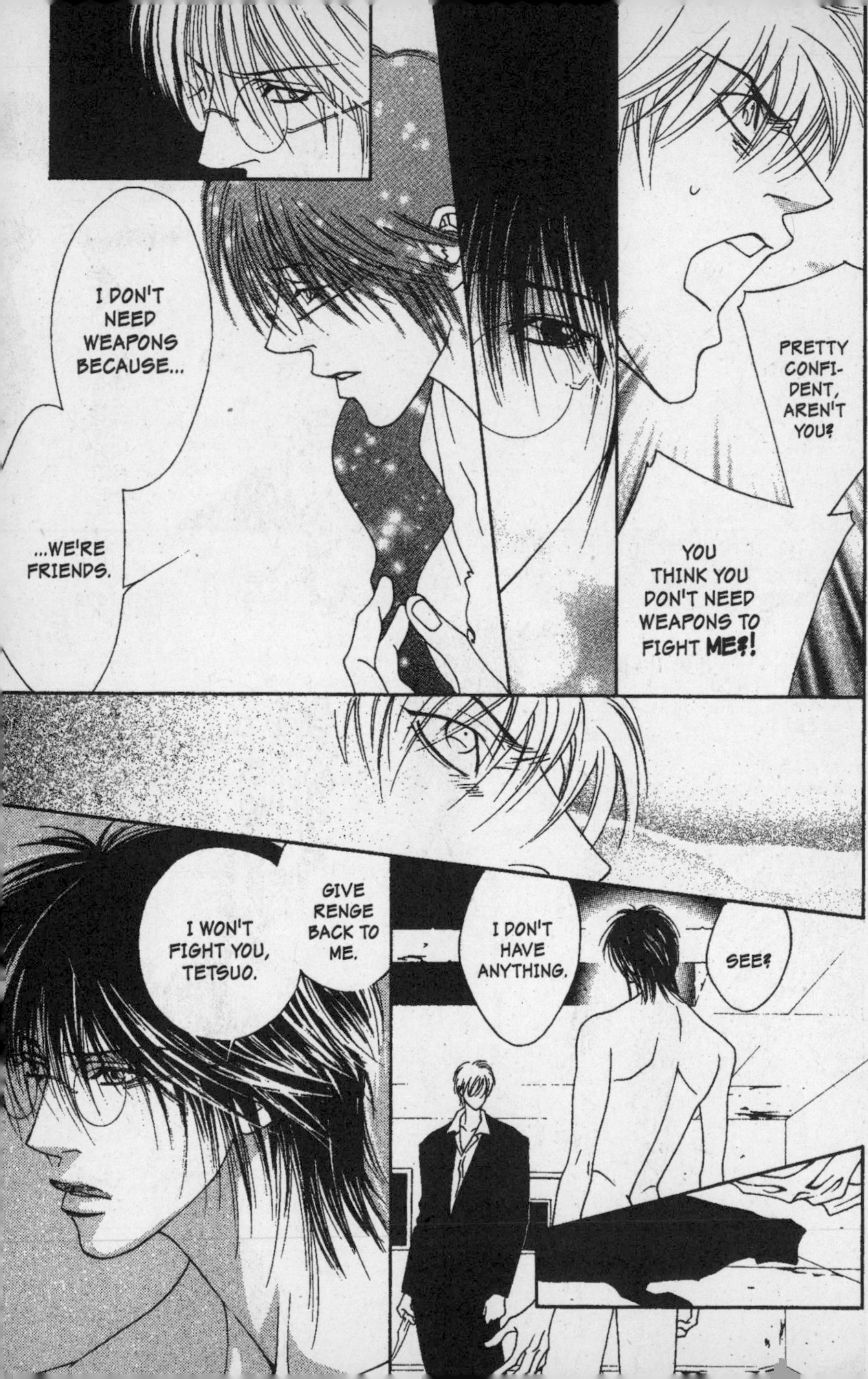
PRETTY CONFIDENT, AREN'T YOU?
YOU THINK YOU DON'T NEED WEAPONS TO FIGHT **ME?!**
I DON'T NEED WEAPONS BECAUSE...
...WE'RE FRIENDS.
I DON'T HAVE ANYTHING.
SEE?
GIVE RENGE BACK TO ME.
I WON'T FIGHT YOU, TETSUO.

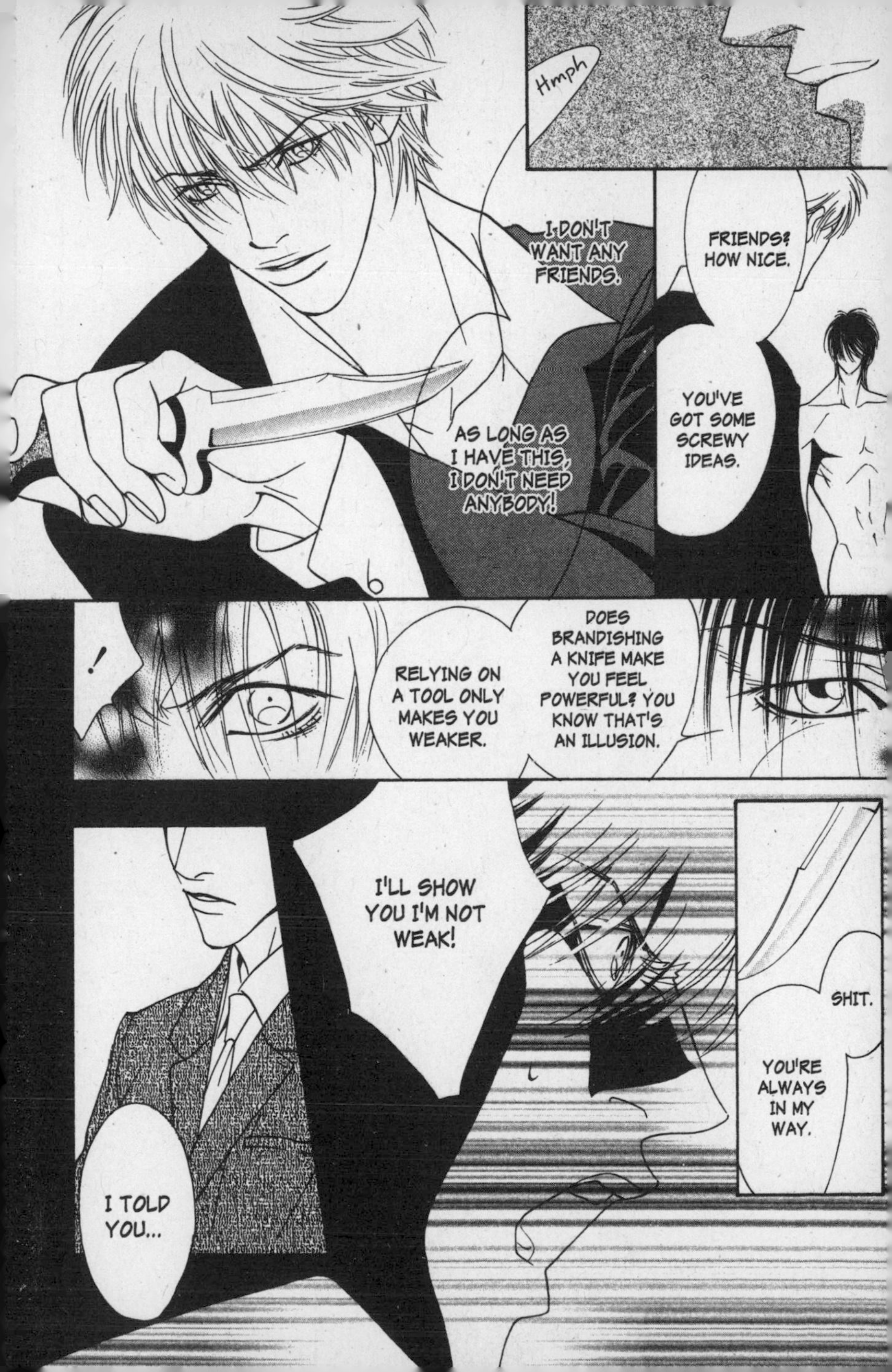
Hmph
FRIENDS? HOW NICE.
YOU'VE GOT SOME SCREWY IDEAS.
I DON'T WANT ANY FRIENDS.
AS LONG AS I HAVE THIS, I DON'T NEED ANYBODY!
DOES BRANDISHING A KNIFE MAKE YOU FEEL POWERFUL? YOU KNOW THAT'S AN ILLUSION.
RELYING ON A TOOL ONLY MAKES YOU WEAKER.
!
SHIT.
YOU'RE ALWAYS IN MY WAY.
I'LL SHOW YOU I'M NOT WEAK!
I TOLD YOU...

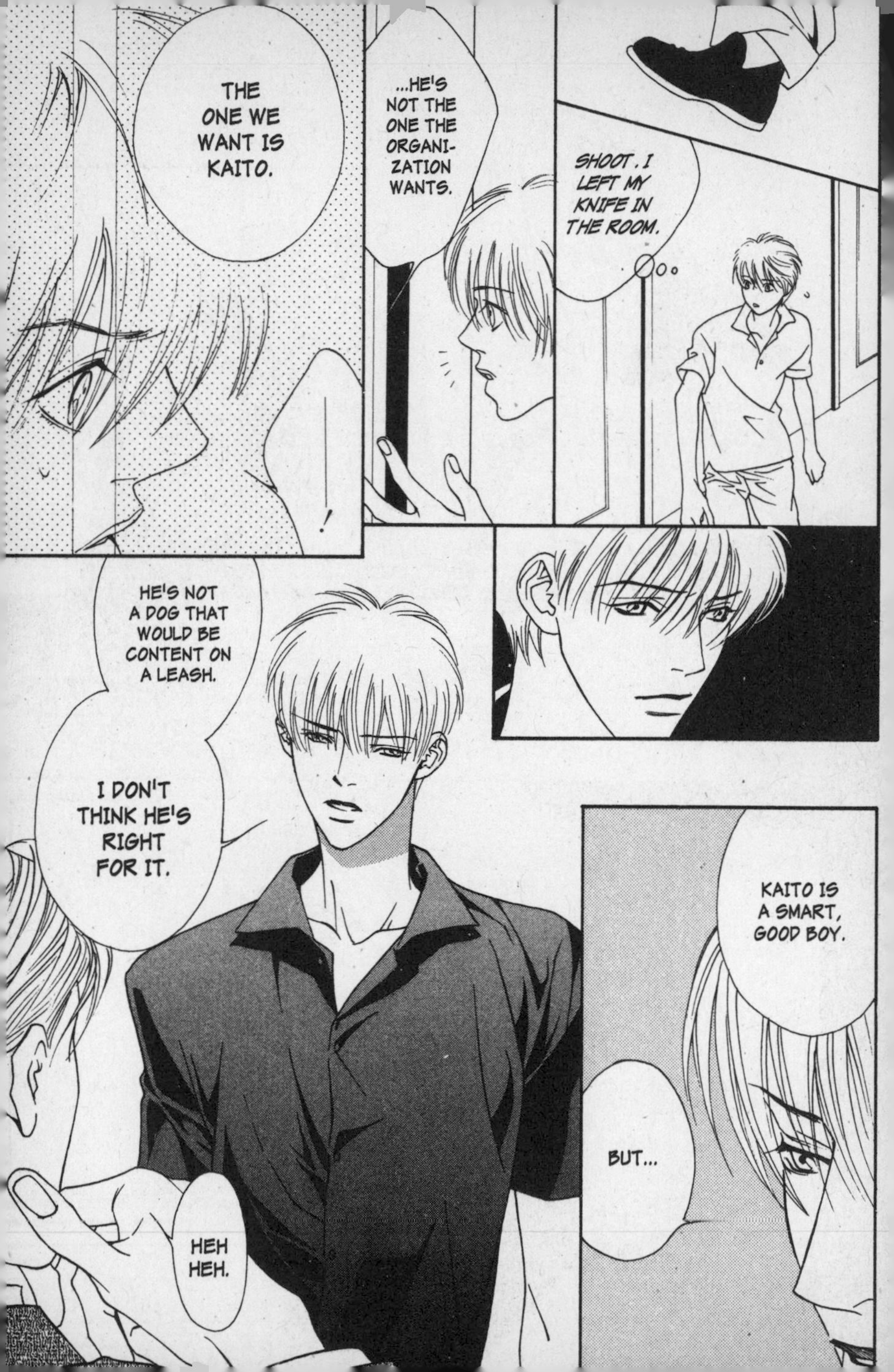
SHOOT. I LEFT MY KNIFE IN THE ROOM.
...HE'S NOT THE ONE THE ORGANI-ZATION WANTS.
THE ONE WE WANT IS KAITO.
KAITO IS A SMART, GOOD BOY.
BUT...
HE'S NOT A DOG THAT WOULD BE CONTENT ON A LEASH.
I DON'T THINK HE'S RIGHT FOR IT.
HEH HEH.

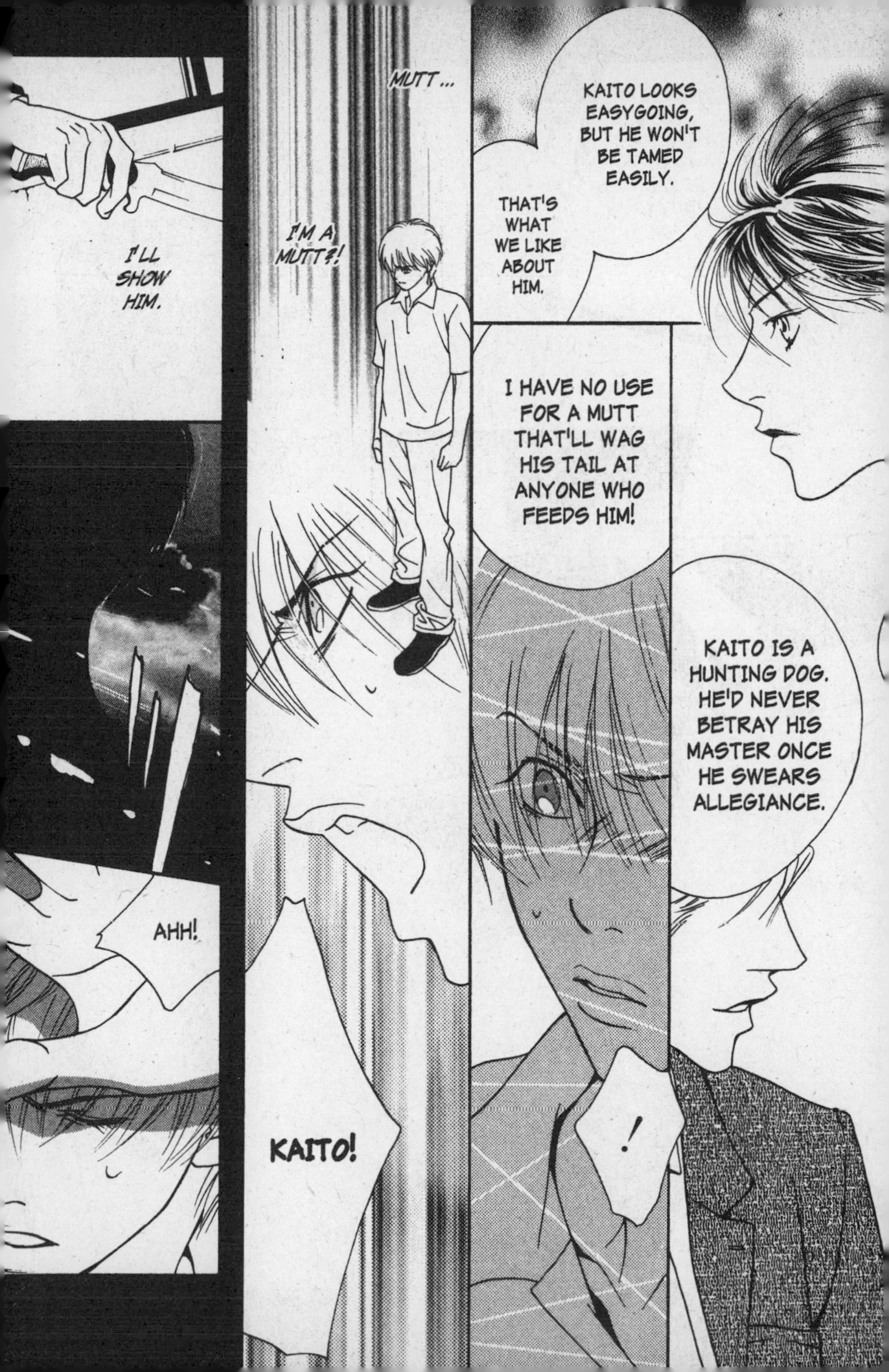
KAITO LOOKS EASYGOING, BUT HE WON'T BE TAMED EASILY.
THAT'S WHAT WE LIKE ABOUT HIM.
KAITO IS A HUNTING DOG. HE'D NEVER BETRAY HIS MASTER ONCE HE SWEARS ALLEGIANCE.
I HAVE NO USE FOR A MUTT THAT'LL WAG HIS TAIL AT ANYONE WHO FEEDS HIM!
!
MUTT...
I'M A MUTT?!
KAITO!
I'LL SHOW HIM.
AHH!

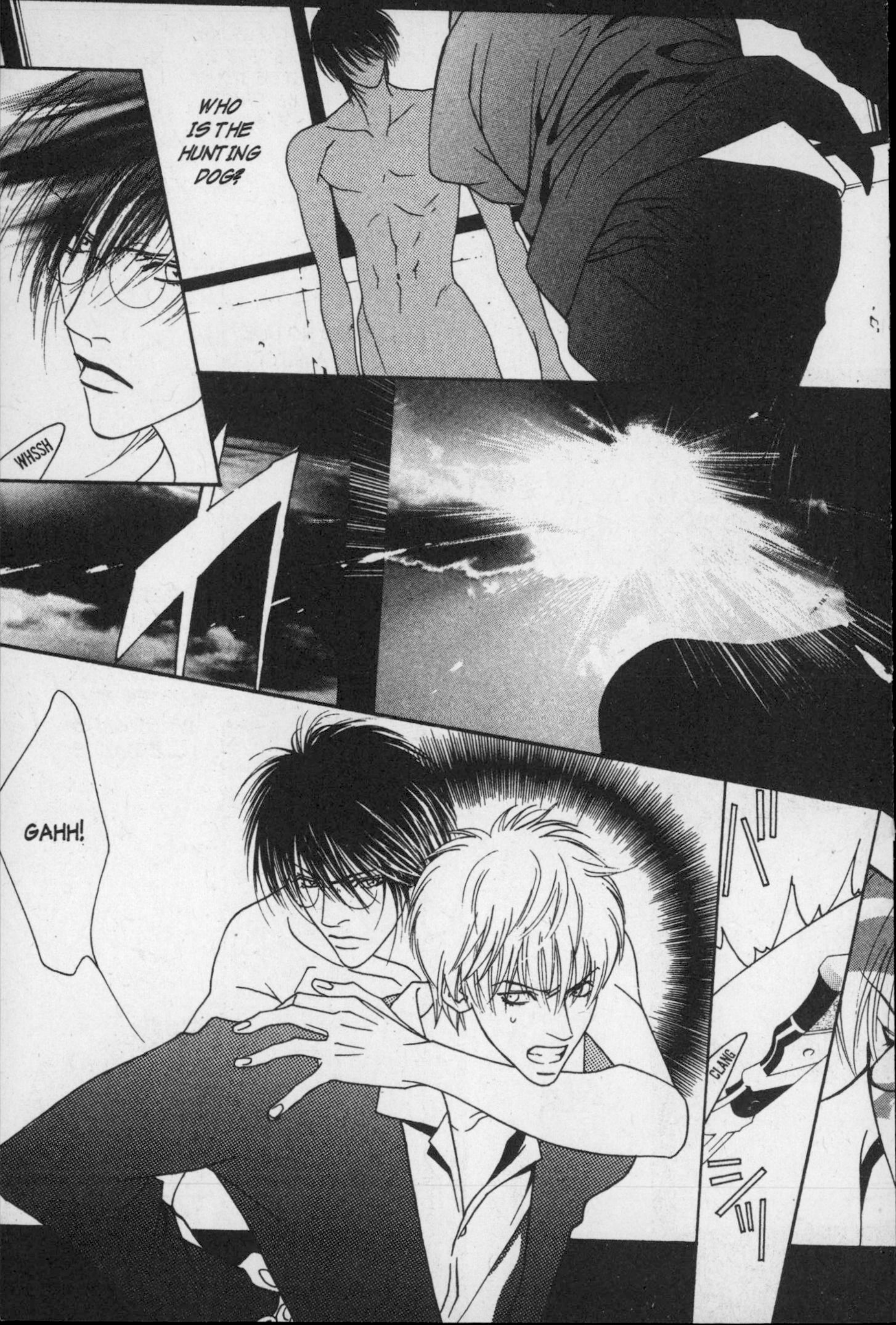
WHO IS THE HUNTING DOG?
WHSSH
CLANG
GAHH!

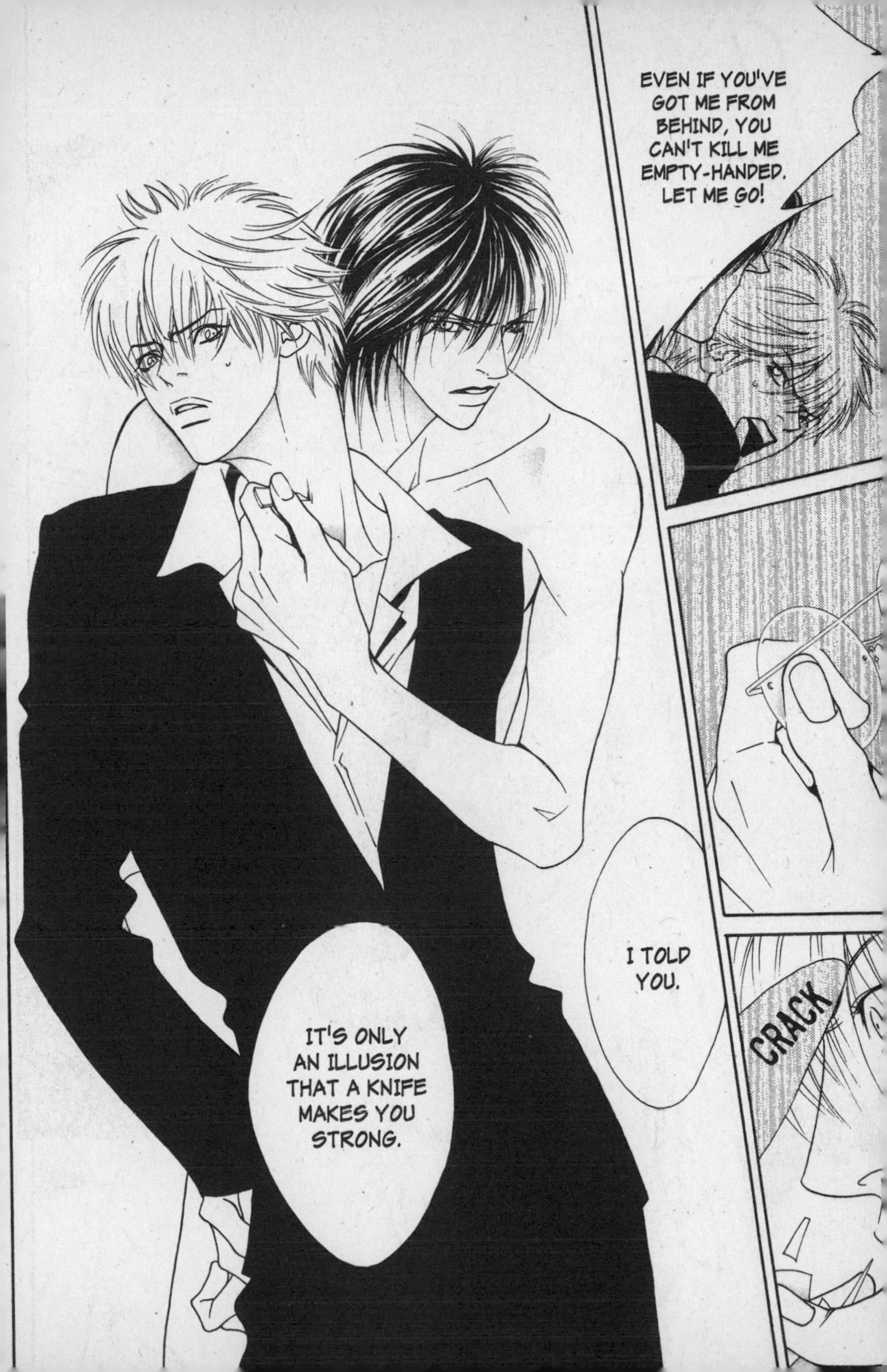
EVEN IF YOU'VE GOT ME FROM BEHIND, YOU CAN'T KILL ME EMPTY-HANDED. LET ME GO!
I TOLD YOU.
CRACK
IT'S ONLY AN ILLUSION THAT A KNIFE MAKES YOU STRONG.

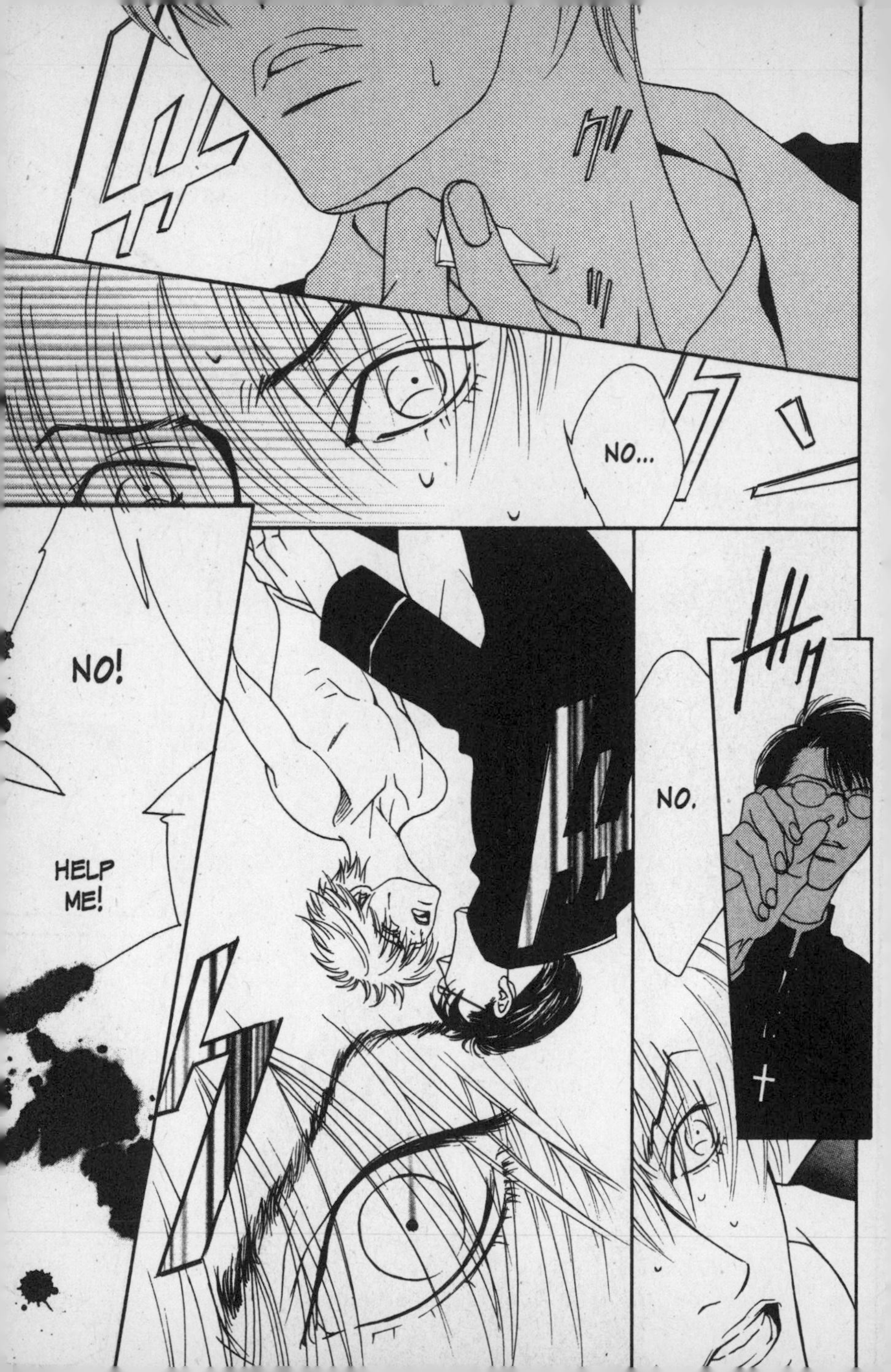
NO...
NO.
NO!
HELP ME!

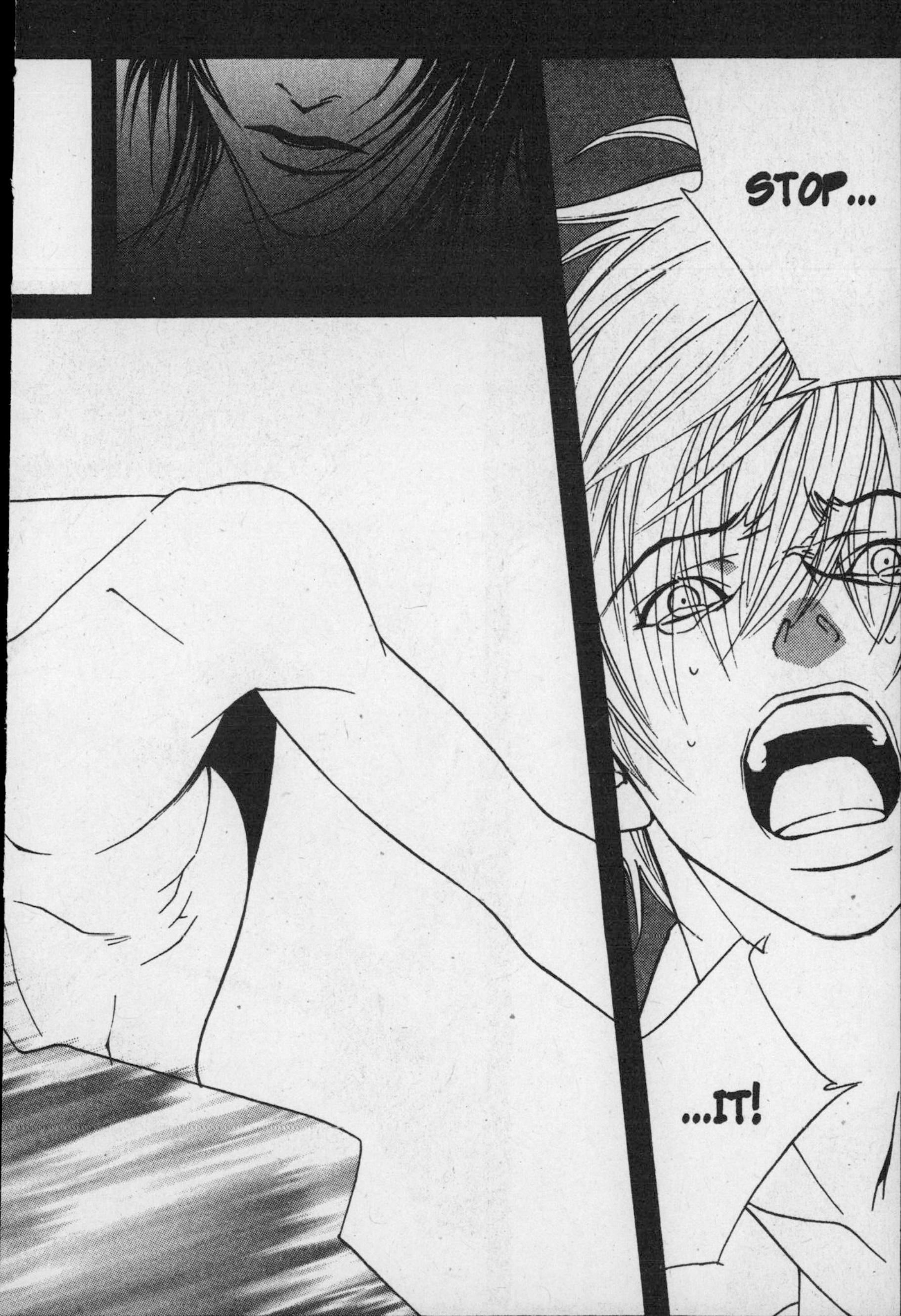
STOP...
...IT!

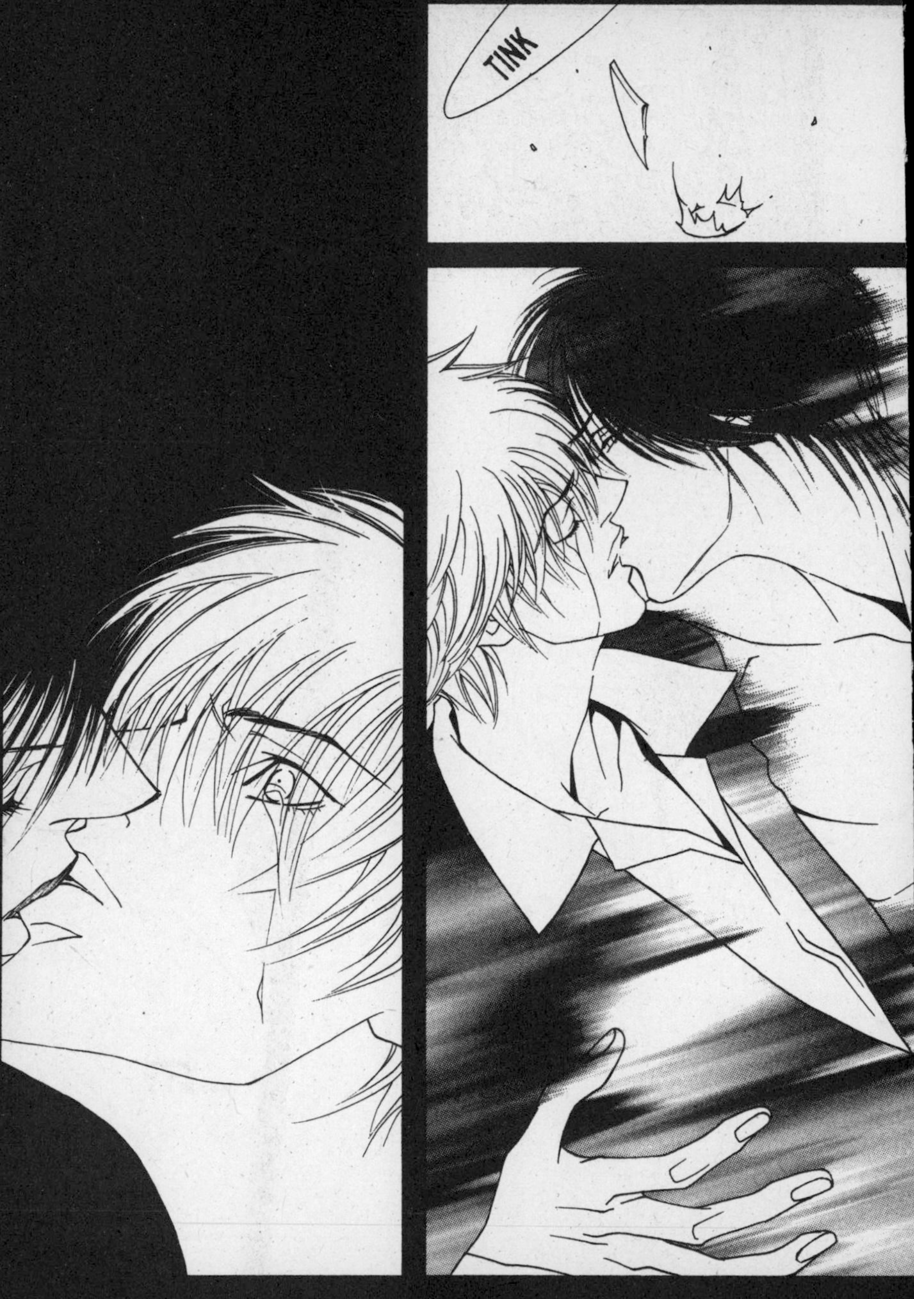
TINK

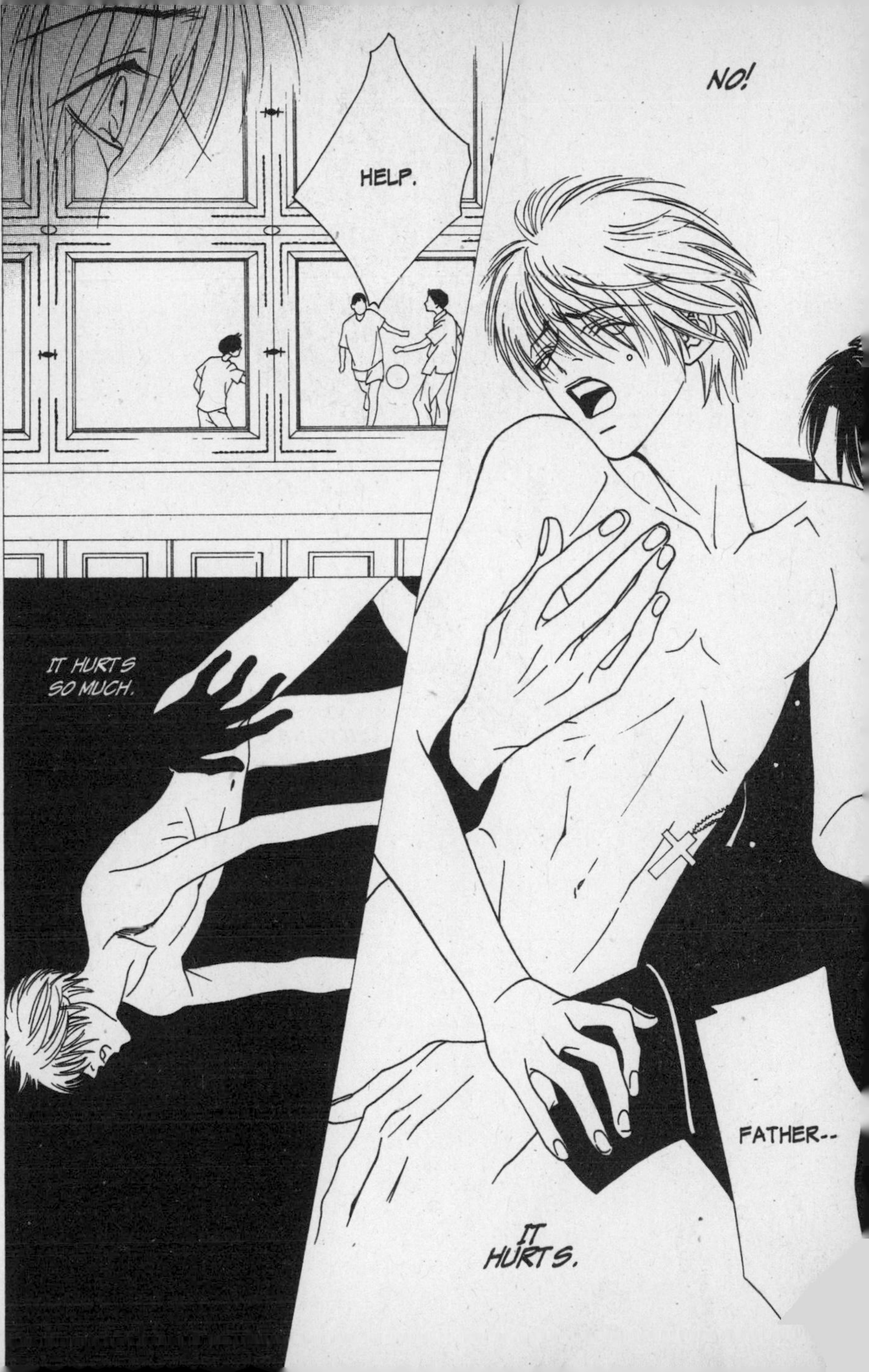
NO!
FATHER--
IT HURTS.
HELP.
IT HURTS SO MUCH.

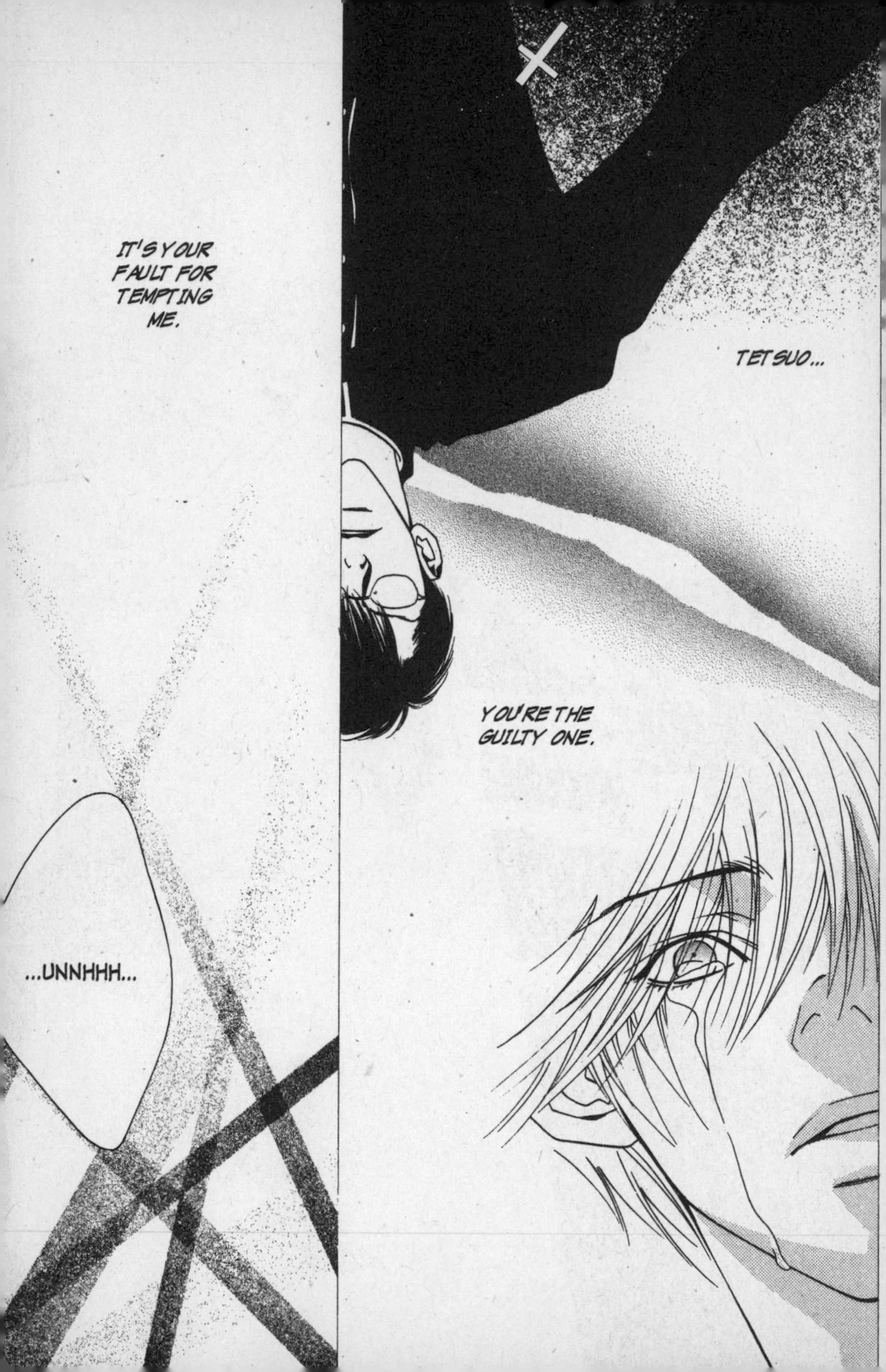
TETSUO...
YOU'RE THE GUILTY ONE.
IT'S YOUR FAULT FOR TEMPTING ME.
...UNNHHH...

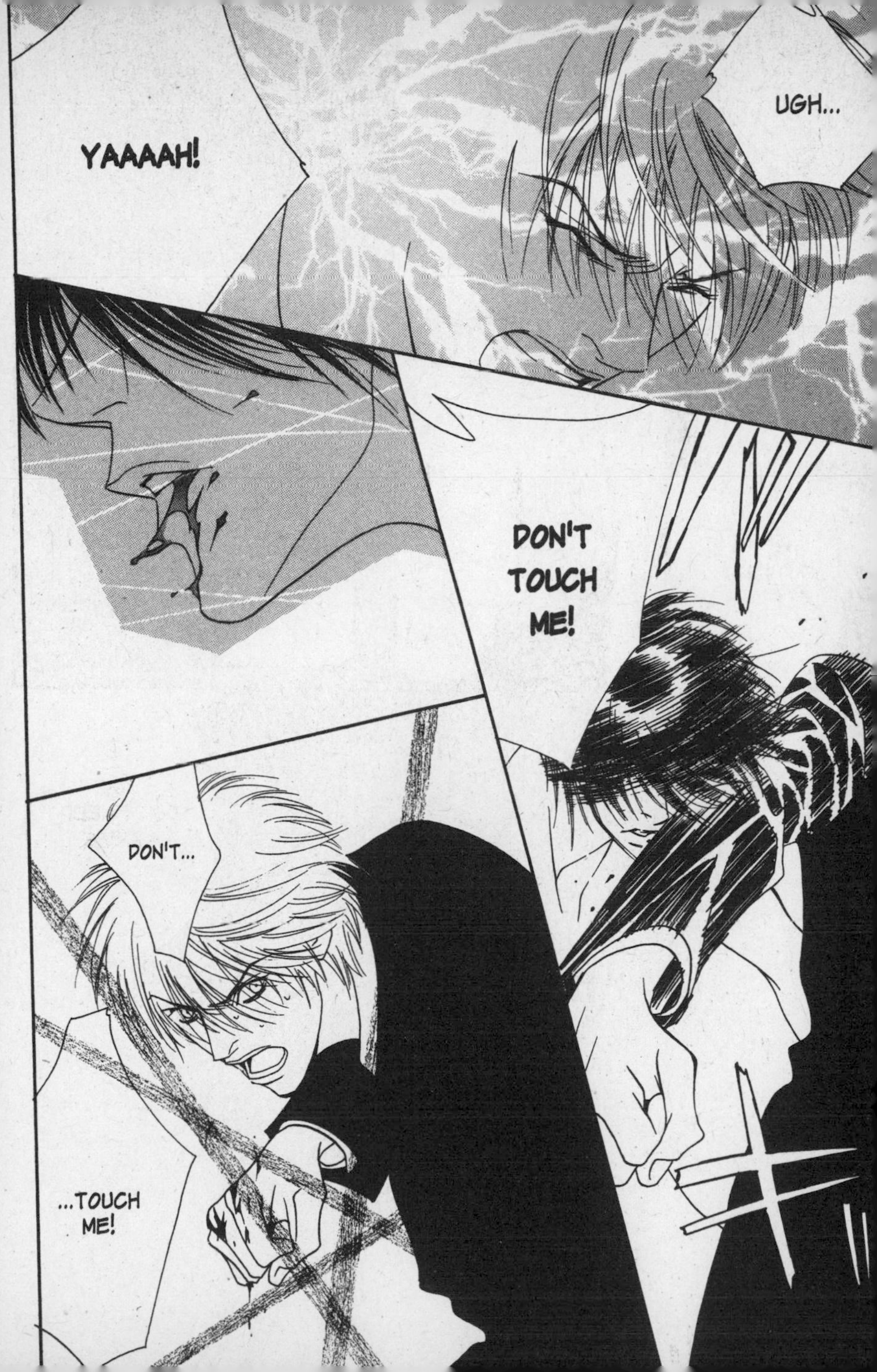
UGH...
YAAAAH!
DON'T TOUCH ME!
DON'T...
...TOUCH ME!

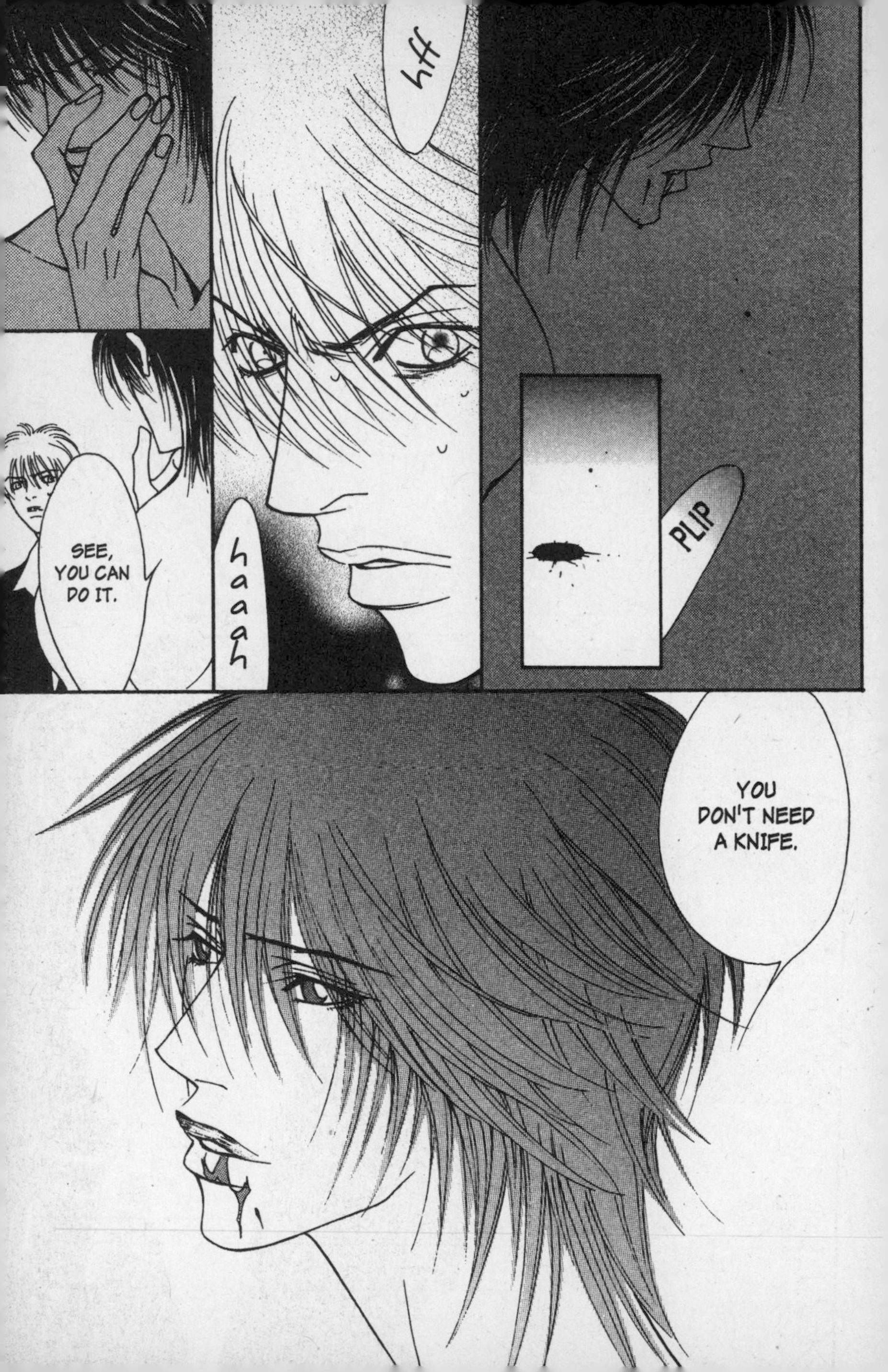
PLIP
hff
haaah
SEE, YOU CAN DO IT.
YOU DON'T NEED A KNIFE.

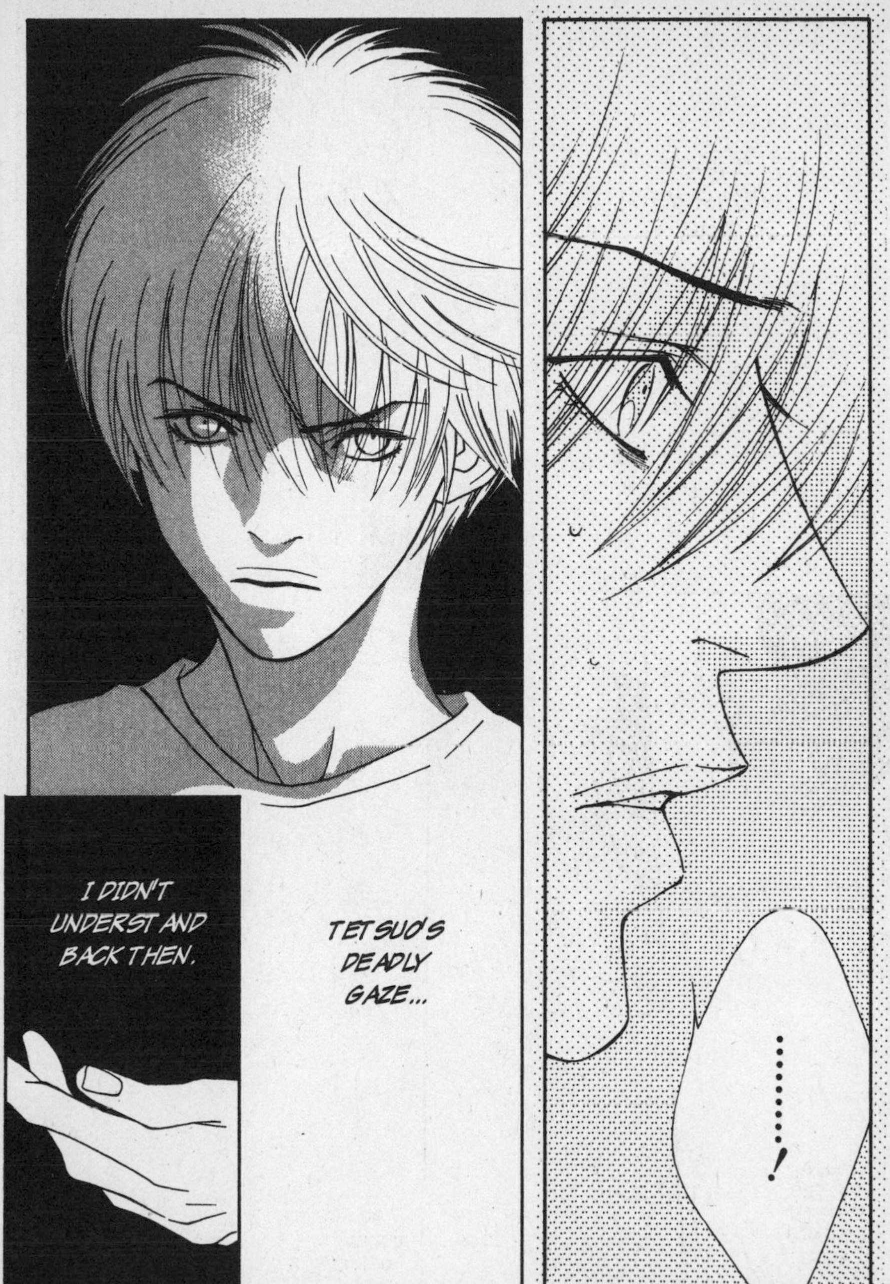
......!
TETSUO'S DEADLY GAZE...
I DIDN'T UNDERSTAND BACK THEN.

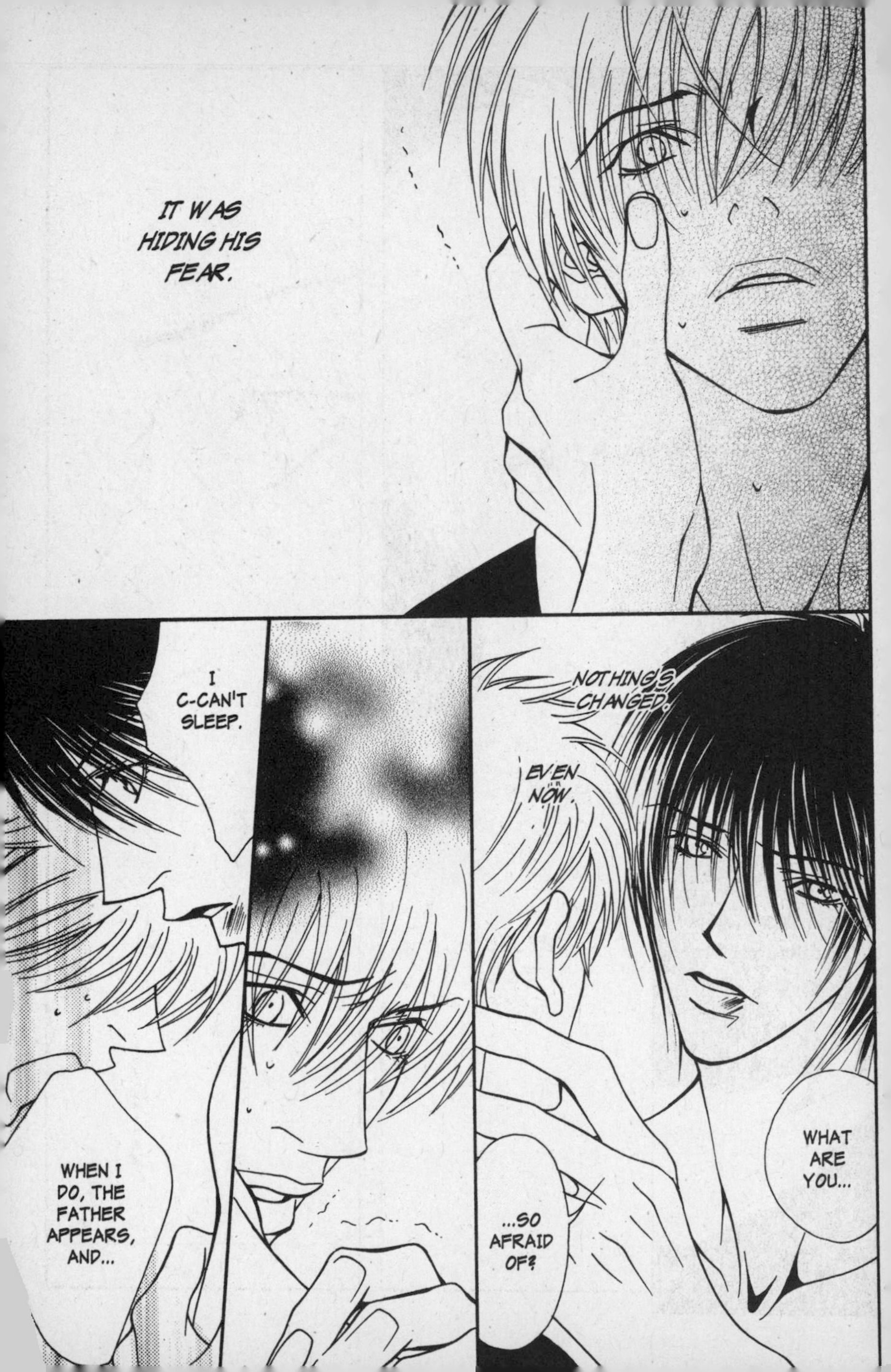
IT WAS HIDING HIS FEAR.
NOTHING'S CHANGED.
EVEN NOW.
WHAT ARE YOU...
...SO AFRAID OF?
I C-CAN'T SLEEP.
WHEN I DO, THE FATHER APPEARS, AND...

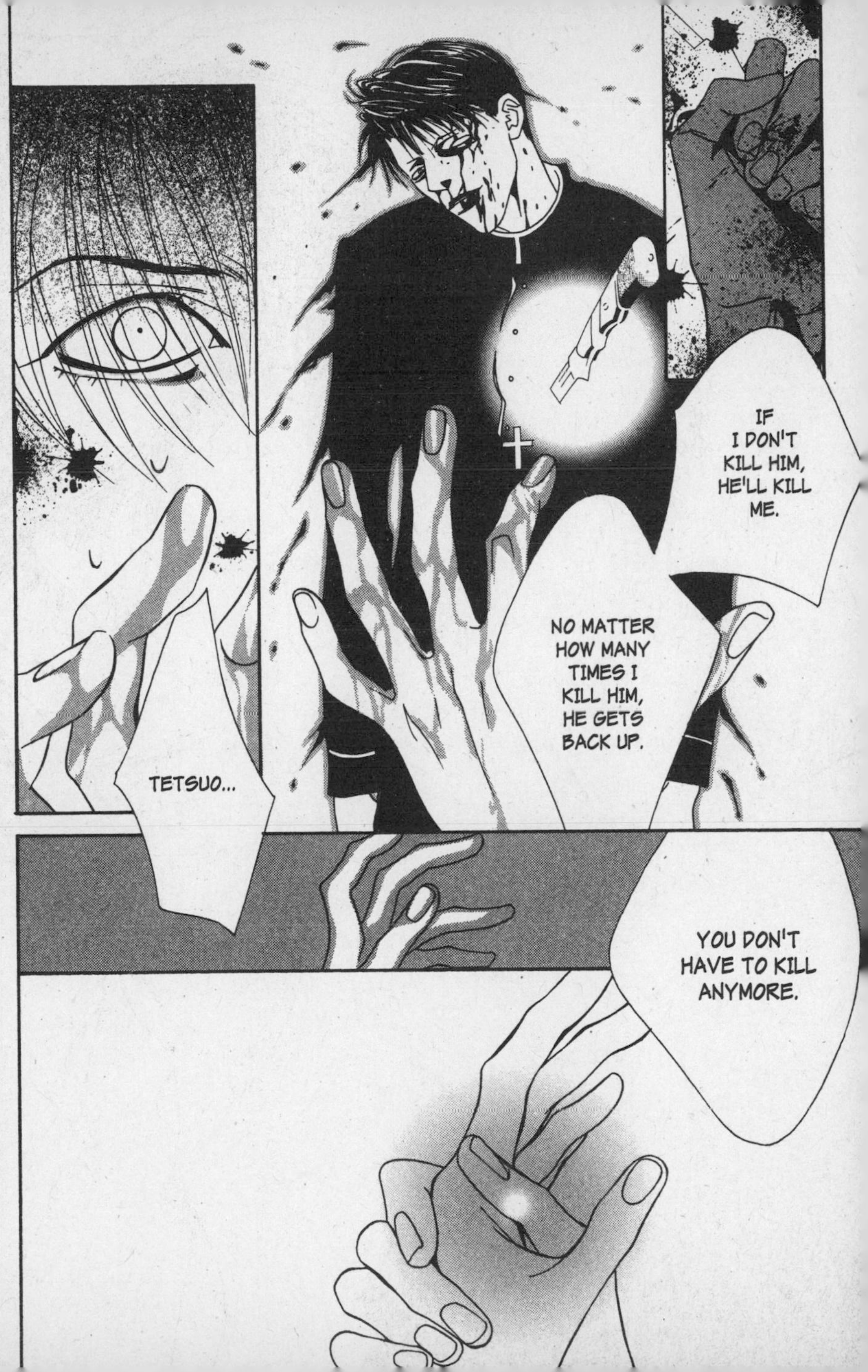
IF I DON'T KILL HIM, HE'LL KILL ME.
NO MATTER HOW MANY TIMES I KILL HIM, HE GETS BACK UP.
TETSUO...
YOU DON'T HAVE TO KILL ANYMORE.

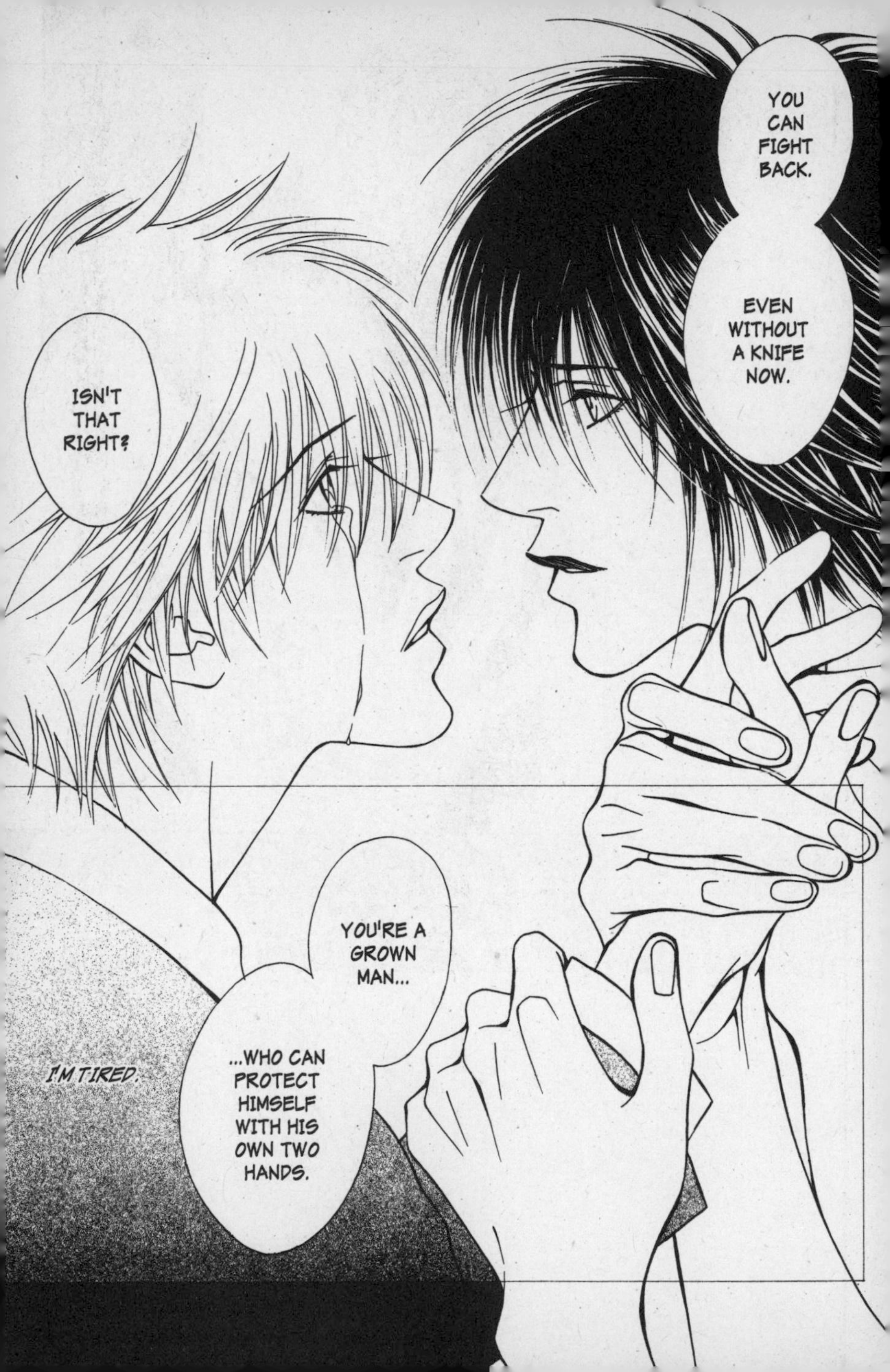
YOU CAN FIGHT BACK.
EVEN WITHOUT A KNIFE NOW.
ISN'T THAT RIGHT?
YOU'RE A GROWN MAN...
...WHO CAN PROTECT HIMSELF WITH HIS OWN TWO HANDS.
I'M TIRED.

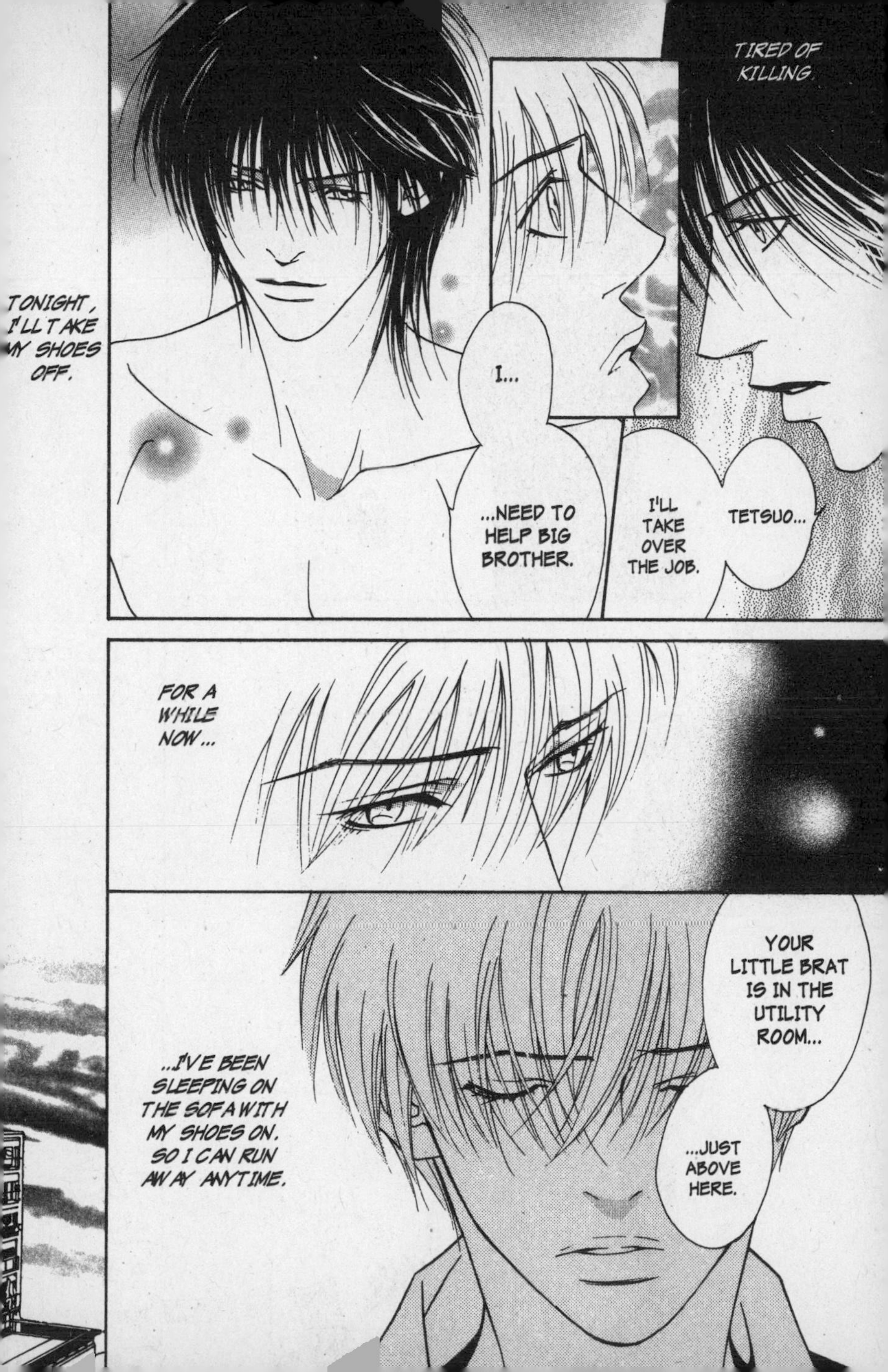
TIRED OF KILLING.
TETSUO...
I'LL TAKE OVER THE JOB.
I...
...NEED TO HELP BIG BROTHER.
TONIGHT, I'LL TAKE MY SHOES OFF.
FOR A WHILE NOW...
YOUR LITTLE BRAT IS IN THE UTILITY ROOM...
...JUST ABOVE HERE.
...I'VE BEEN SLEEPING ON THE SOFA WITH MY SHOES ON. SO I CAN RUN AWAY ANYTIME.

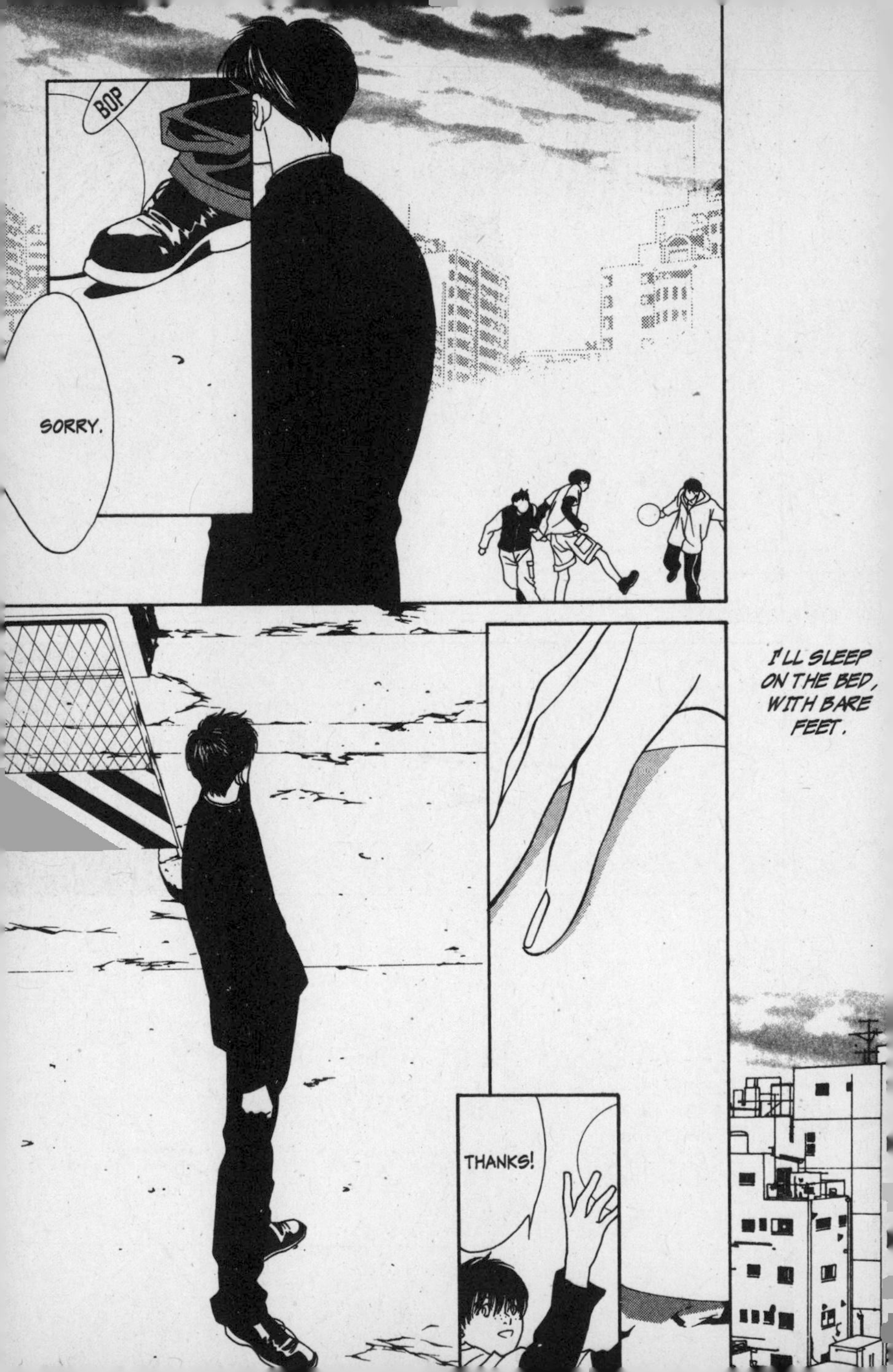
BOP
SORRY.
I'LL SLEEP ON THE BED, WITH BARE FEET.
THANKS!

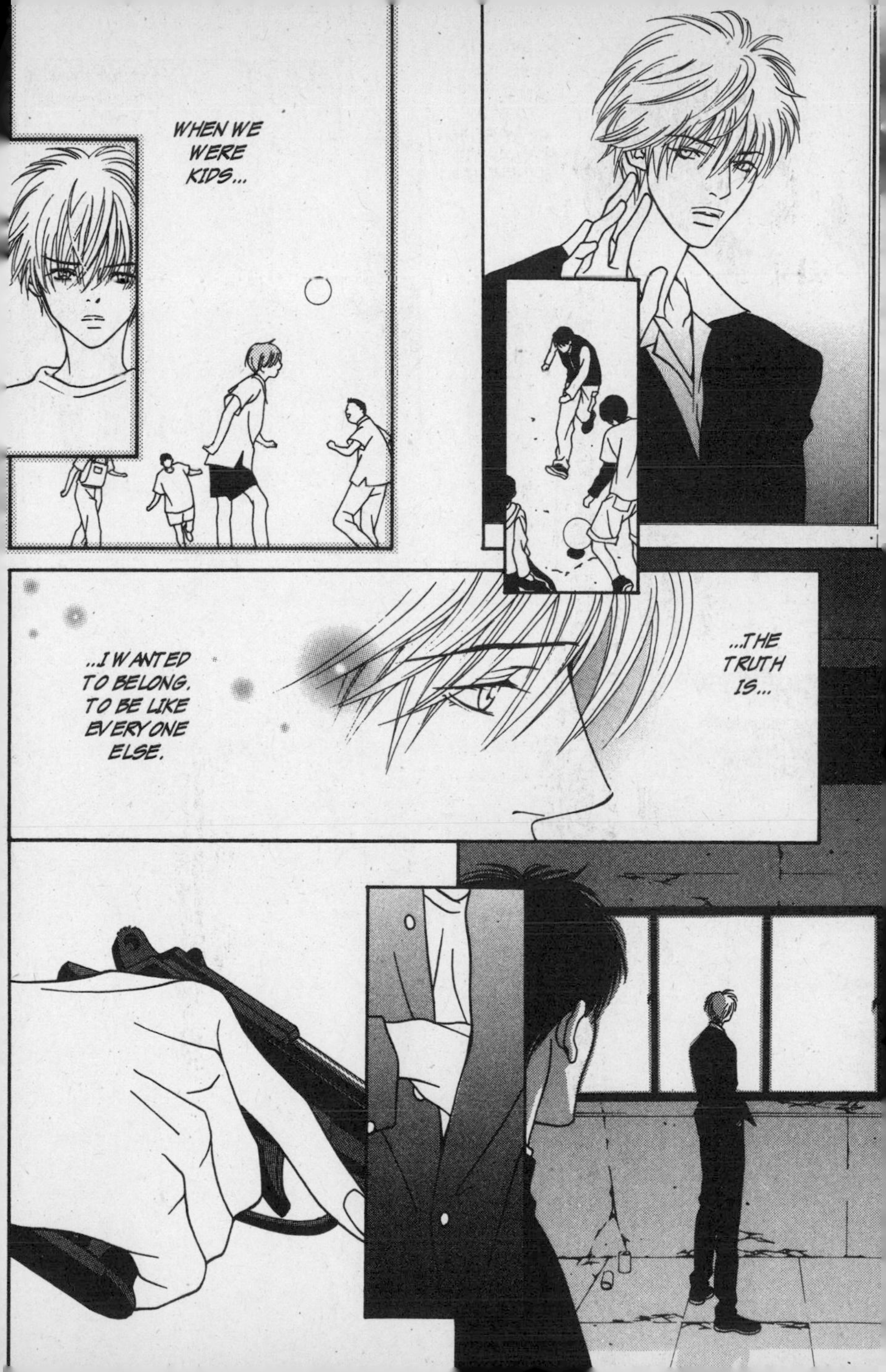
WHEN WE WERE KIDS...
...THE TRUTH IS...
...I WANTED TO BELONG. TO BE LIKE EVERYONE ELSE.

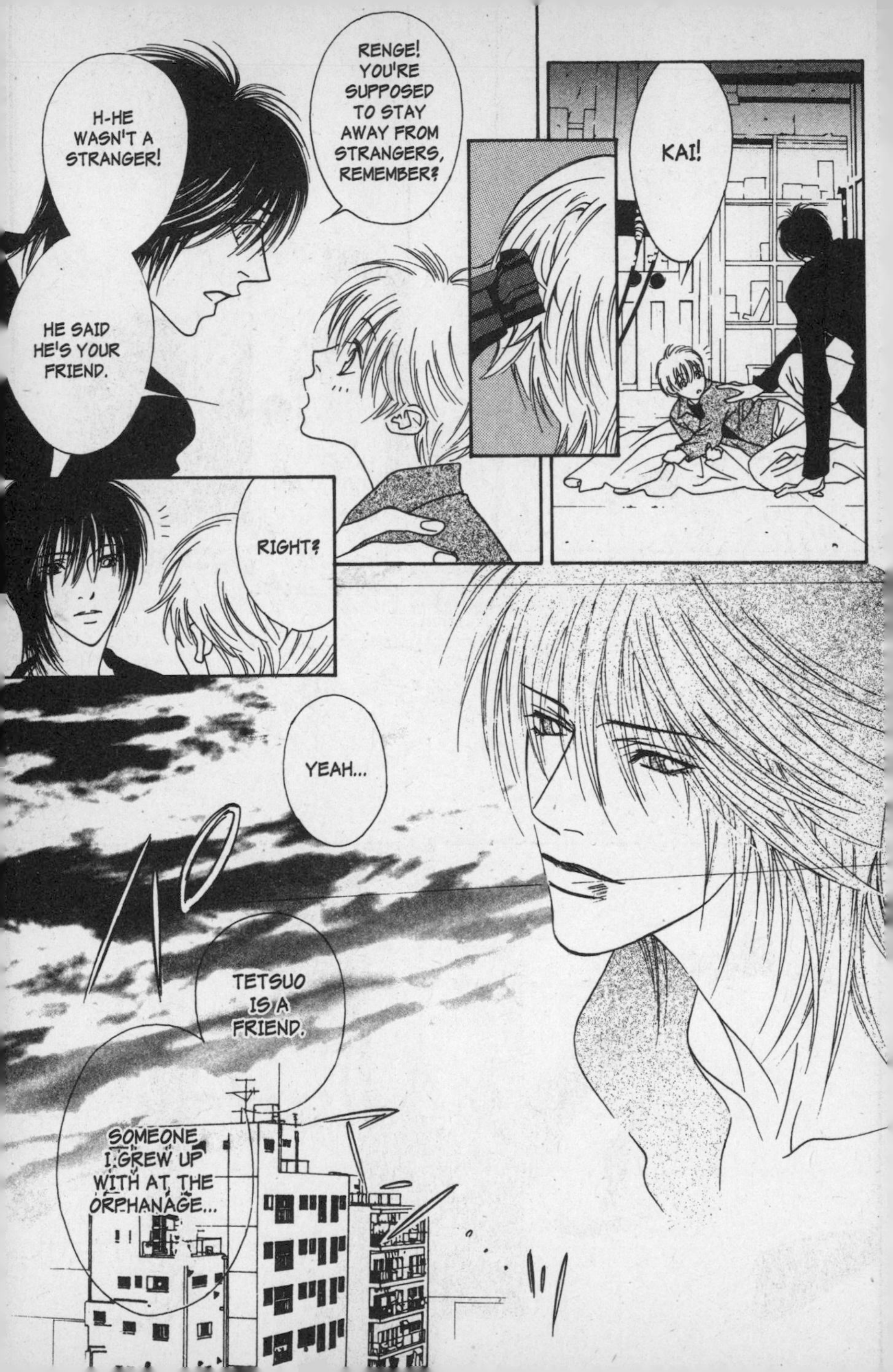
KAI!
RENGE! YOU'RE SUPPOSED TO STAY AWAY FROM STRANGERS, REMEMBER?
H-HE WASN'T A STRANGER!
HE SAID HE'S YOUR FRIEND.
RIGHT?
YEAH...
TETSUO IS A FRIEND.
SOMEONE I GREW UP WITH AT THE ORPHANAGE...

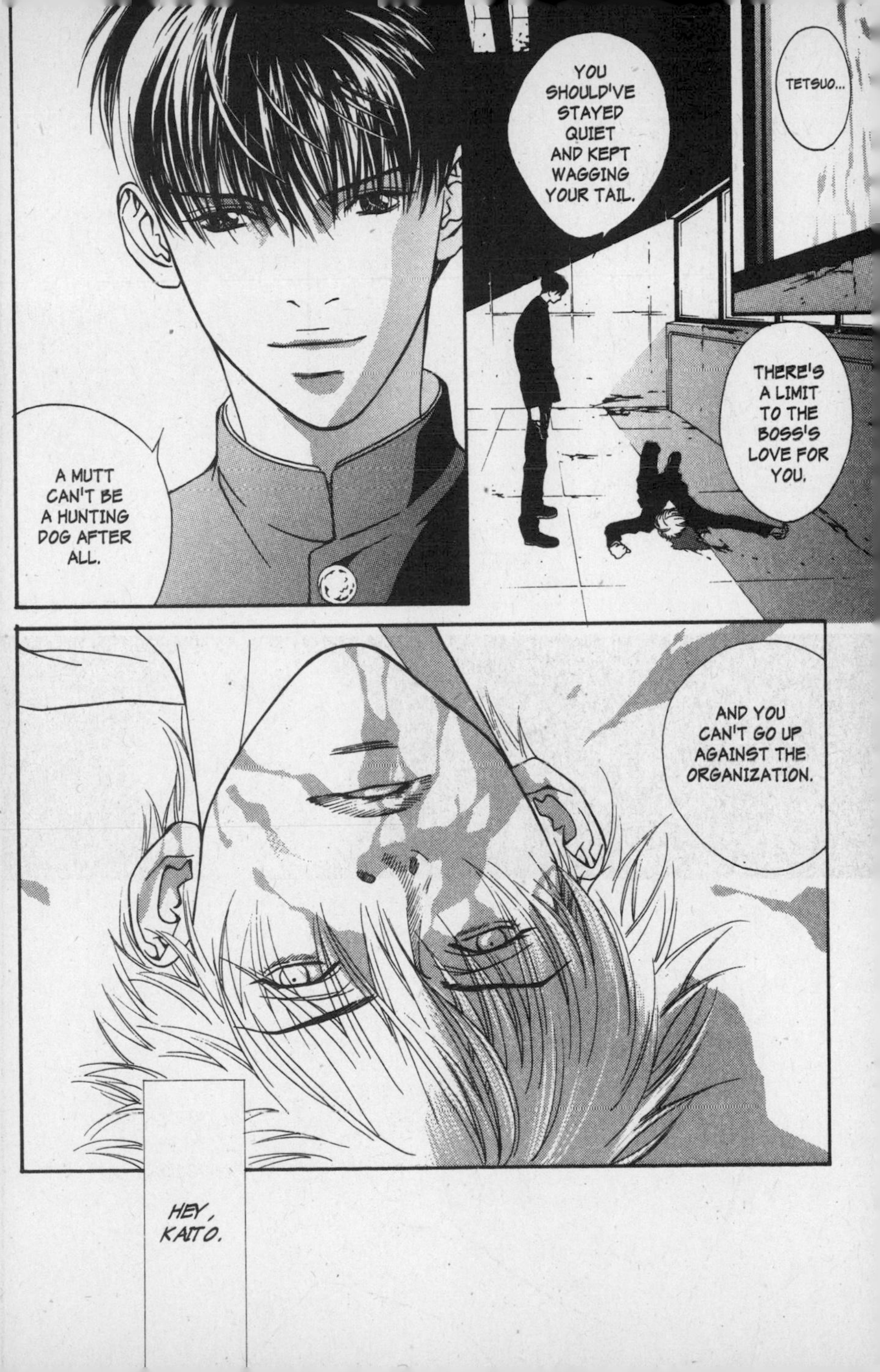
TETSUO...
YOU SHOULD'VE STAYED QUIET AND KEPT WAGGING YOUR TAIL.
THERE'S A LIMIT TO THE BOSS'S LOVE FOR YOU.
A MUTT CAN'T BE A HUNTING DOG AFTER ALL.
AND YOU CAN'T GO UP AGAINST THE ORGANIZATION.
HEY, KAITO.

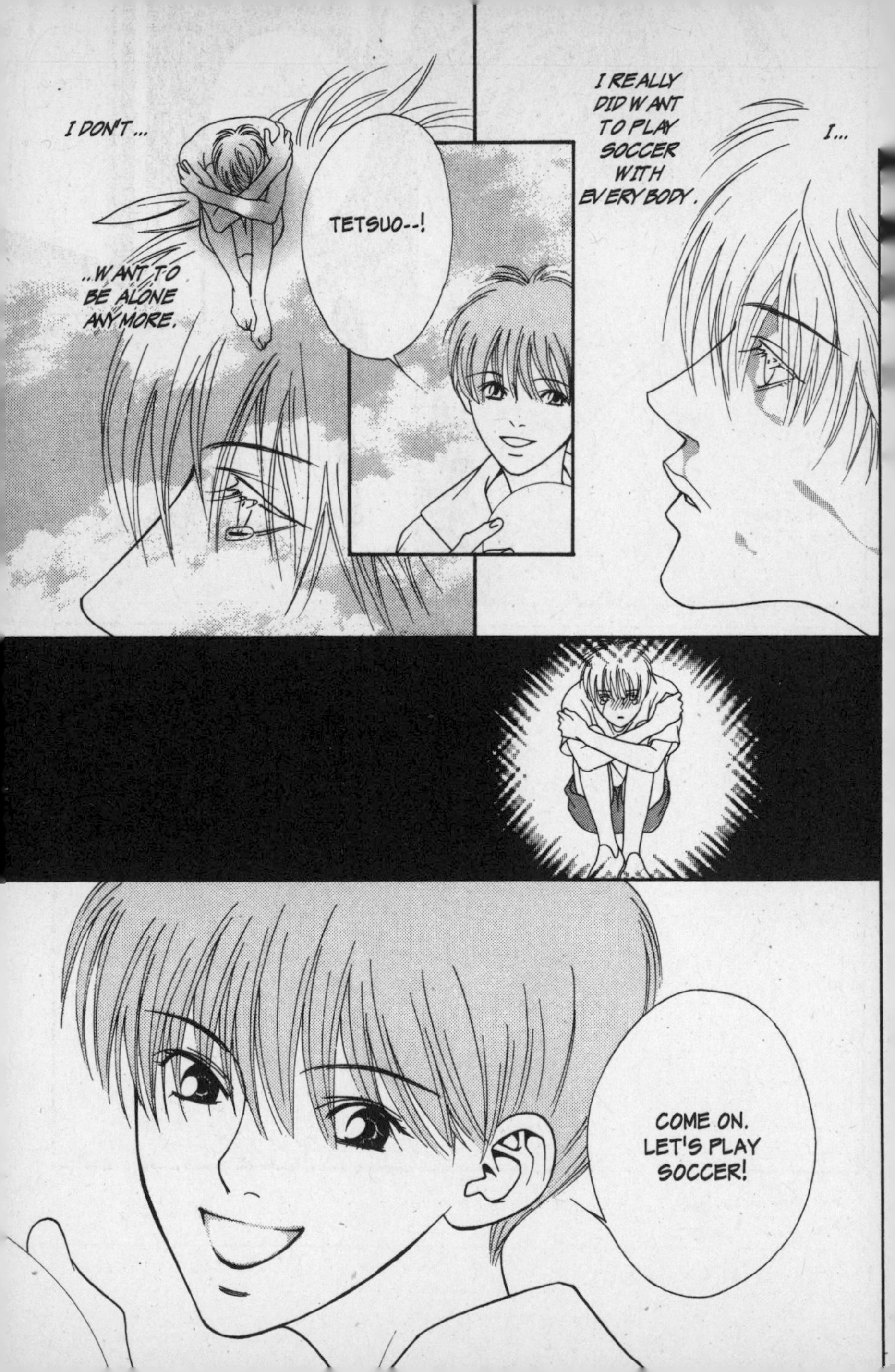

I...
I REALLY DID WANT TO PLAY SOCCER WITH EVERYBODY.
TETSUO--!
I DON'T ...
..WANT TO BE ALONE ANYMORE.
COME ON. LET'S PLAY SOCCER!

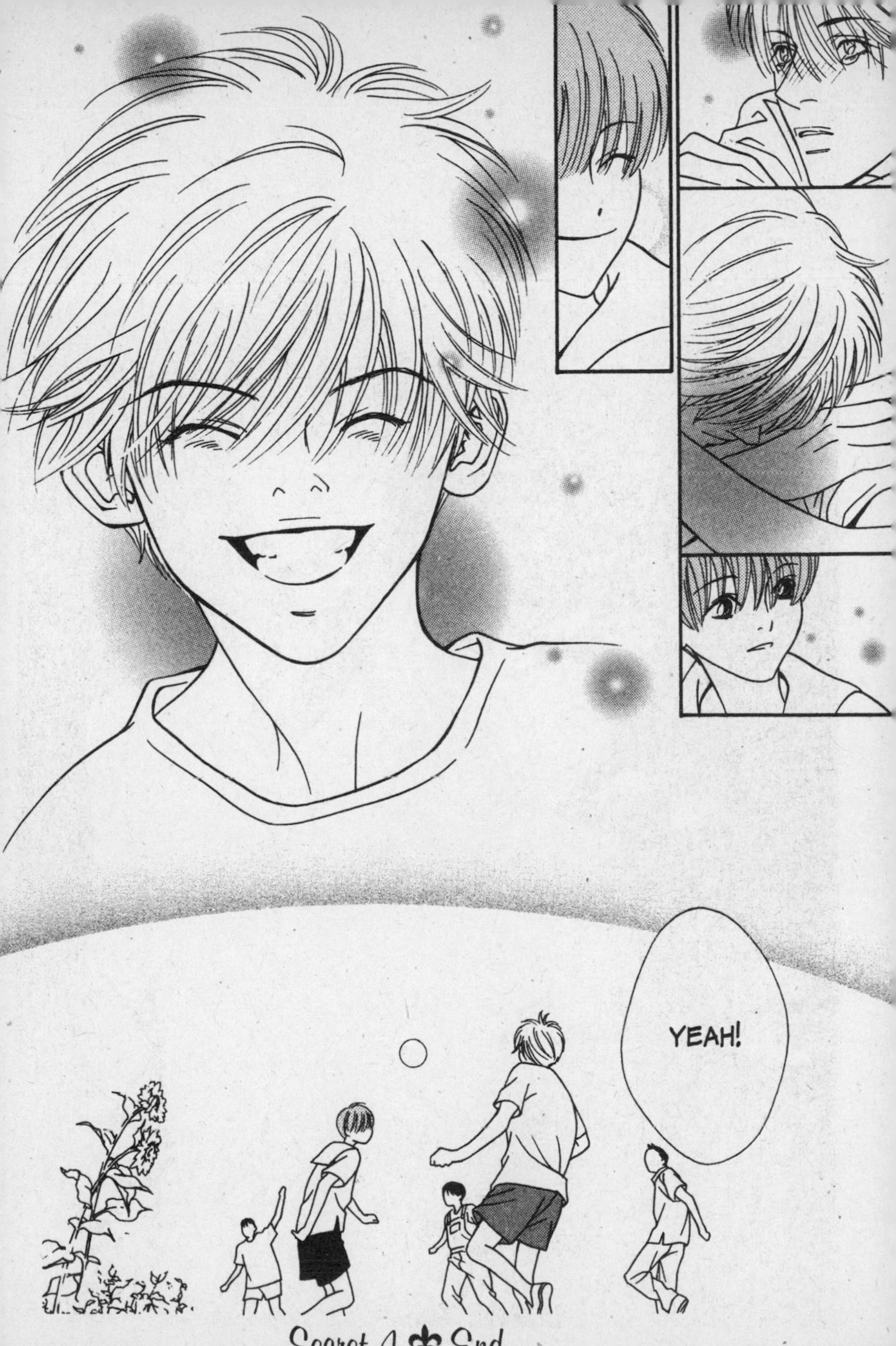
YEAH!

Secret 4 ✤ End

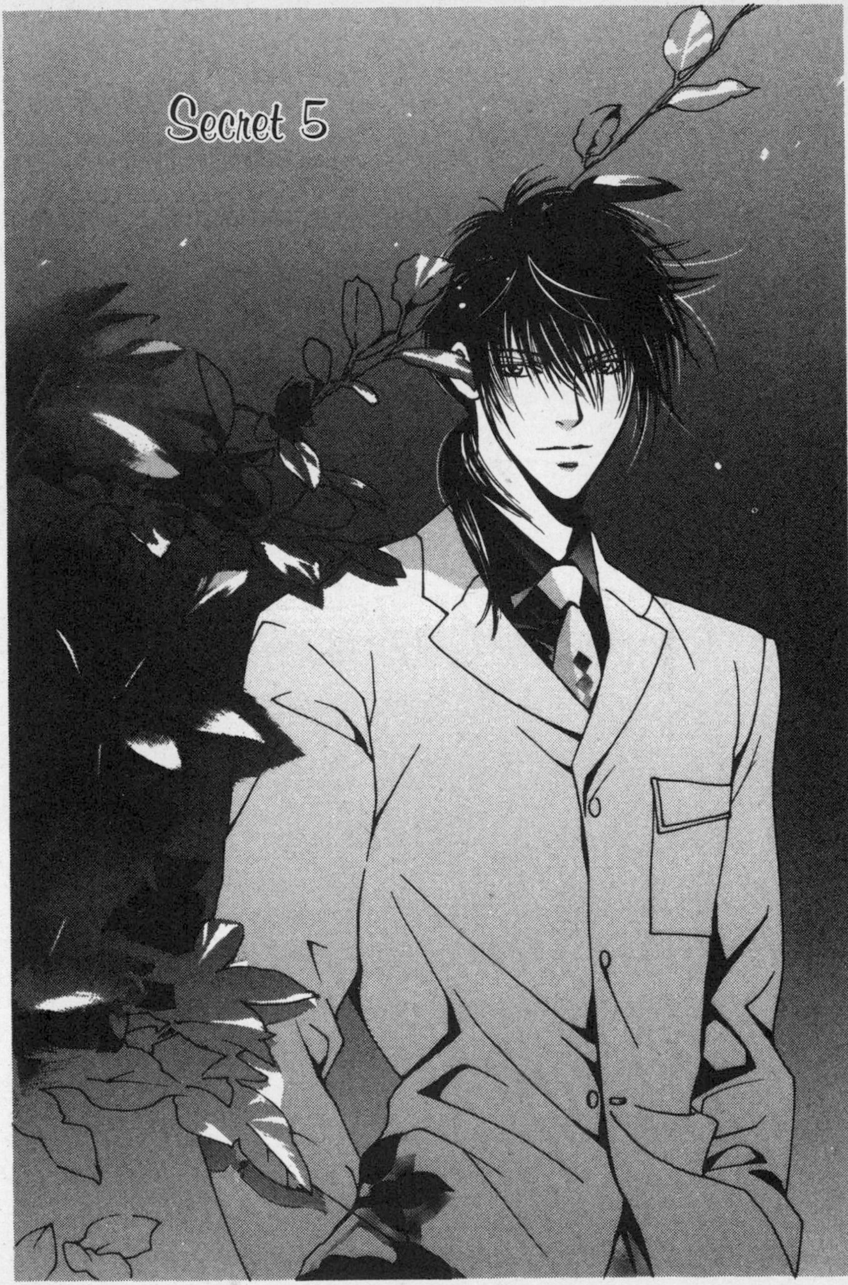
Secret 5

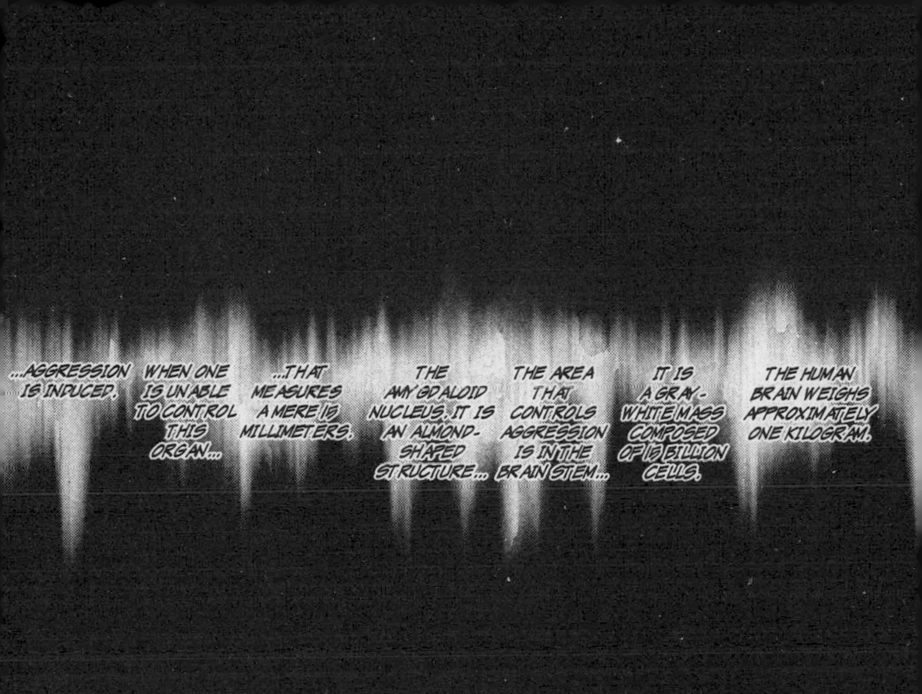
THE HUMAN BRAIN WEIGHS APPROXIMATELY ONE KILOGRAM.
IT IS A GRAY-WHITE MASS COMPOSED OF 15 BILLION CELLS.
THE AREA THAT CONTROLS AGGRESSION IS IN THE BRAIN STEM...
THE AMYGDALOID NUCLEUS. IT IS AN ALMOND-SHAPED STRUCTURE...
...THAT MEASURES A MERE 15 MILLIMETERS.
WHEN ONE IS UNABLE TO CONTROL THIS ORGAN...
...AGGRESSION IS INDUCED.

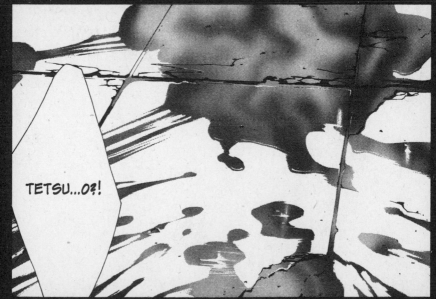

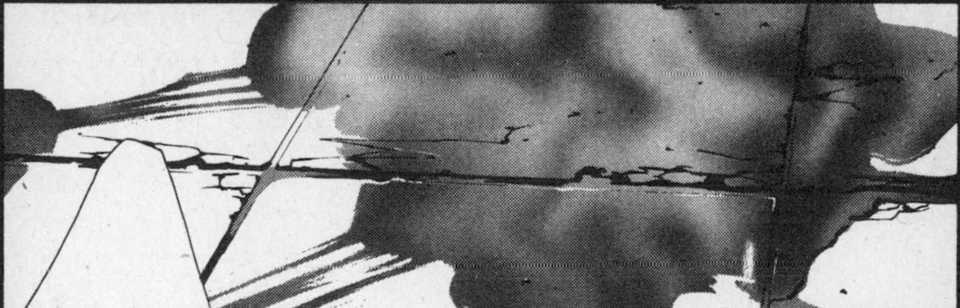
TETSU...O?!

Exerpt from Psychology of Crime Analysis Manual (Dobun Press)

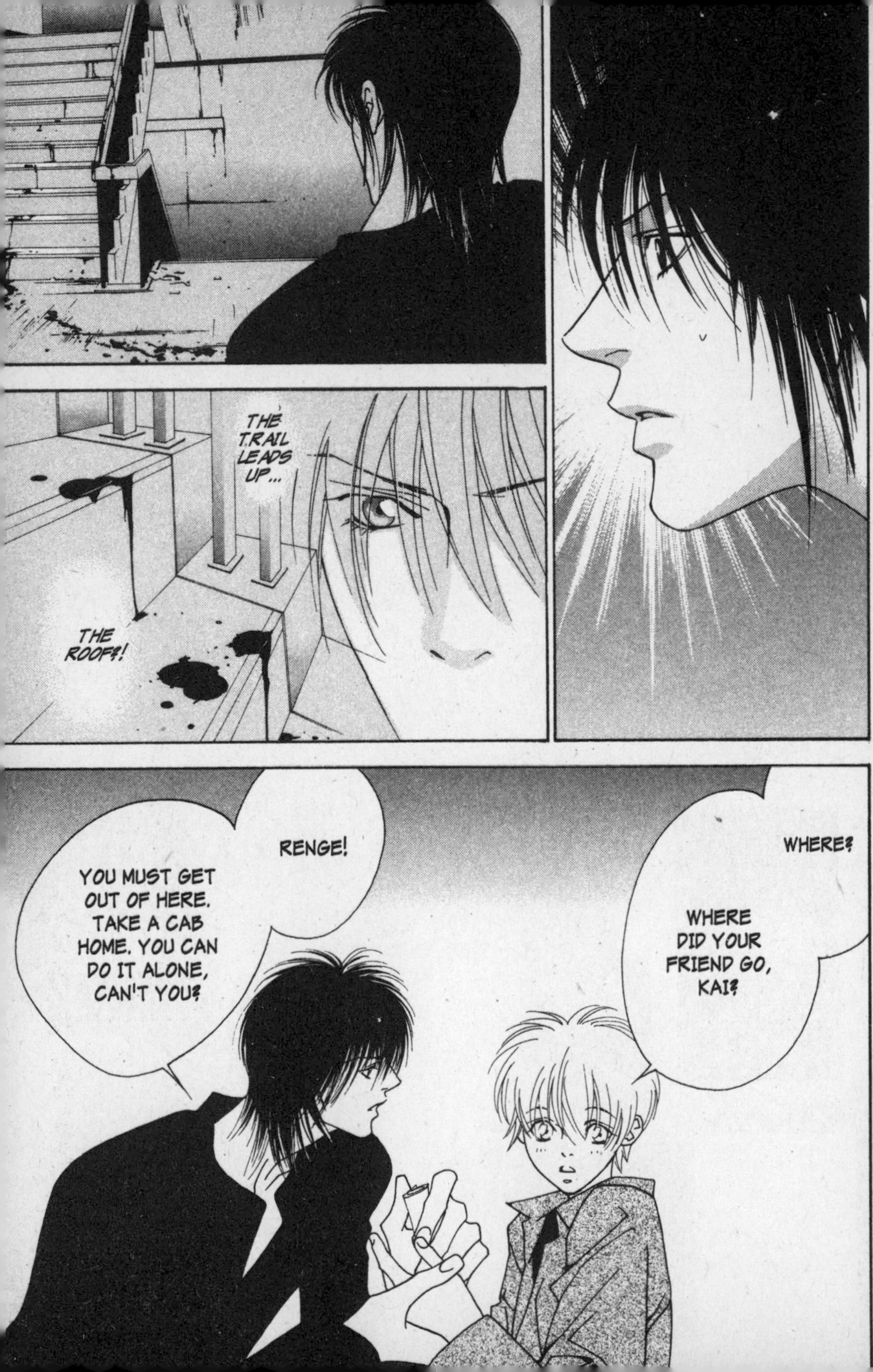
THE TRAIL LEADS UP...
THE ROOF?!
WHERE?
WHERE DID YOUR FRIEND GO, KAI?
RENGE!
YOU MUST GET OUT OF HERE. TAKE A CAB HOME. YOU CAN DO IT ALONE, CAN'T YOU?

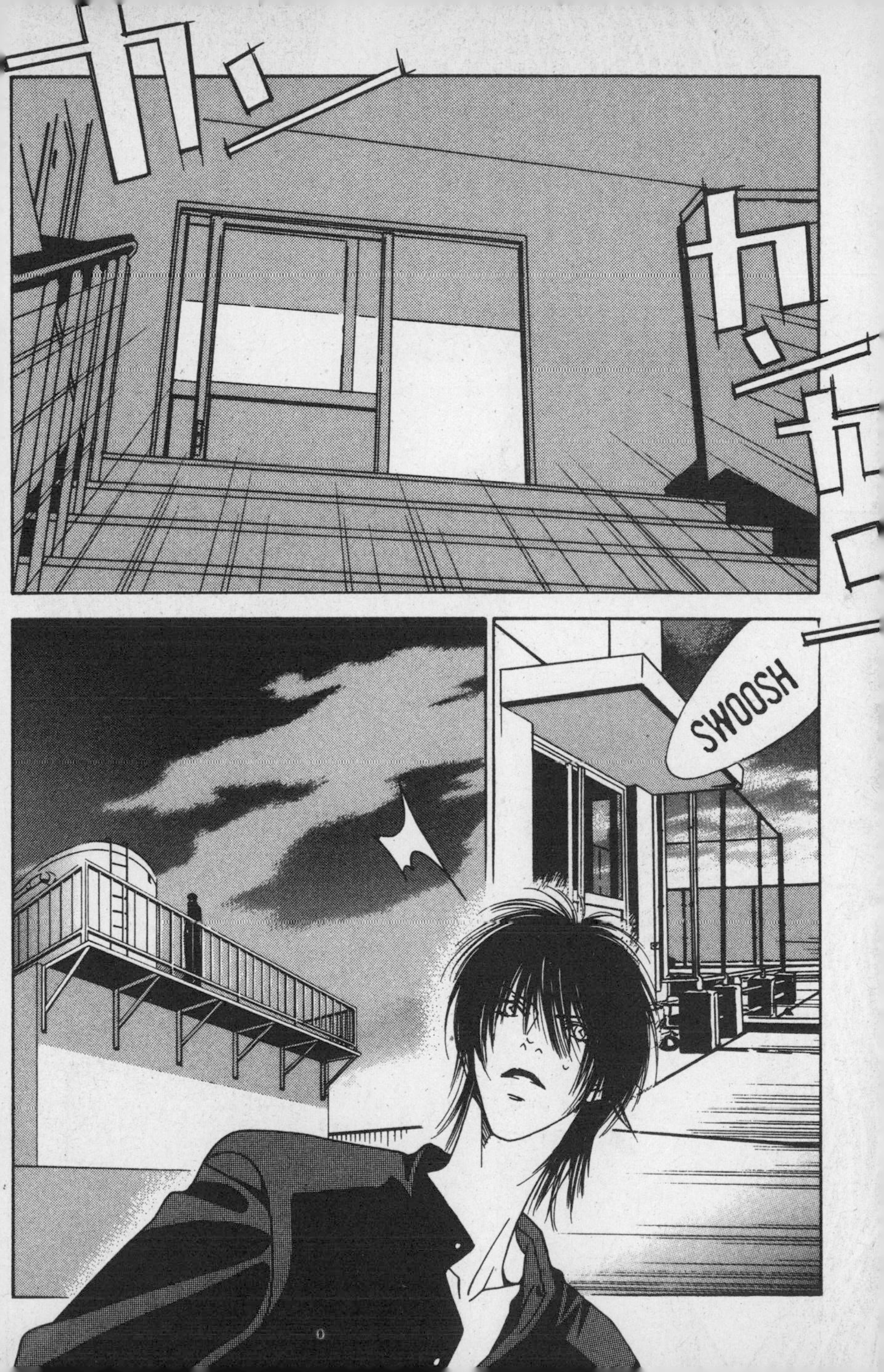
SWOOSH

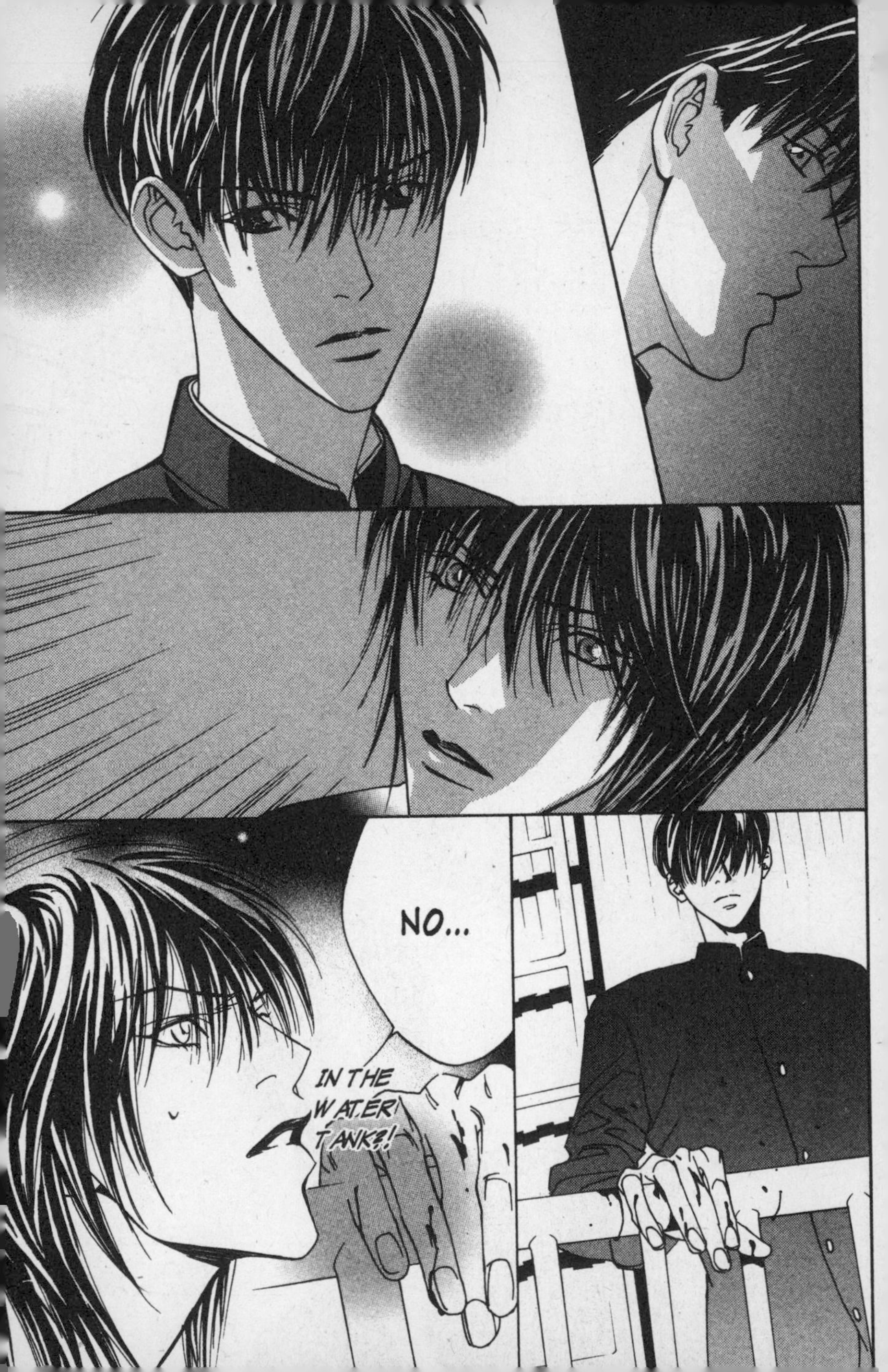
NO...
IN THE WATER TANK?!

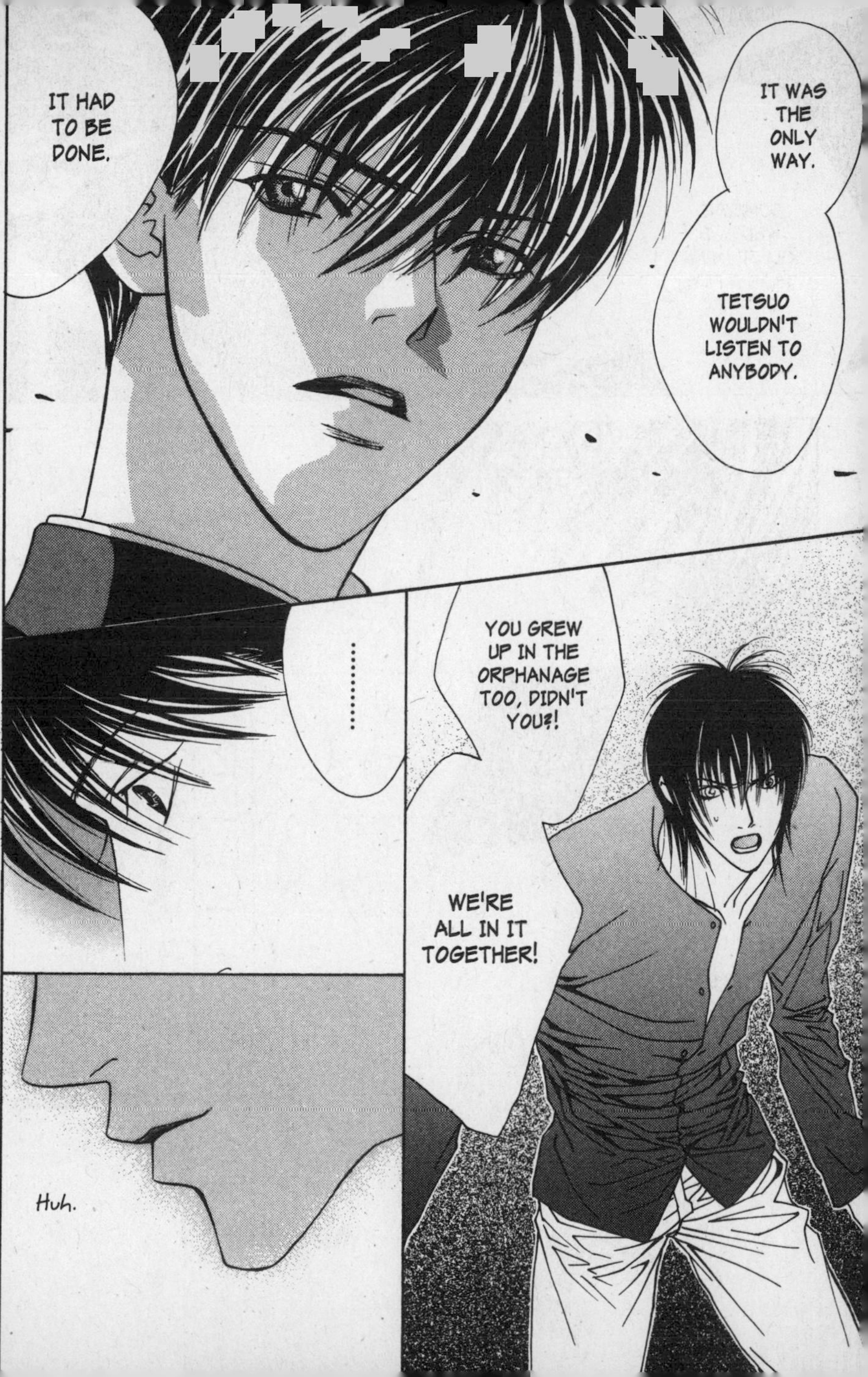

IT WAS THE ONLY WAY.
TETSUO WOULDN'T LISTEN TO ANYBODY.
IT HAD TO BE DONE.
YOU GREW UP IN THE ORPHANAGE TOO, DIDN'T YOU?!
WE'RE ALL IN IT TOGETHER!
....
Huh.

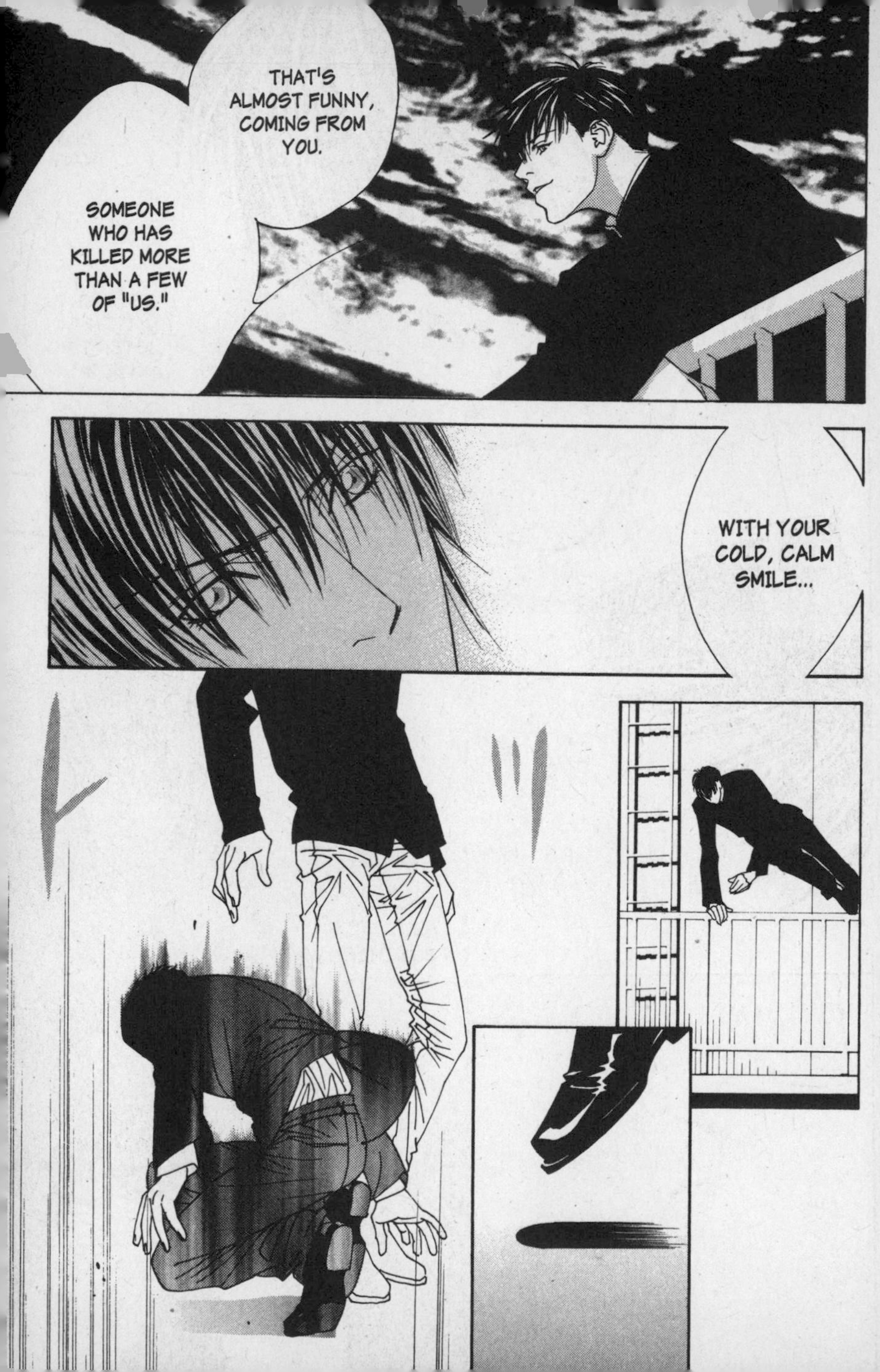
THAT'S ALMOST FUNNY, COMING FROM YOU.
SOMEONE WHO HAS KILLED MORE THAN A FEW OF "US."
WITH YOUR COLD, CALM SMILE...

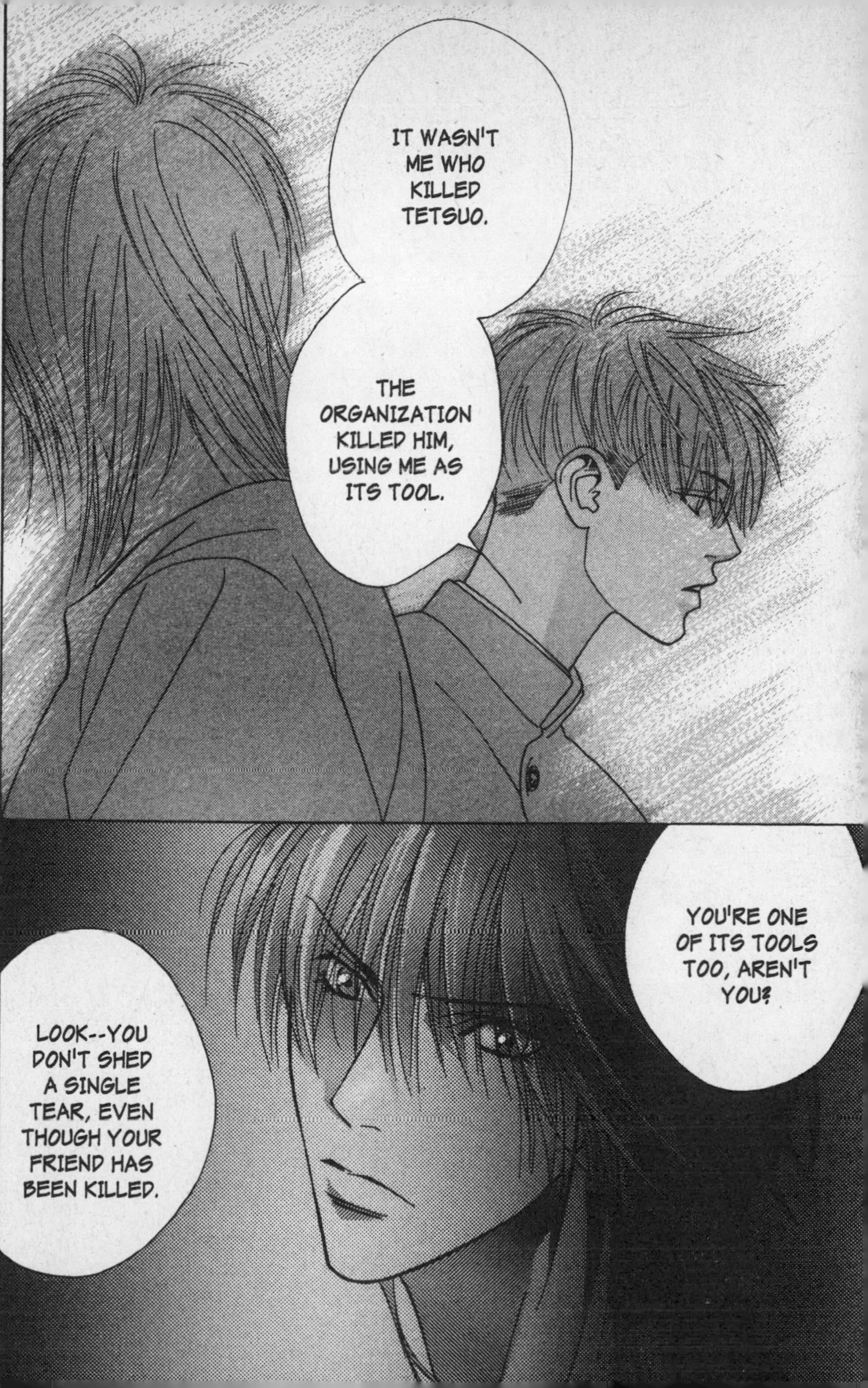
IT WASN'T ME WHO KILLED TETSUO.
THE ORGANIZATION KILLED HIM, USING ME AS ITS TOOL.
YOU'RE ONE OF ITS TOOLS TOO, AREN'T YOU?
LOOK--YOU DON'T SHED A SINGLE TEAR, EVEN THOUGH YOUR FRIEND HAS BEEN KILLED.

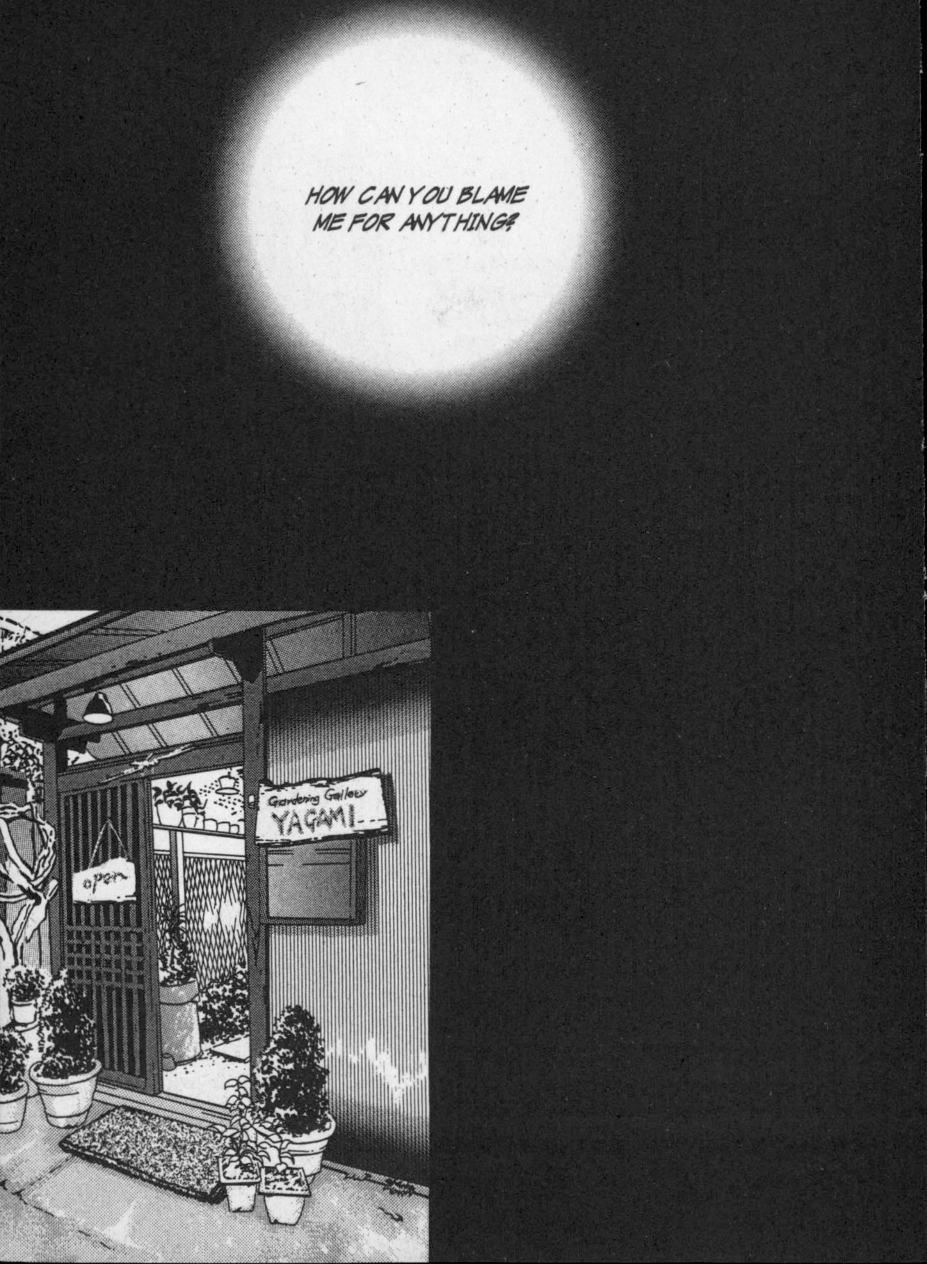
HOW CAN YOU BLAME ME FOR ANYTHING?
Gardening Gallery
YAGAMI
open

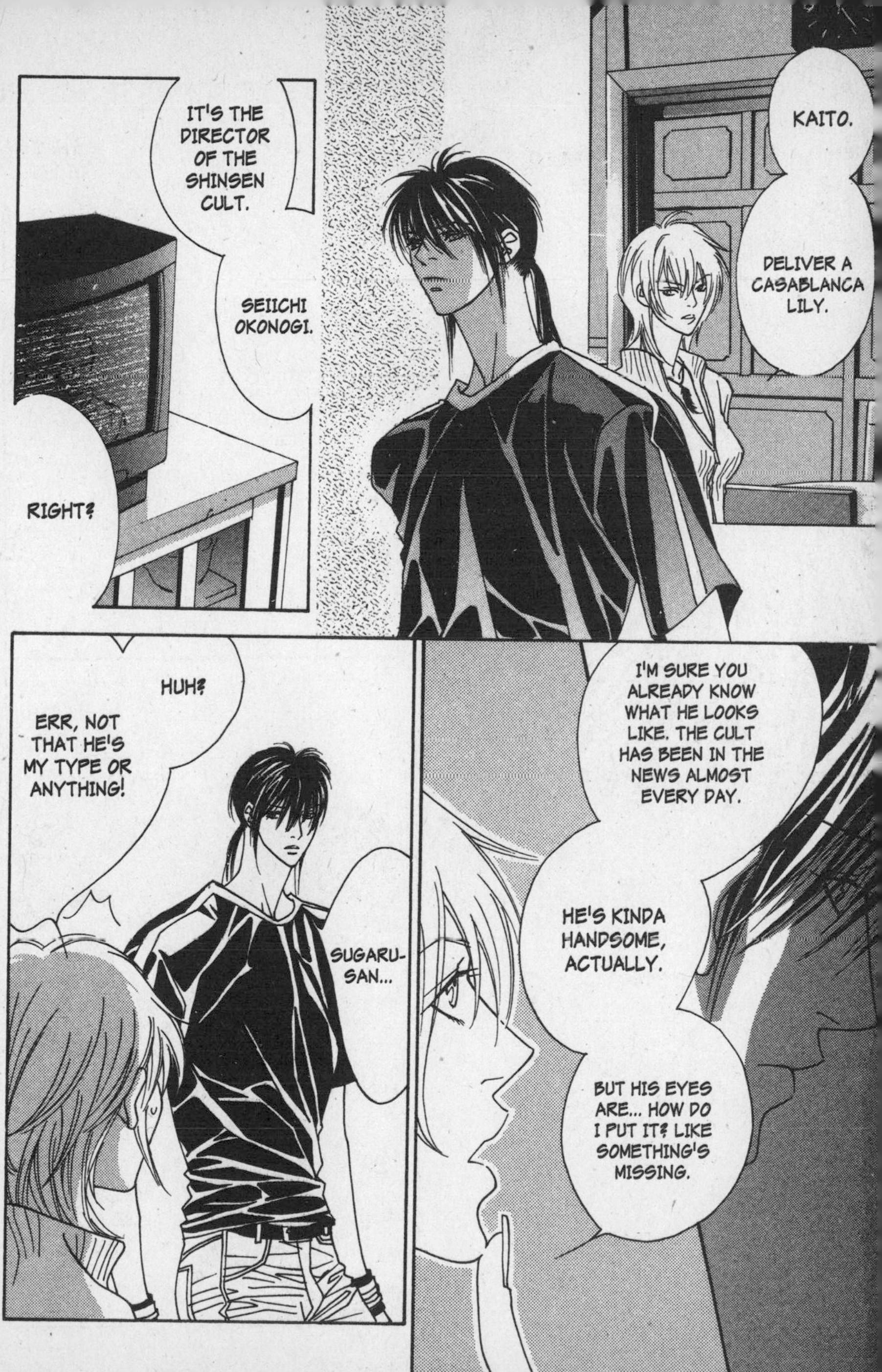
KAITO.
DELIVER A CASABLANCA LILY.
IT'S THE DIRECTOR OF THE SHINSEN CULT.
SEIICHI OKONOGI.
RIGHT?
I'M SURE YOU ALREADY KNOW WHAT HE LOOKS LIKE. THE CULT HAS BEEN IN THE NEWS ALMOST EVERY DAY.
HE'S KINDA HANDSOME, ACTUALLY.
BUT HIS EYES ARE... HOW DO I PUT IT? LIKE SOMETHING'S MISSING.
SUGARU-SAN...
HUH?
ERR, NOT THAT HE'S MY TYPE OR ANYTHING!

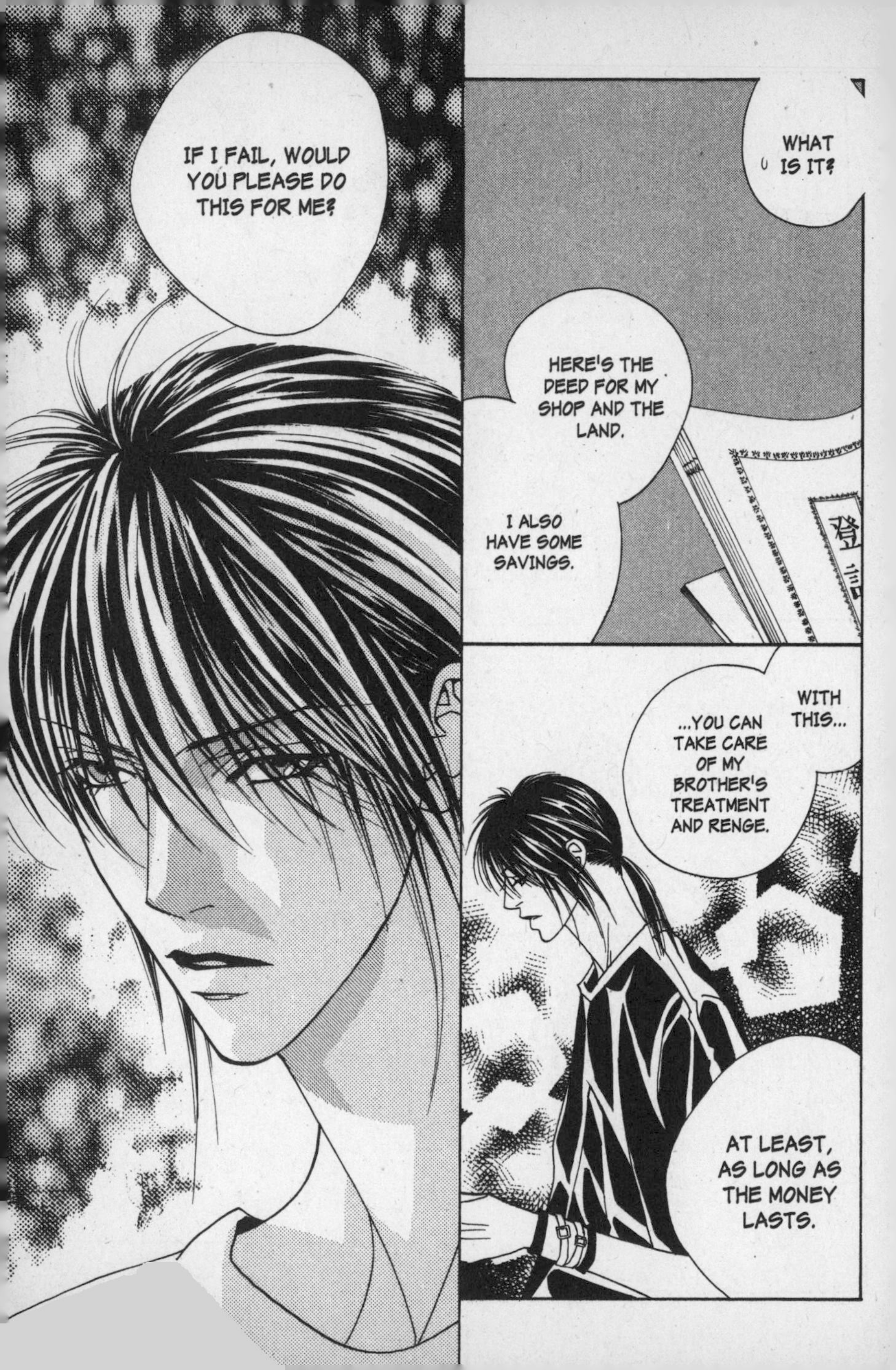
IF I FAIL, WOULD YOU PLEASE DO THIS FOR ME?
WHAT IS IT?
HERE'S THE DEED FOR MY SHOP AND THE LAND.
I ALSO HAVE SOME SAVINGS.
WITH THIS...
...YOU CAN TAKE CARE OF MY BROTHER'S TREATMENT AND RENGE.
AT LEAST, AS LONG AS THE MONEY LASTS.

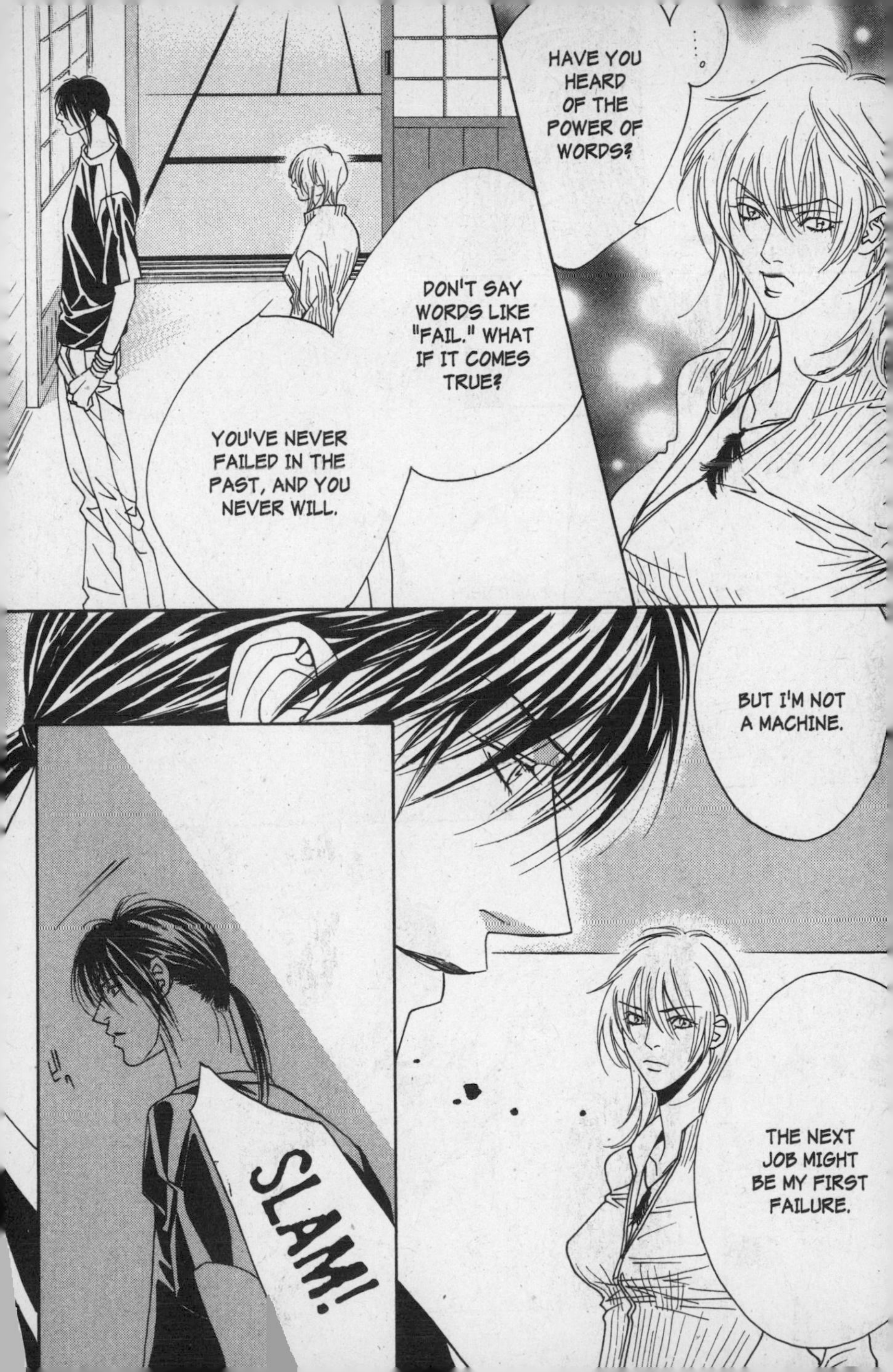
.....
HAVE YOU HEARD OF THE POWER OF WORDS?
DON'T SAY WORDS LIKE "FAIL." WHAT IF IT COMES TRUE?
YOU'VE NEVER FAILED IN THE PAST, AND YOU NEVER WILL.
BUT I'M NOT A MACHINE.
THE NEXT JOB MIGHT BE MY FIRST FAILURE.
SLAM!

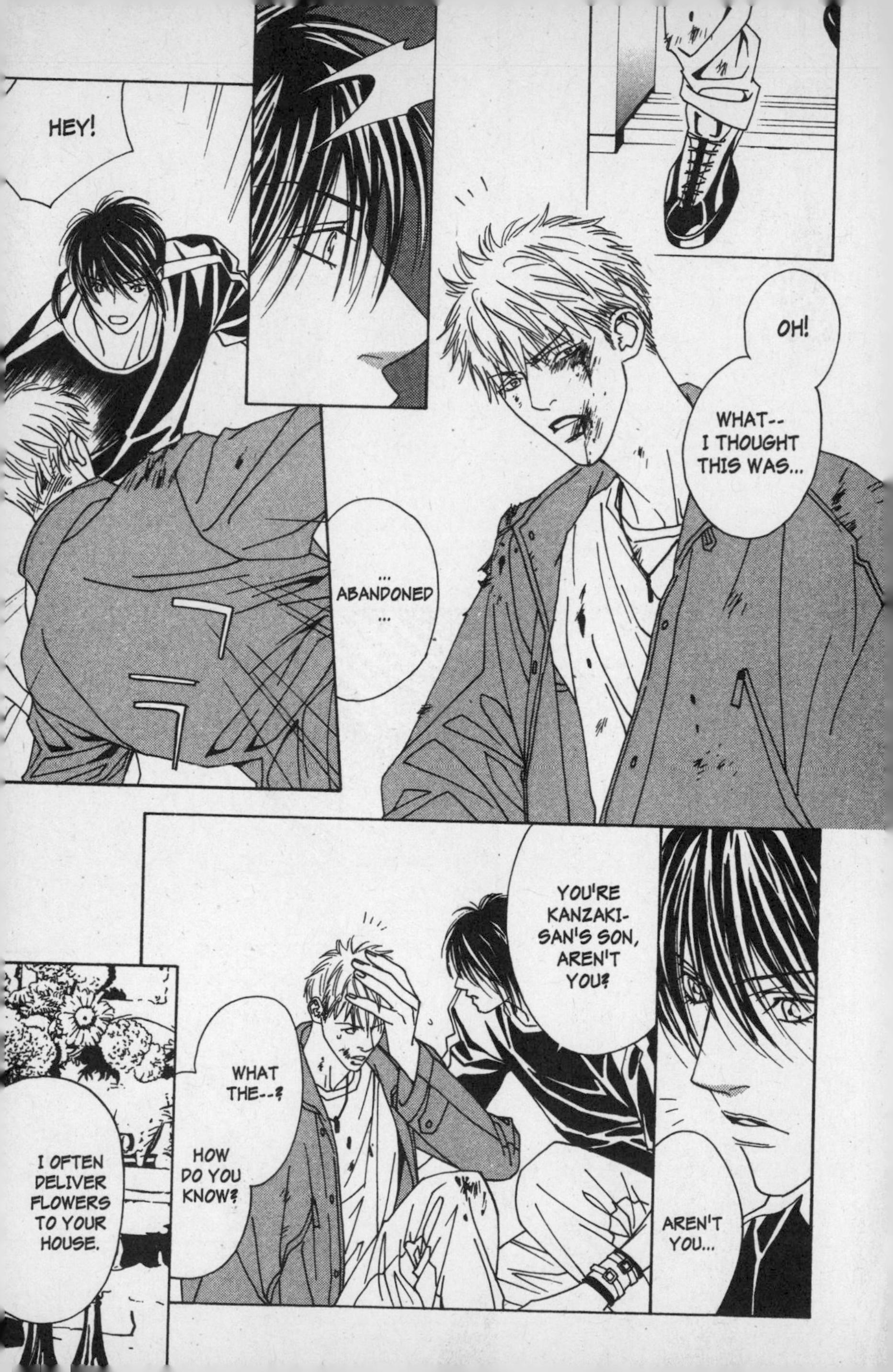
HEY!
OH!
WHAT-- I THOUGHT THIS WAS...
... ABANDONED ...
AREN'T YOU...
YOU'RE KANZAKI-SAN'S SON, AREN'T YOU?
WHAT THE--?
HOW DO YOU KNOW?
I OFTEN DELIVER FLOWERS TO YOUR HOUSE.

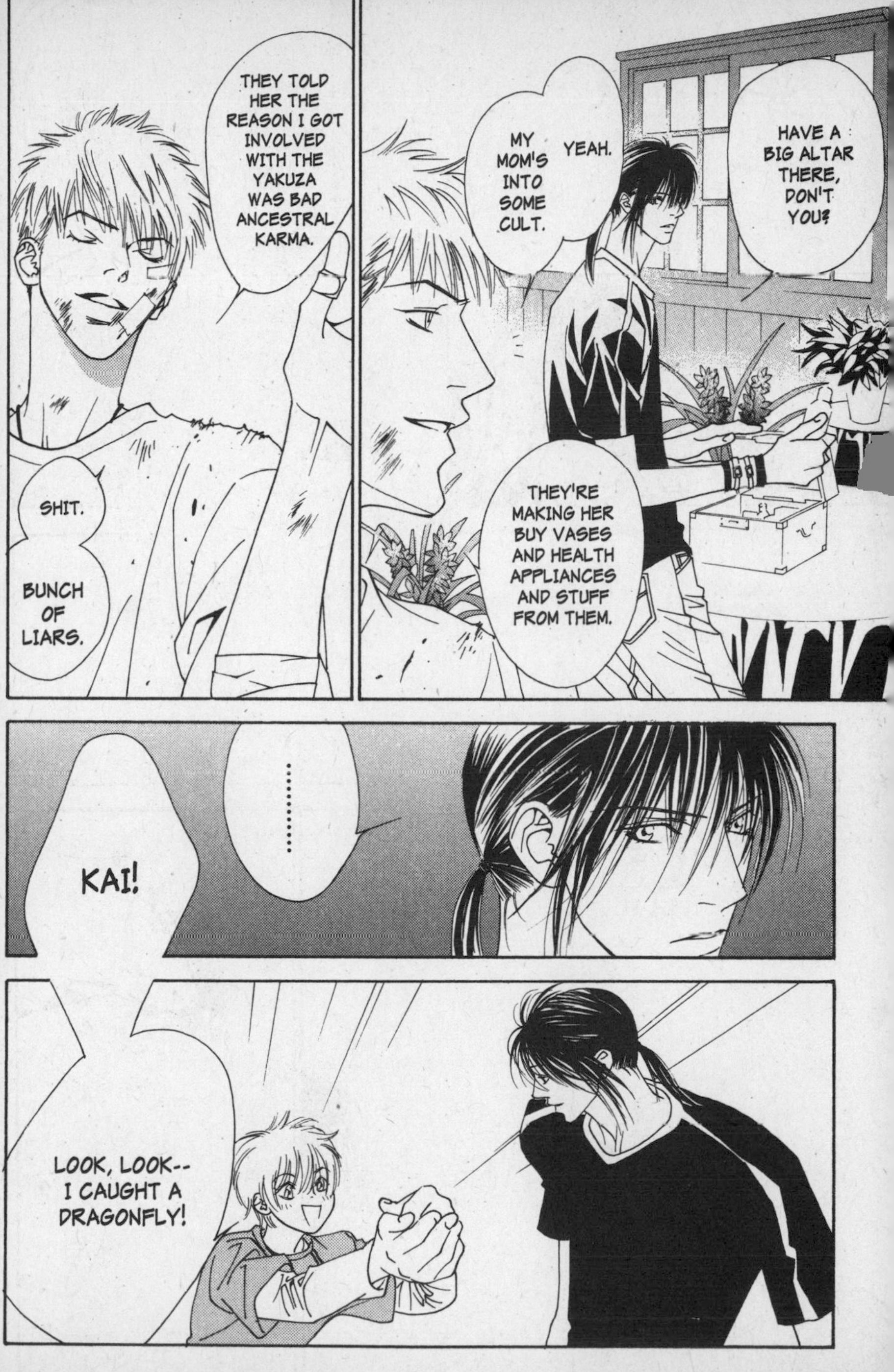
HAVE A BIG ALTAR THERE, DON'T YOU?
YEAH.
MY MOM'S INTO SOME CULT.
THEY'RE MAKING HER BUY VASES AND HEALTH APPLIANCES AND STUFF FROM THEM.
THEY TOLD HER THE REASON I GOT INVOLVED WITH THE YAKUZA WAS BAD ANCESTRAL KARMA.
SHIT.
BUNCH OF LIARS.
......
KAI!
LOOK, LOOK-- I CAUGHT A DRAGONFLY!

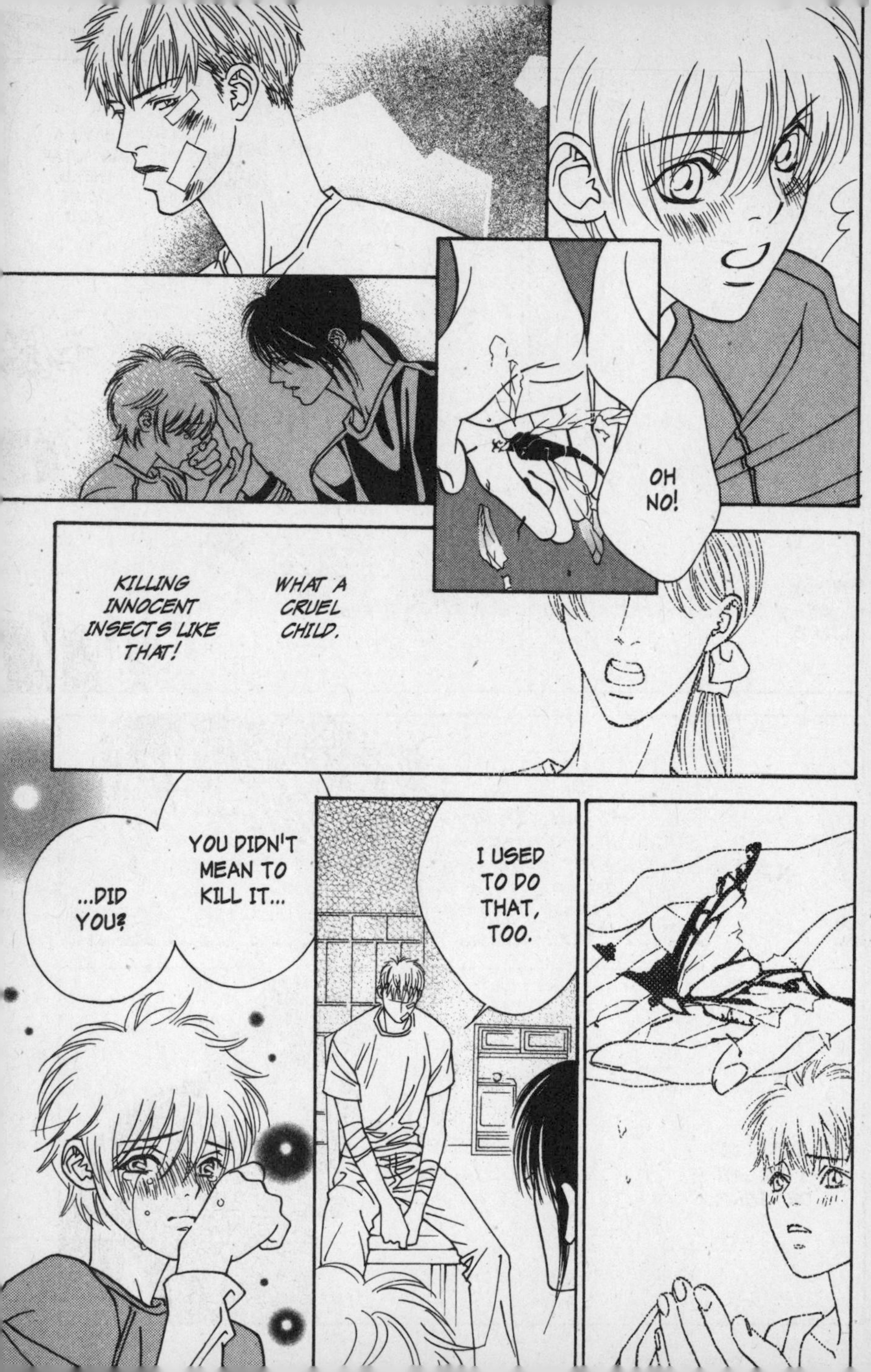
OH NO!
WHAT A CRUEL CHILD.
KILLING INNOCENT INSECTS LIKE THAT!
I USED TO DO THAT, TOO.
YOU DIDN'T MEAN TO KILL IT...
...DID YOU?

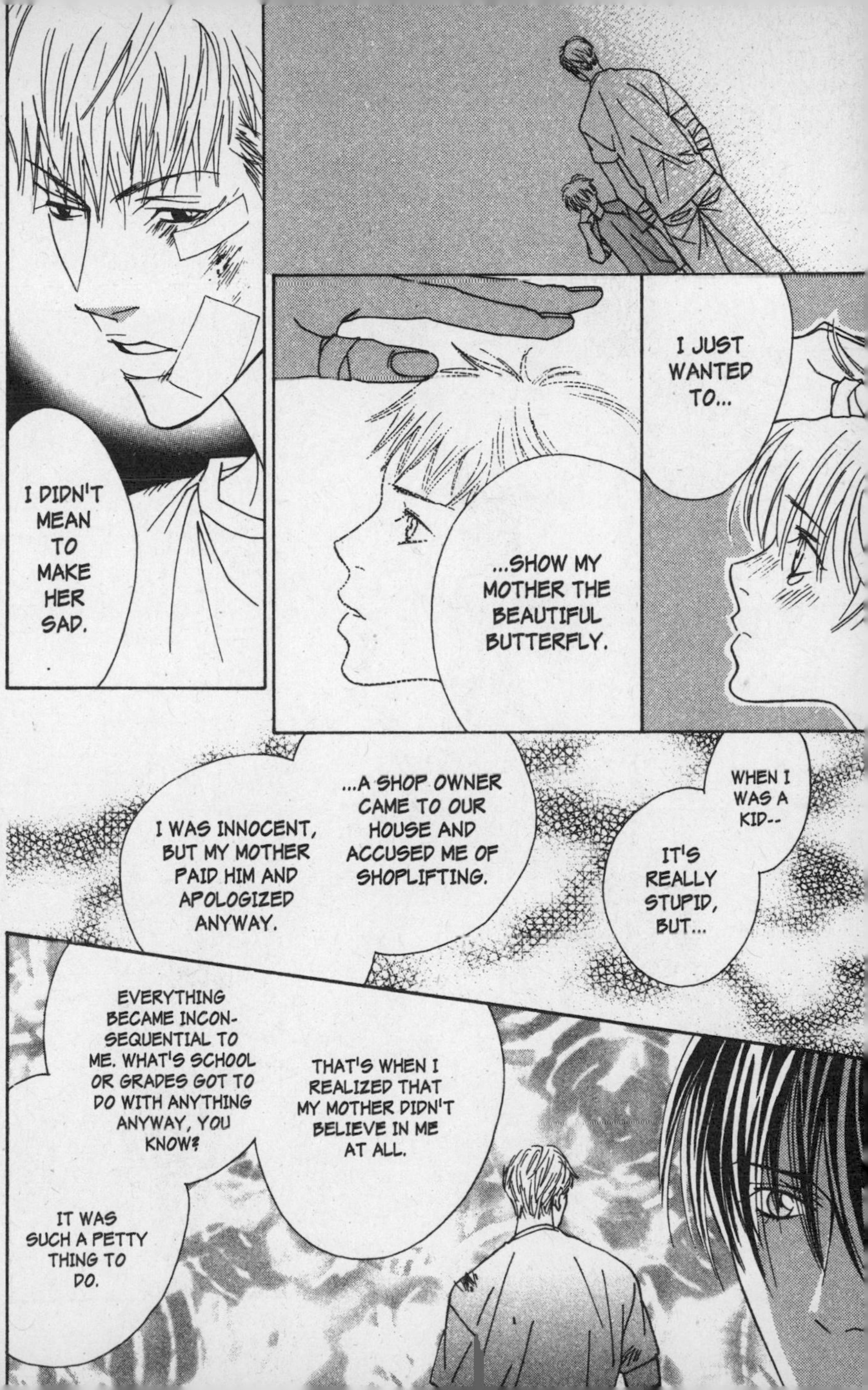
I JUST WANTED TO...
...SHOW MY MOTHER THE BEAUTIFUL BUTTERFLY.
I DIDN'T MEAN TO MAKE HER SAD.
WHEN I WAS A KID--
IT'S REALLY STUPID, BUT...
...A SHOP OWNER CAME TO OUR HOUSE AND ACCUSED ME OF SHOPLIFTING.
I WAS INNOCENT, BUT MY MOTHER PAID HIM AND APOLOGIZED ANYWAY.
THAT'S WHEN I REALIZED THAT MY MOTHER DIDN'T BELIEVE IN ME AT ALL.
EVERYTHING BECAME INCON-SEQUENTIAL TO ME. WHAT'S SCHOOL OR GRADES GOT TO DO WITH ANYTHING ANYWAY, YOU KNOW?
IT WAS SUCH A PETTY THING TO DO.

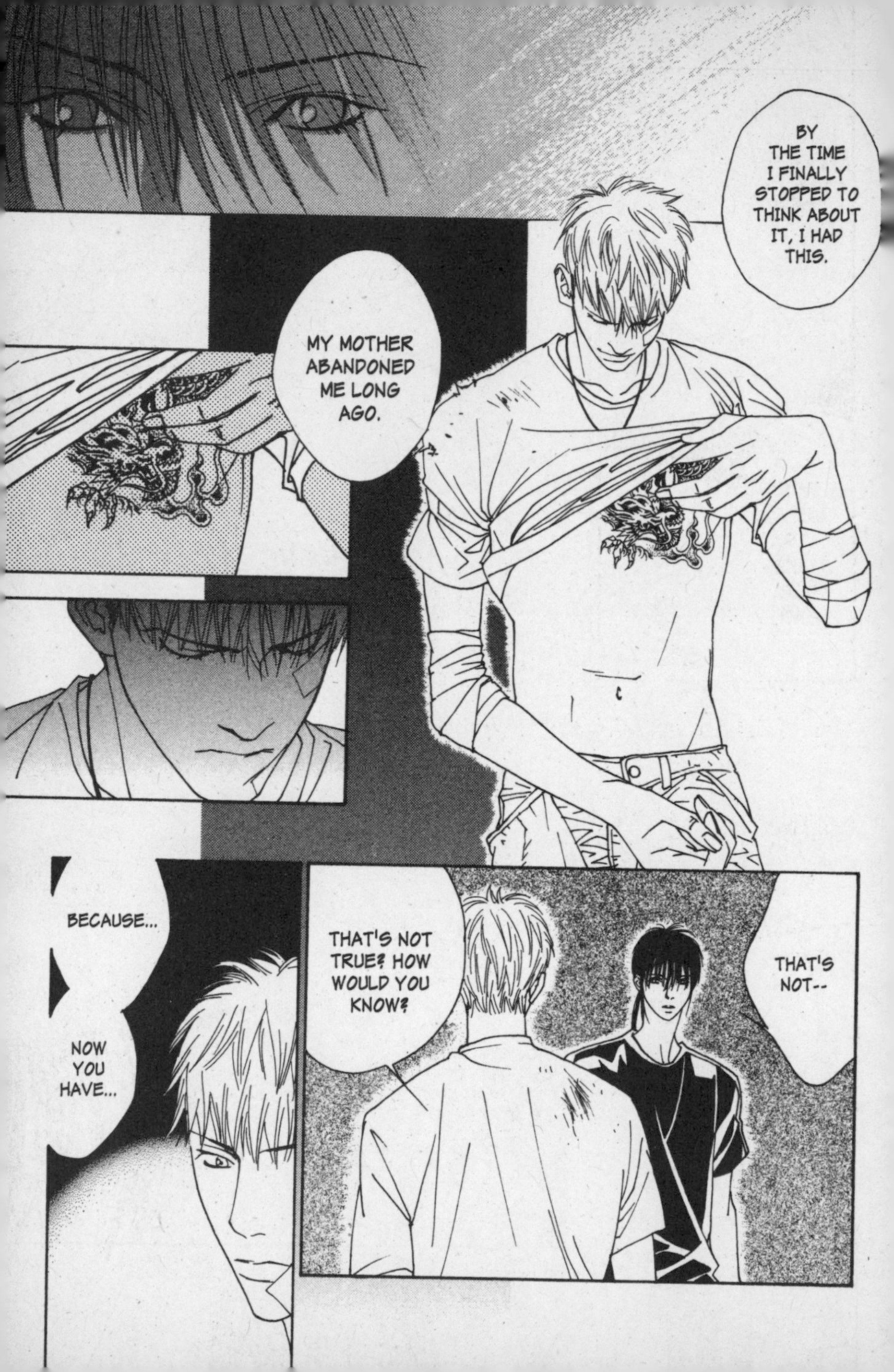
BY THE TIME I FINALLY STOPPED TO THINK ABOUT IT, I HAD THIS.
MY MOTHER ABANDONED ME LONG AGO.
THAT'S NOT--
THAT'S NOT TRUE? HOW WOULD YOU KNOW?
BECAUSE...
NOW YOU HAVE...

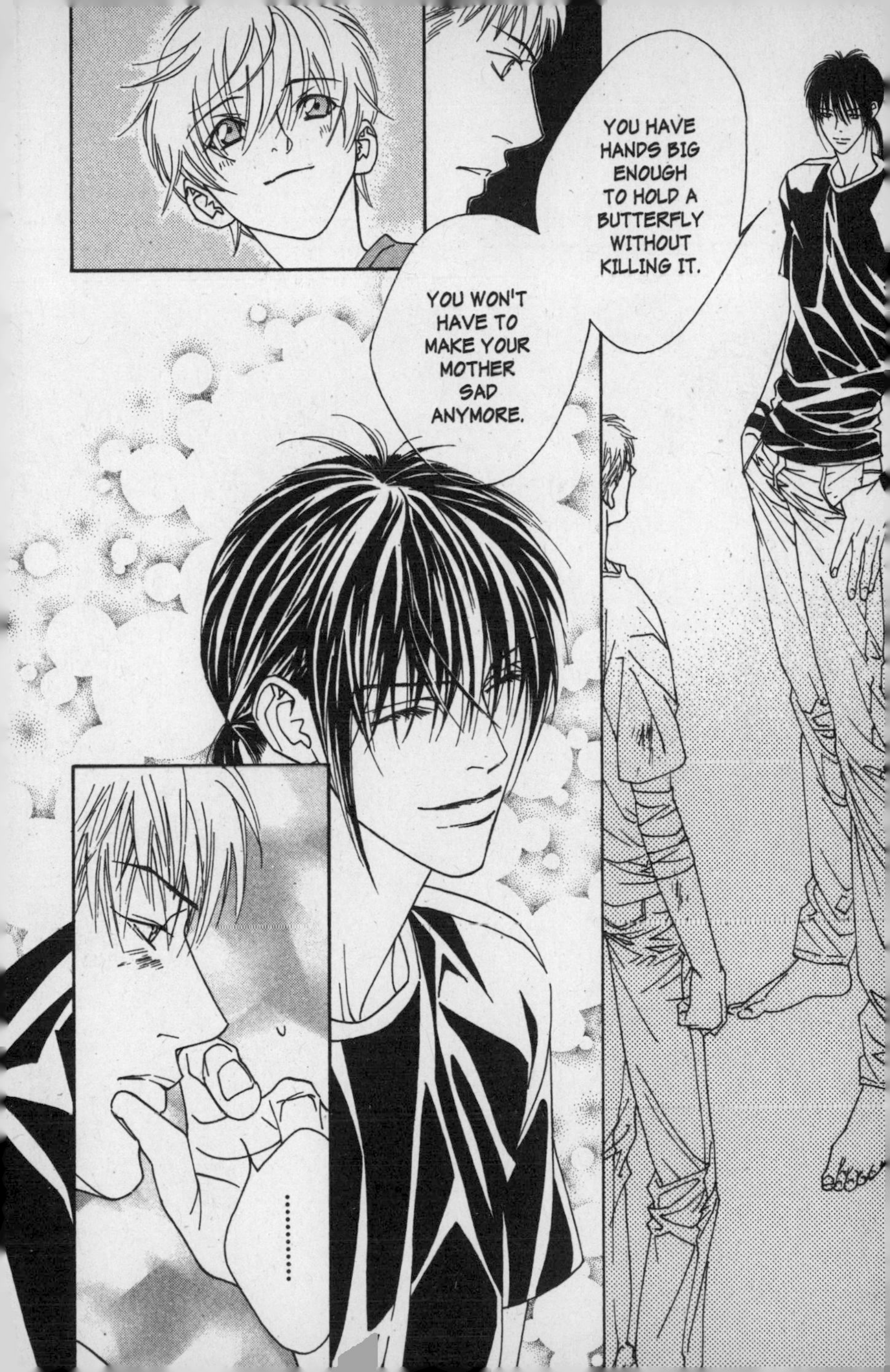
YOU HAVE HANDS BIG ENOUGH TO HOLD A BUTTERFLY WITHOUT KILLING IT.
YOU WON'T HAVE TO MAKE YOUR MOTHER SAD ANYMORE.
......

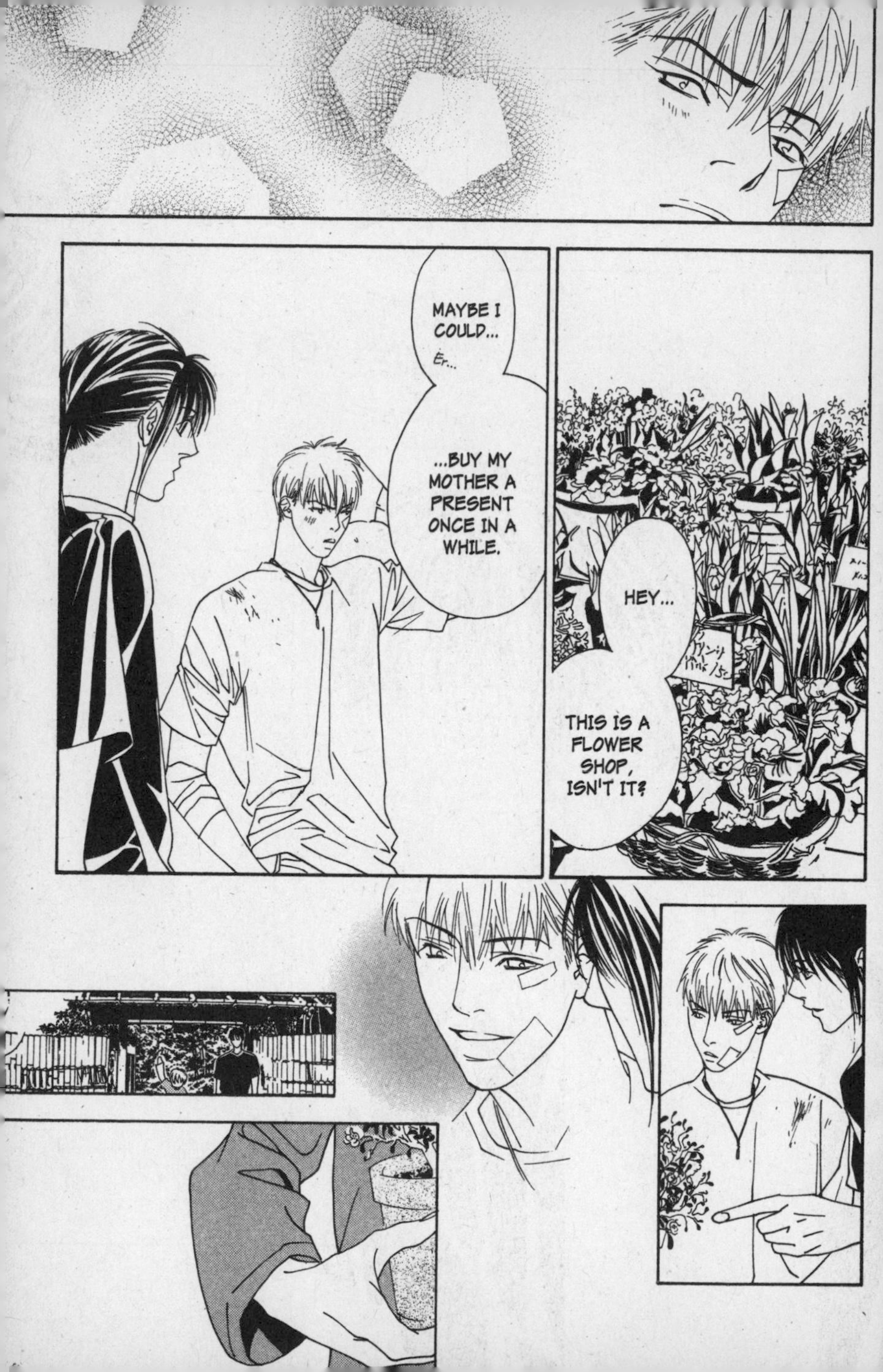
HEY...
THIS IS A FLOWER SHOP, ISN'T IT?
MAYBE I COULD...
Er...
...BUY MY MOTHER A PRESENT ONCE IN A WHILE.

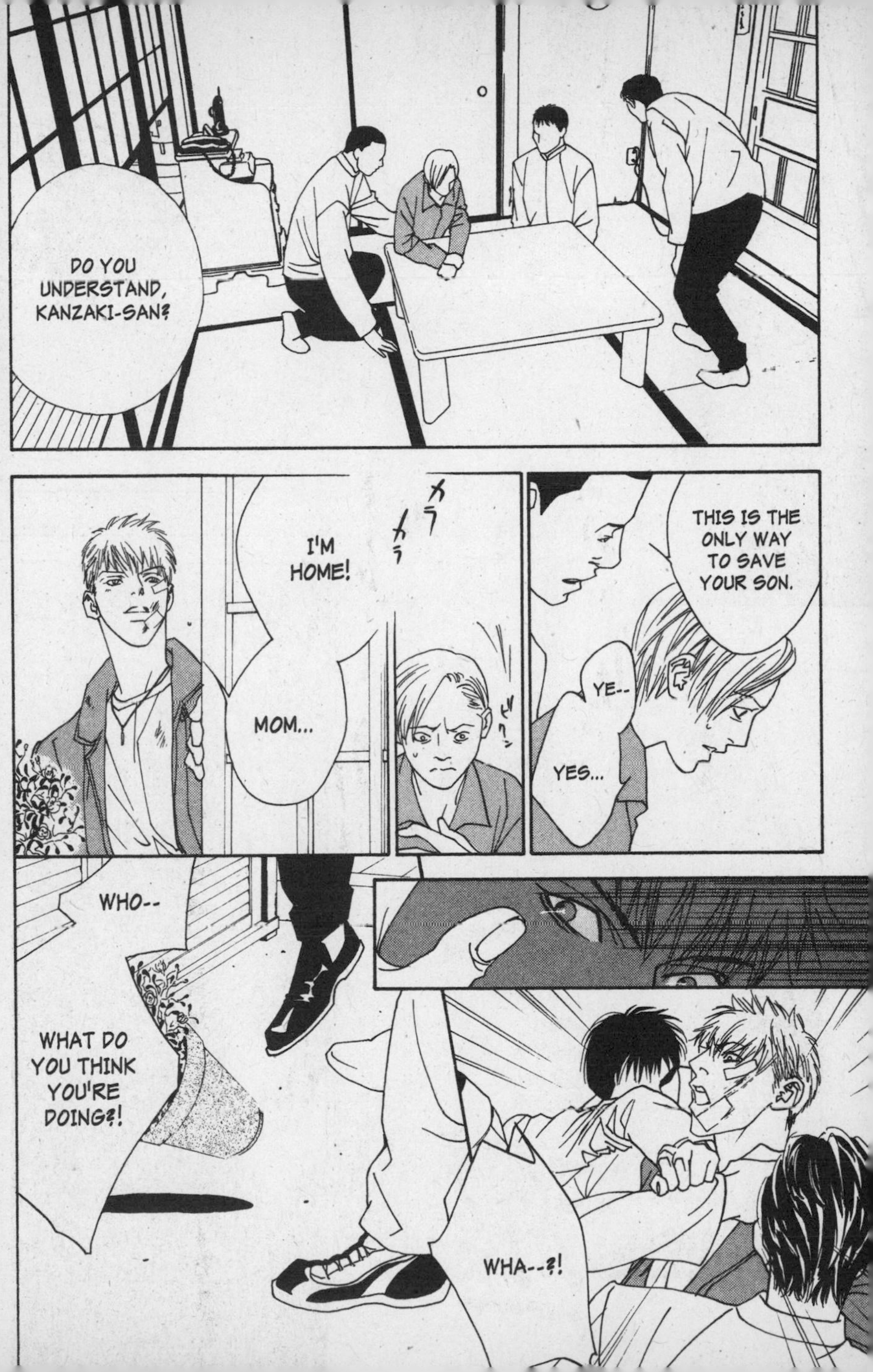
DO YOU UNDERSTAND, KANZAKI-SAN?
THIS IS THE ONLY WAY TO SAVE YOUR SON.
YE--
YES...
I'M HOME!
MOM...
WHA--?!
WHO--
WHAT DO YOU THINK YOU'RE DOING?!

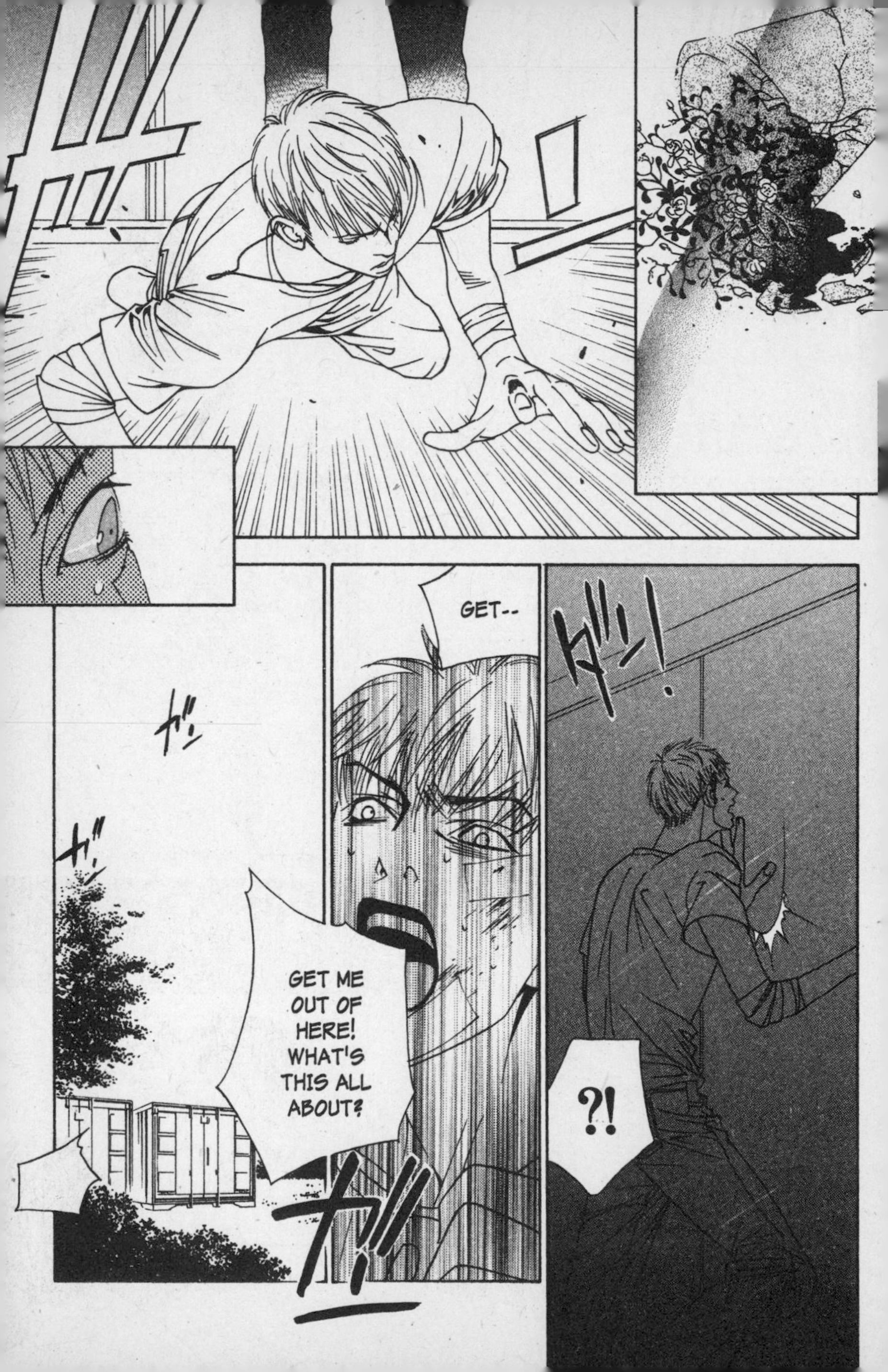
?!
GET--
GET ME OUT OF HERE! WHAT'S THIS ALL ABOUT?

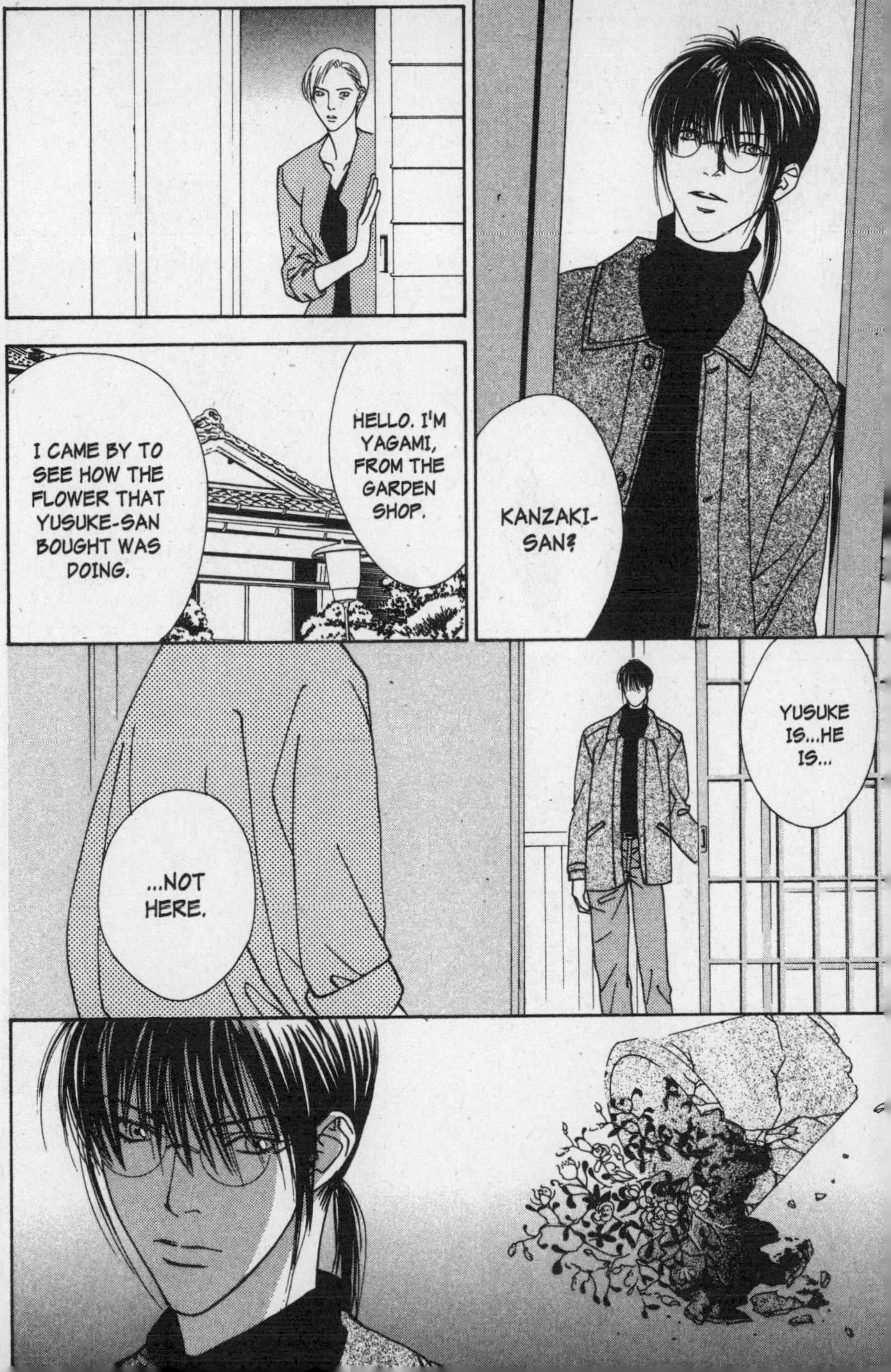
KANZAKI-SAN?
HELLO. I'M YAGAMI, FROM THE GARDEN SHOP.
I CAME BY TO SEE HOW THE FLOWER THAT YUSUKE-SAN BOUGHT WAS DOING.
YUSUKE IS...HE IS...
...NOT HERE.

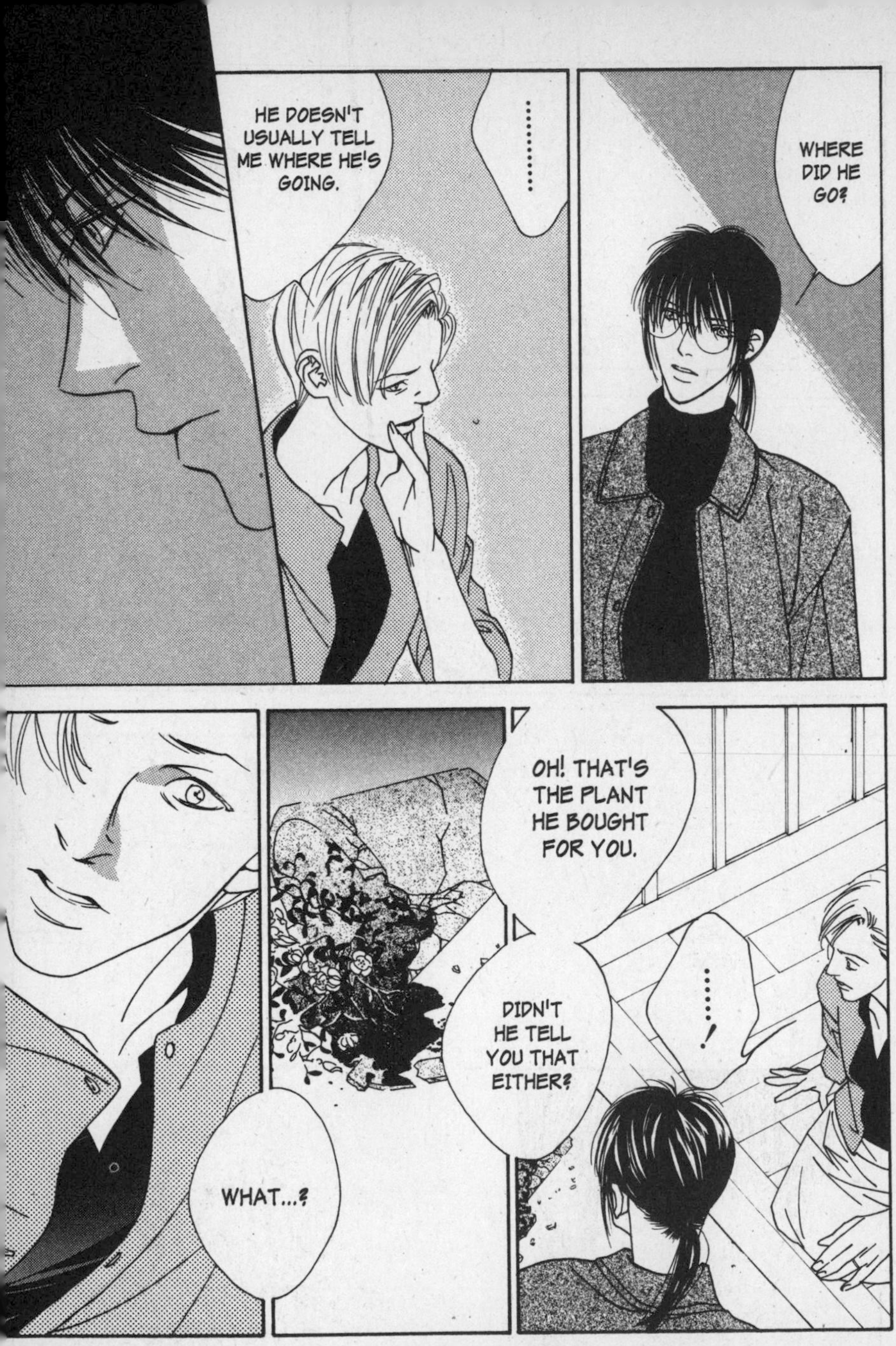
WHERE DID HE GO?
......
HE DOESN'T USUALLY TELL ME WHERE HE'S GOING.
OH! THAT'S THE PLANT HE BOUGHT FOR YOU.
......!
DIDN'T HE TELL YOU THAT EITHER?
WHAT...?

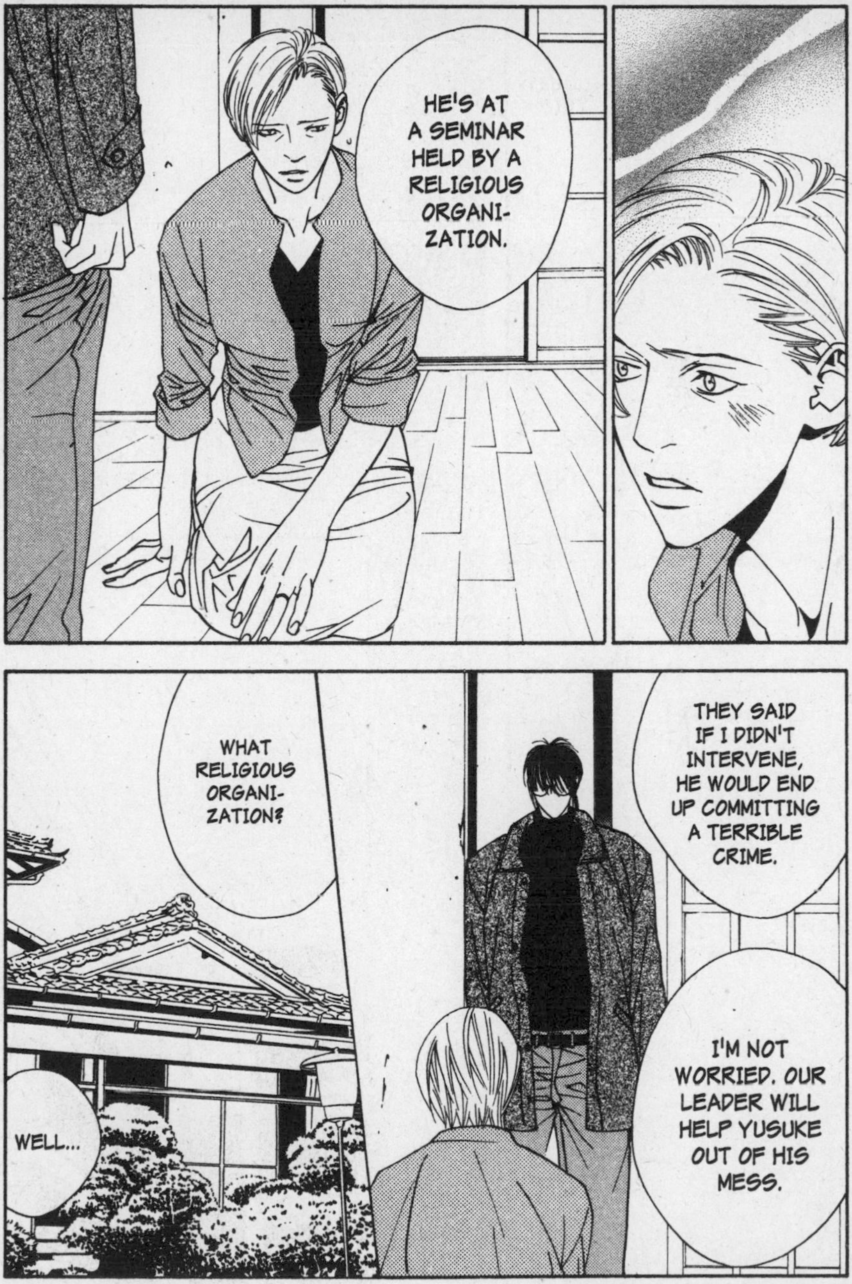
HE'S AT A SEMINAR HELD BY A RELIGIOUS ORGANI-ZATION.
THEY SAID IF I DIDN'T INTERVENE, HE WOULD END UP COMMITTING A TERRIBLE CRIME.
WHAT RELIGIOUS ORGANI-ZATION?
I'M NOT WORRIED. OUR LEADER WILL HELP YUSUKE OUT OF HIS MESS.
WELL...

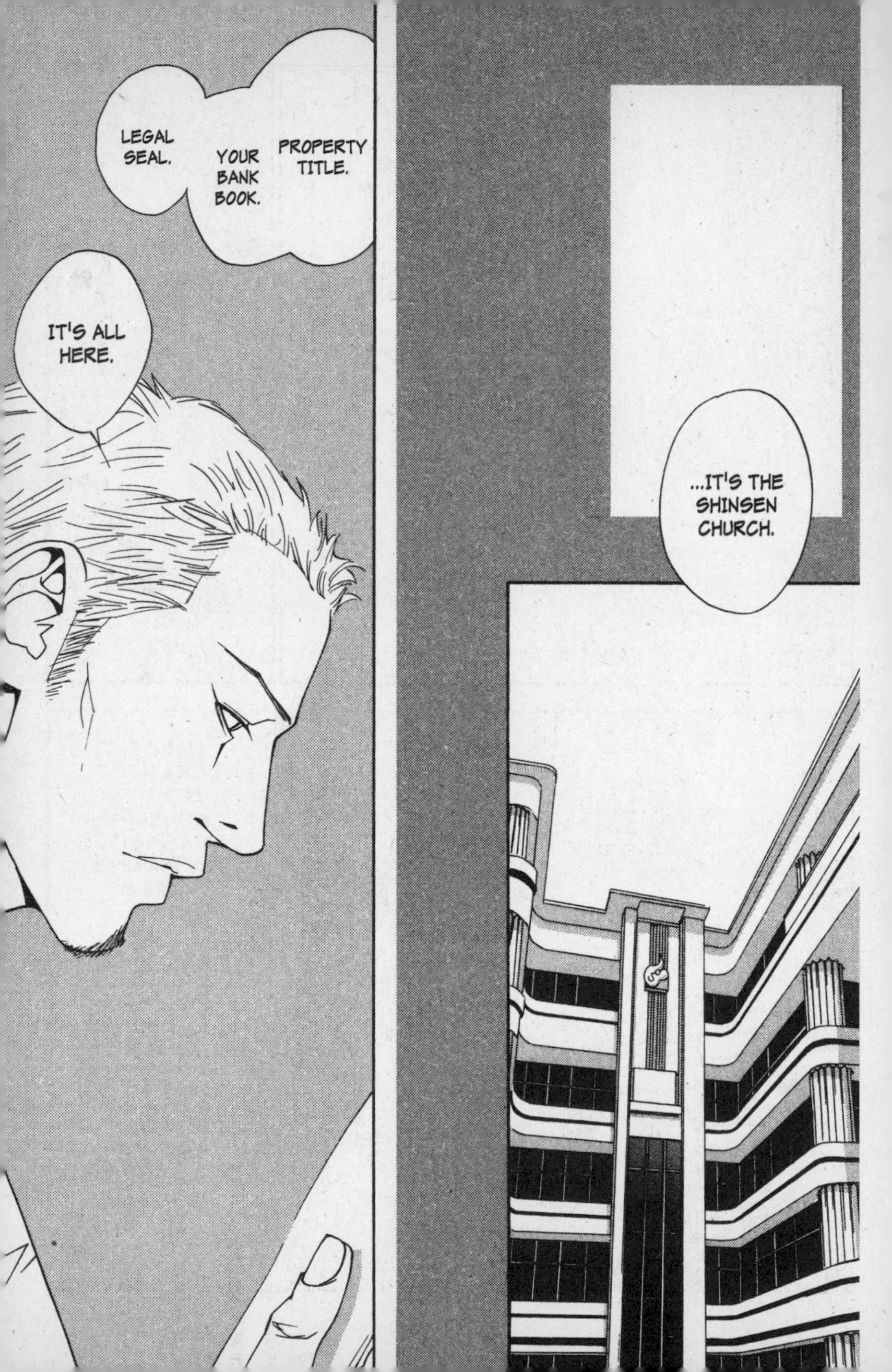
...IT'S THE SHINSEN CHURCH.
PROPERTY TITLE.
YOUR BANK BOOK.
LEGAL SEAL.
IT'S ALL HERE.

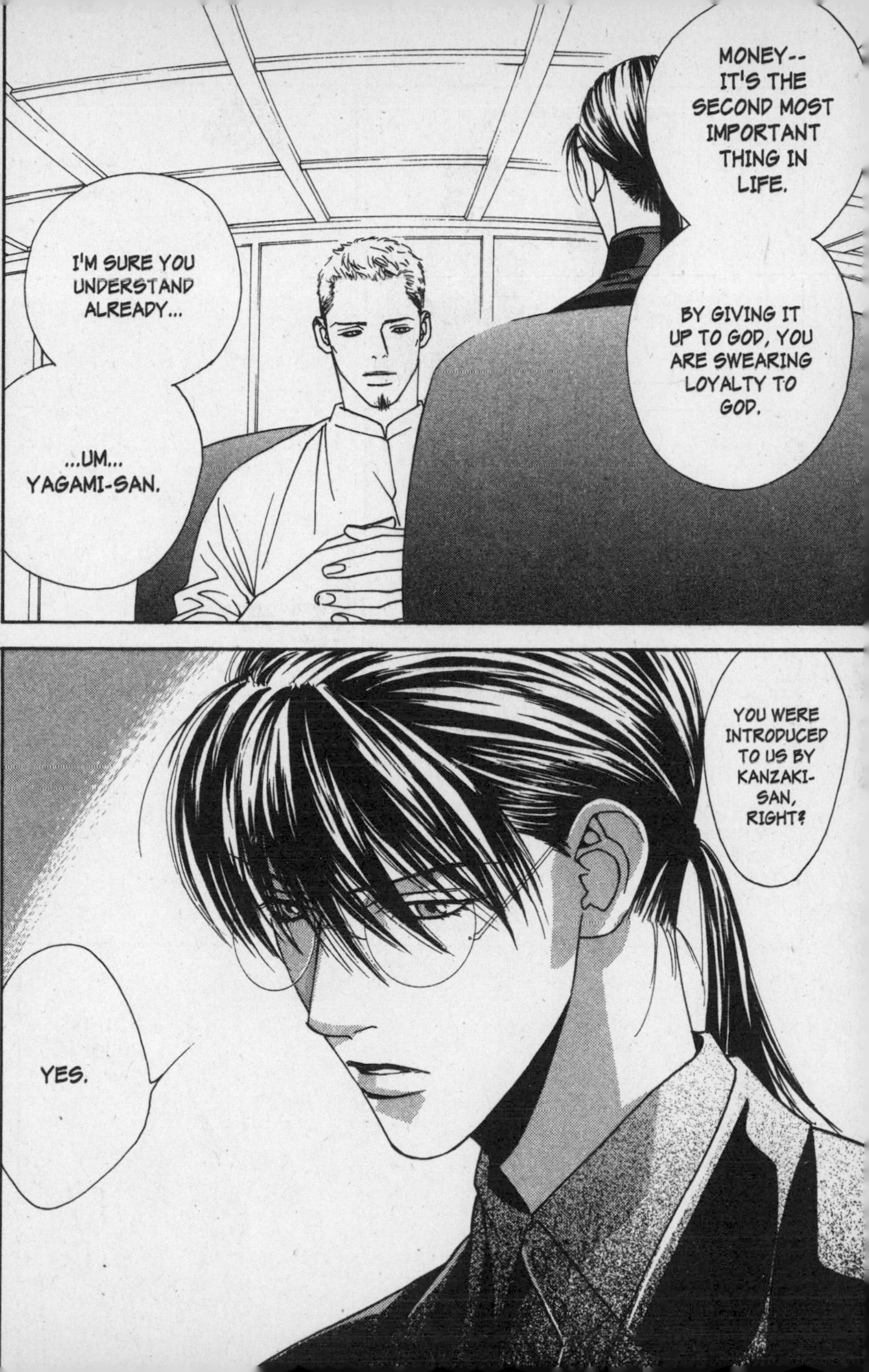
MONEY-- IT'S THE SECOND MOST IMPORTANT THING IN LIFE.
BY GIVING IT UP TO GOD, YOU ARE SWEARING LOYALTY TO GOD.
I'M SURE YOU UNDERSTAND ALREADY...
...UM... YAGAMI-SAN.
YOU WERE INTRODUCED TO US BY KANZAKI-SAN, RIGHT?
YES.

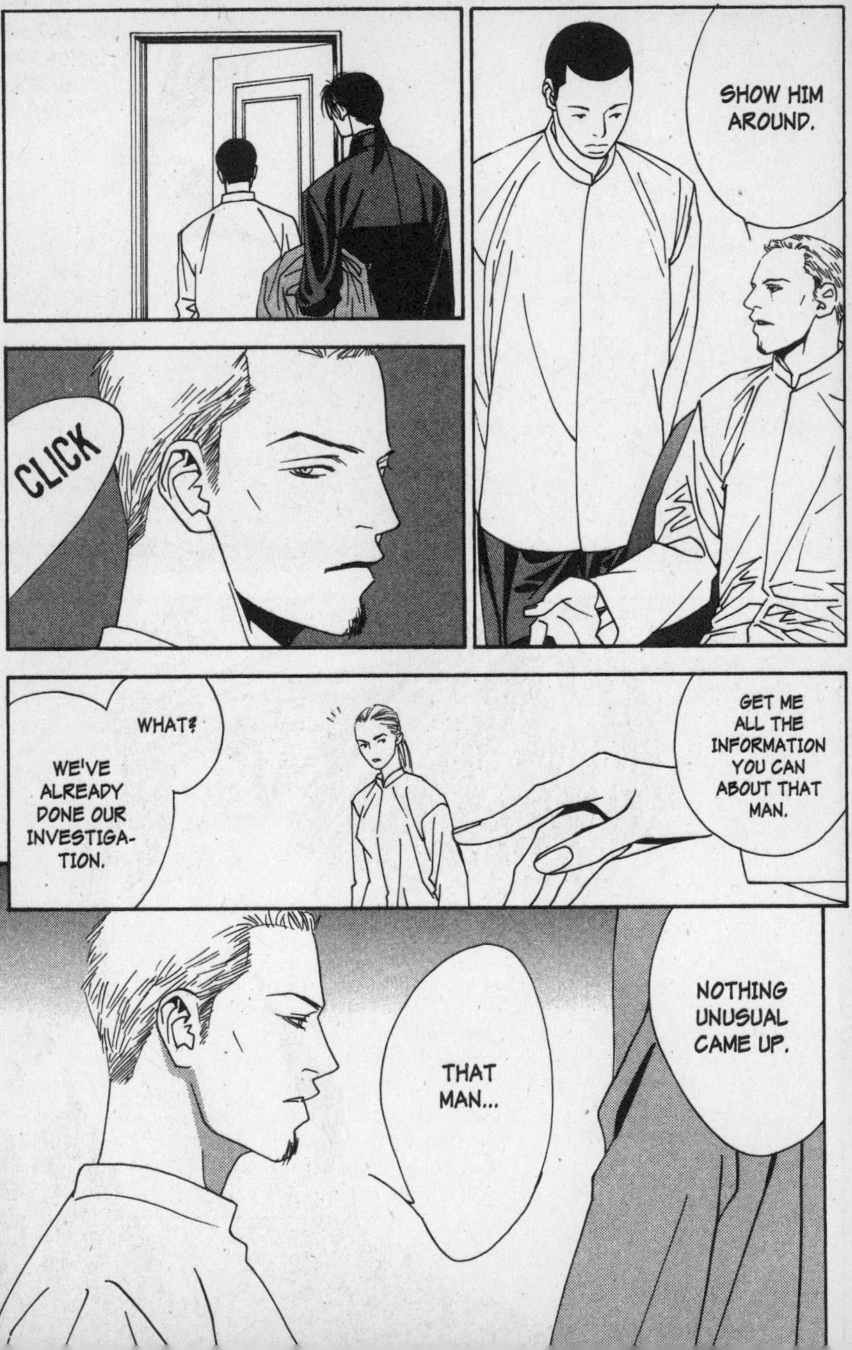
SHOW HIM AROUND.
CLICK
GET ME ALL THE INFORMATION YOU CAN ABOUT THAT MAN.
WHAT?
WE'VE ALREADY DONE OUR INVESTIGA-TION.
NOTHING UNUSUAL CAME UP.
THAT MAN...

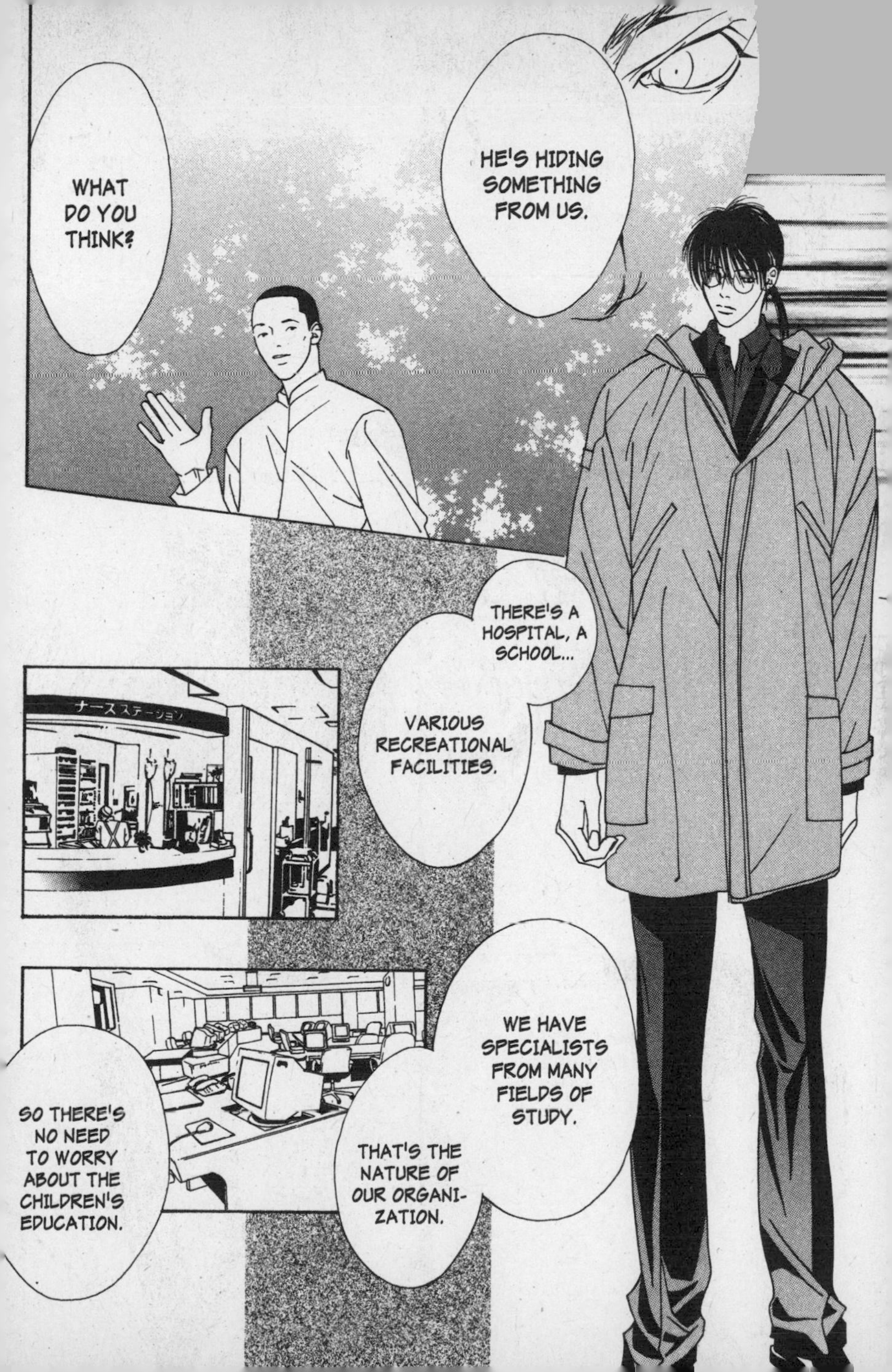
HE'S HIDING SOMETHING FROM US.
WHAT DO YOU THINK?
THERE'S A HOSPITAL, A SCHOOL...
VARIOUS RECREATIONAL FACILITIES.
ナースステーション
WE HAVE SPECIALISTS FROM MANY FIELDS OF STUDY.
THAT'S THE NATURE OF OUR ORGANI-ZATION.
SO THERE'S NO NEED TO WORRY ABOUT THE CHILDREN'S EDUCATION.

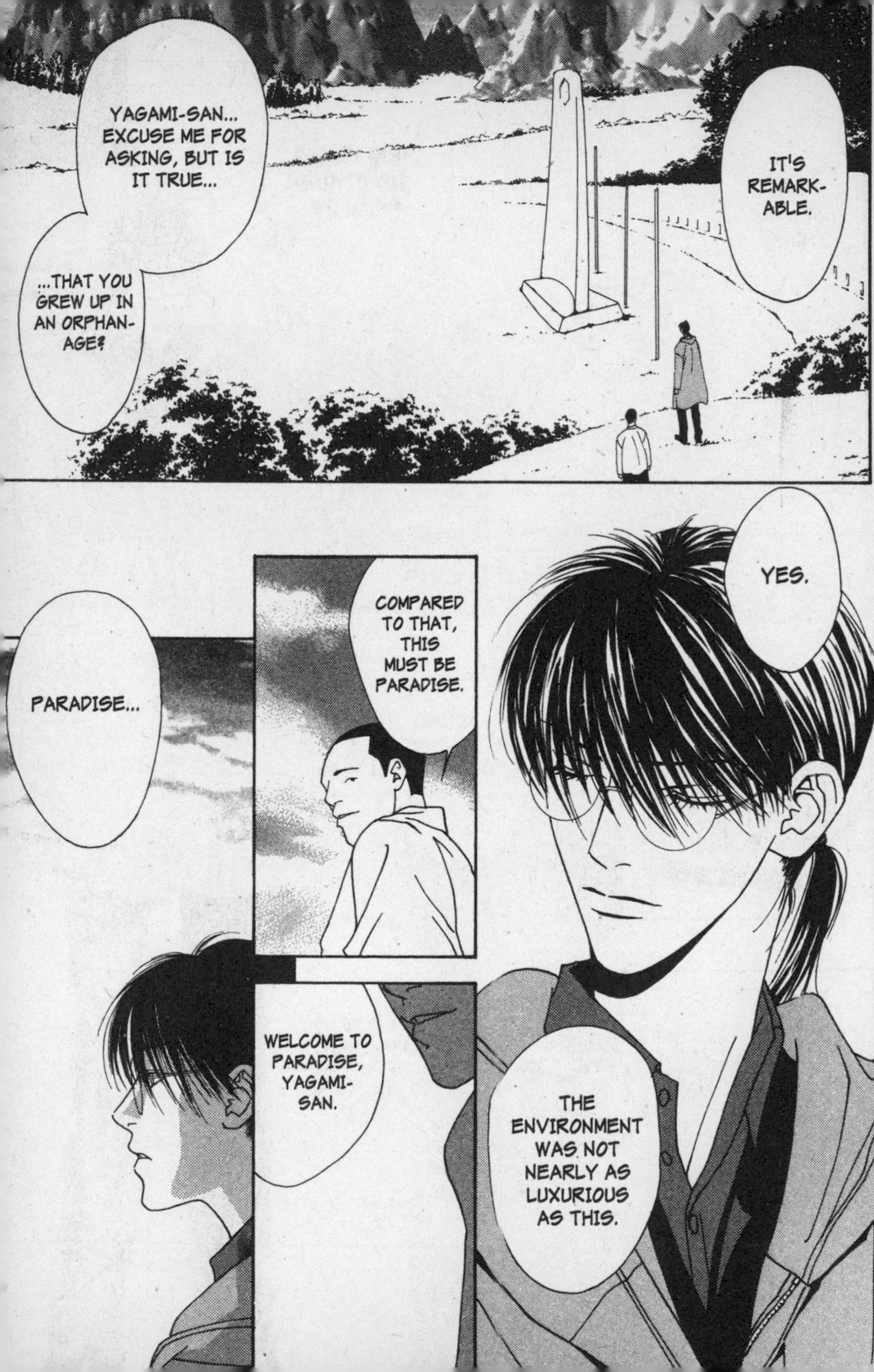
IT'S REMARK-ABLE.
YAGAMI-SAN... EXCUSE ME FOR ASKING, BUT IS IT TRUE...
...THAT YOU GREW UP IN AN ORPHAN-AGE?
YES.
THE ENVIRONMENT WAS NOT NEARLY AS LUXURIOUS AS THIS.
COMPARED TO THAT, THIS MUST BE PARADISE.
WELCOME TO PARADISE, YAGAMI-SAN.
PARADISE...

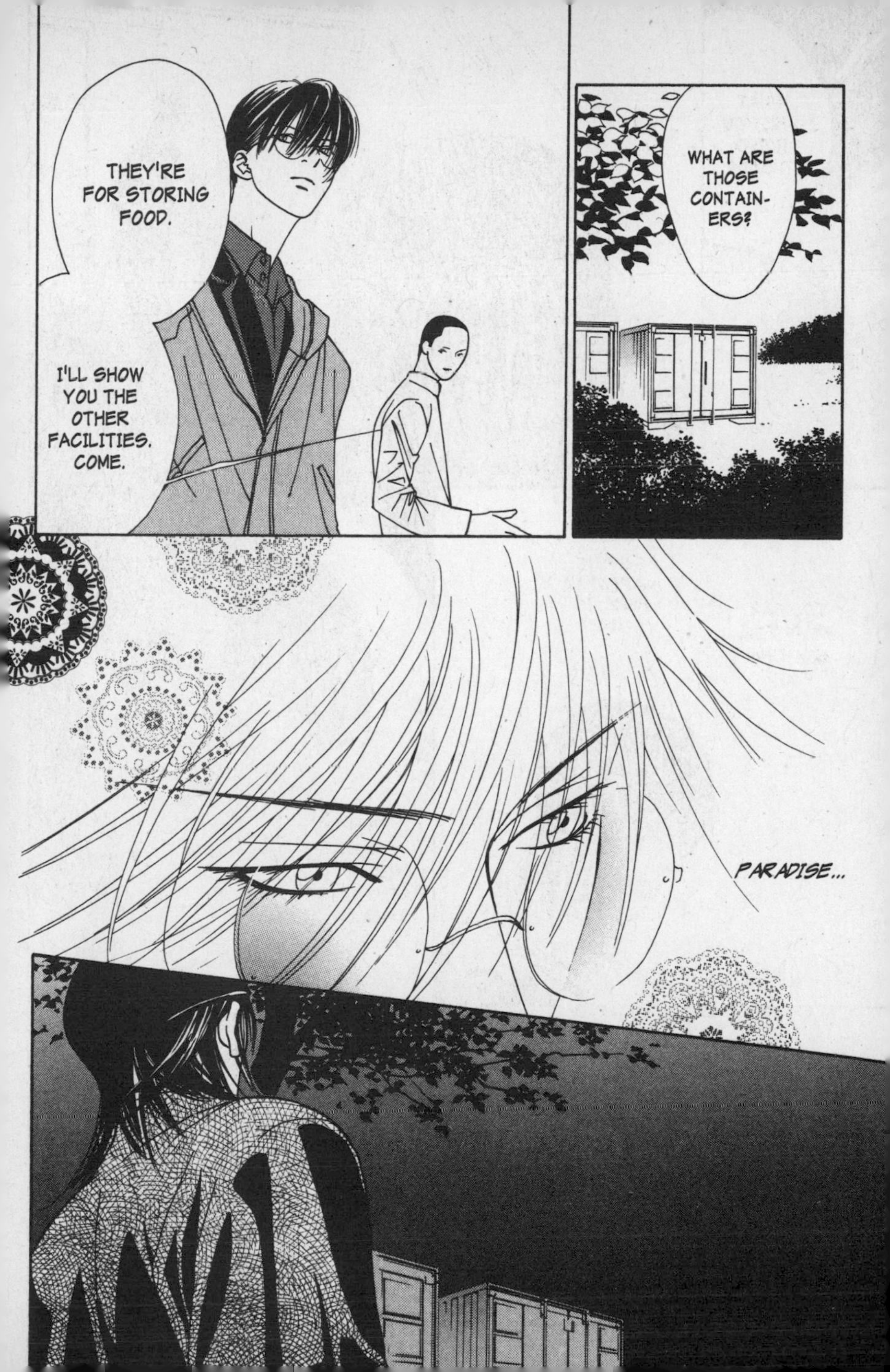
WHAT ARE THOSE CONTAINERS?
THEY'RE FOR STORING FOOD.
I'LL SHOW YOU THE OTHER FACILITIES. COME.
PARADISE...

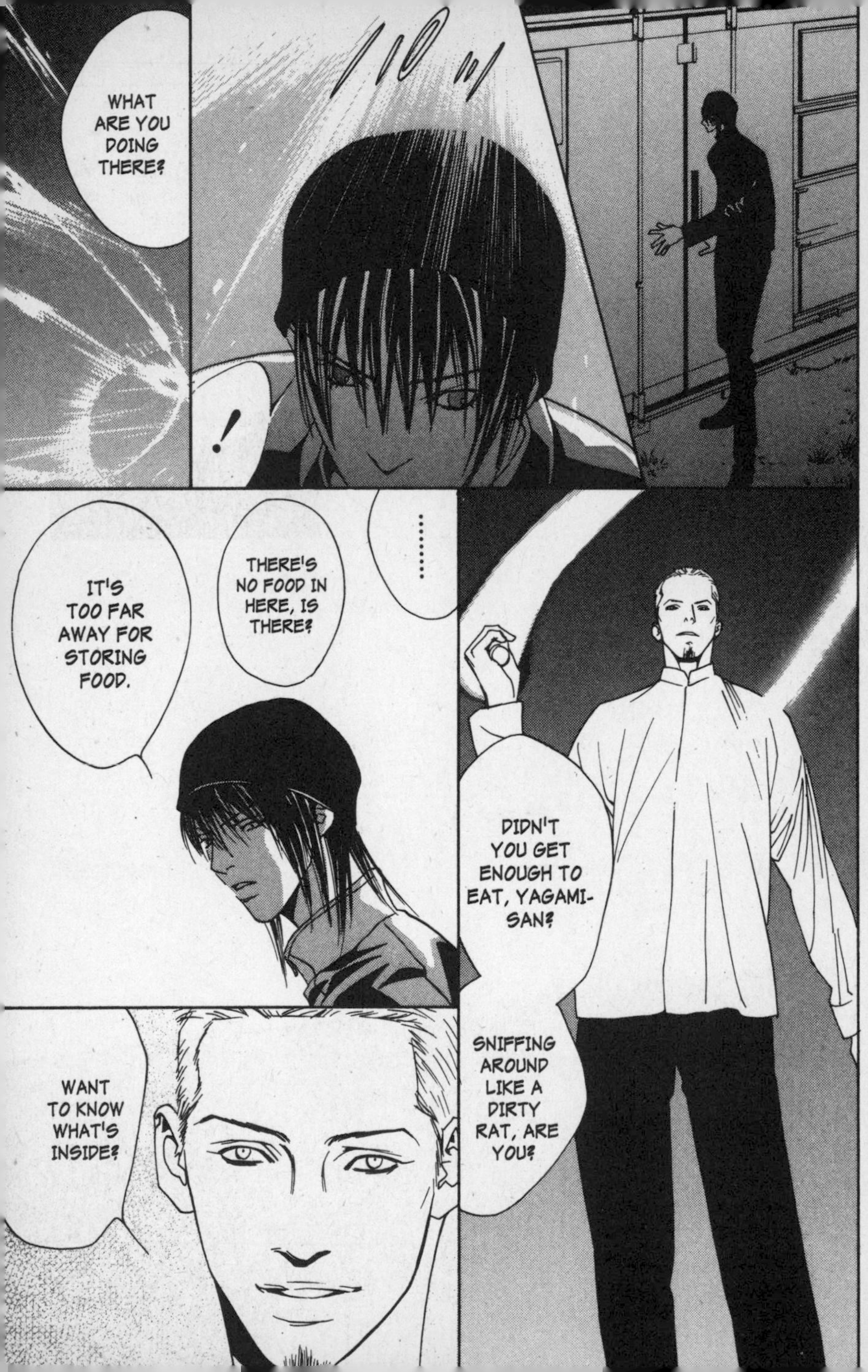
!
WHAT ARE YOU DOING THERE?
DIDN'T YOU GET ENOUGH TO EAT, YAGAMI-SAN?
SNIFFING AROUND LIKE A DIRTY RAT, ARE YOU?
....
THERE'S NO FOOD IN HERE, IS THERE?
IT'S TOO FAR AWAY FOR STORING FOOD.
WANT TO KNOW WHAT'S INSIDE?

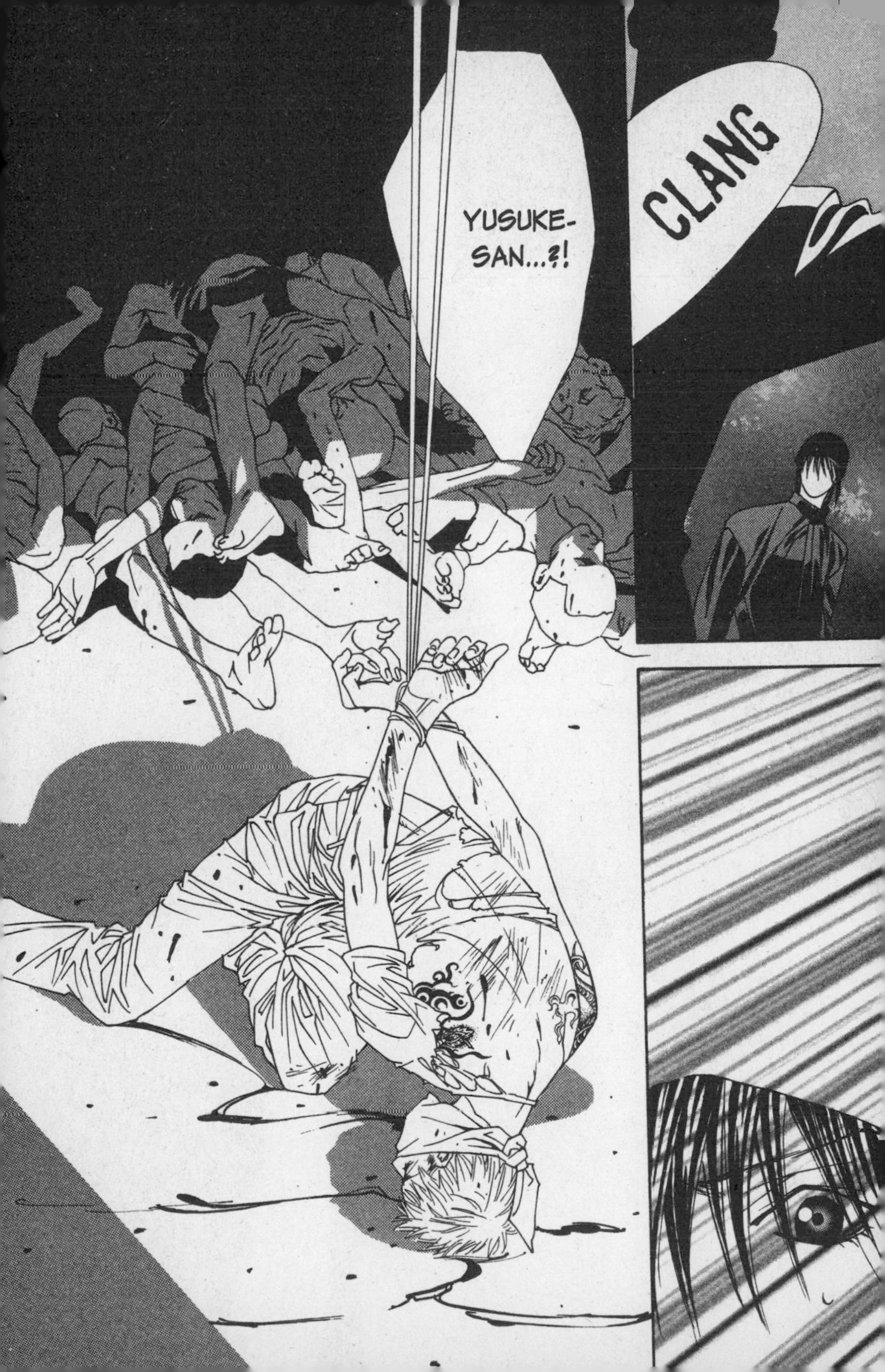
CLANG
YUSUKE-SAN...?!

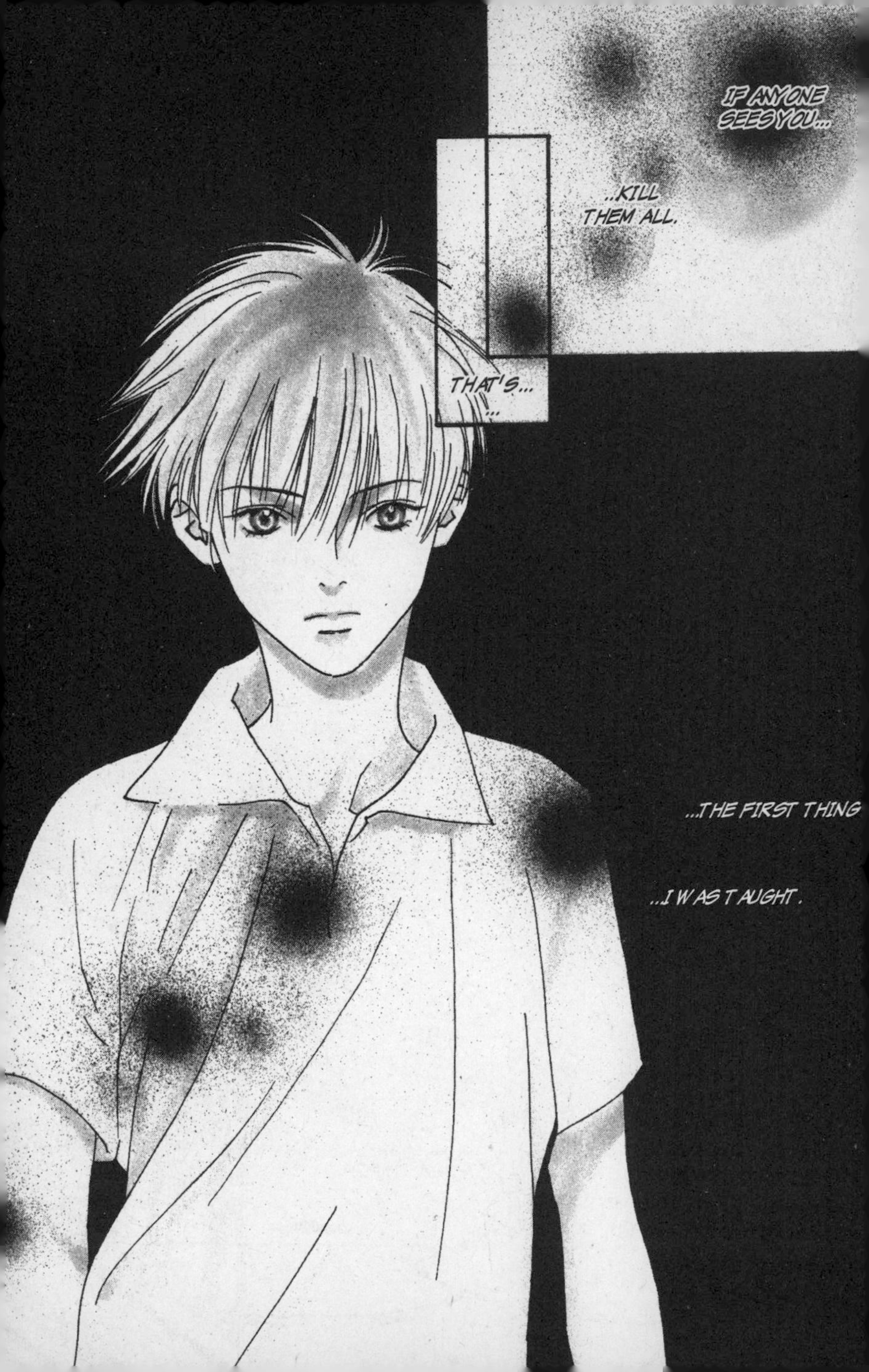
IF ANYONE SEES YOU...
...KILL THEM ALL.
THAT'S... ...
...THE FIRST THING
...I WAS TAUGHT.

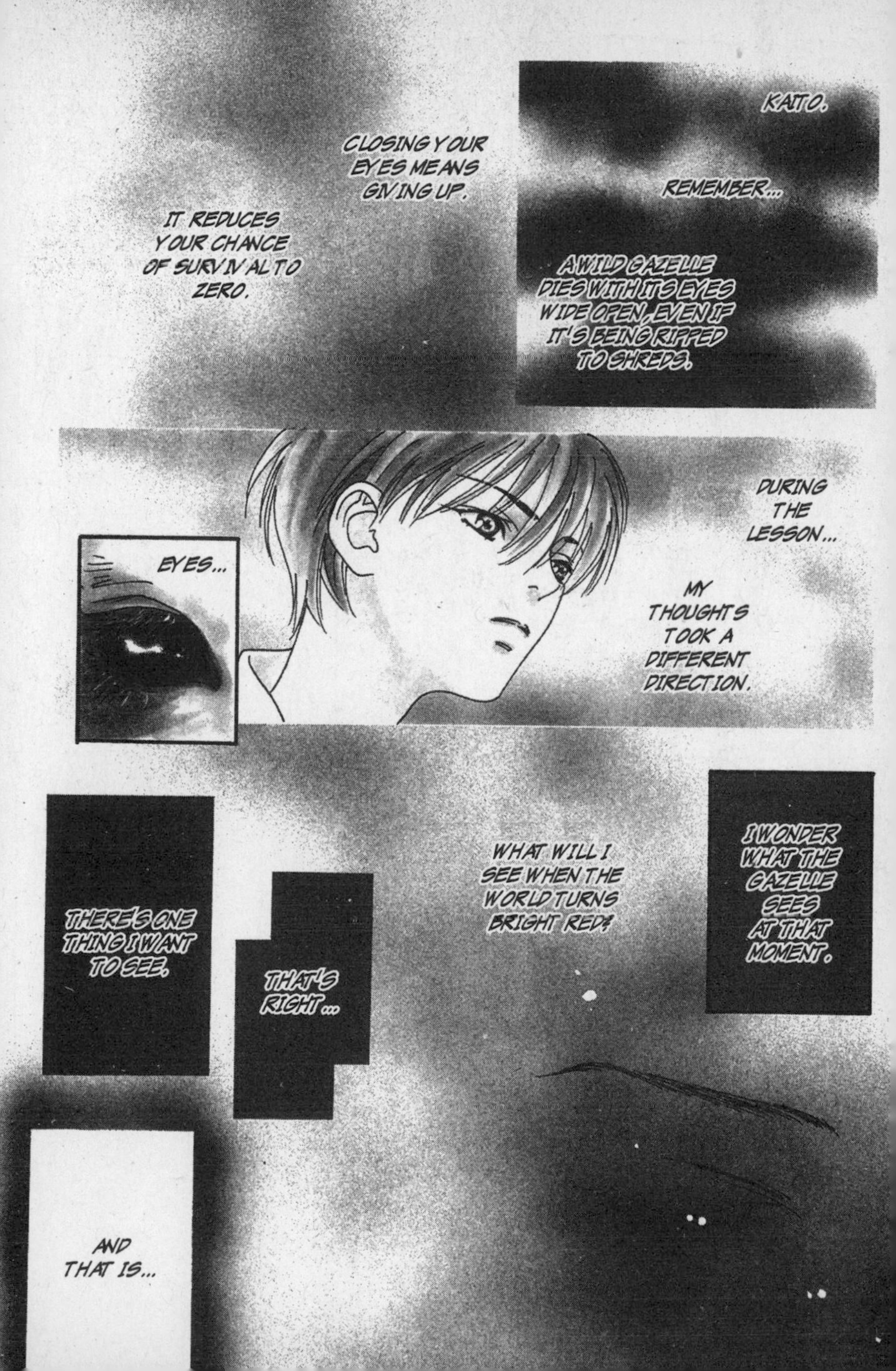
KAITO.
REMEMBER...
A WILD GAZELLE DIES WITH ITS EYES WIDE OPEN, EVEN IF IT'S BEING RIPPED TO SHREDS.
CLOSING YOUR EYES MEANS GIVING UP.
IT REDUCES YOUR CHANCE OF SURVIVAL TO ZERO.
DURING THE LESSON...
MY THOUGHTS TOOK A DIFFERENT DIRECTION.
EYES...
I WONDER WHAT THE GAZELLE SEES AT THAT MOMENT.
WHAT WILL I SEE WHEN THE WORLD TURNS BRIGHT RED?
THAT'S RIGHT...
THERE'S ONE THING I WANT TO SEE.
AND THAT IS...

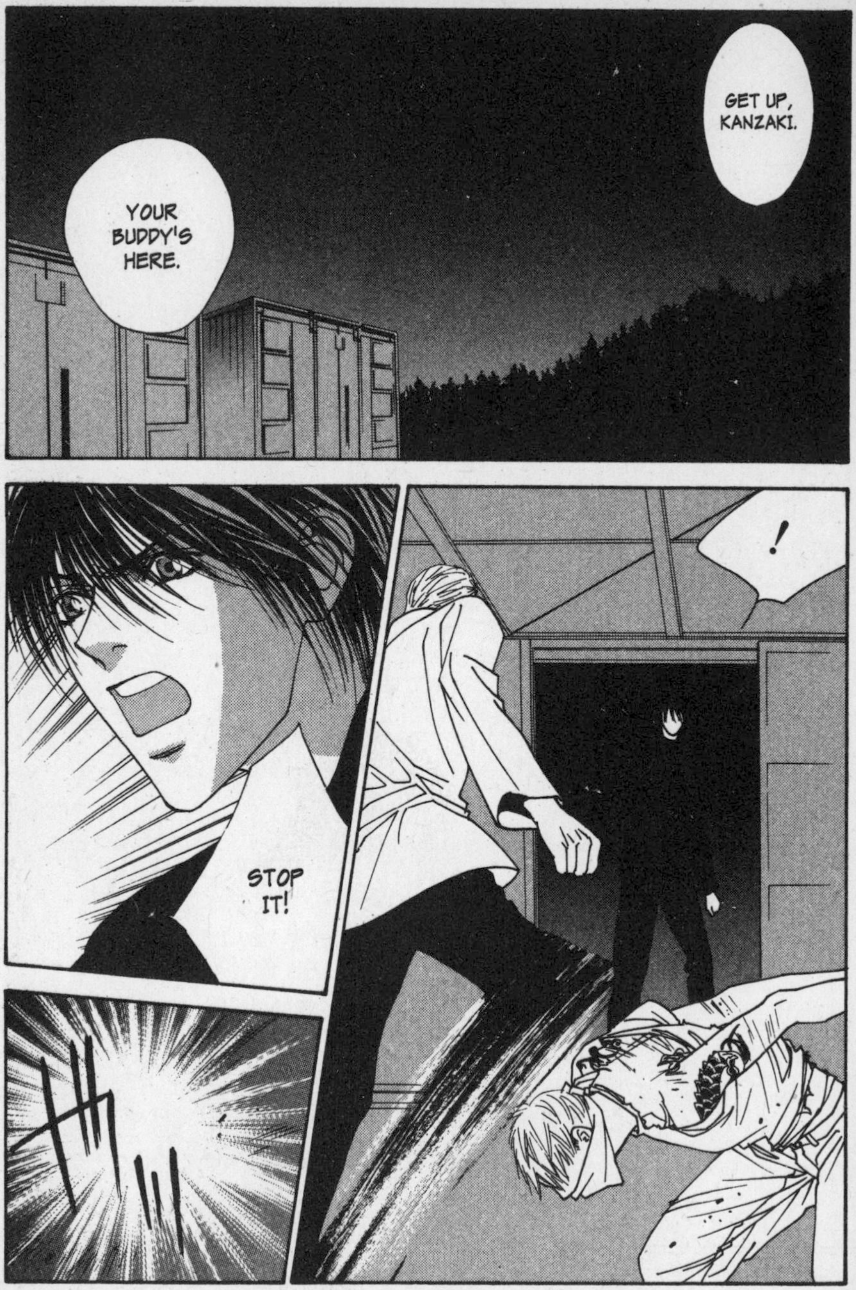
GET UP, KANZAKI.
YOUR BUDDY'S HERE.
!
STOP IT!

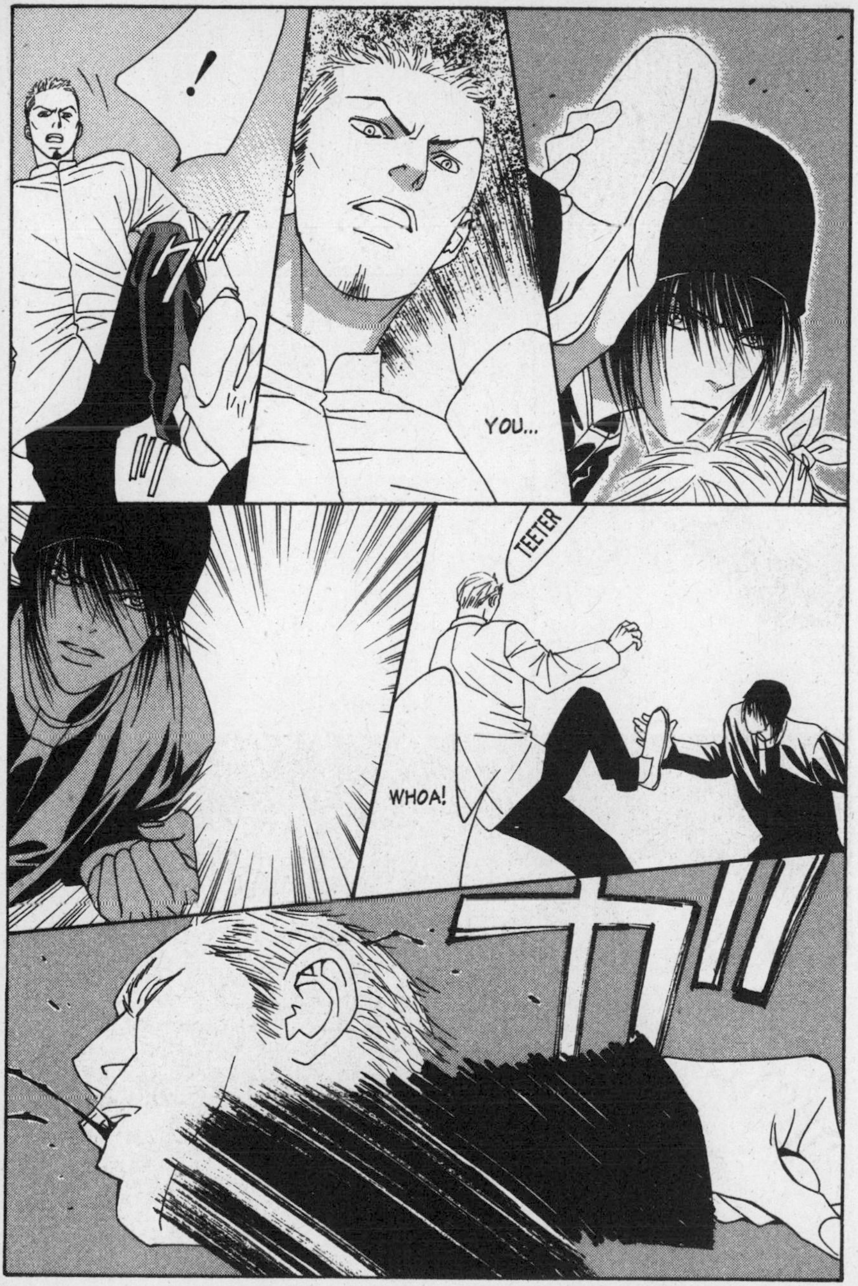
YOU...
!
TEETER
WHOA!

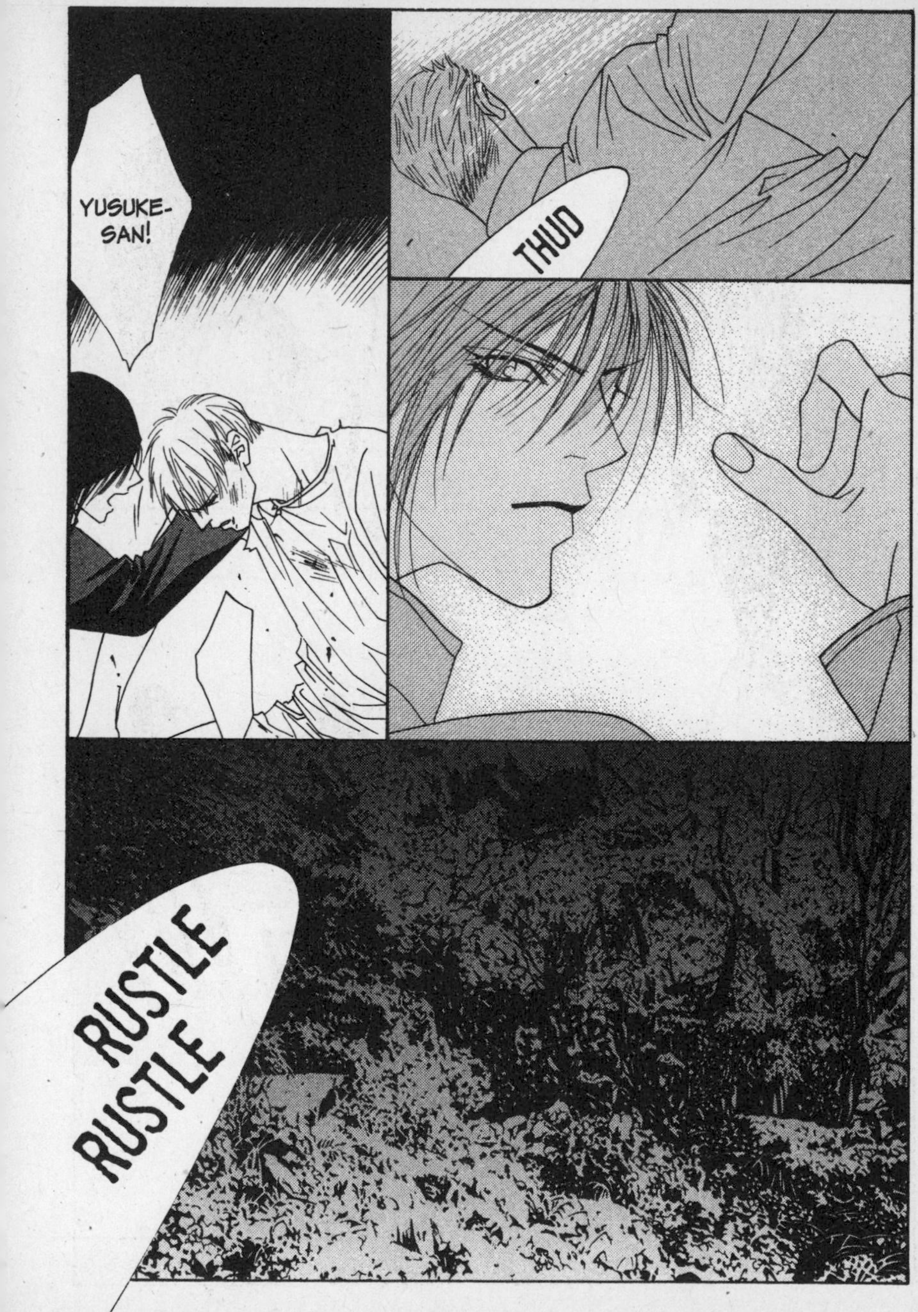
THUD
YUSUKE-SAN!
RUSTLE RUSTLE

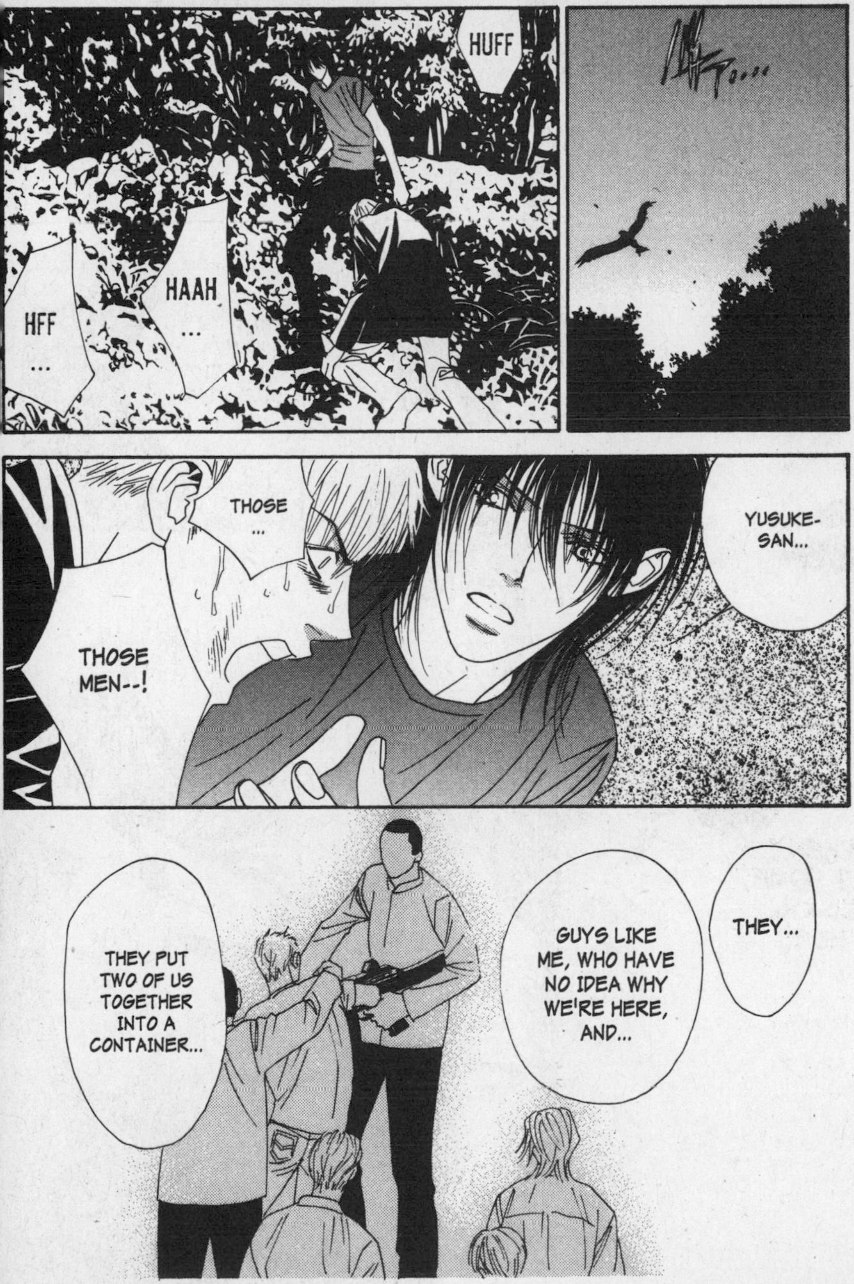
HUFF
HAAH ...
HFF ...
YUSUKE-SAN...
THOSE ...
THOSE MEN--!
THEY...
GUYS LIKE ME, WHO HAVE NO IDEA WHY WE'RE HERE, AND...
THEY PUT TWO OF US TOGETHER INTO A CONTAINER...

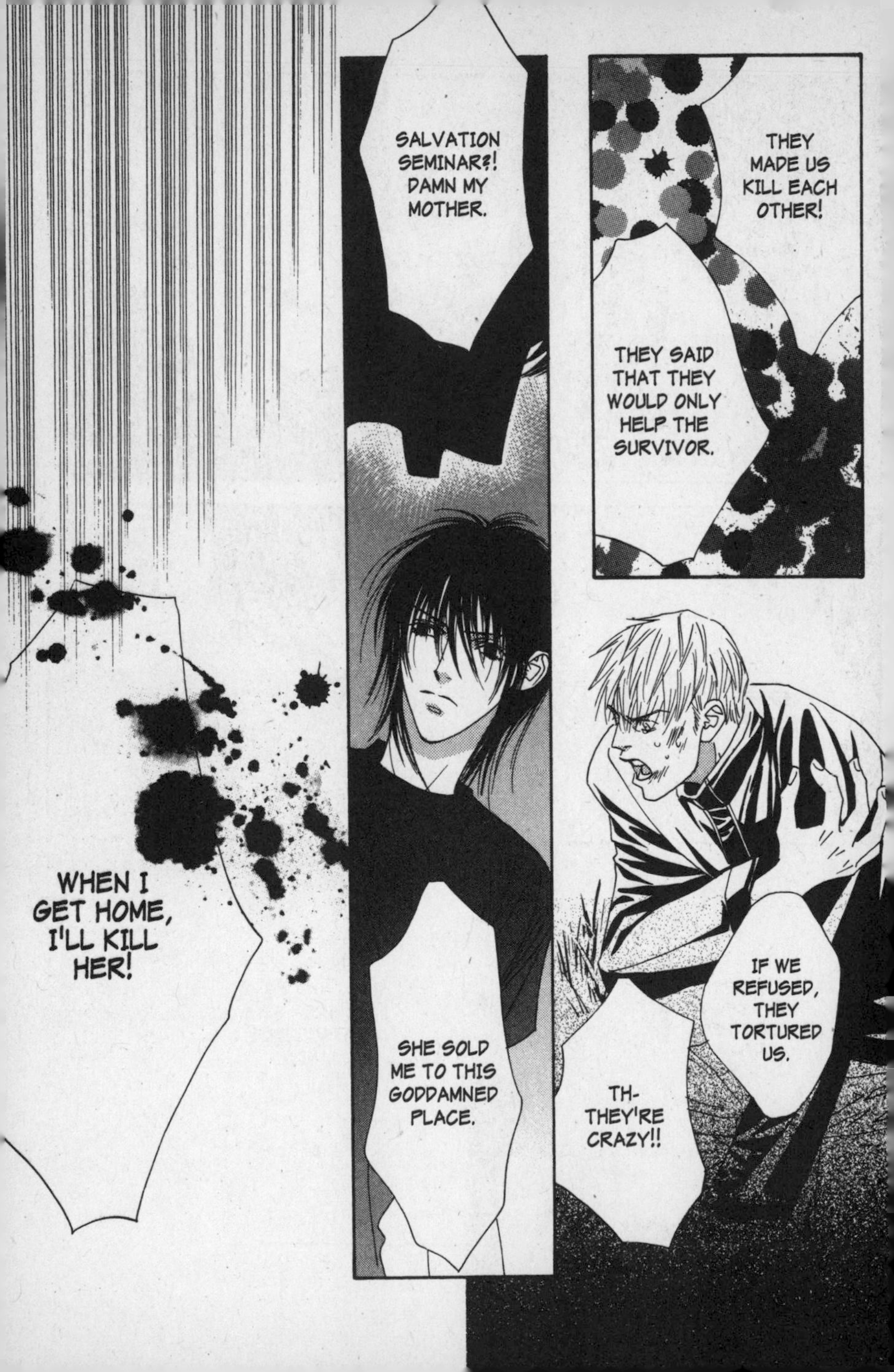
THEY MADE US KILL EACH OTHER!
THEY SAID THAT THEY WOULD ONLY HELP THE SURVIVOR.
IF WE REFUSED, THEY TORTURED US.
TH- THEY'RE CRAZY!!
SALVATION SEMINAR?! DAMN MY MOTHER.
SHE SOLD ME TO THIS GODDAMNED PLACE.
WHEN I GET HOME, I'LL KILL HER!

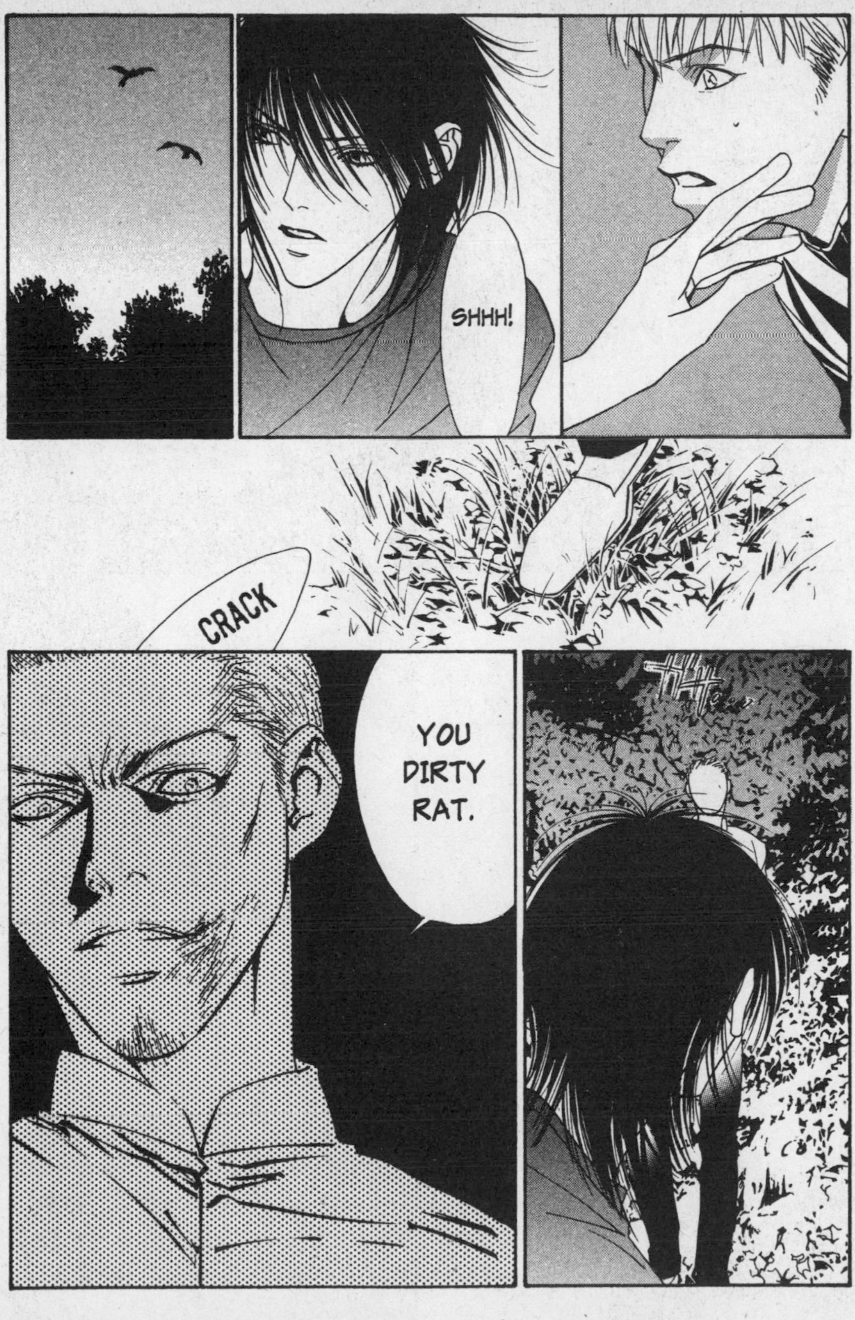
SHHH!
CRACK
YOU DIRTY RAT.

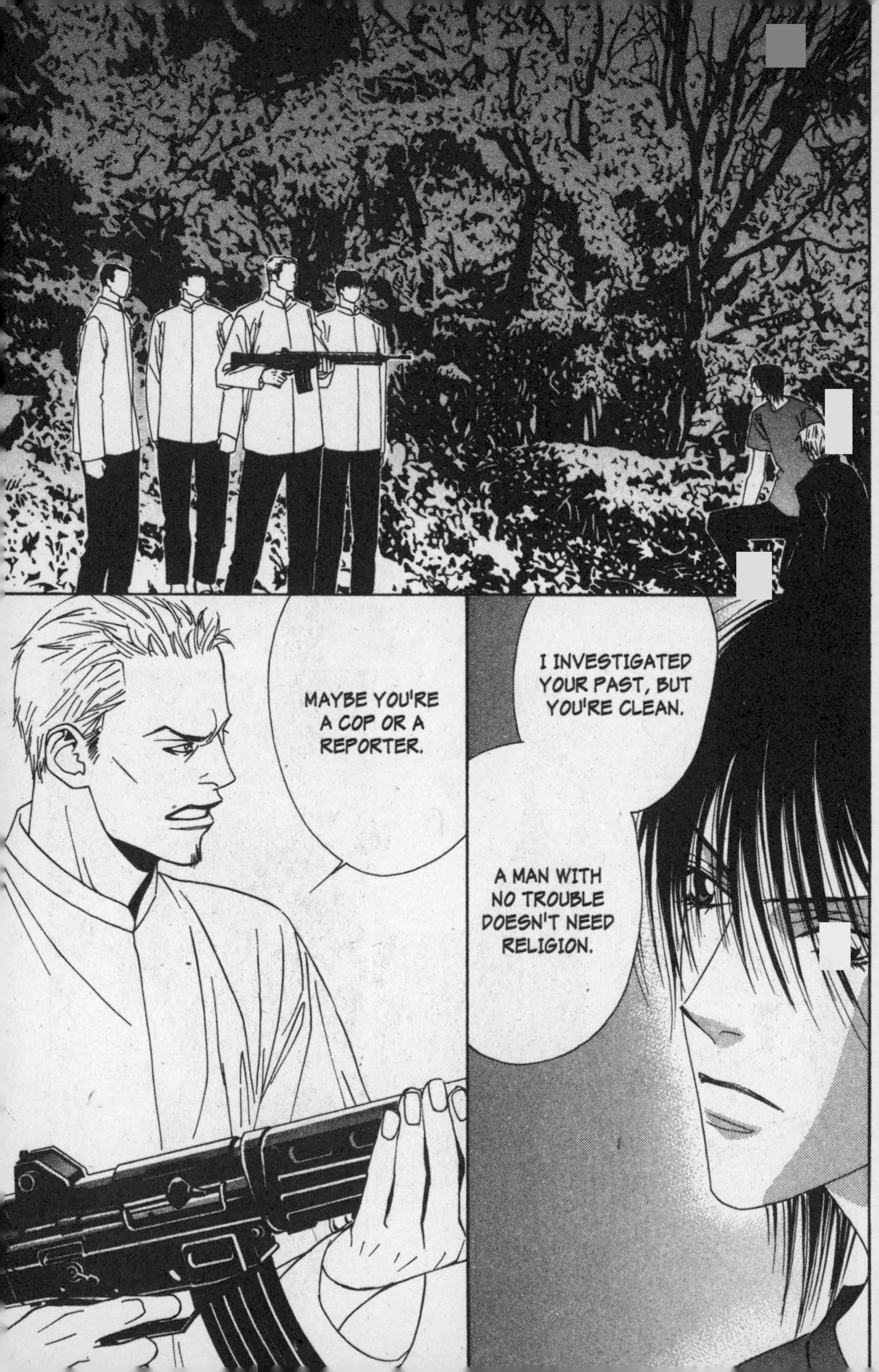
I INVESTIGATED YOUR PAST, BUT YOU'RE CLEAN.
A MAN WITH NO TROUBLE DOESN'T NEED RELIGION.
MAYBE YOU'RE A COP OR A REPORTER.

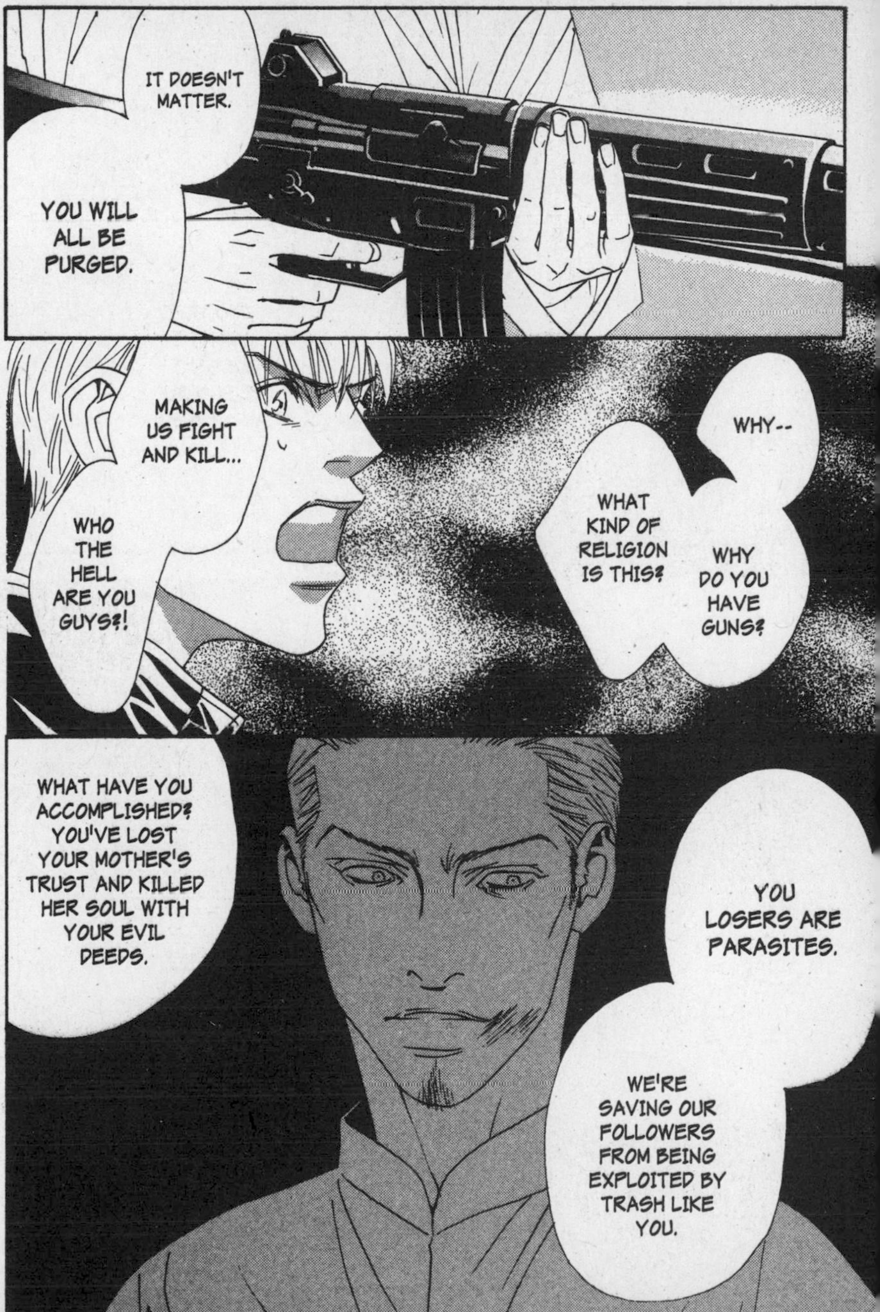
IT DOESN'T MATTER.
YOU WILL ALL BE PURGED.
WHY--
WHY DO YOU HAVE GUNS?
WHAT KIND OF RELIGION IS THIS?
MAKING US FIGHT AND KILL...
WHO THE HELL ARE YOU GUYS?!
YOU LOSERS ARE PARASITES.
WE'RE SAVING OUR FOLLOWERS FROM BEING EXPLOITED BY TRASH LIKE YOU.
WHAT HAVE YOU ACCOMPLISHED? YOU'VE LOST YOUR MOTHER'S TRUST AND KILLED HER SOUL WITH YOUR EVIL DEEDS.

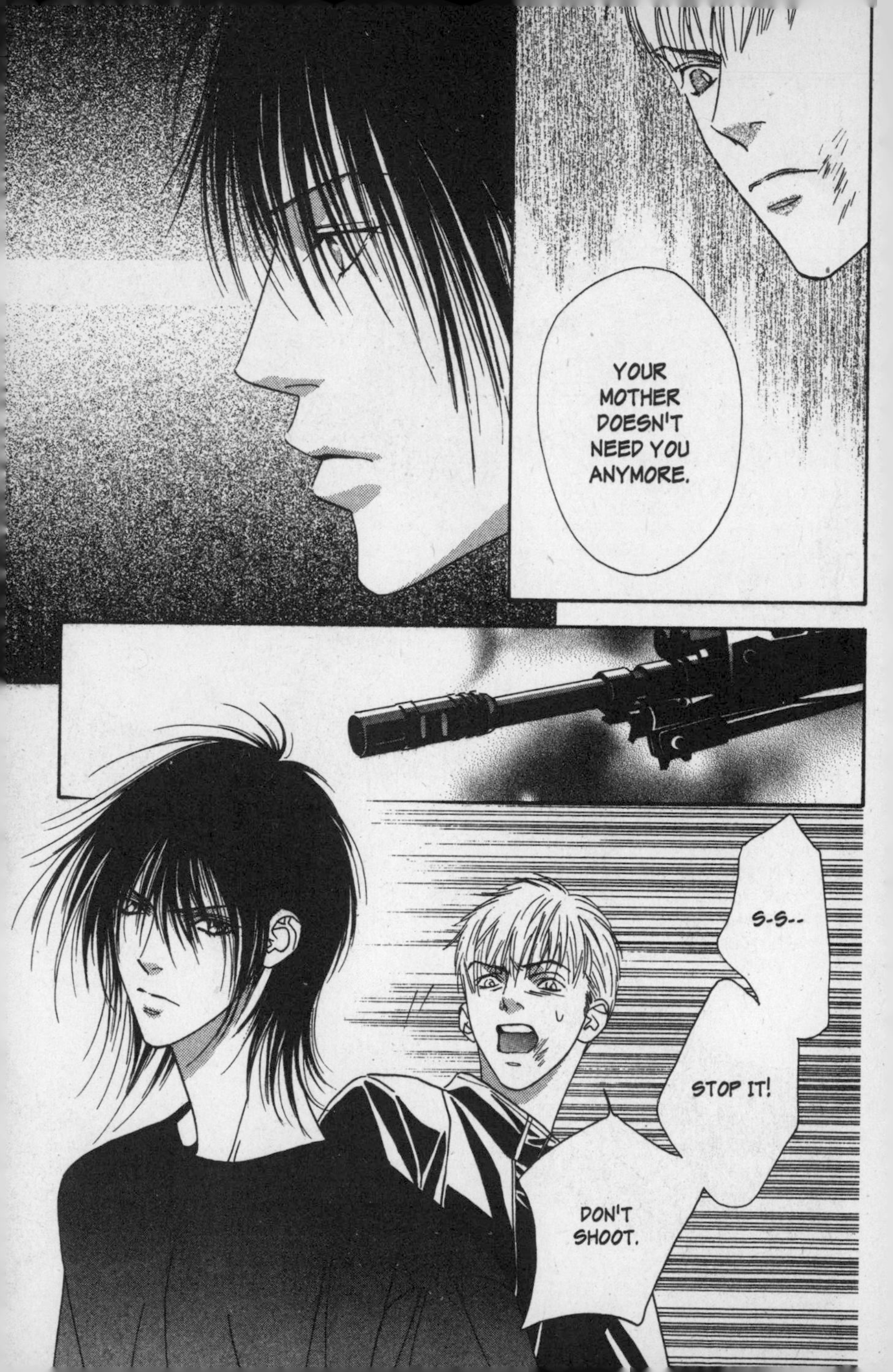
YOUR MOTHER DOESN'T NEED YOU ANYMORE.
S-S--
STOP IT!
DON'T SHOOT.

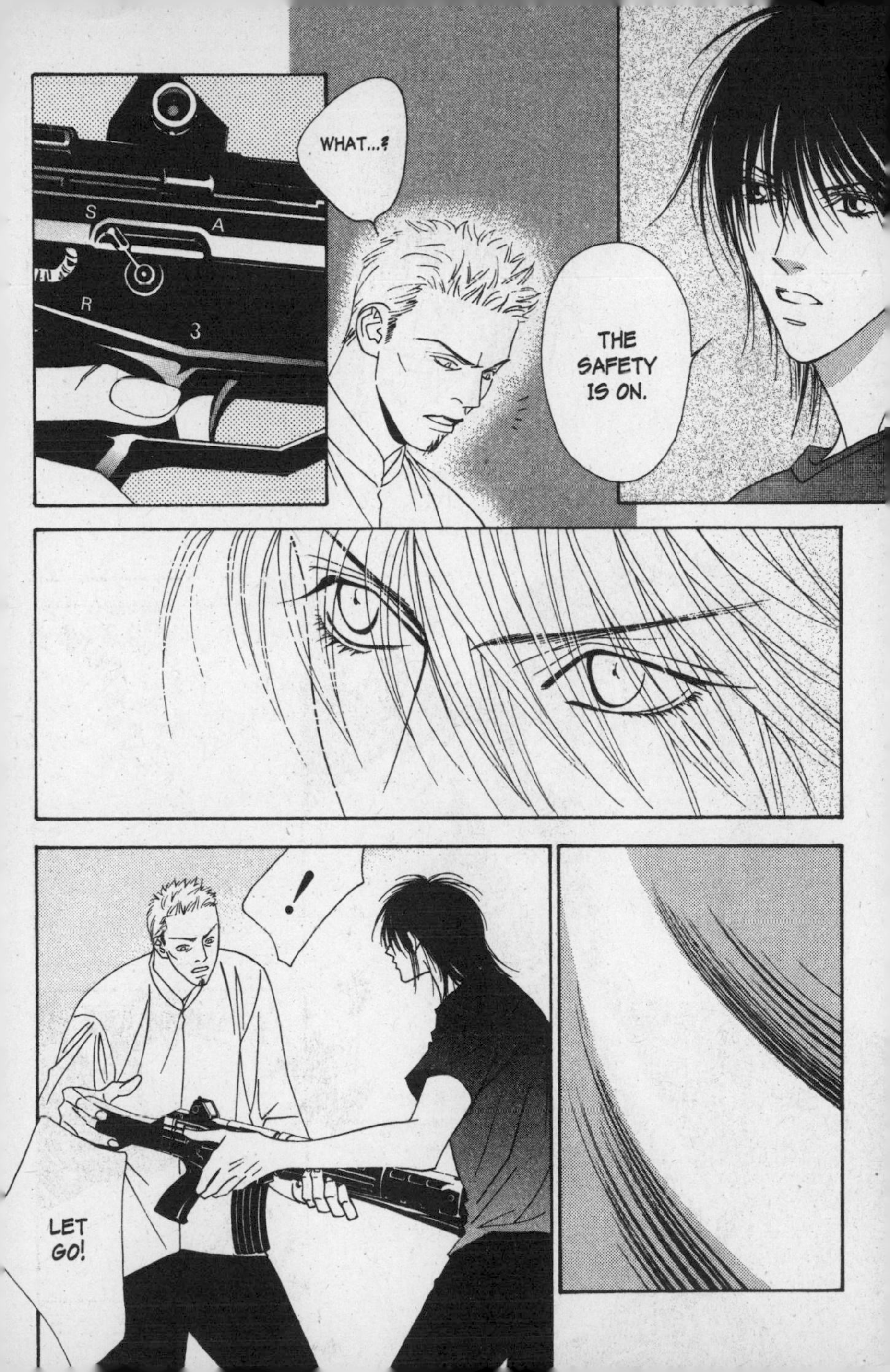
THE SAFETY IS ON.
WHAT...?
S
A
R
3
!
LET GO!

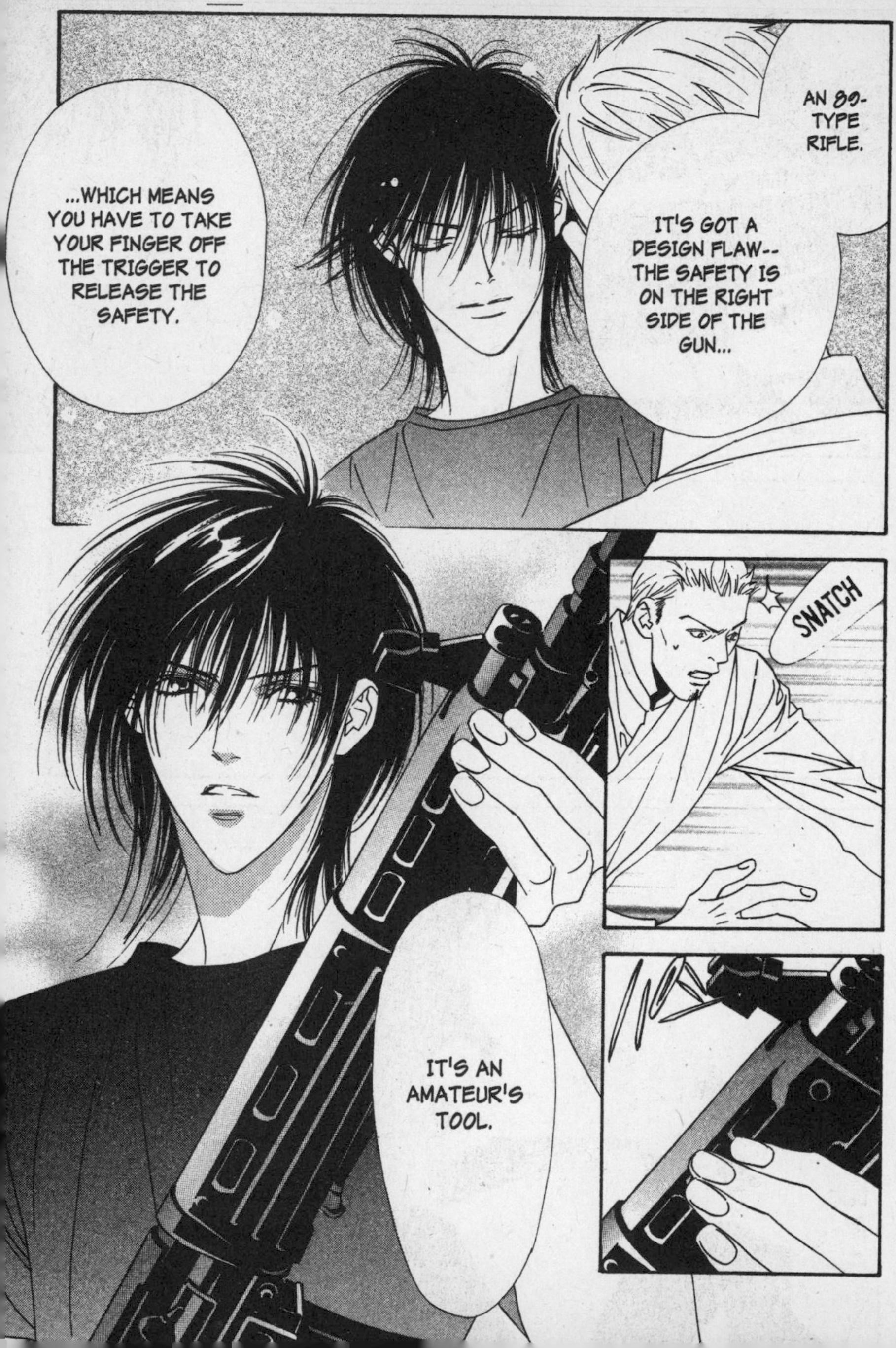
AN 89-TYPE RIFLE.
IT'S GOT A DESIGN FLAW-- THE SAFETY IS ON THE RIGHT SIDE OF THE GUN...
...WHICH MEANS YOU HAVE TO TAKE YOUR FINGER OFF THE TRIGGER TO RELEASE THE SAFETY.
SNATCH
IT'S AN AMATEUR'S TOOL.

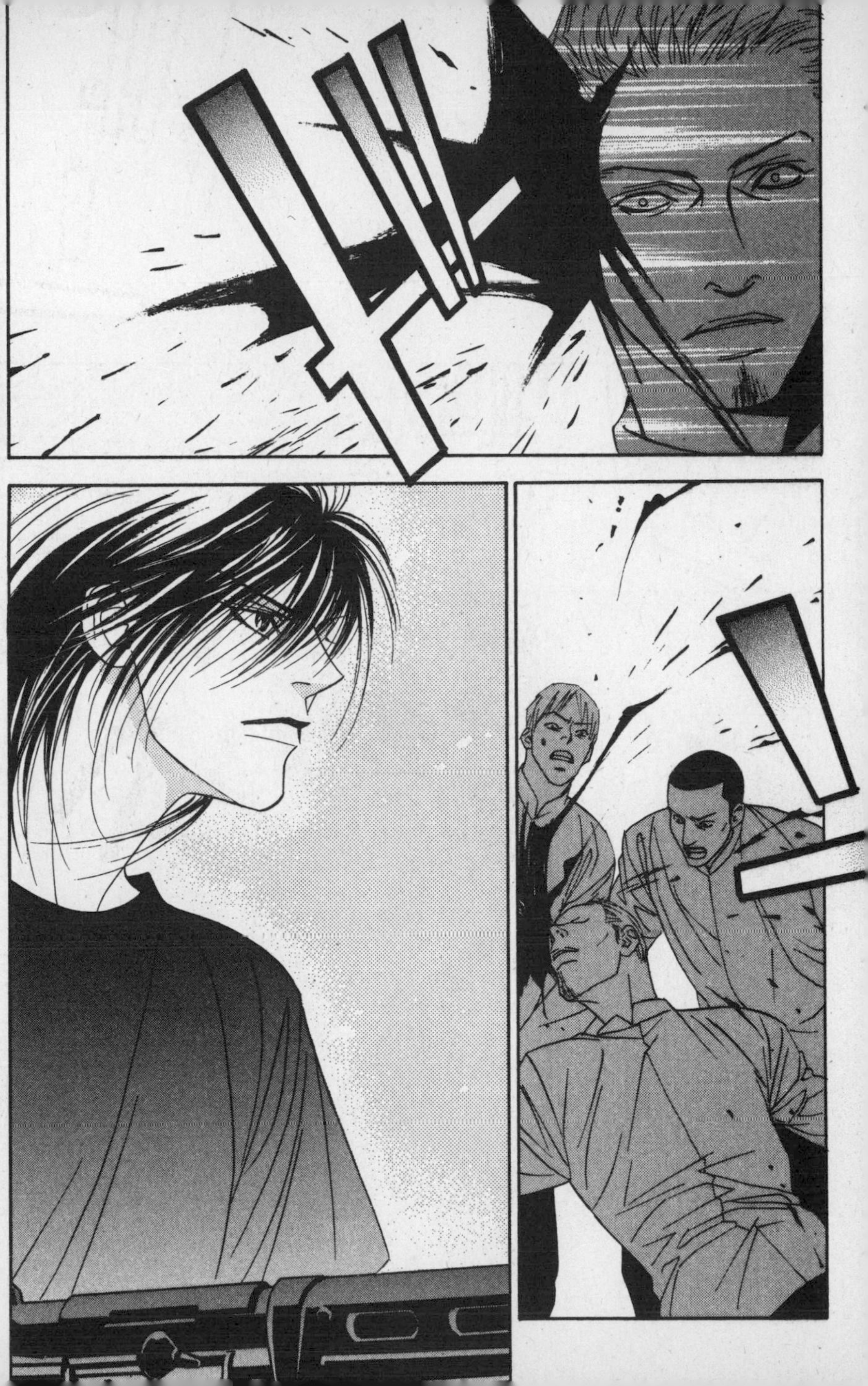
!!
!!

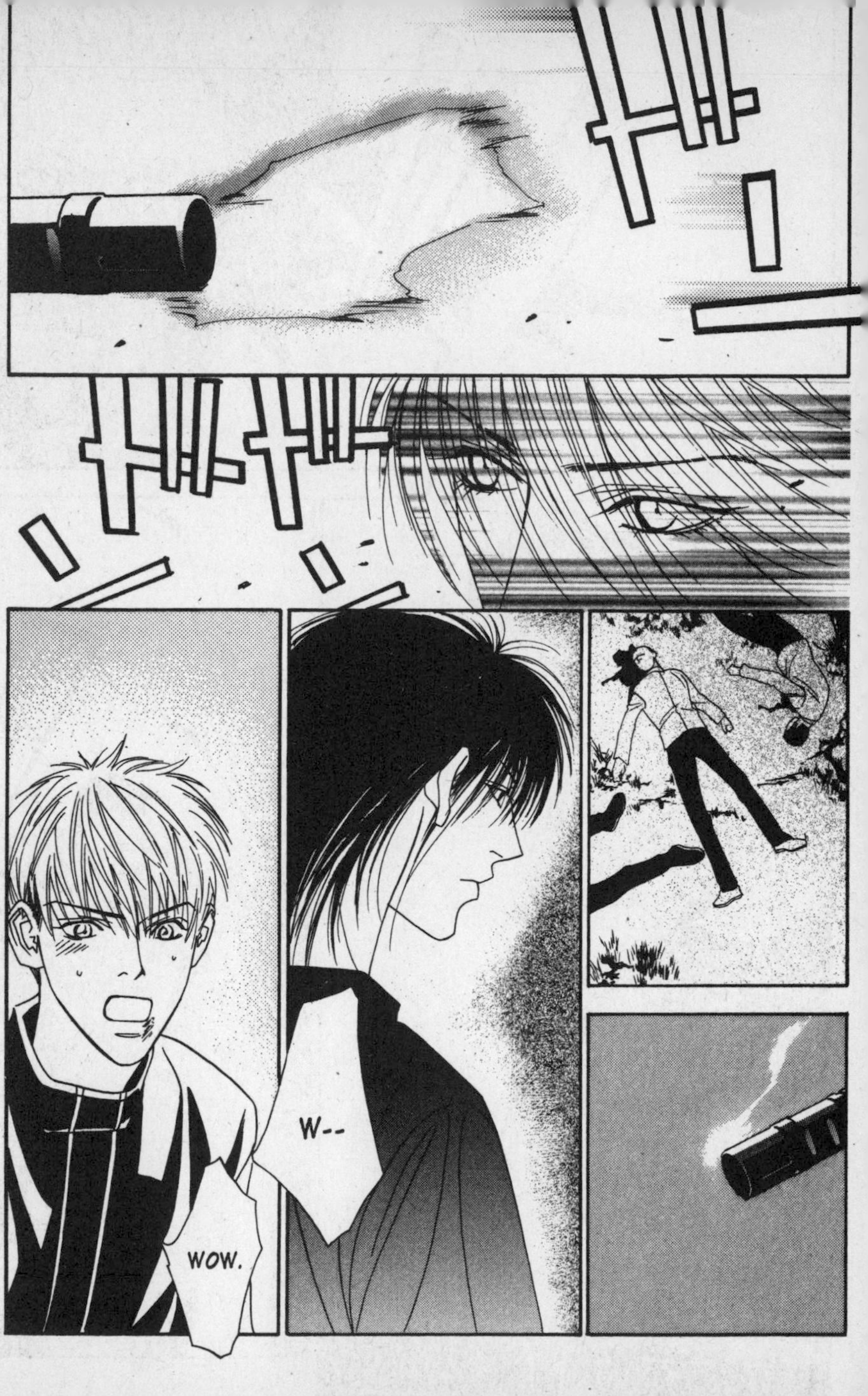
W--
WOW.

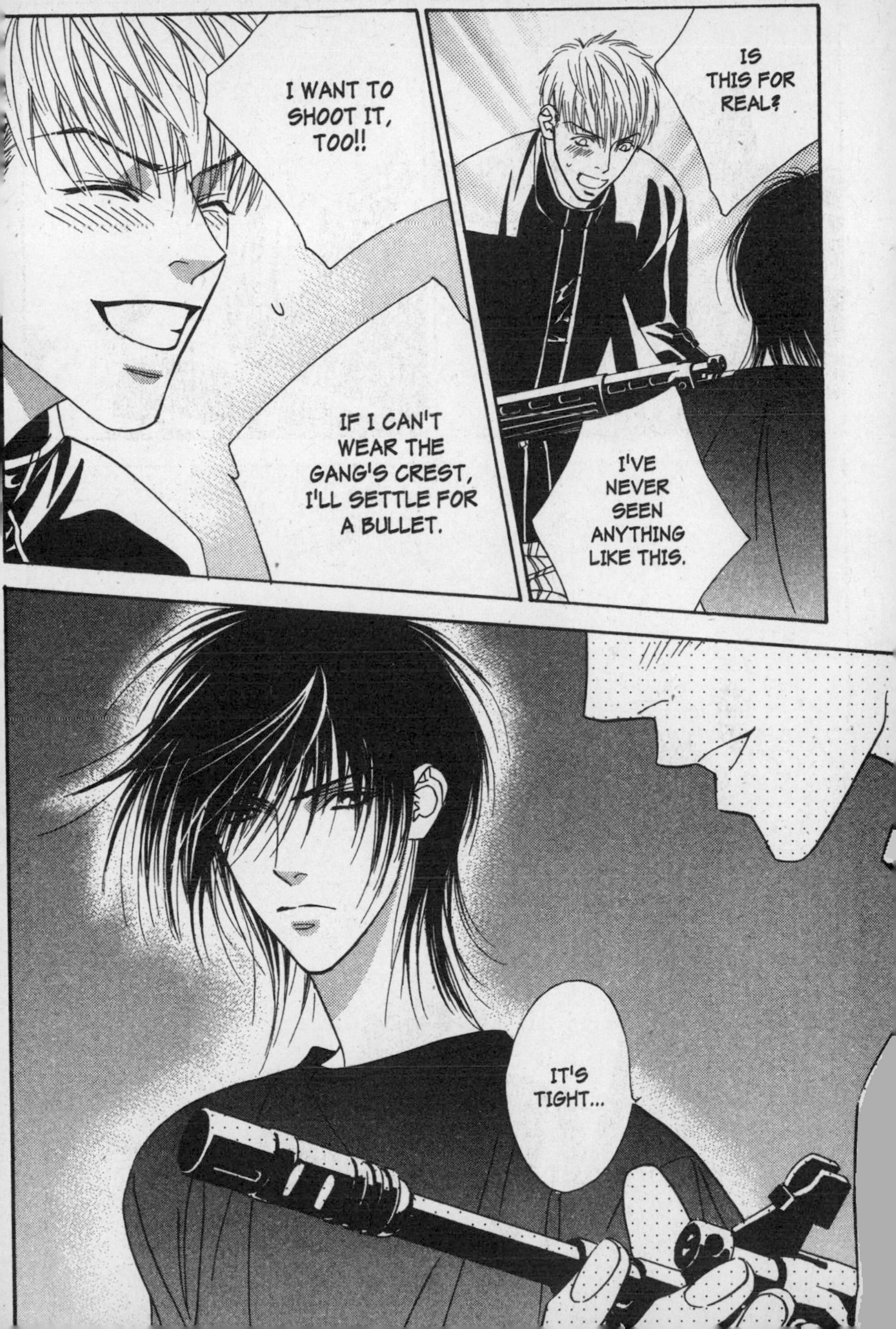
IS THIS FOR REAL?
I'VE NEVER SEEN ANYTHING LIKE THIS.
I WANT TO SHOOT IT, TOO!!
IF I CAN'T WEAR THE GANG'S CREST, I'LL SETTLE FOR A BULLET.
IT'S TIGHT...

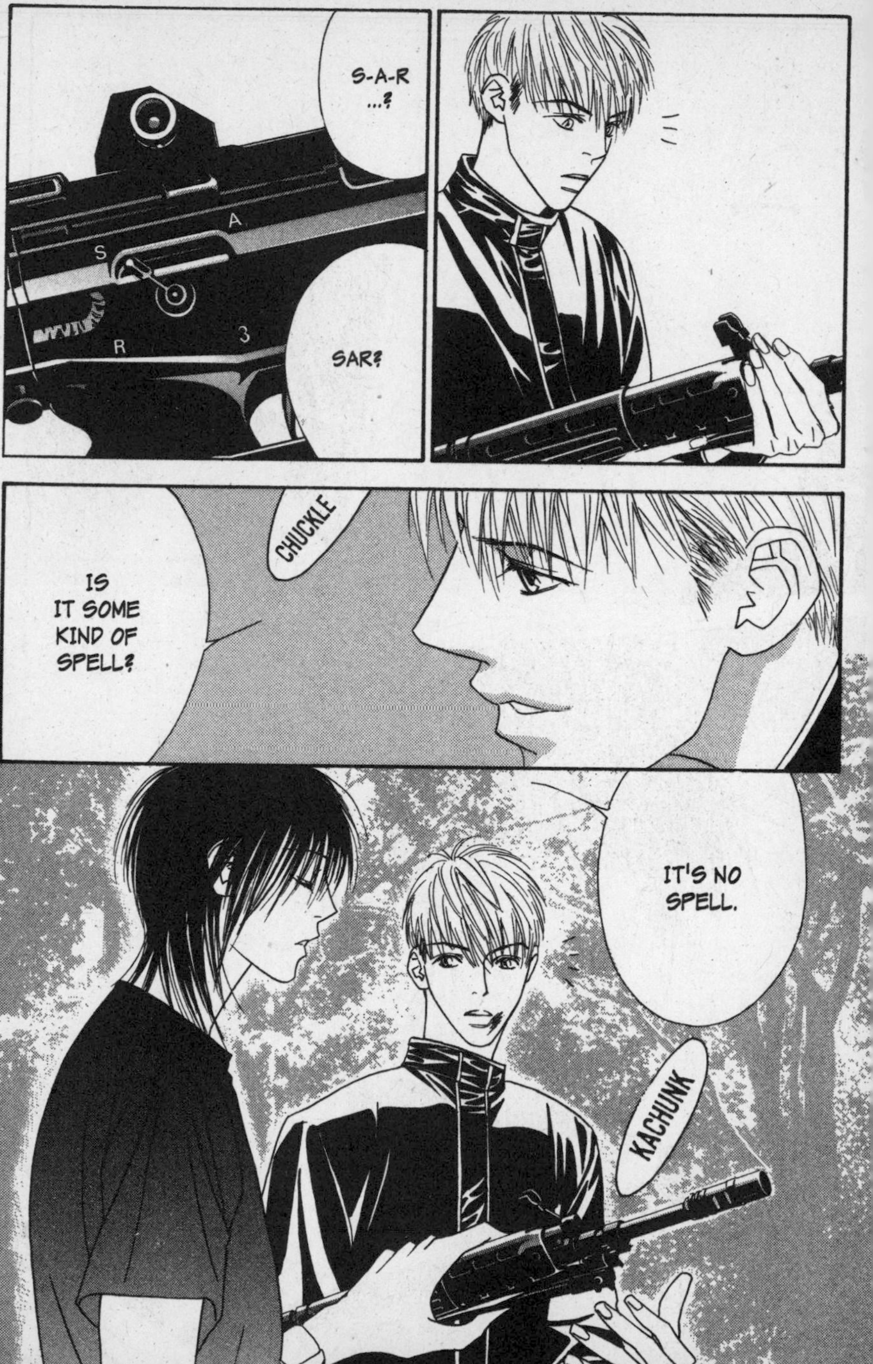
S-A-R ...?
SAR?
CHUCKLE
IS IT SOME KIND OF SPELL?
IT'S NO SPELL.
KACHUNK

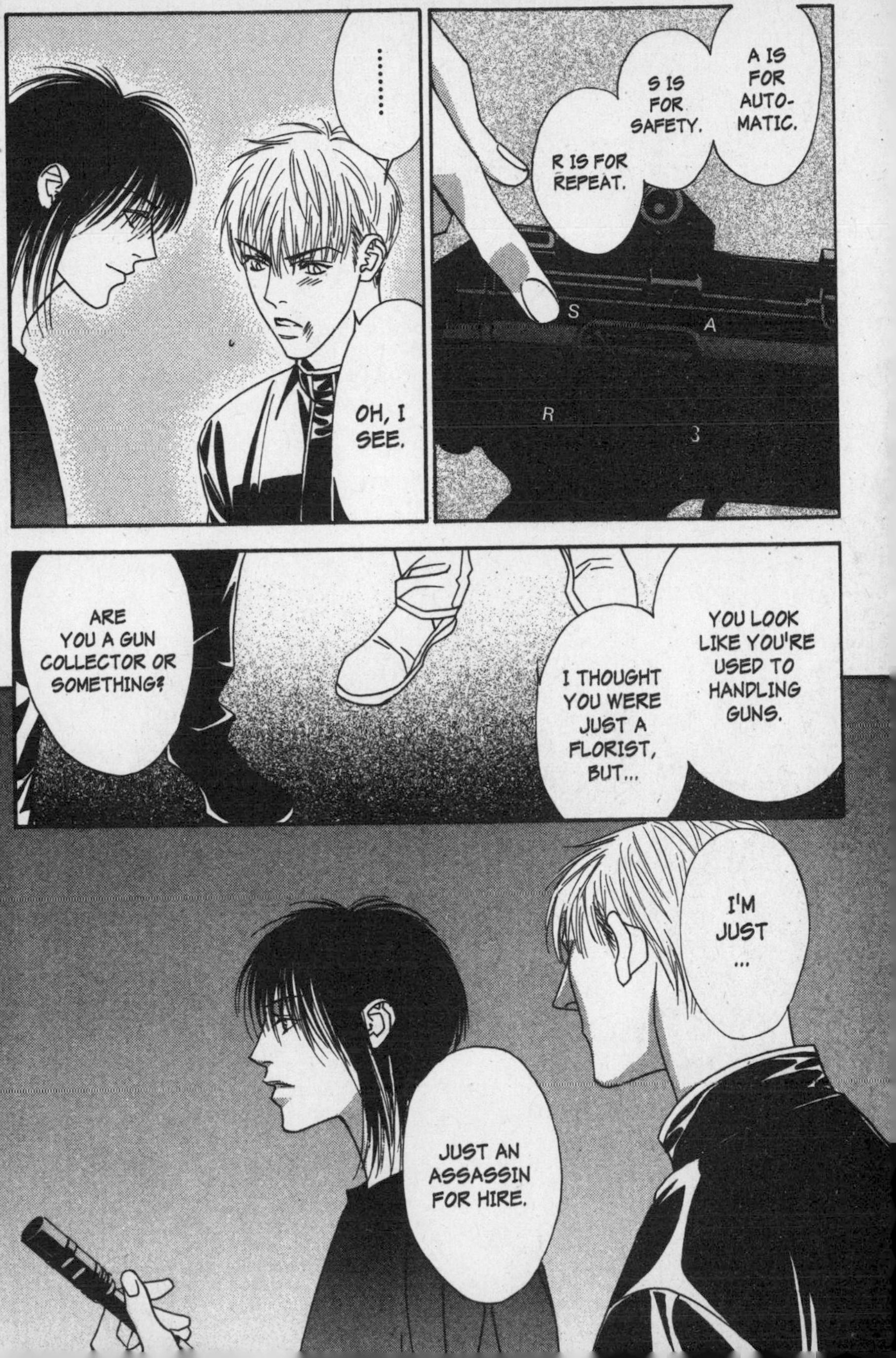
A IS FOR AUTO-MATIC.
S IS FOR SAFETY.
R IS FOR REPEAT.
S
A
R
3
………
OH, I SEE.
YOU LOOK LIKE YOU'RE USED TO HANDLING GUNS.
I THOUGHT YOU WERE JUST A FLORIST, BUT...
ARE YOU A GUN COLLECTOR OR SOMETHING?
I'M JUST ...
JUST AN ASSASSIN FOR HIRE.

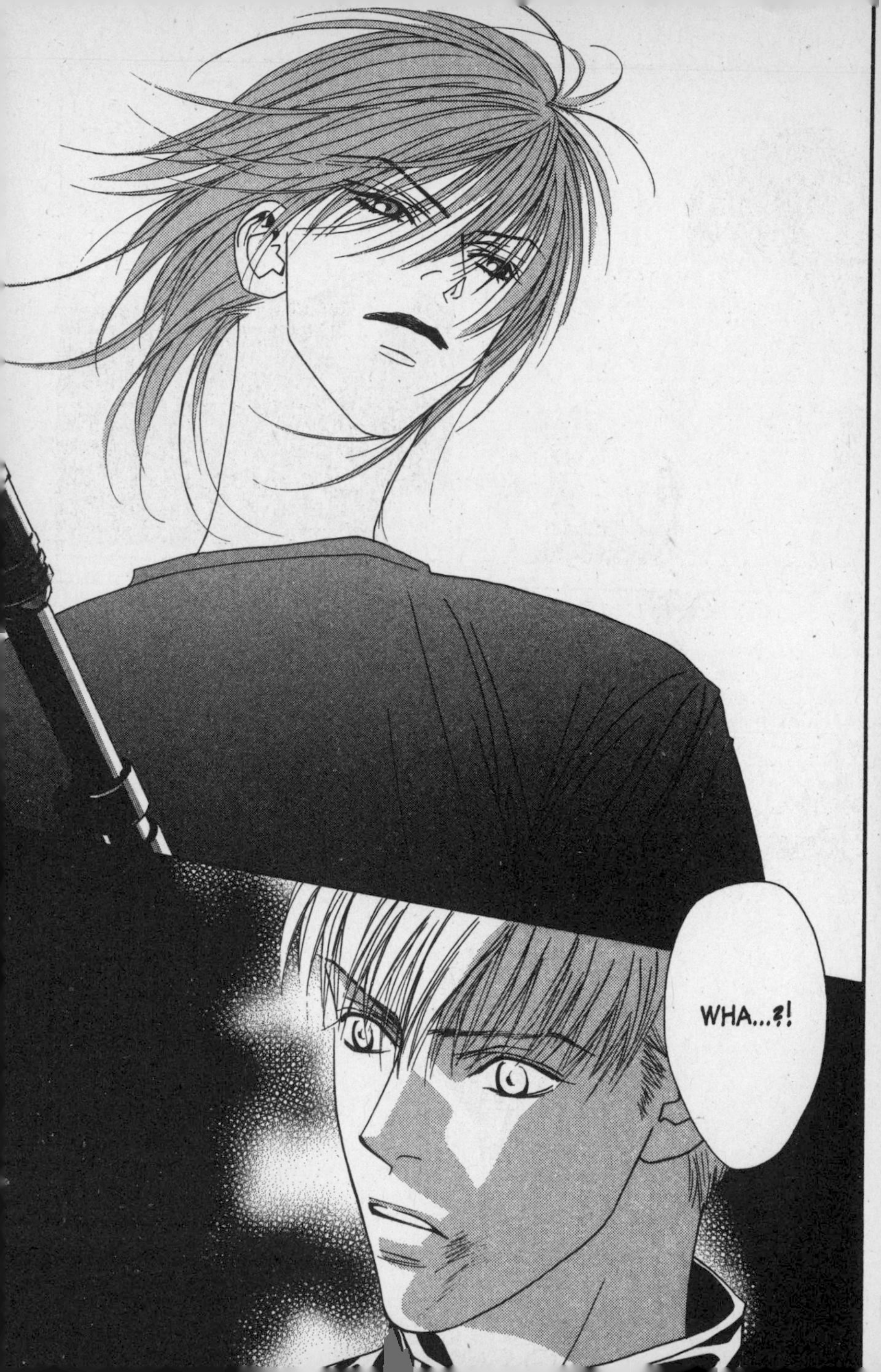
WHA...?!

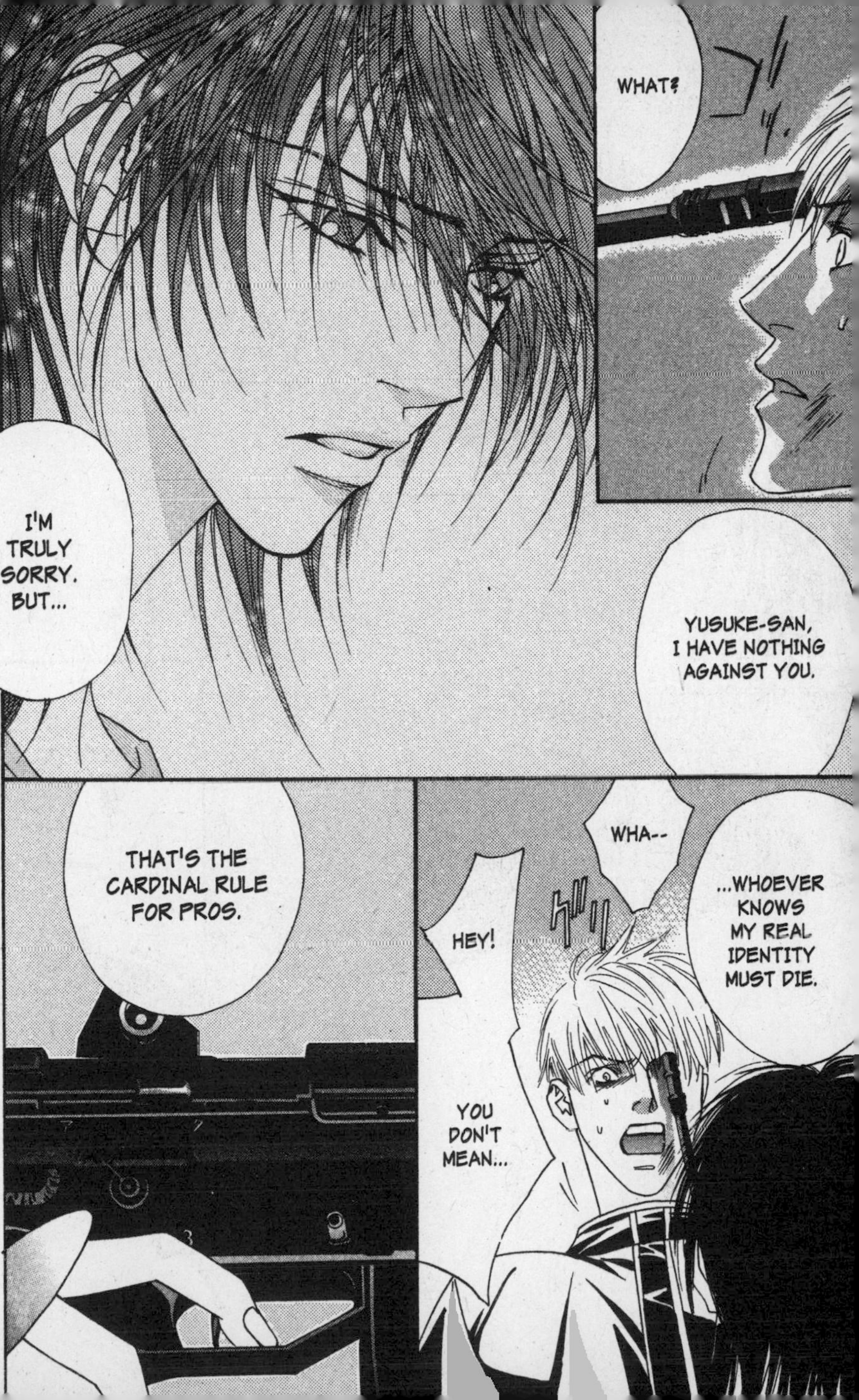
WHAT?
YUSUKE-SAN, I HAVE NOTHING AGAINST YOU.
I'M TRULY SORRY. BUT...
...WHOEVER KNOWS MY REAL IDENTITY MUST DIE.
WHA--
HEY!
YOU DON'T MEAN...
THAT'S THE CARDINAL RULE FOR PROS.

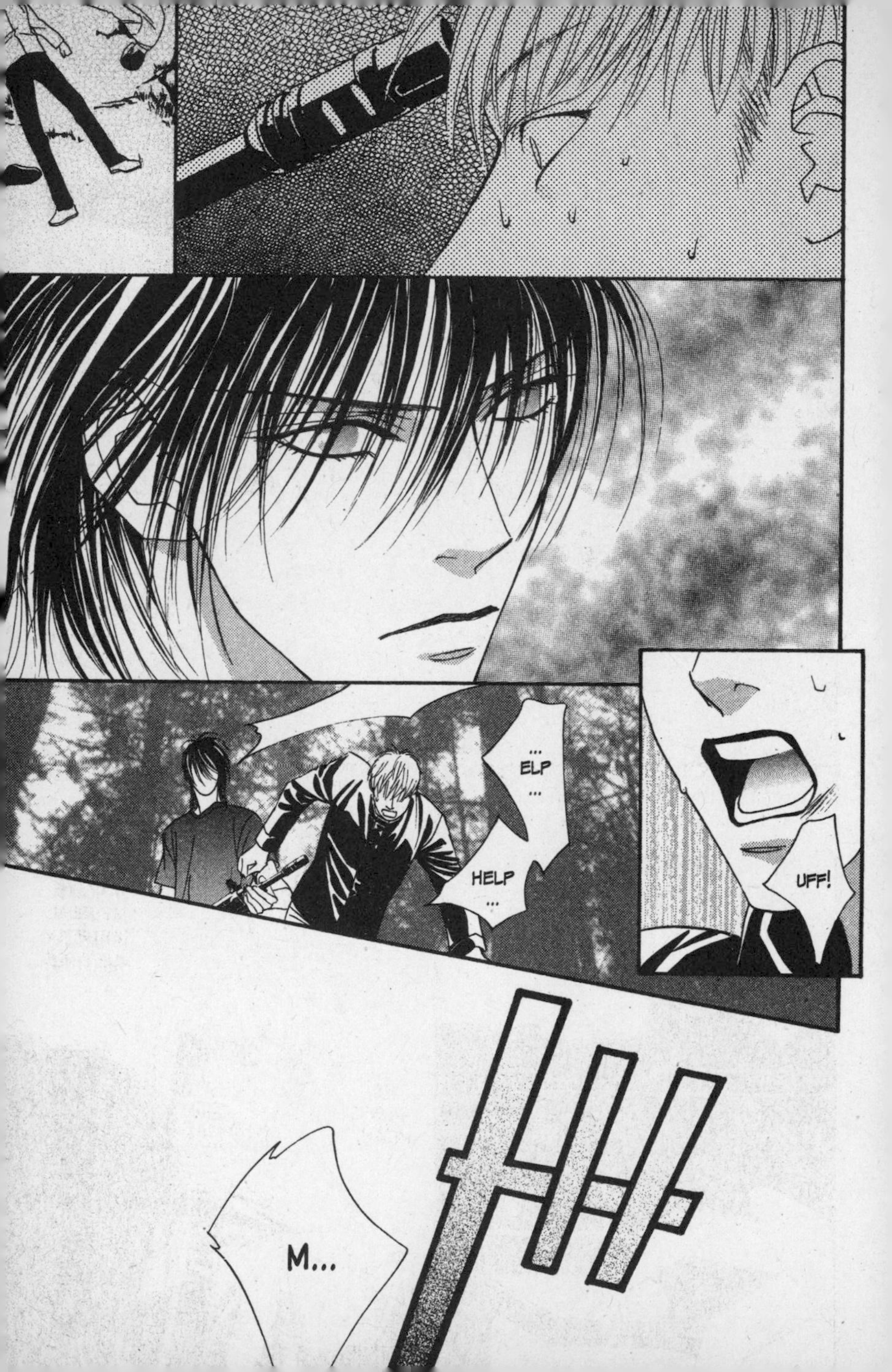
UFF!
... ELP ...
HELP ...
M...

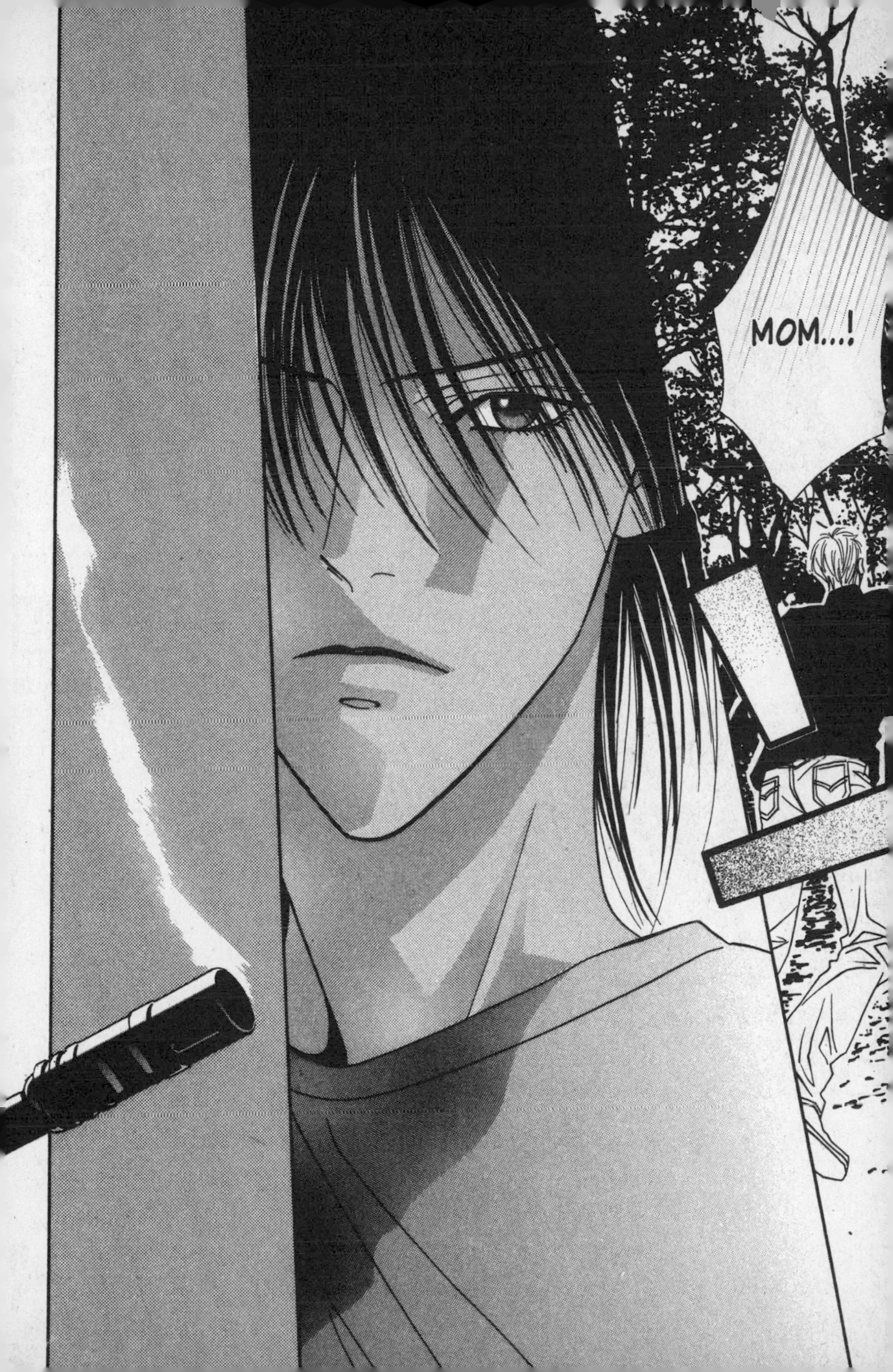
MOM...!

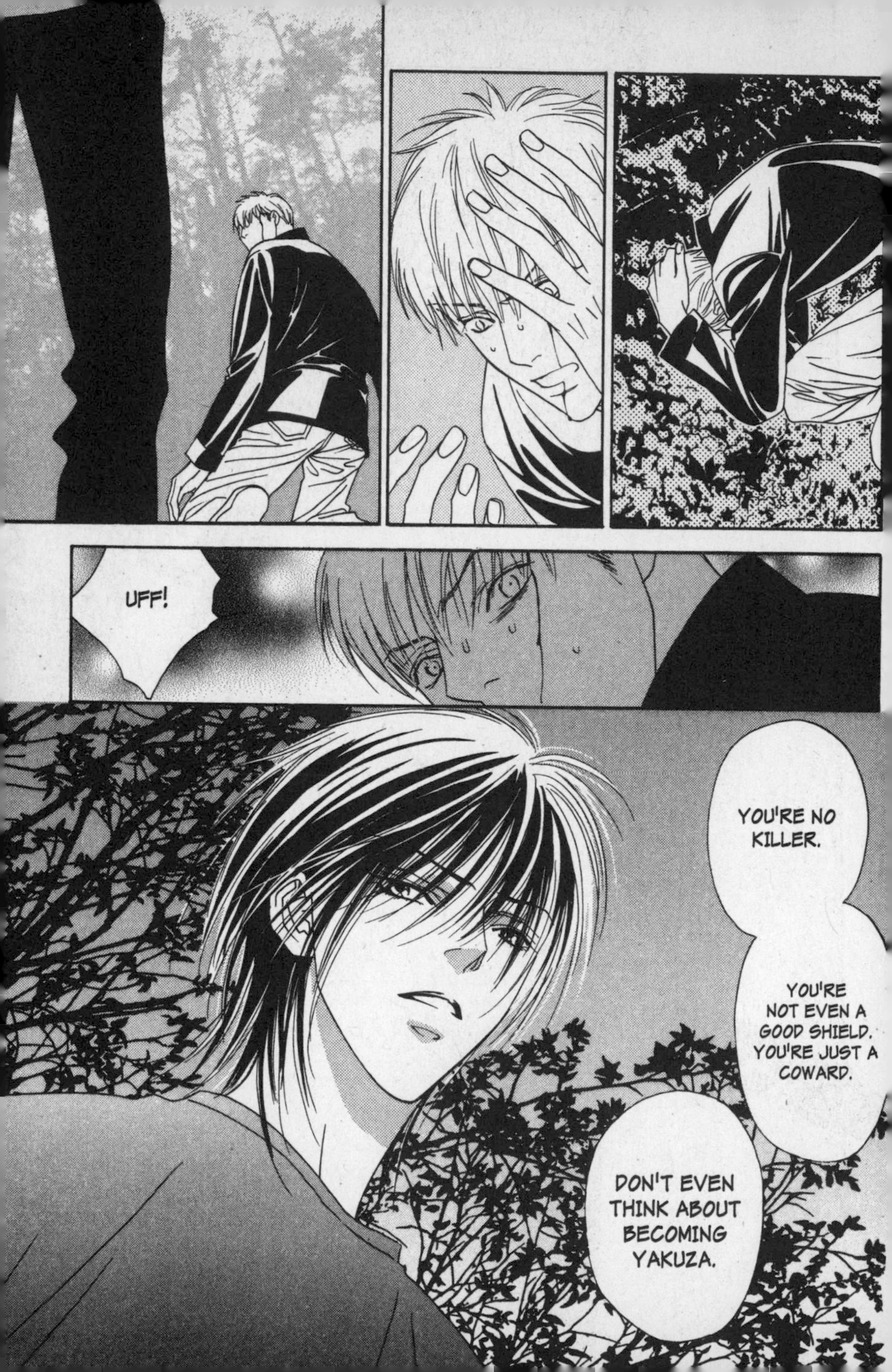
UFF!
YOU'RE NO KILLER.
YOU'RE NOT EVEN A GOOD SHIELD. YOU'RE JUST A COWARD.
DON'T EVEN THINK ABOUT BECOMING YAKUZA.

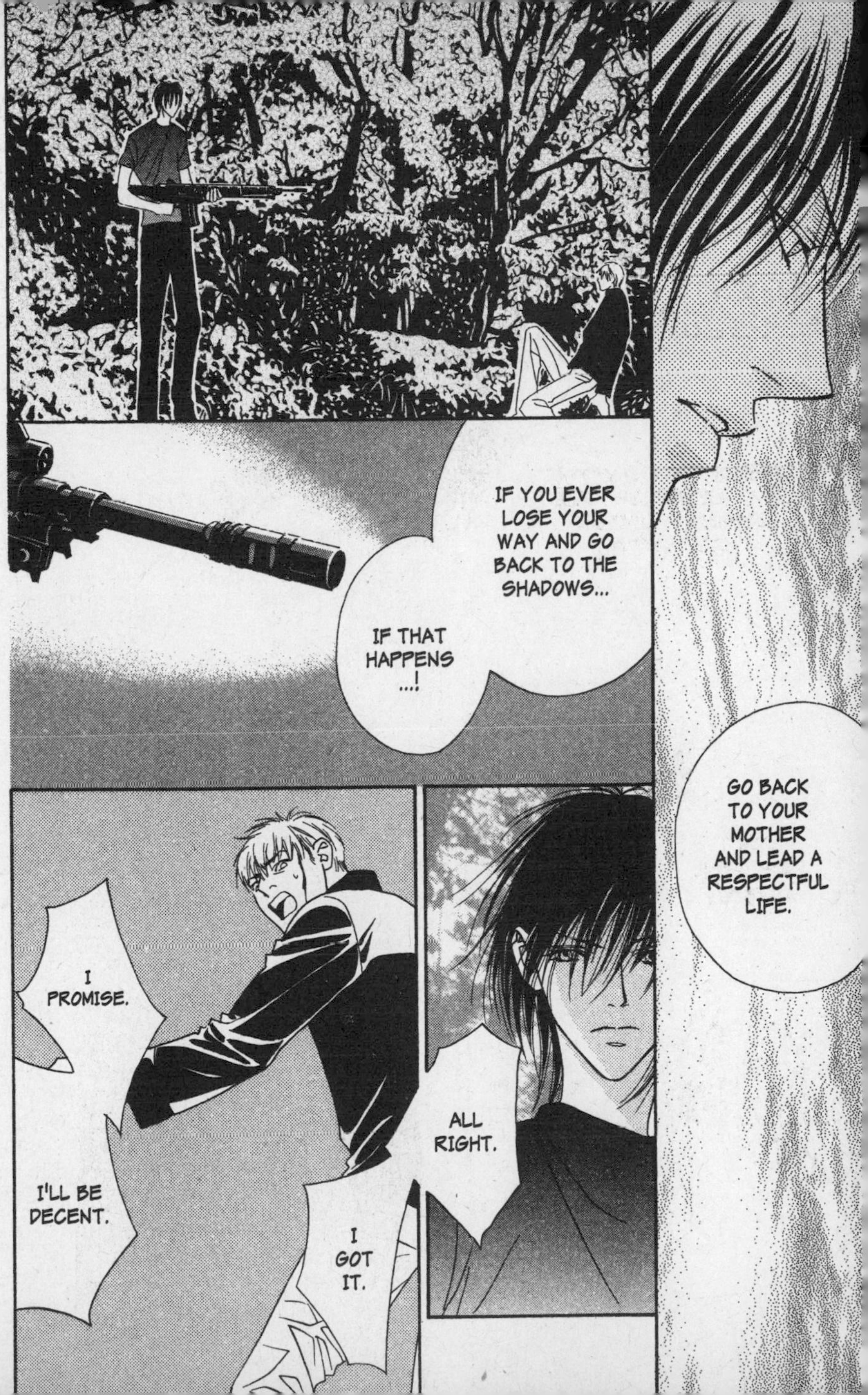
GO BACK TO YOUR MOTHER AND LEAD A RESPECTFUL LIFE.
IF YOU EVER LOSE YOUR WAY AND GO BACK TO THE SHADOWS...
IF THAT HAPPENS ...!
ALL RIGHT.
I PROMISE.
I'LL BE DECENT.
I GOT IT.

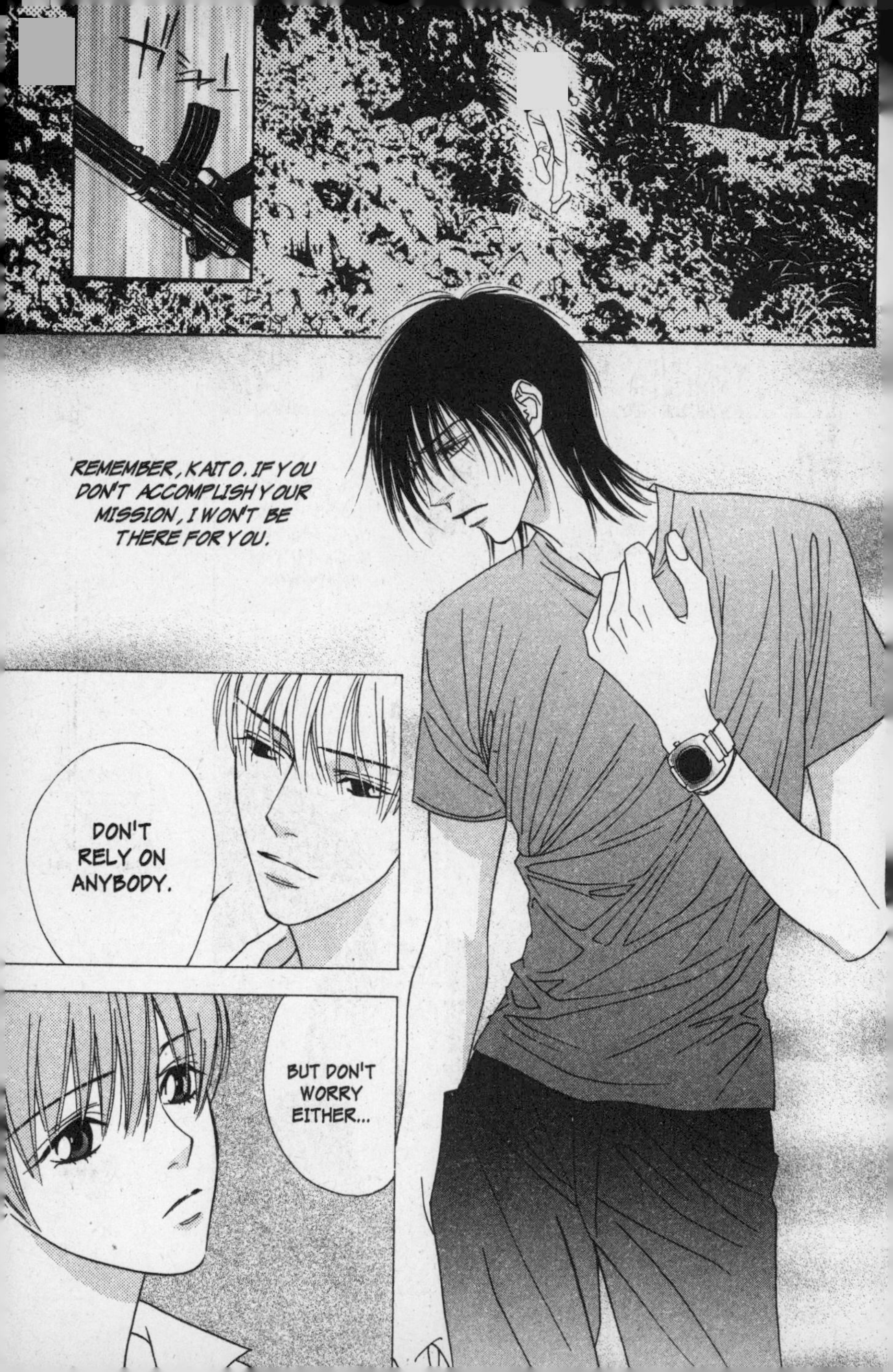
REMEMBER, KAITO. IF YOU DON'T ACCOMPLISH YOUR MISSION, I WON'T BE THERE FOR YOU.
DON'T RELY ON ANYBODY.
BUT DON'T WORRY EITHER...

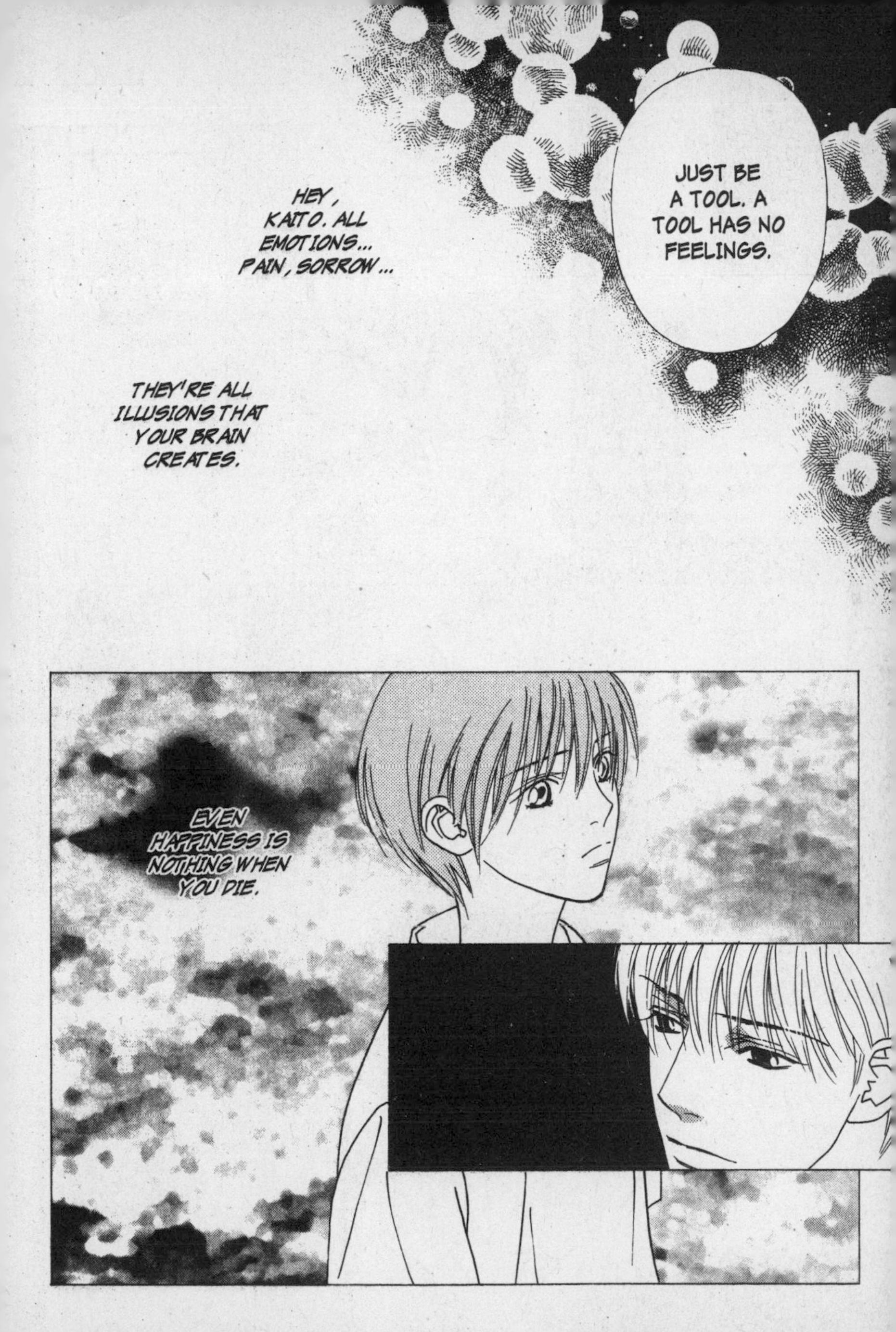
JUST BE A TOOL. A TOOL HAS NO FEELINGS.
HEY, KAITO. ALL EMOTIONS... PAIN, SORROW...
THEY'RE ALL ILLUSIONS THAT YOUR BRAIN CREATES.
EVEN HAPPINESS IS NOTHING WHEN YOU DIE.

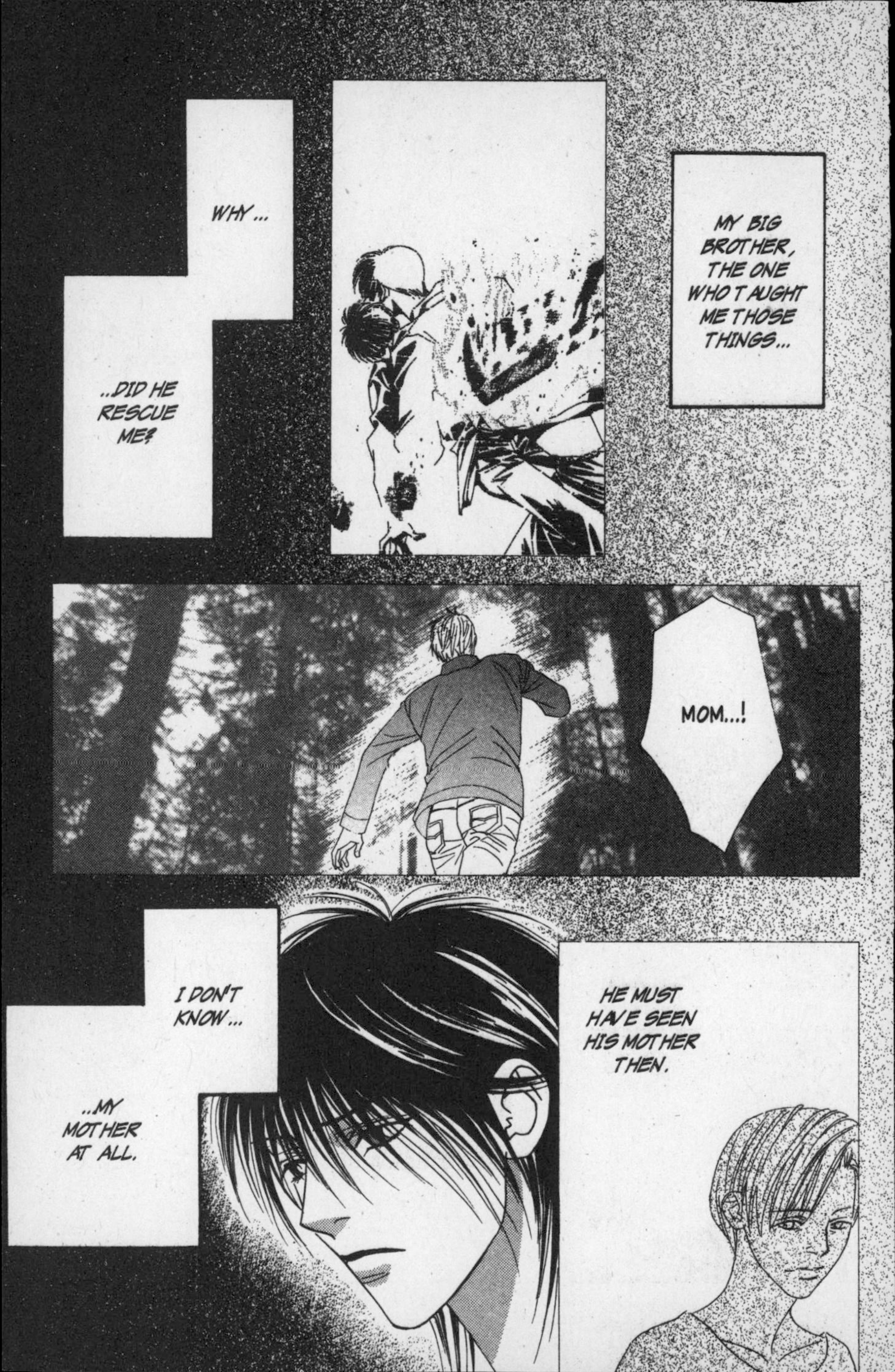
MY BIG BROTHER, THE ONE WHO TAUGHT ME THOSE THINGS...
WHY...
...DID HE RESCUE ME?
MOM...!
HE MUST HAVE SEEN HIS MOTHER THEN.
I DON'T KNOW...
...MY MOTHER AT ALL.

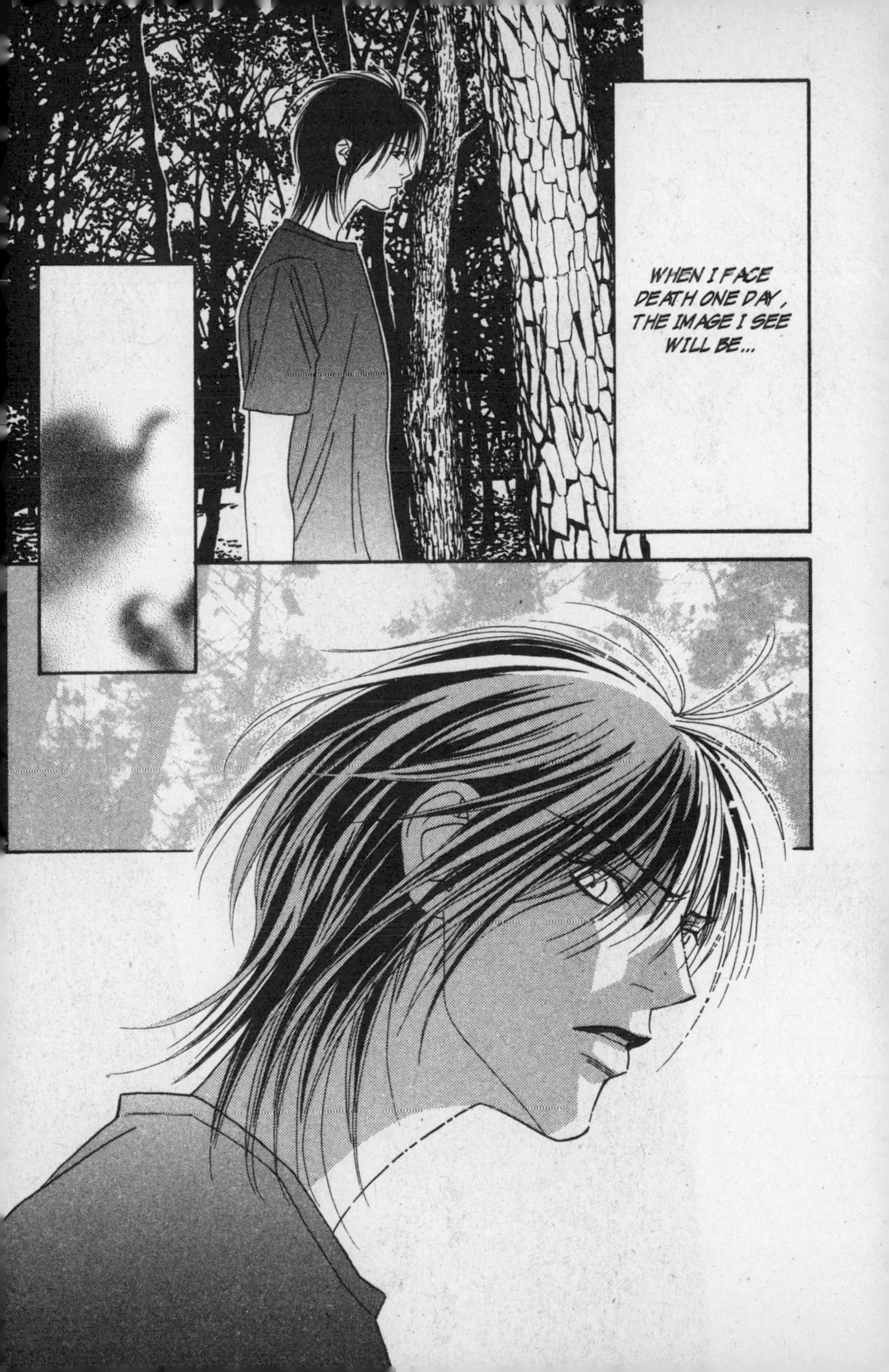
WHEN I FACE DEATH ONE DAY, THE IMAGE I SEE WILL BE...

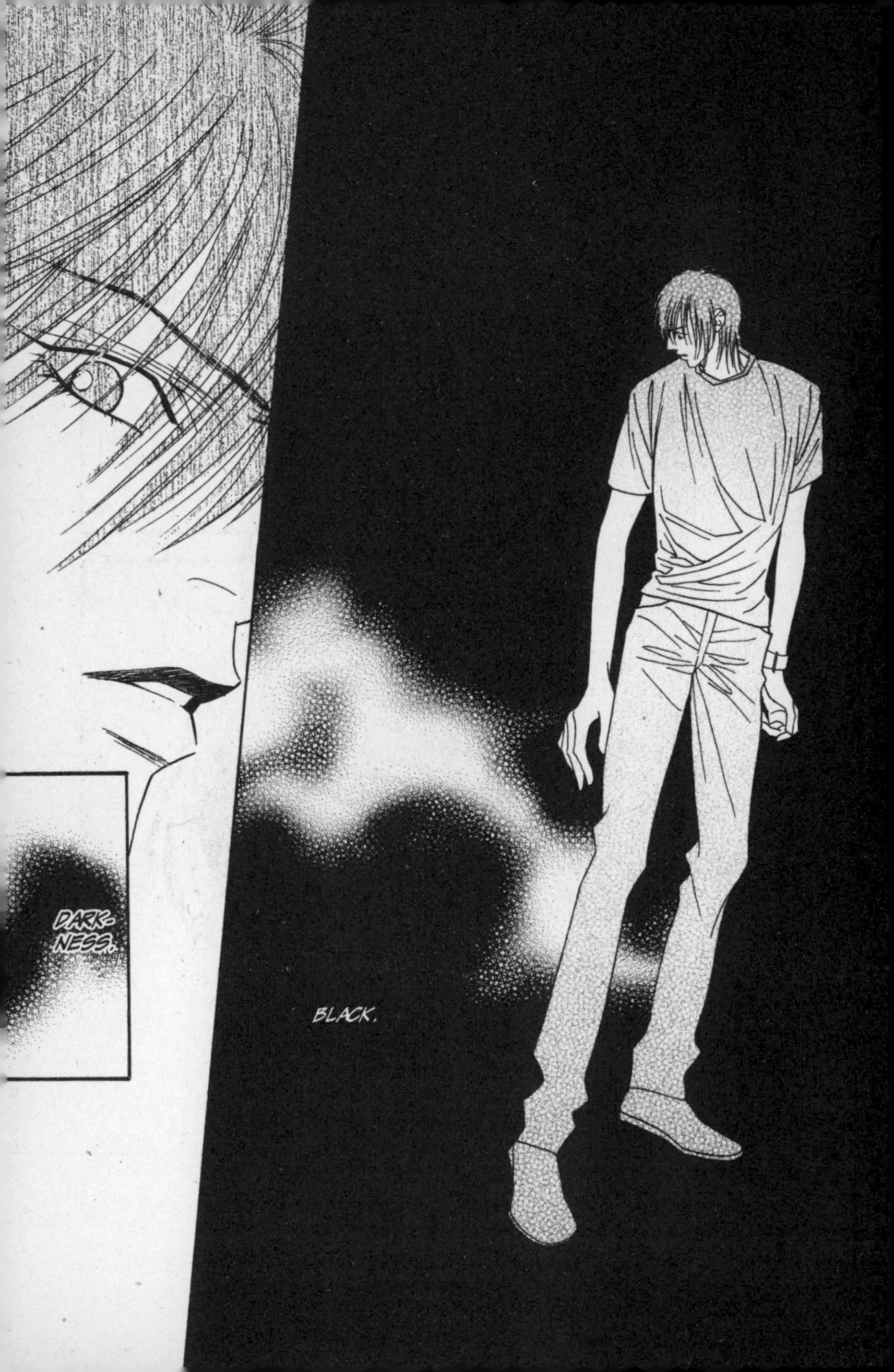
BLACK.
DARK-
NESS.

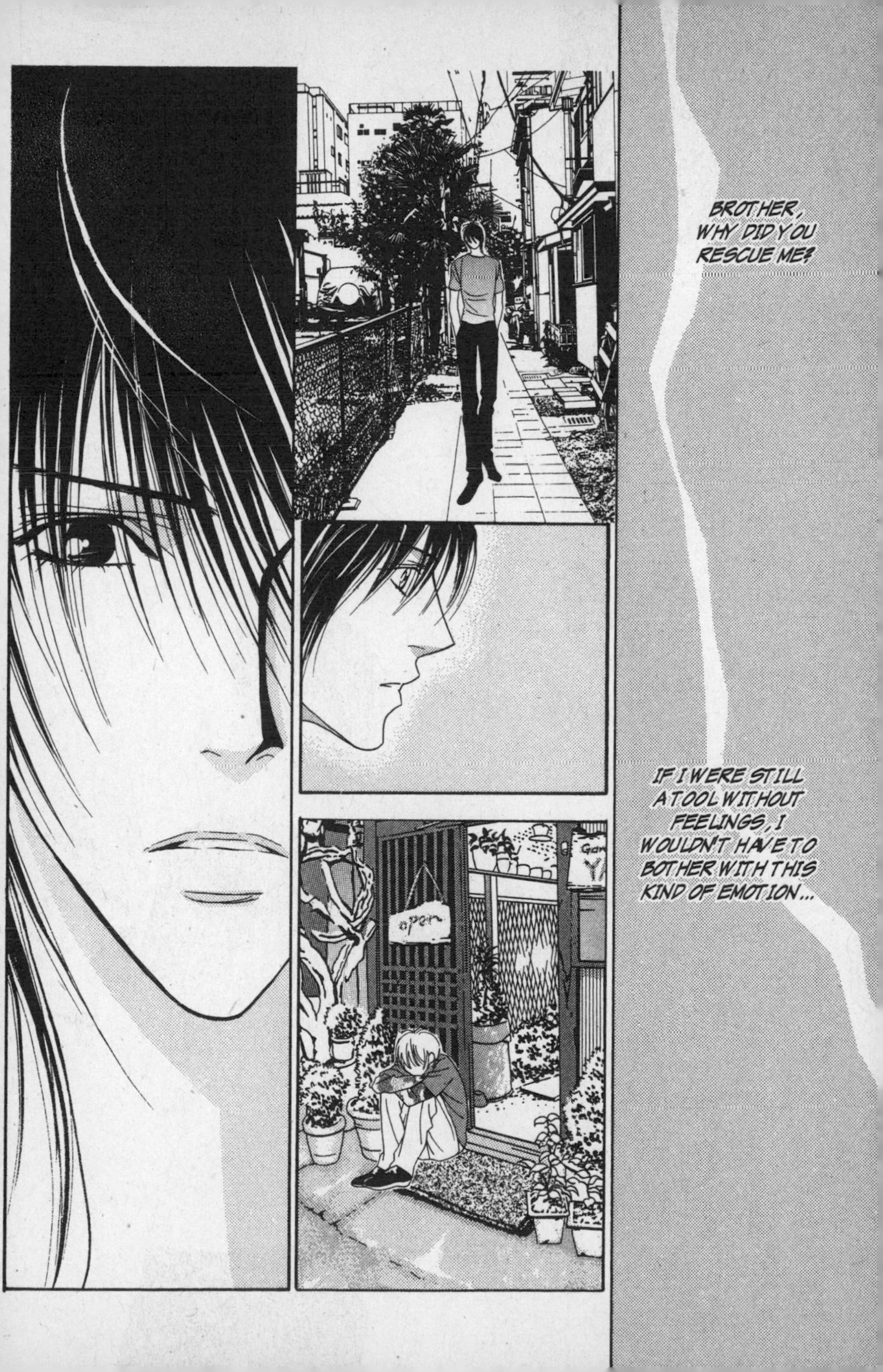
BROTHER, WHY DID YOU RESCUE ME?
IF I WERE STILL A TOOL WITHOUT FEELINGS, I WOULDN'T HAVE TO BOTHER WITH THIS KIND OF EMOTION...
open

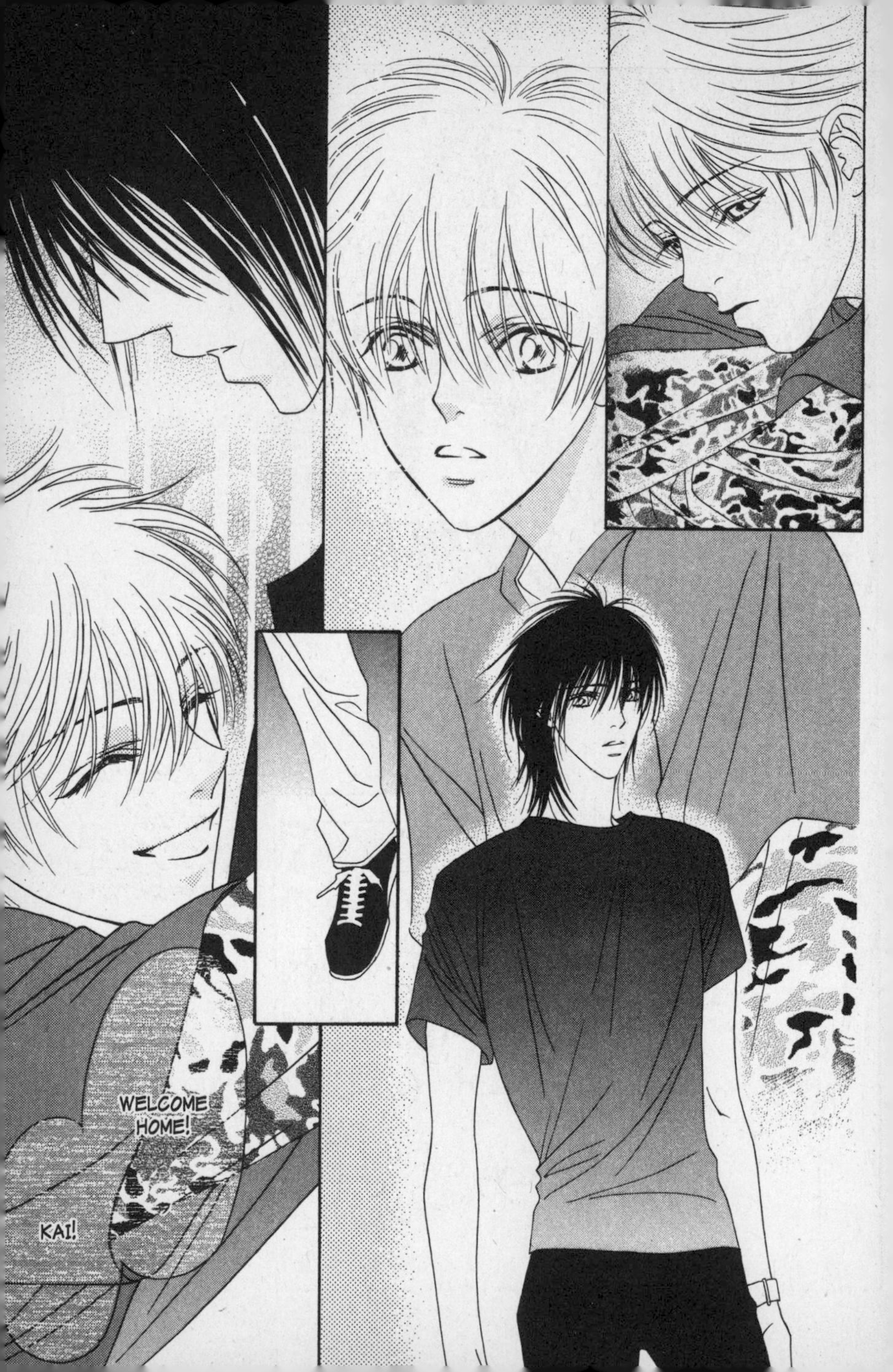
WELCOME HOME!
KAI!

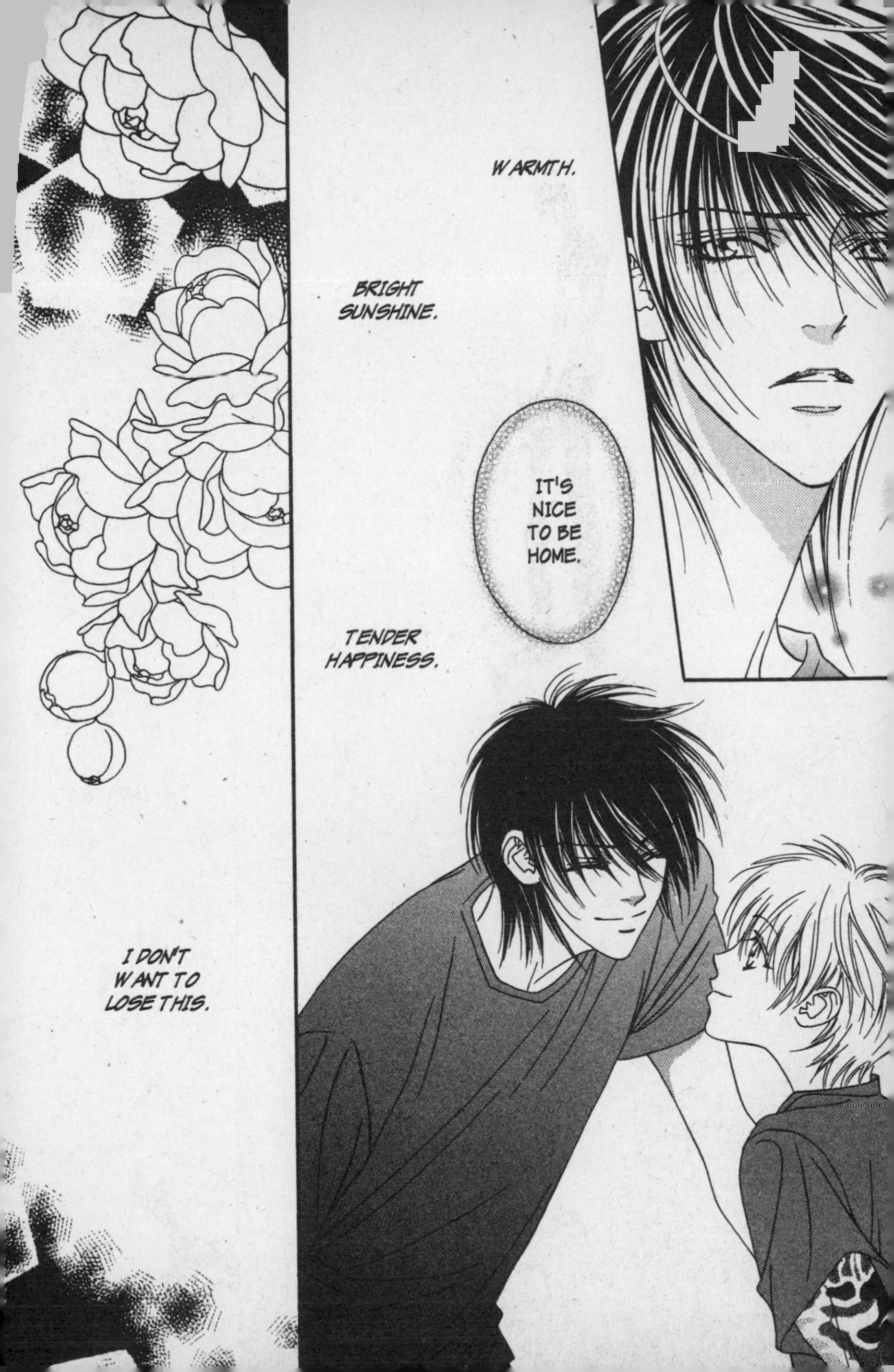
WARMTH.
BRIGHT SUNSHINE.
IT'S NICE TO BE HOME.
TENDER HAPPINESS.
I DON'T WANT TO LOSE THIS.

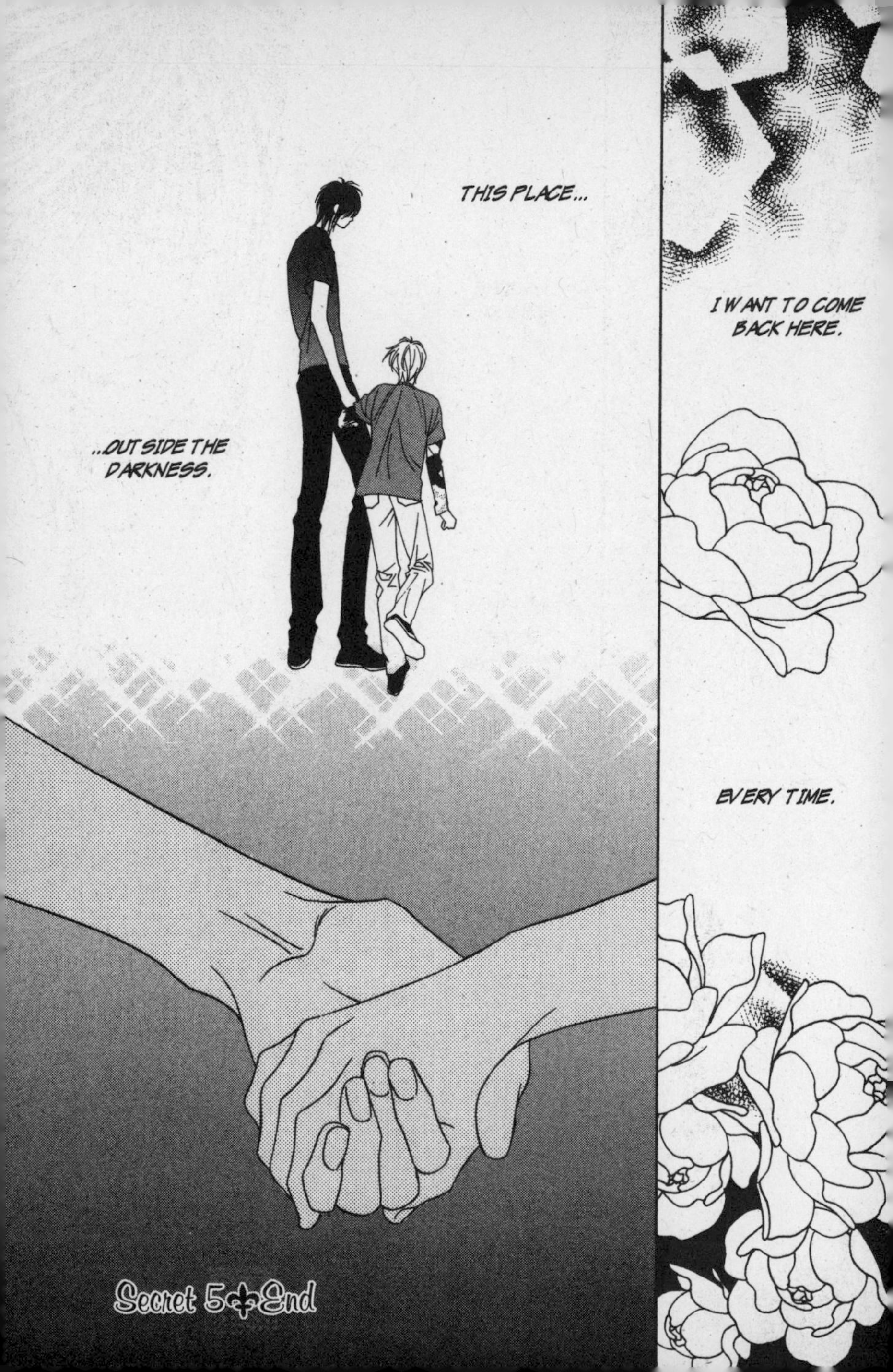
I WANT TO COME BACK HERE.
EVERY TIME.
THIS PLACE...
...OUT SIDE THE DARKNESS.
Secret 5 End

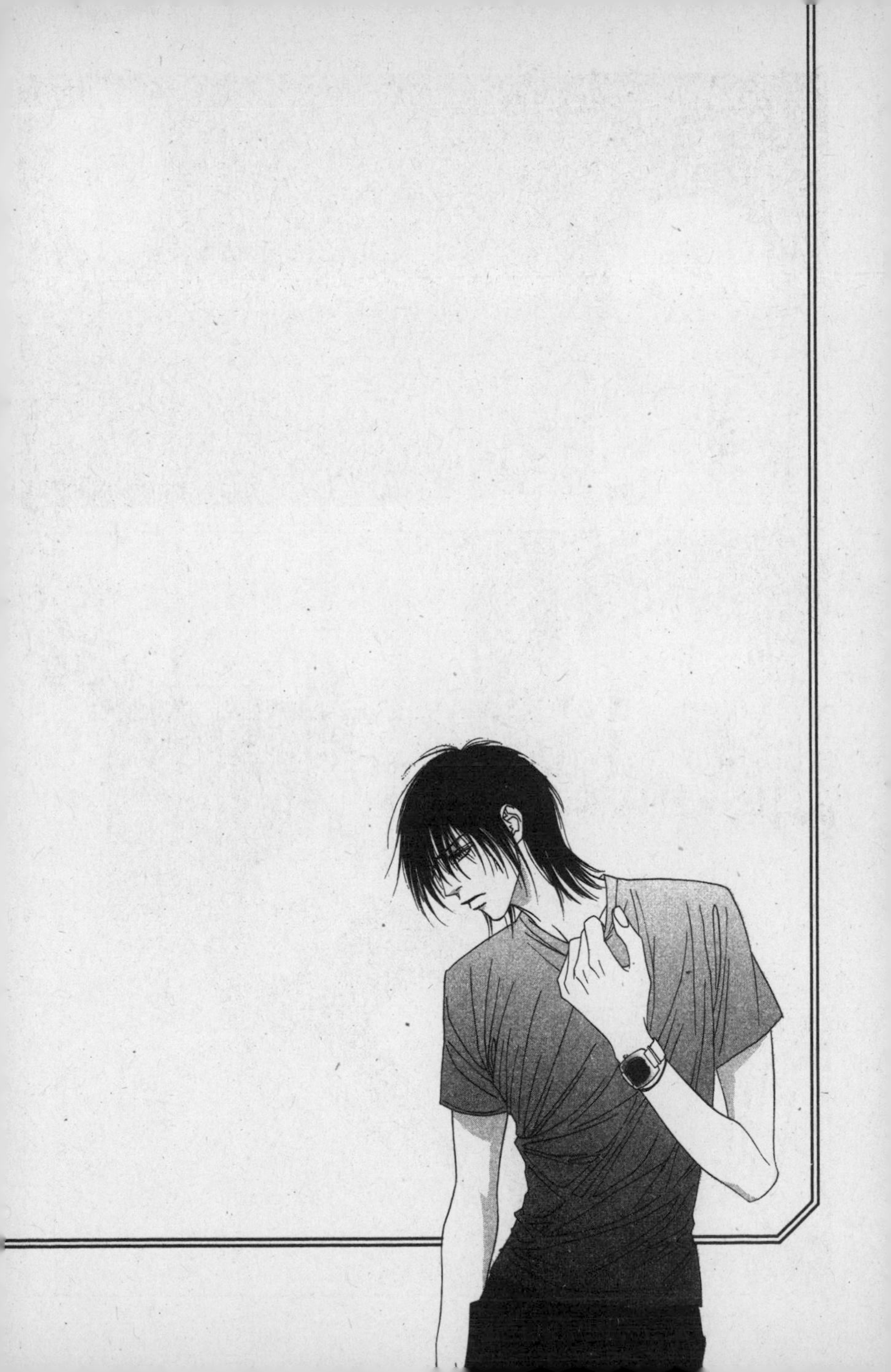

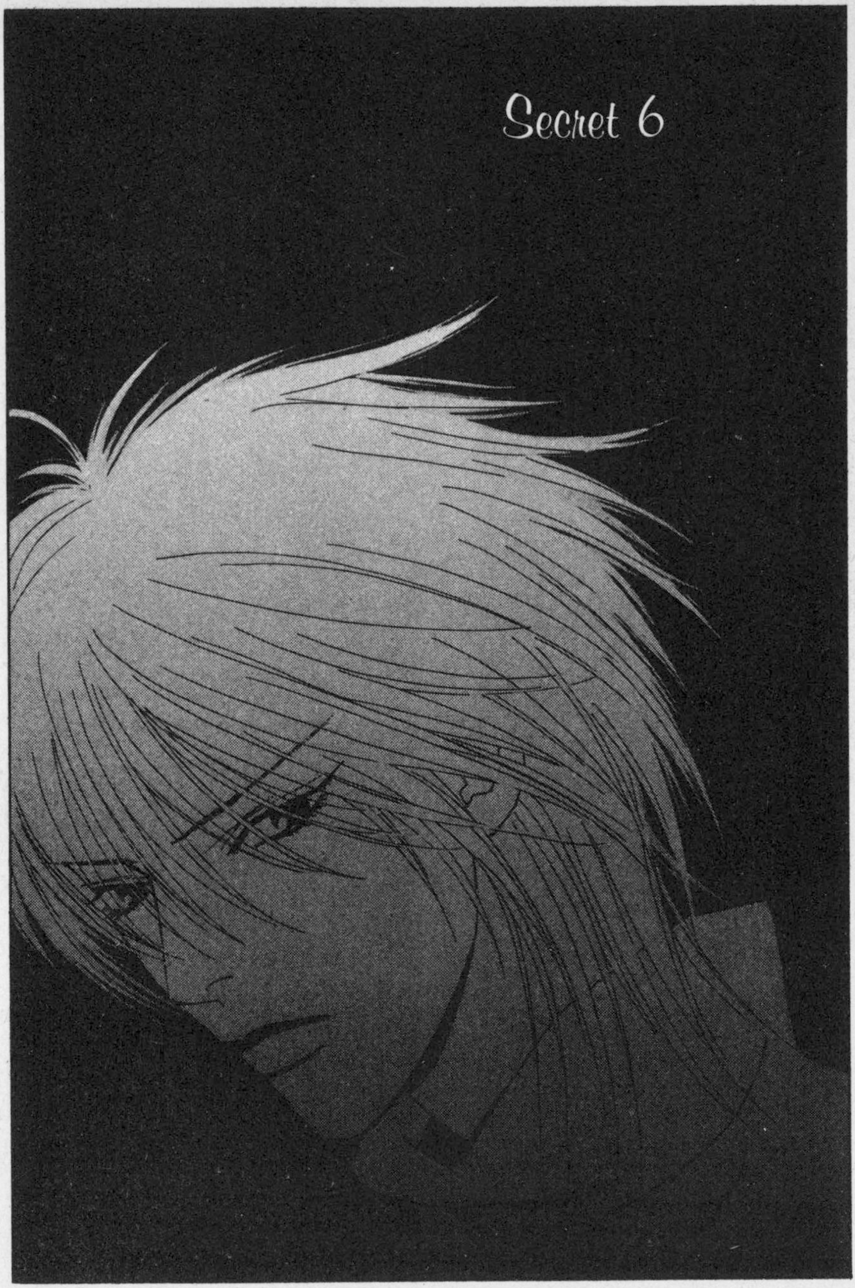
Secret 6

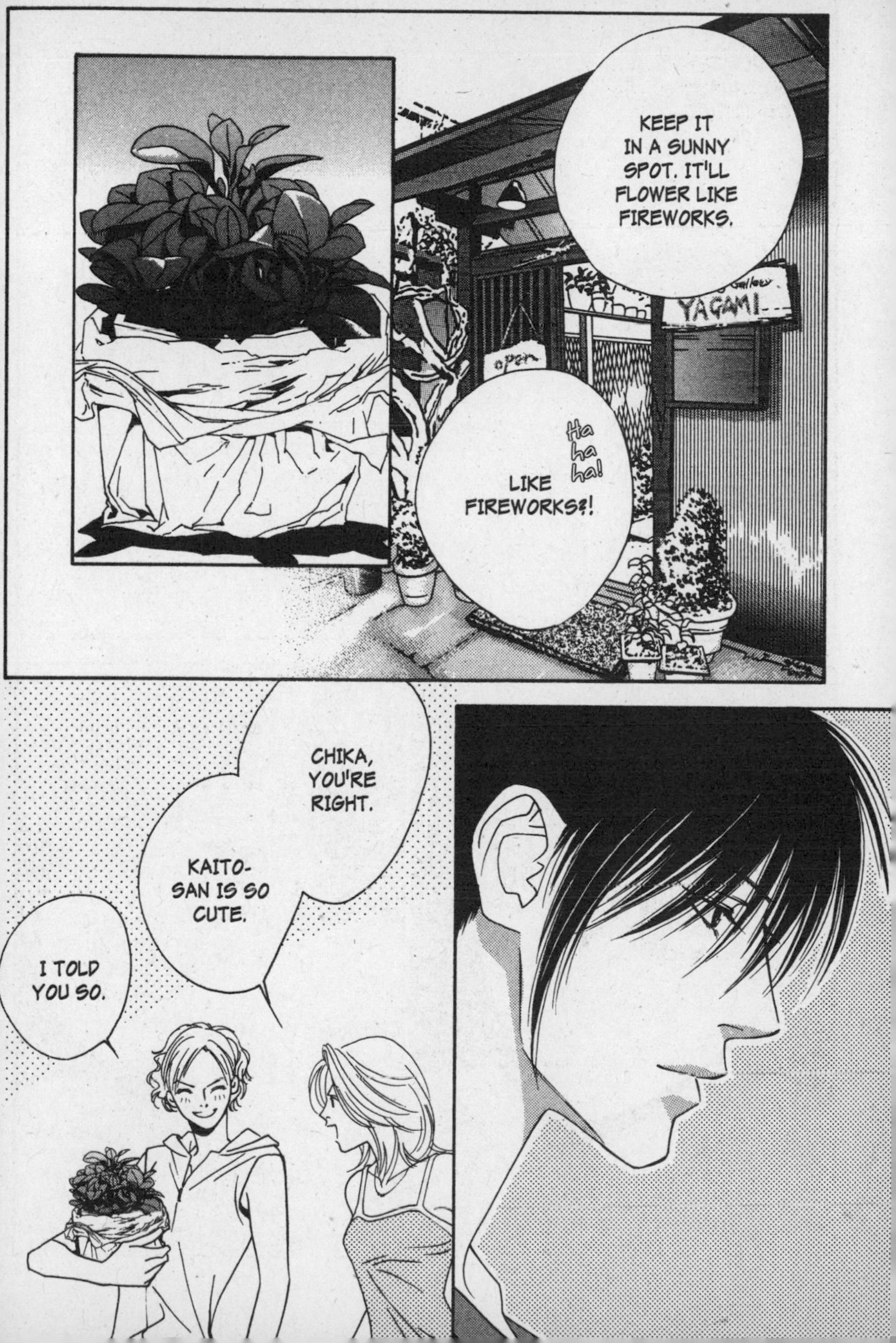
KEEP IT IN A SUNNY SPOT. IT'LL FLOWER LIKE FIREWORKS.
YAGAMI
open
Ha ha ha!
LIKE FIREWORKS?!
CHIKA, YOU'RE RIGHT.
KAITO-SAN IS SO CUTE.
I TOLD YOU SO.

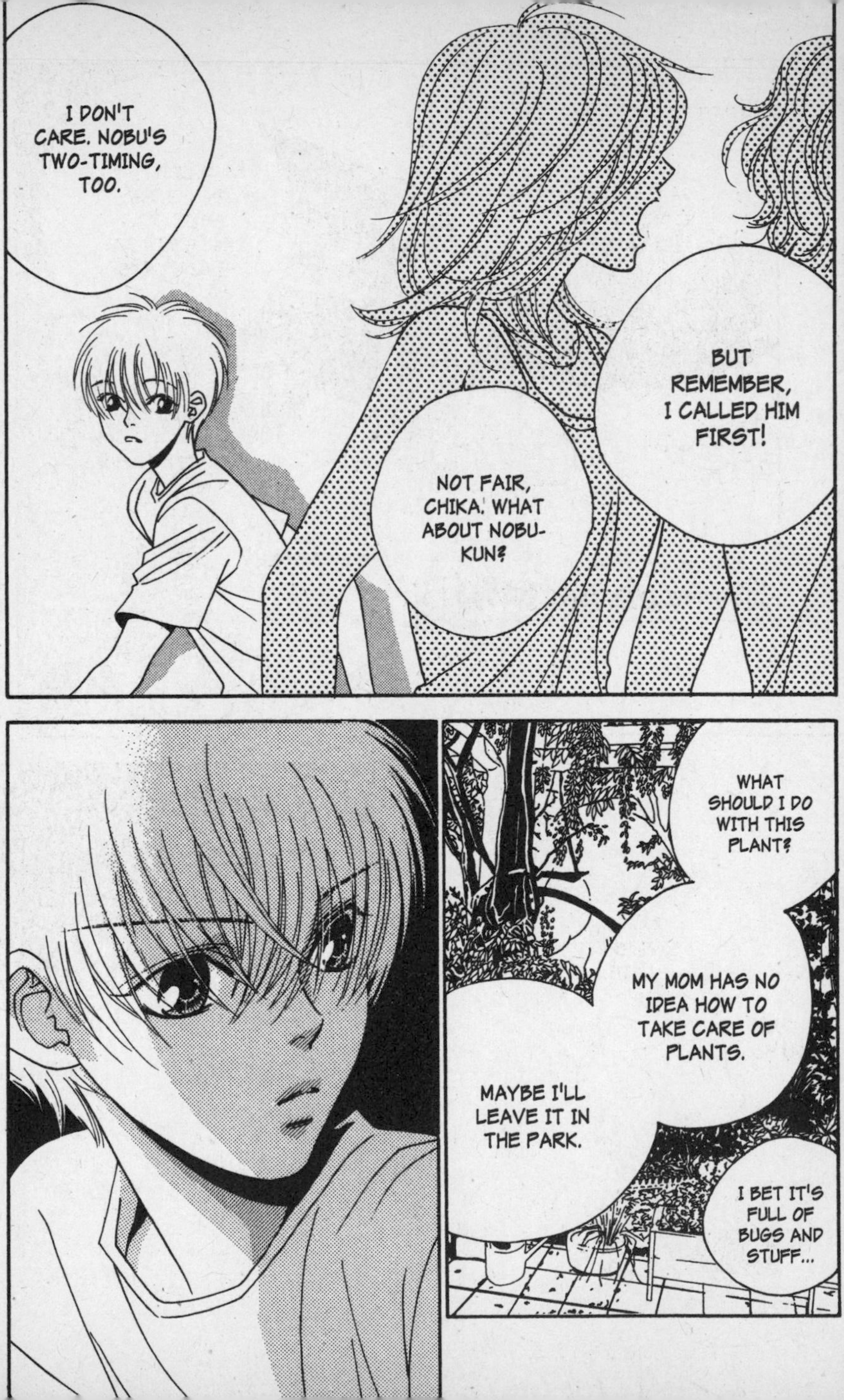
BUT REMEMBER, I CALLED HIM FIRST!
NOT FAIR, CHIKA! WHAT ABOUT NOBU-KUN?
I DON'T CARE. NOBU'S TWO-TIMING, TOO.
WHAT SHOULD I DO WITH THIS PLANT?
MY MOM HAS NO IDEA HOW TO TAKE CARE OF PLANTS.
I BET IT'S FULL OF BUGS AND STUFF...
MAYBE I'LL LEAVE IT IN THE PARK.

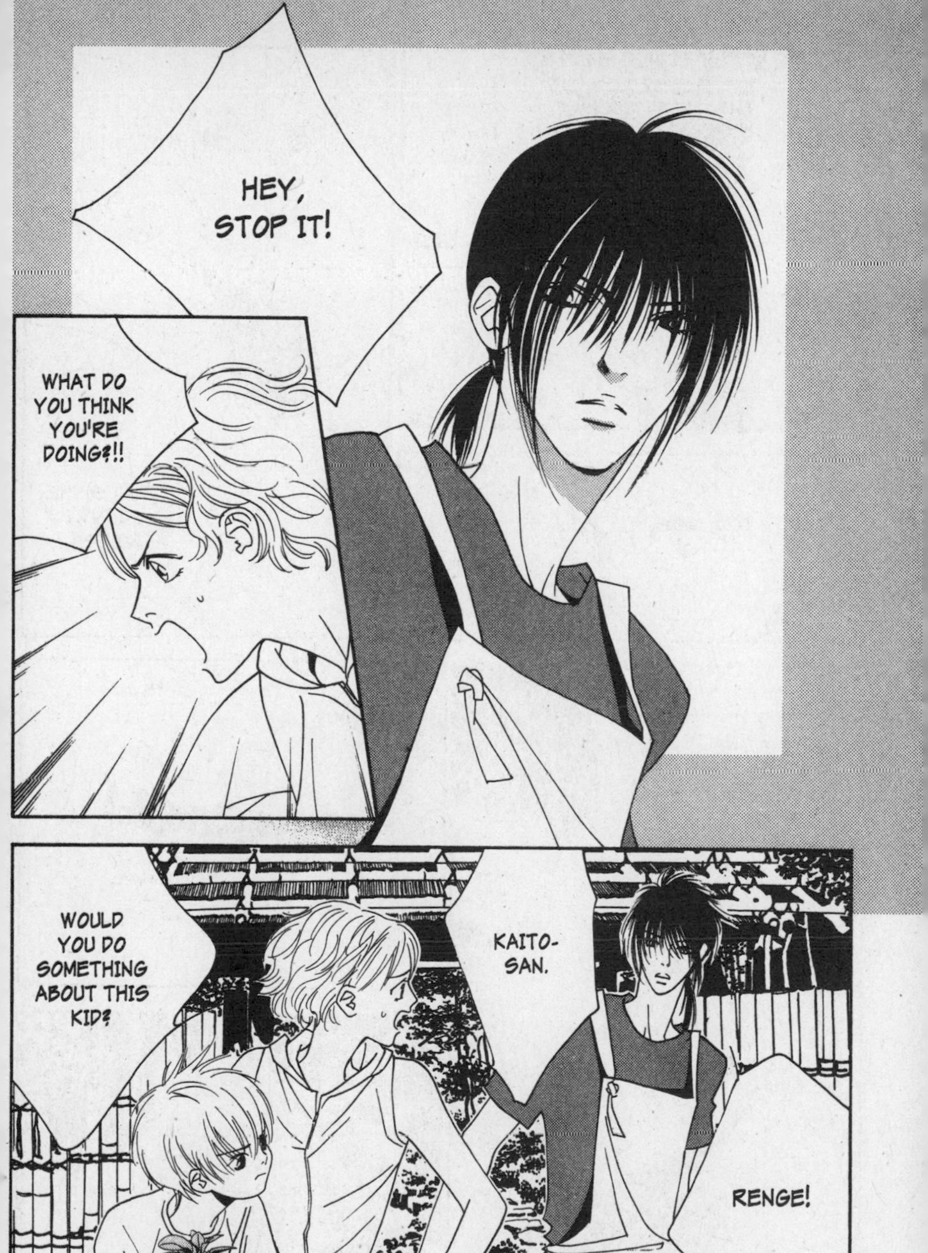
HEY, STOP IT!
WHAT DO YOU THINK YOU'RE DOING?!!
KAITO-SAN.
WOULD YOU DO SOMETHING ABOUT THIS KID?
RENGE!

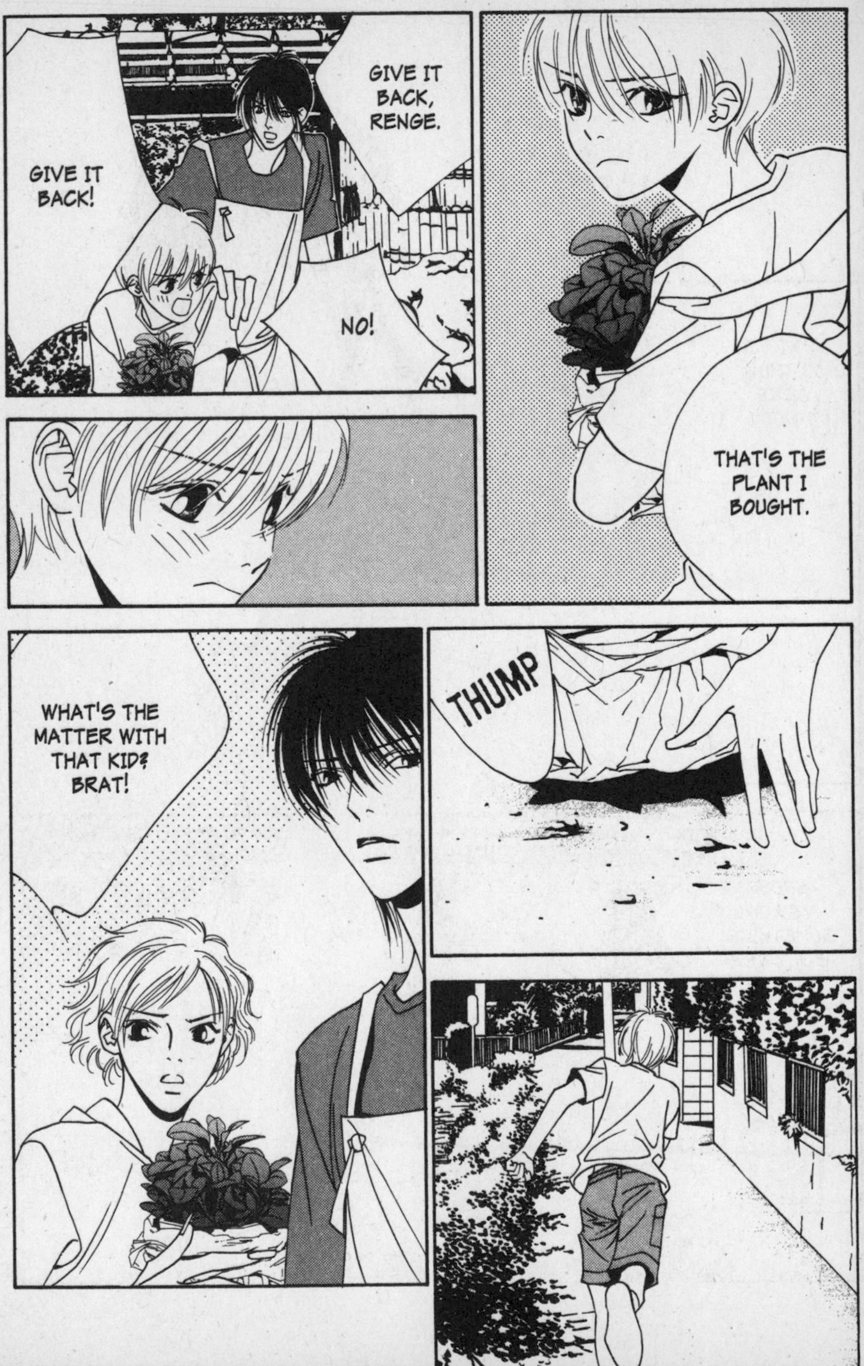
THAT'S THE PLANT I BOUGHT.
GIVE IT BACK, RENGE.
GIVE IT BACK!
NO!
THUMP
WHAT'S THE MATTER WITH THAT KID? BRAT!

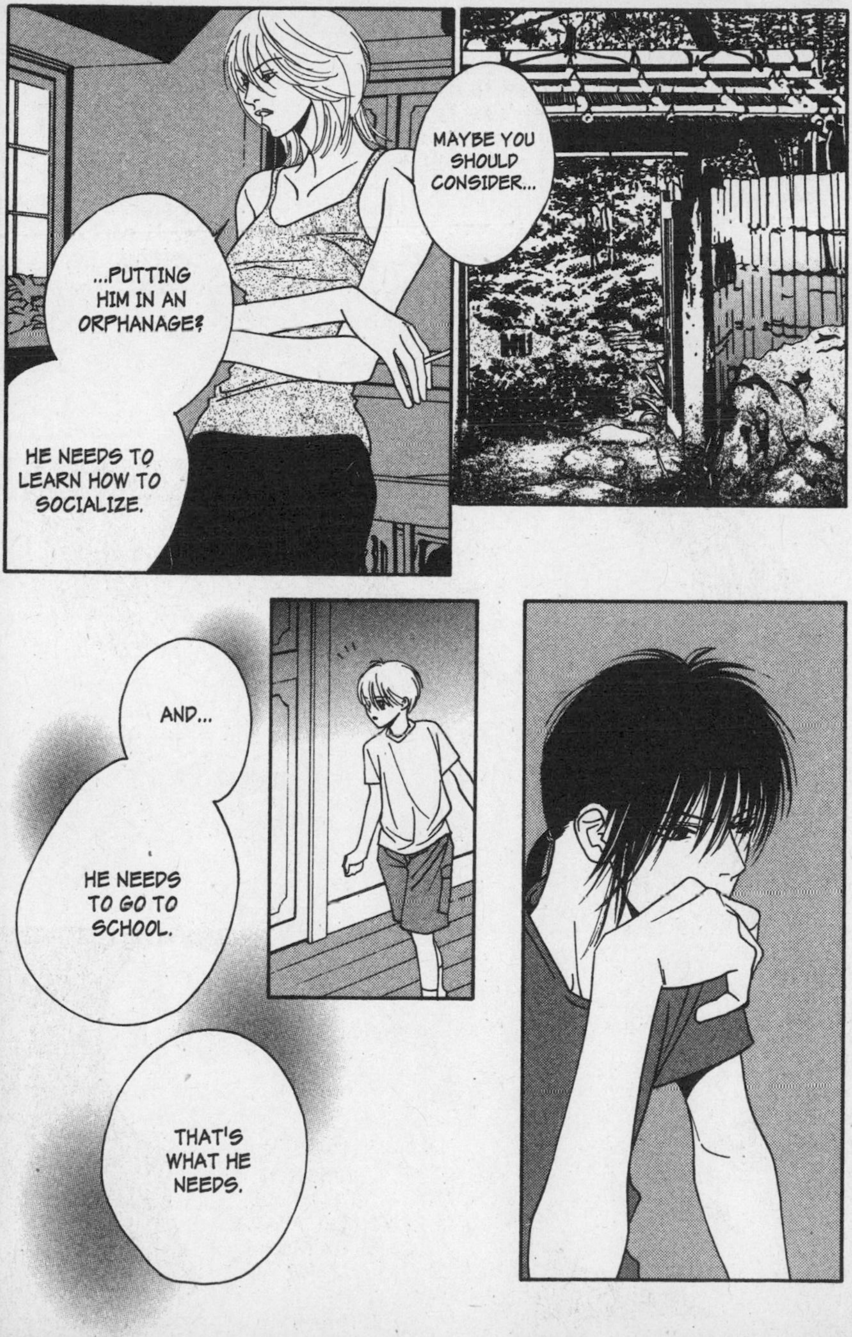
MAYBE YOU SHOULD CONSIDER...
...PUTTING HIM IN AN ORPHANAGE?
HE NEEDS TO LEARN HOW TO SOCIALIZE.
AND...
HE NEEDS TO GO TO SCHOOL.
THAT'S WHAT HE NEEDS.

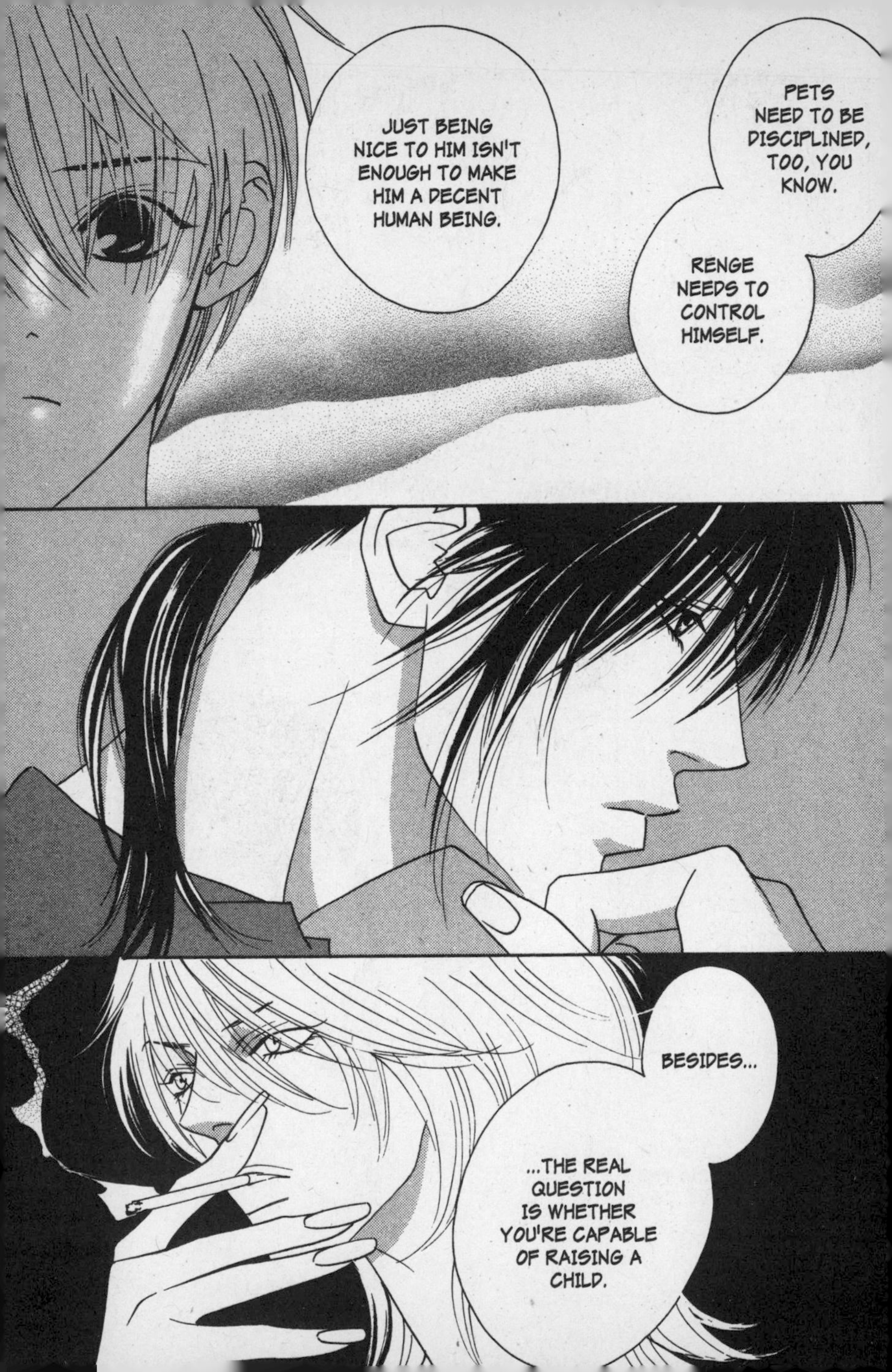
PETS NEED TO BE DISCIPLINED, TOO, YOU KNOW.
RENGE NEEDS TO CONTROL HIMSELF.
JUST BEING NICE TO HIM ISN'T ENOUGH TO MAKE HIM A DECENT HUMAN BEING.
BESIDES...
...THE REAL QUESTION IS WHETHER YOU'RE CAPABLE OF RAISING A CHILD.

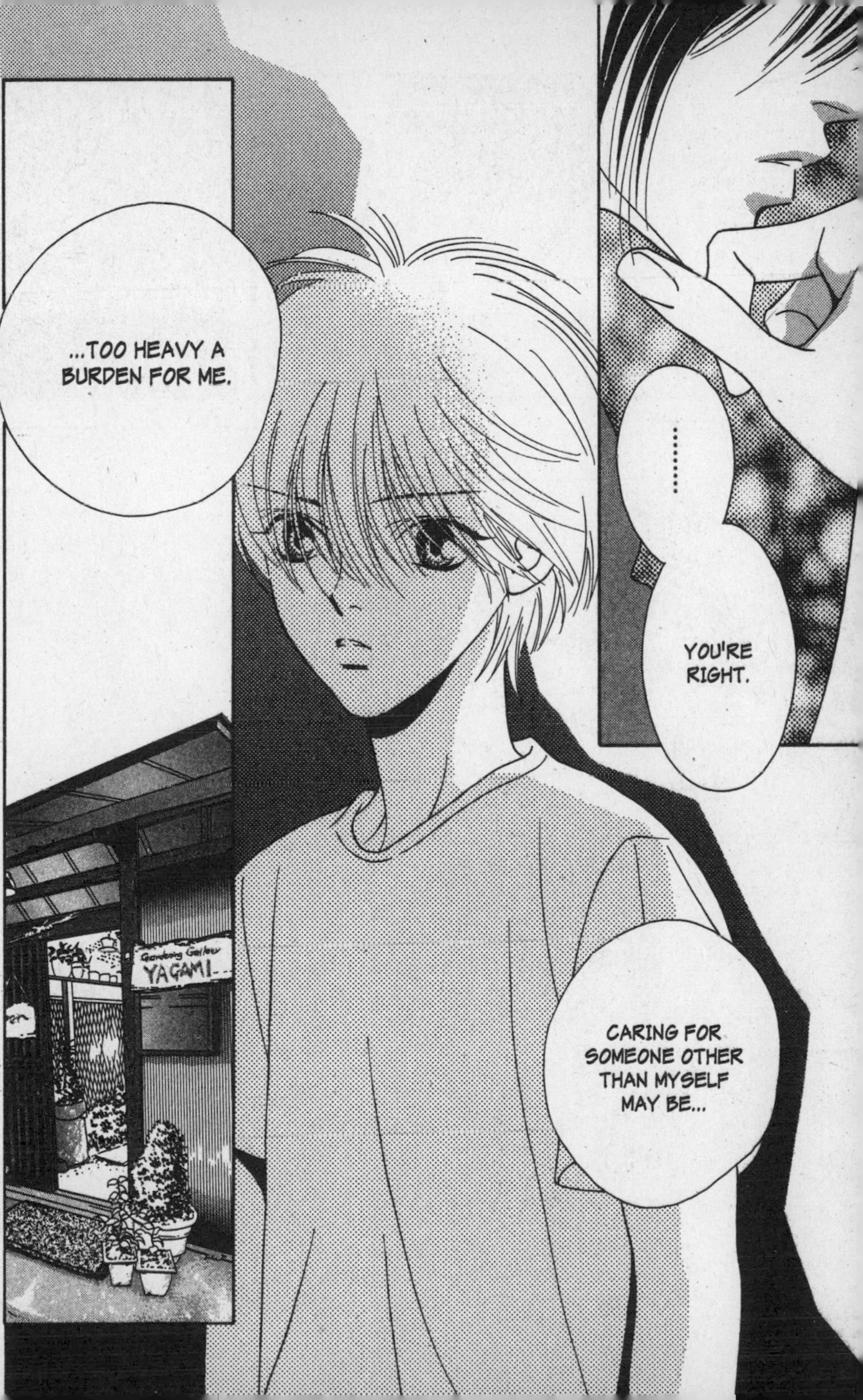
......
YOU'RE RIGHT.
CARING FOR SOMEONE OTHER THAN MYSELF MAY BE...
...TOO HEAVY A BURDEN FOR ME.
Gardening Gallery YAGAMI

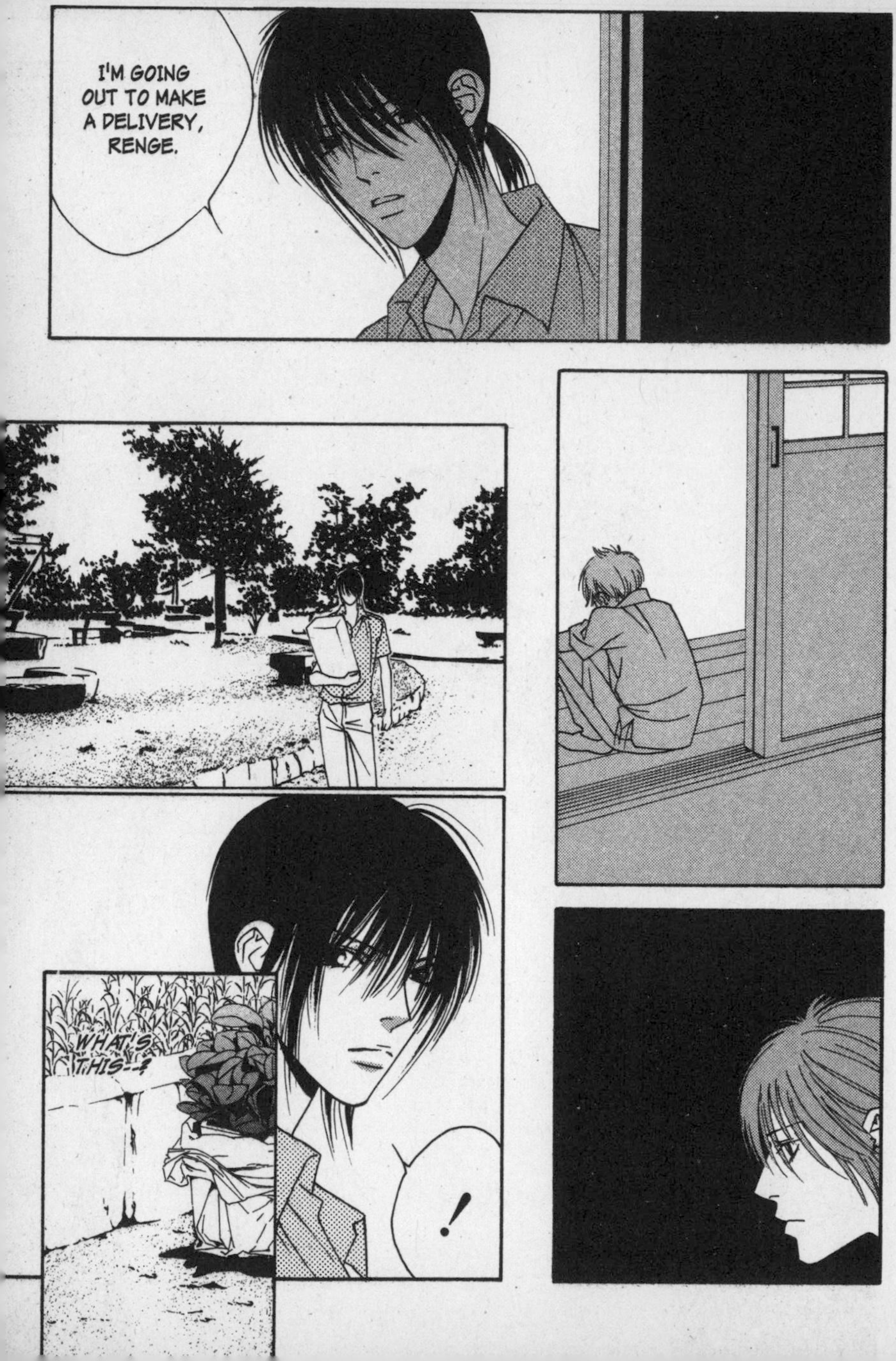
I'M GOING OUT TO MAKE A DELIVERY, RENGE.
!
WHAT'S THIS--?

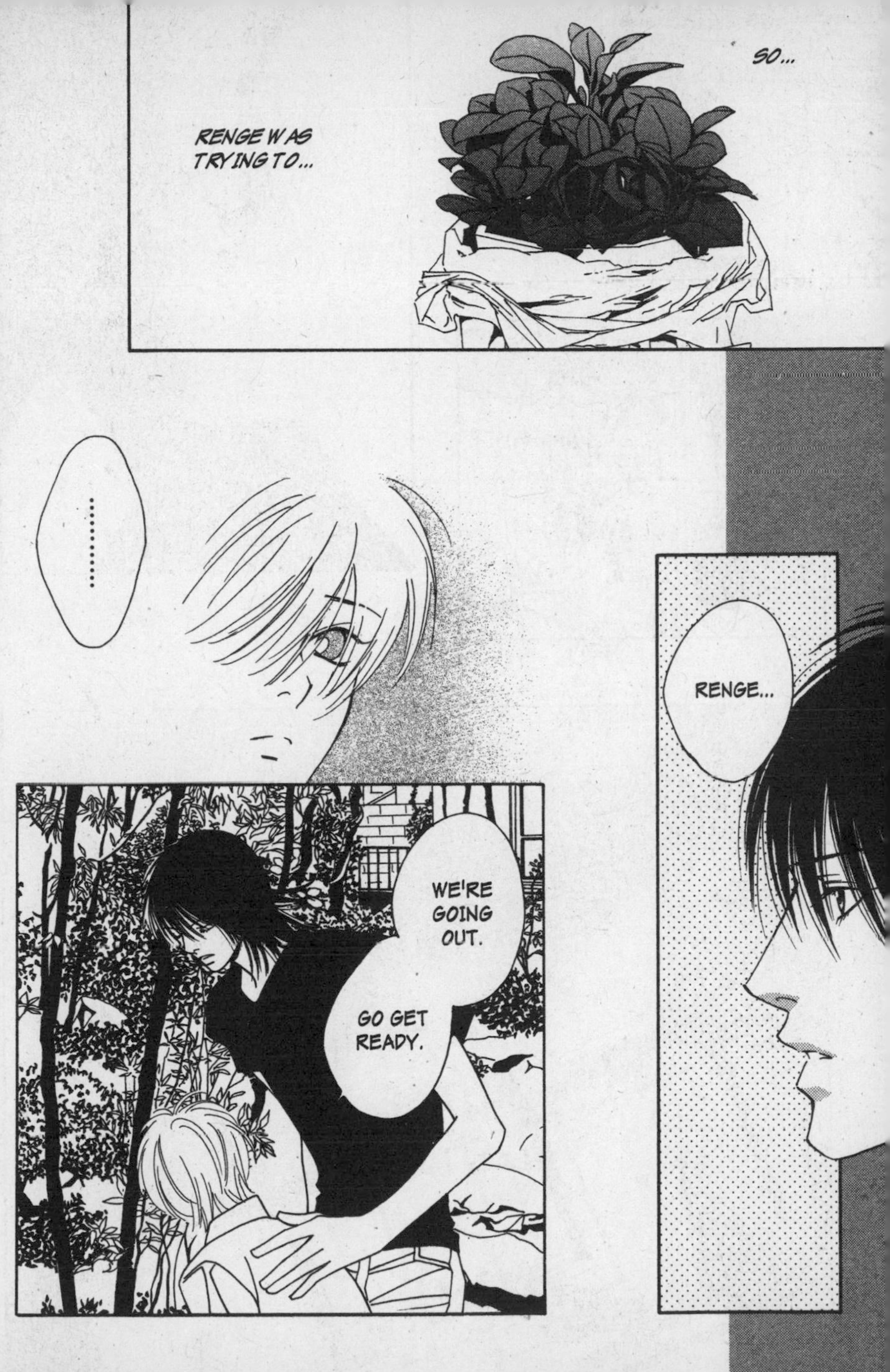
SO...
RENGE WAS TRYING TO...
RENGE...
......
WE'RE GOING OUT.
GO GET READY.

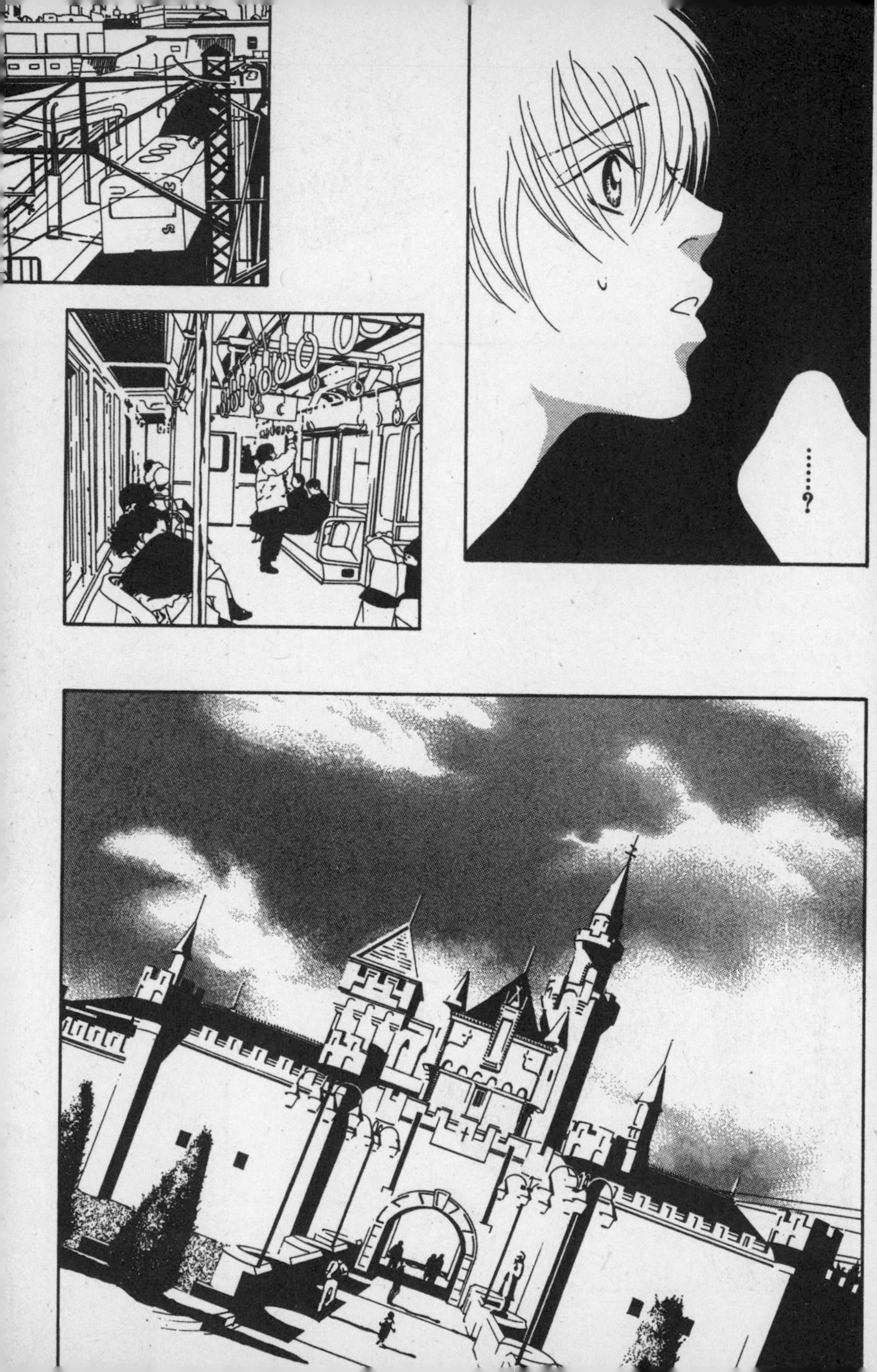
……?

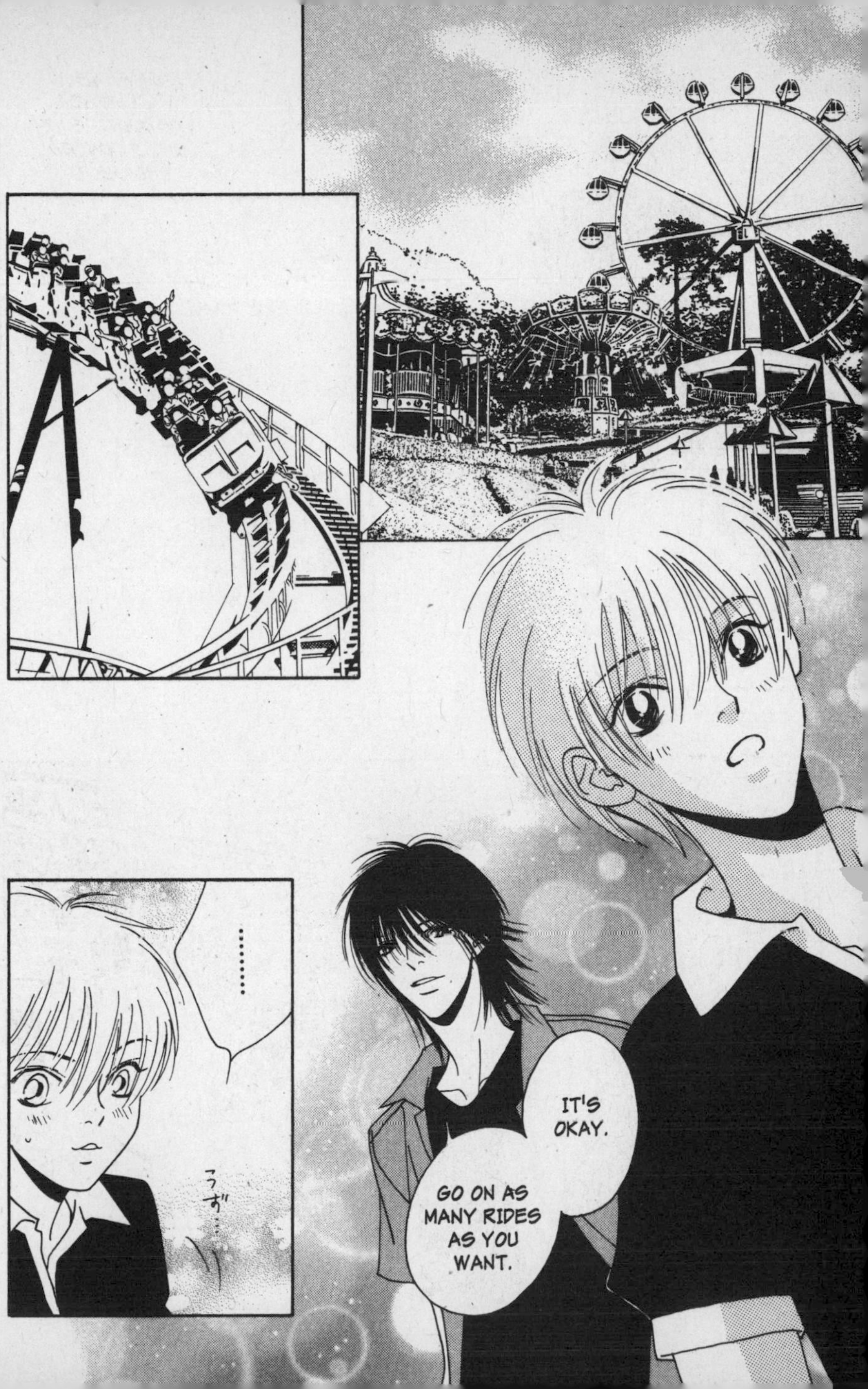
IT'S OKAY.
GO ON AS MANY RIDES AS YOU WANT.
......
こず…

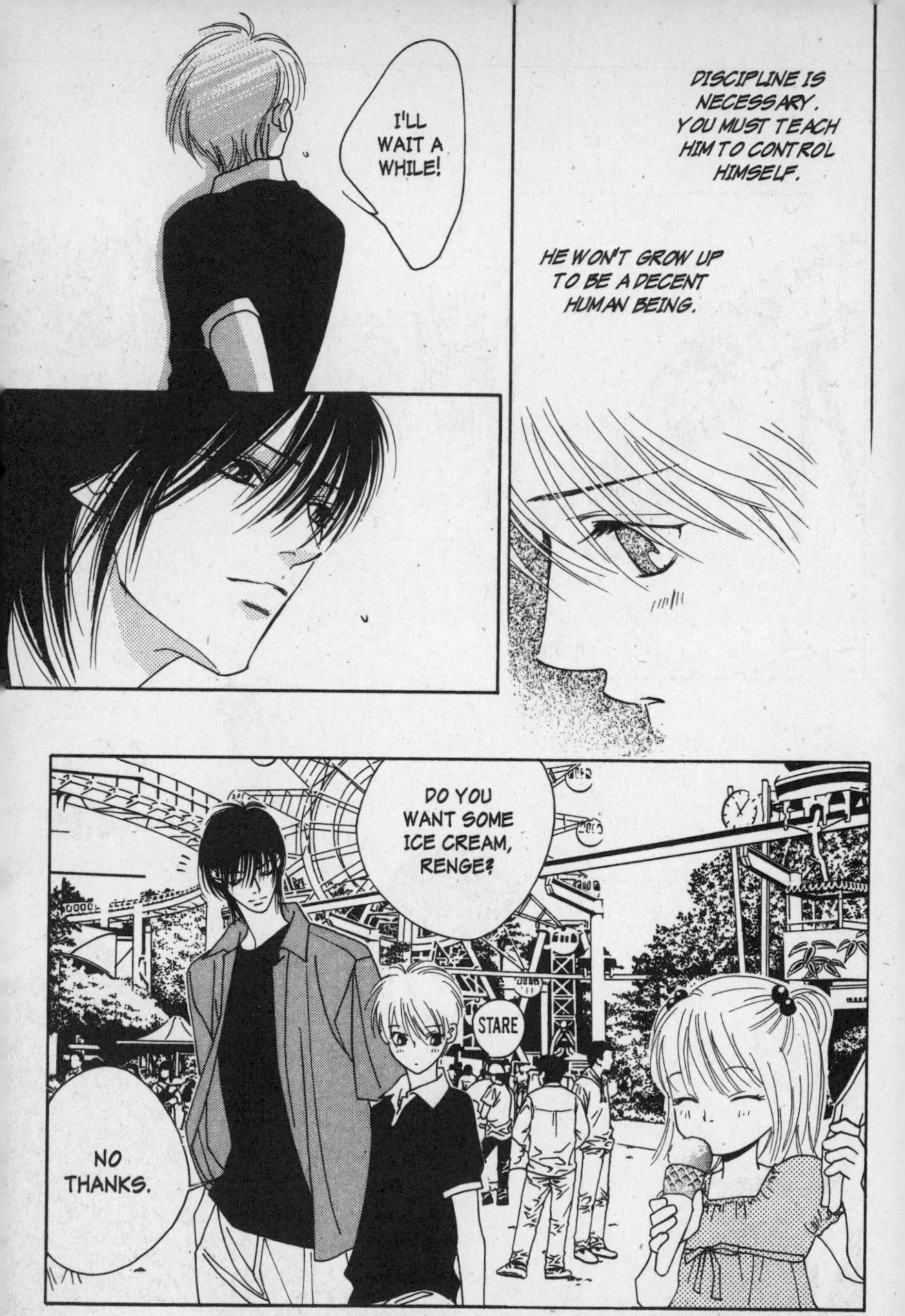
DISCIPLINE IS NECESSARY. YOU MUST TEACH HIM TO CONTROL HIMSELF.
HE WON'T GROW UP TO BE A DECENT HUMAN BEING.
I'LL WAIT A WHILE!
DO YOU WANT SOME ICE CREAM, RENGE?
STARE
NO THANKS.

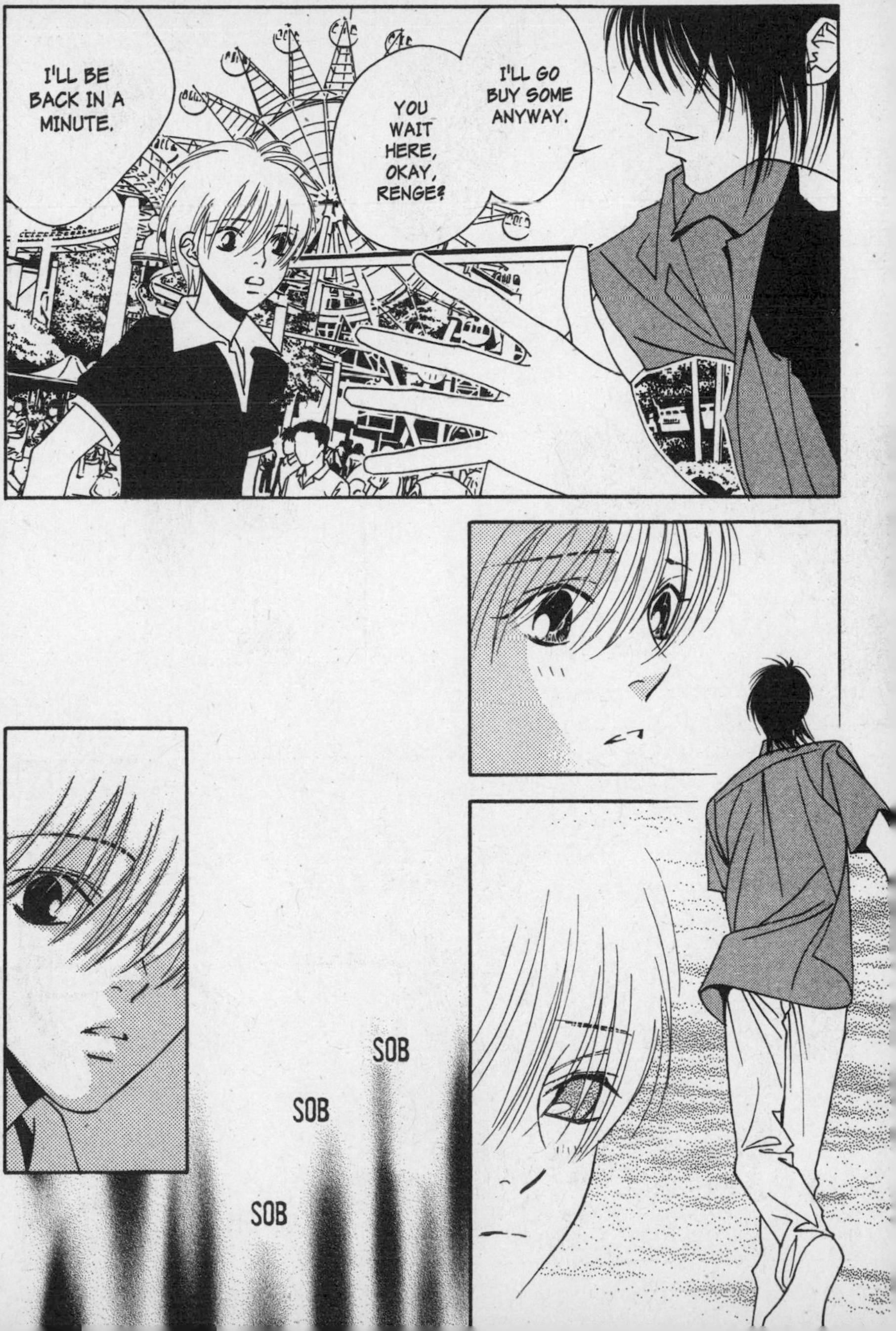
I'LL GO BUY SOME ANYWAY.
YOU WAIT HERE, OKAY, RENGE?
I'LL BE BACK IN A MINUTE.
SOB
SOB
SOB

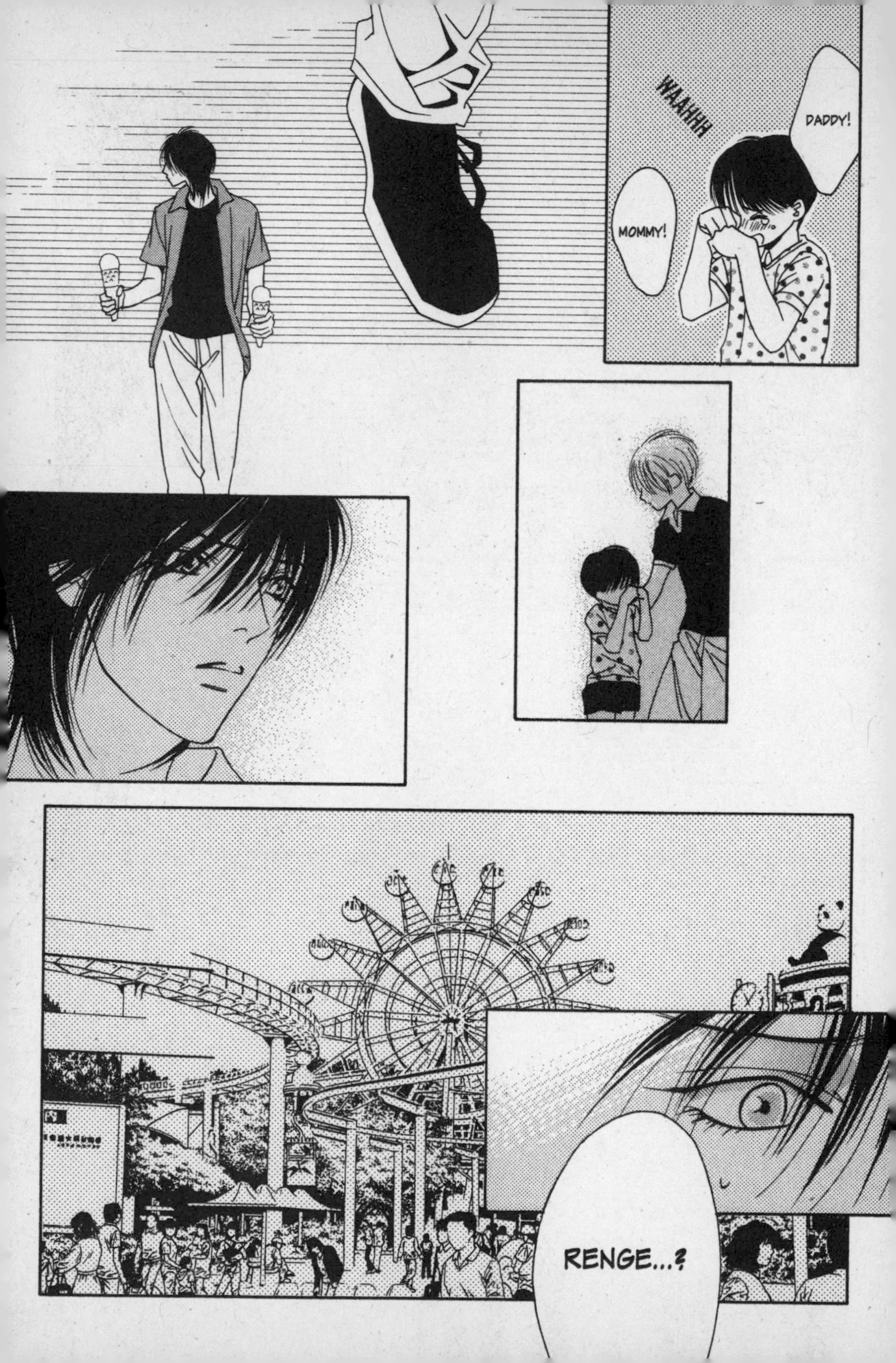
DADDY!
WAAHHH
MOMMY!
RENGE...?

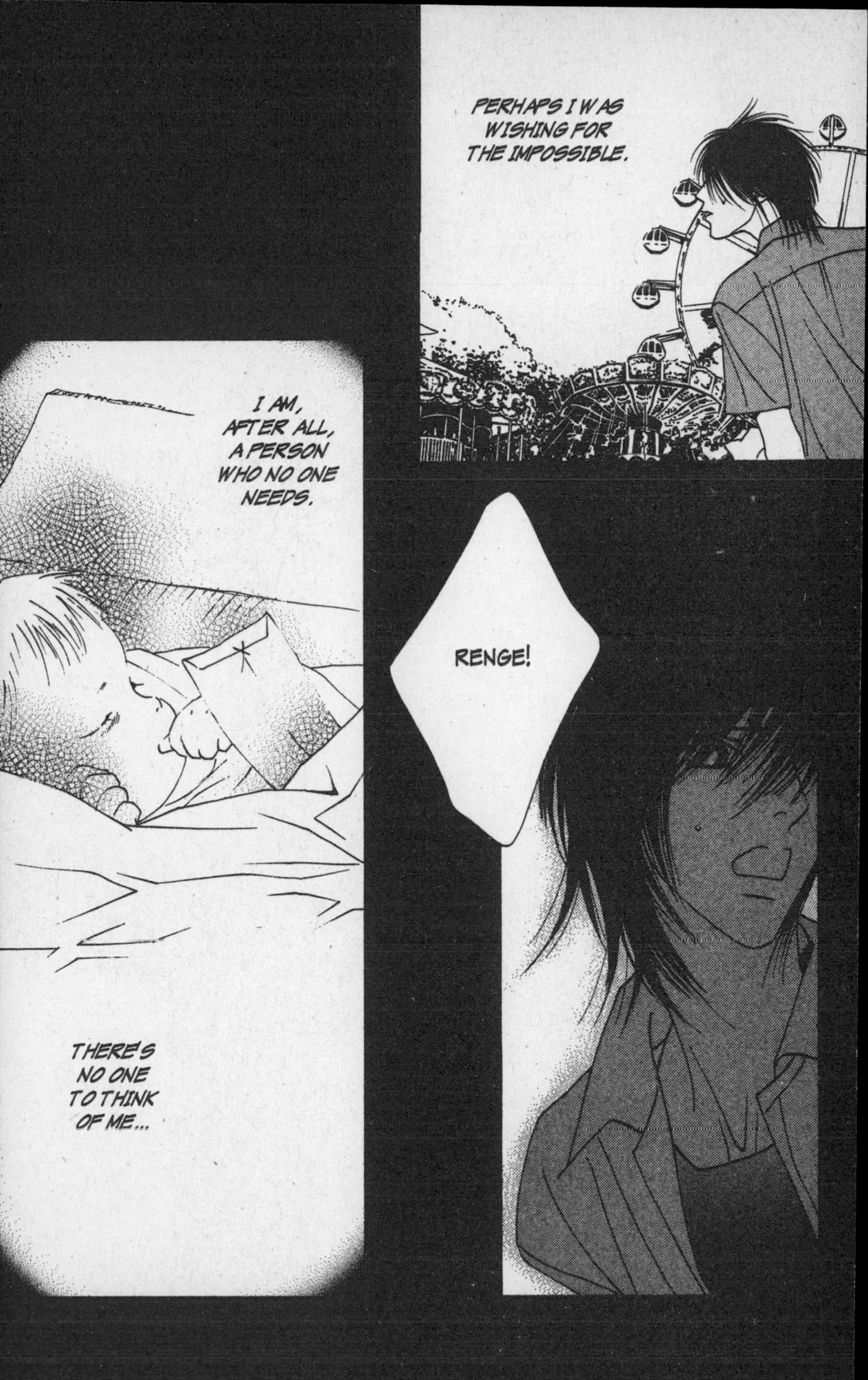
PERHAPS I WAS WISHING FOR THE IMPOSSIBLE.
I AM, AFTER ALL, A PERSON WHO NO ONE NEEDS.
THERE'S NO ONE TO THINK OF ME...
RENGE!

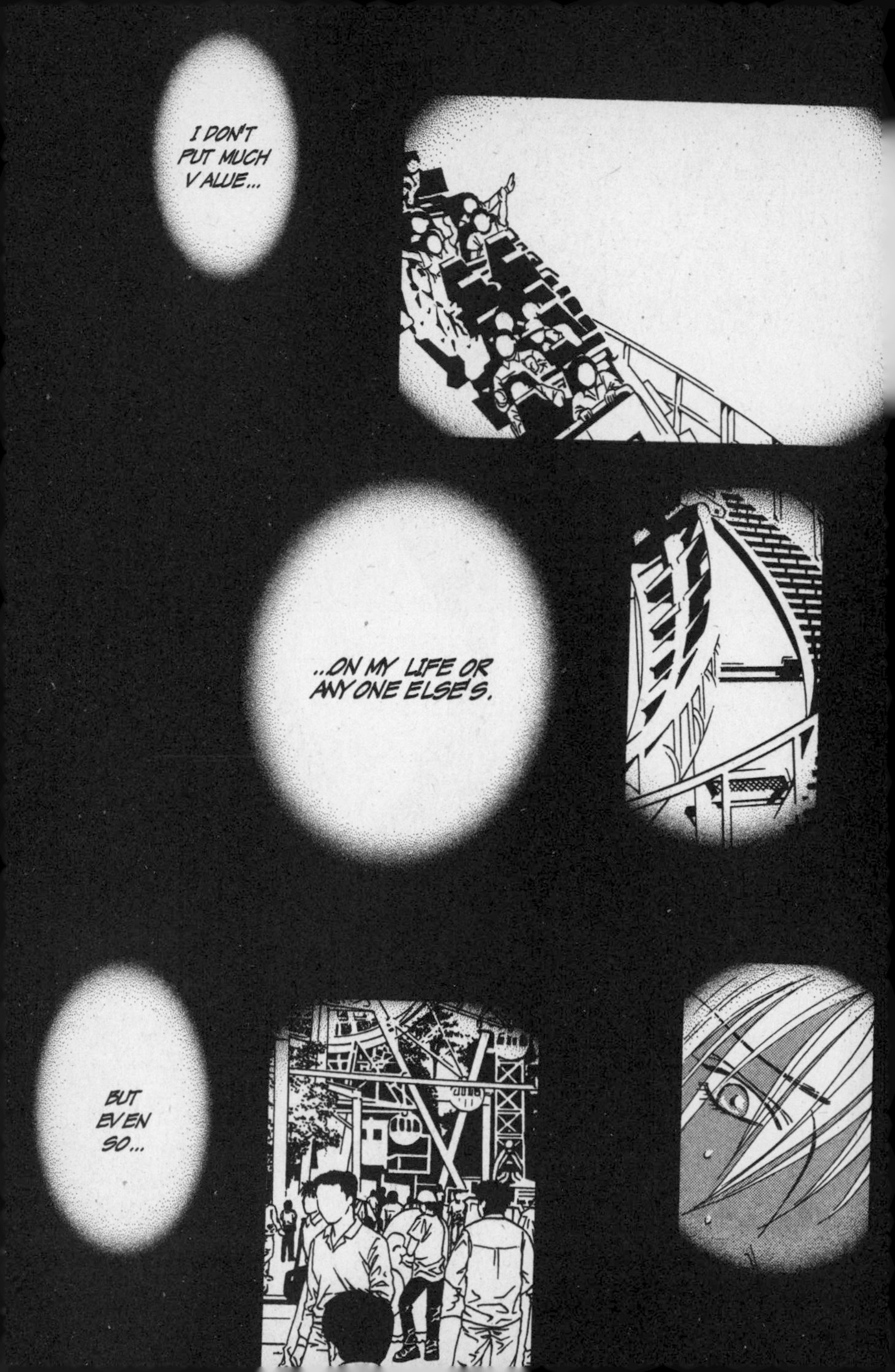
I DON'T PUT MUCH VALUE...
...ON MY LIFE OR ANYONE ELSE'S.
BUT EVEN SO...

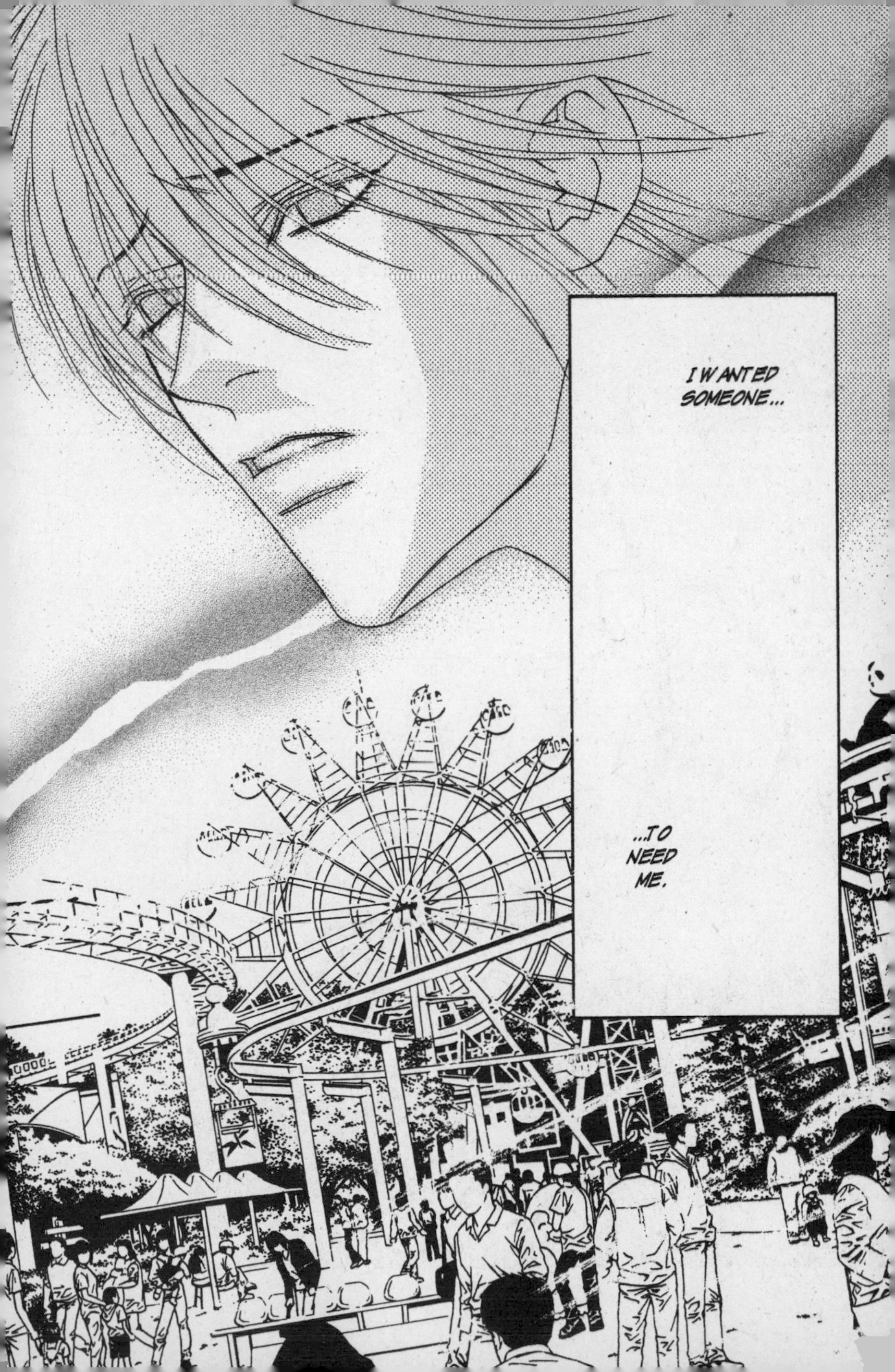
I WANTED SOMEONE...
...TO NEED ME.

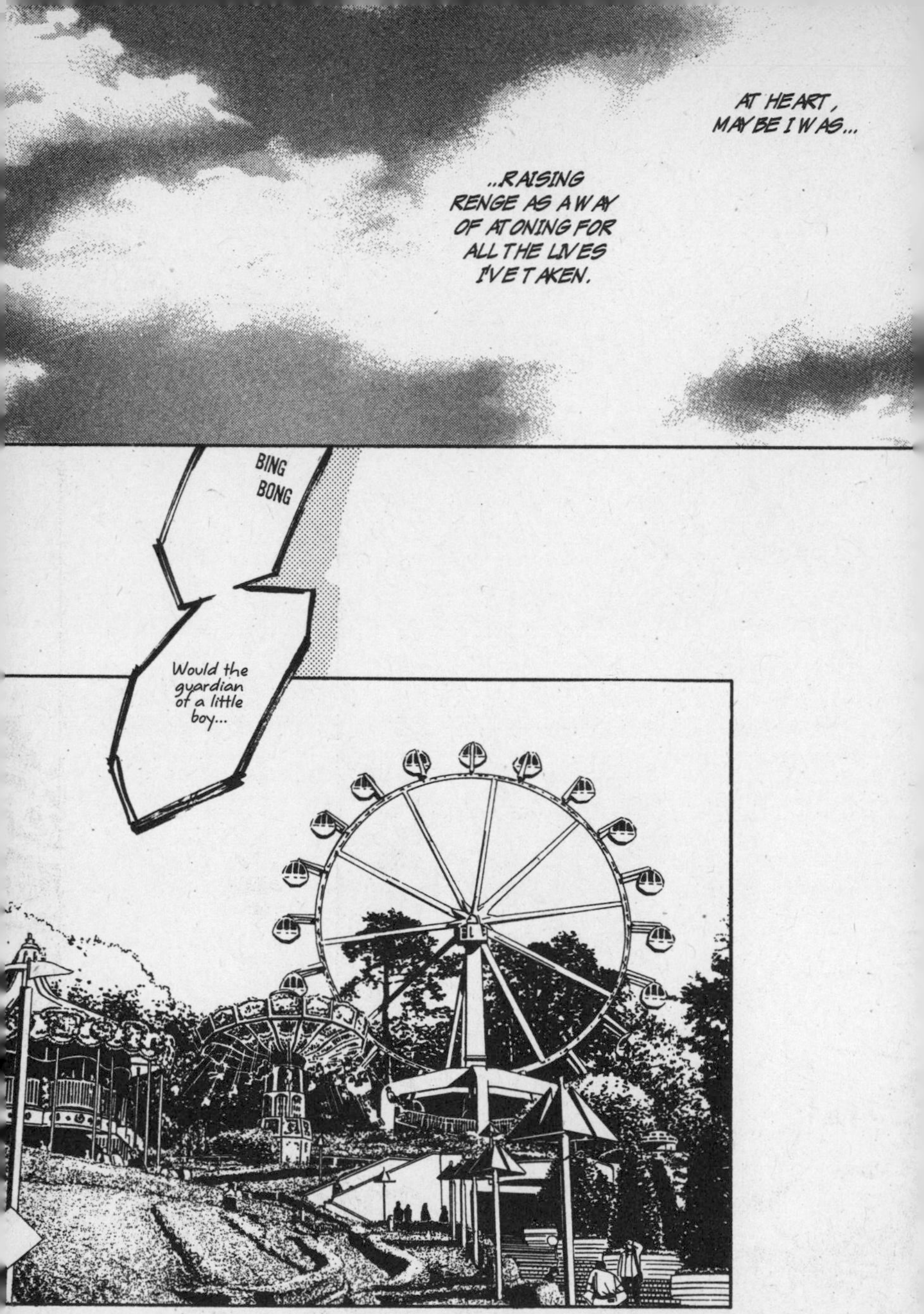
AT HEART, MAYBE I WAS...
...RAISING RENGE AS A WAY OF ATONING FOR ALL THE LIVES I'VE TAKEN.
BING BONG
Would the guardian of a little boy...

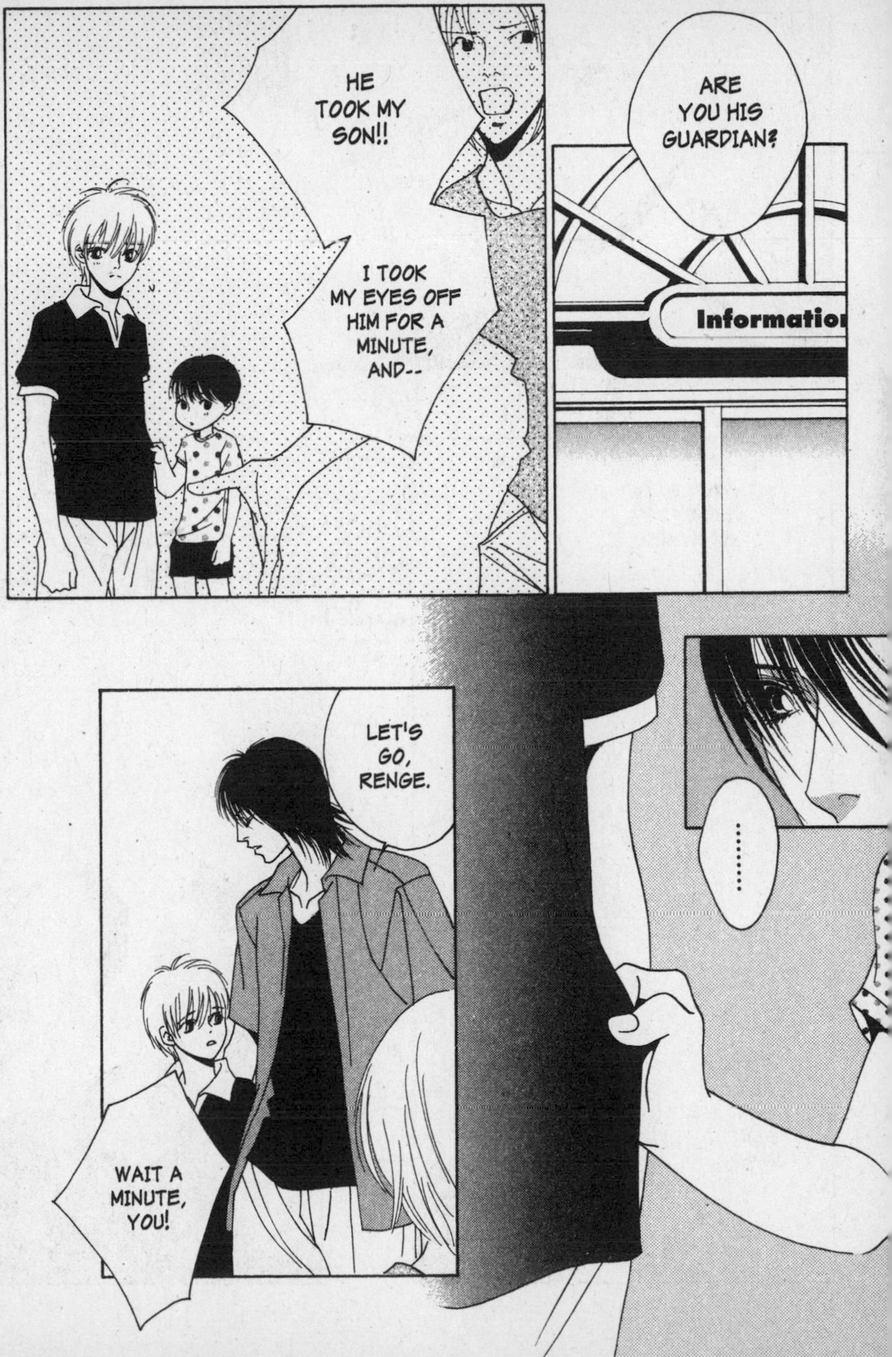
ARE YOU HIS GUARDIAN?
Information
HE TOOK MY SON!!
I TOOK MY EYES OFF HIM FOR A MINUTE, AND--
......
LET'S GO, RENGE.
WAIT A MINUTE, YOU!

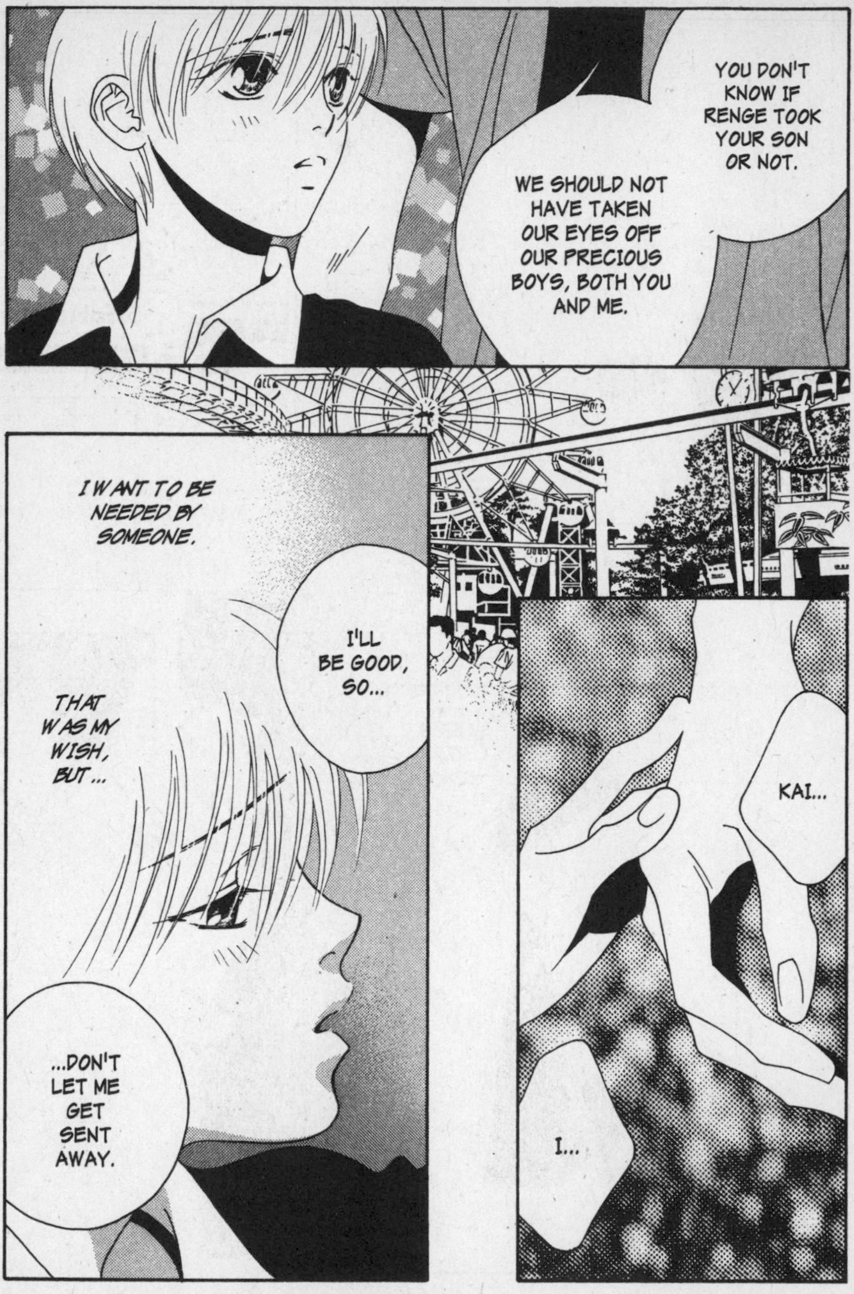
YOU DON'T KNOW IF RENGE TOOK YOUR SON OR NOT.
WE SHOULD NOT HAVE TAKEN OUR EYES OFF OUR PRECIOUS BOYS, BOTH YOU AND ME.
KAI...
I...
I WANT TO BE NEEDED BY SOMEONE.
I'LL BE GOOD, SO...
THAT WAS MY WISH, BUT...
...DON'T LET ME GET SENT AWAY.

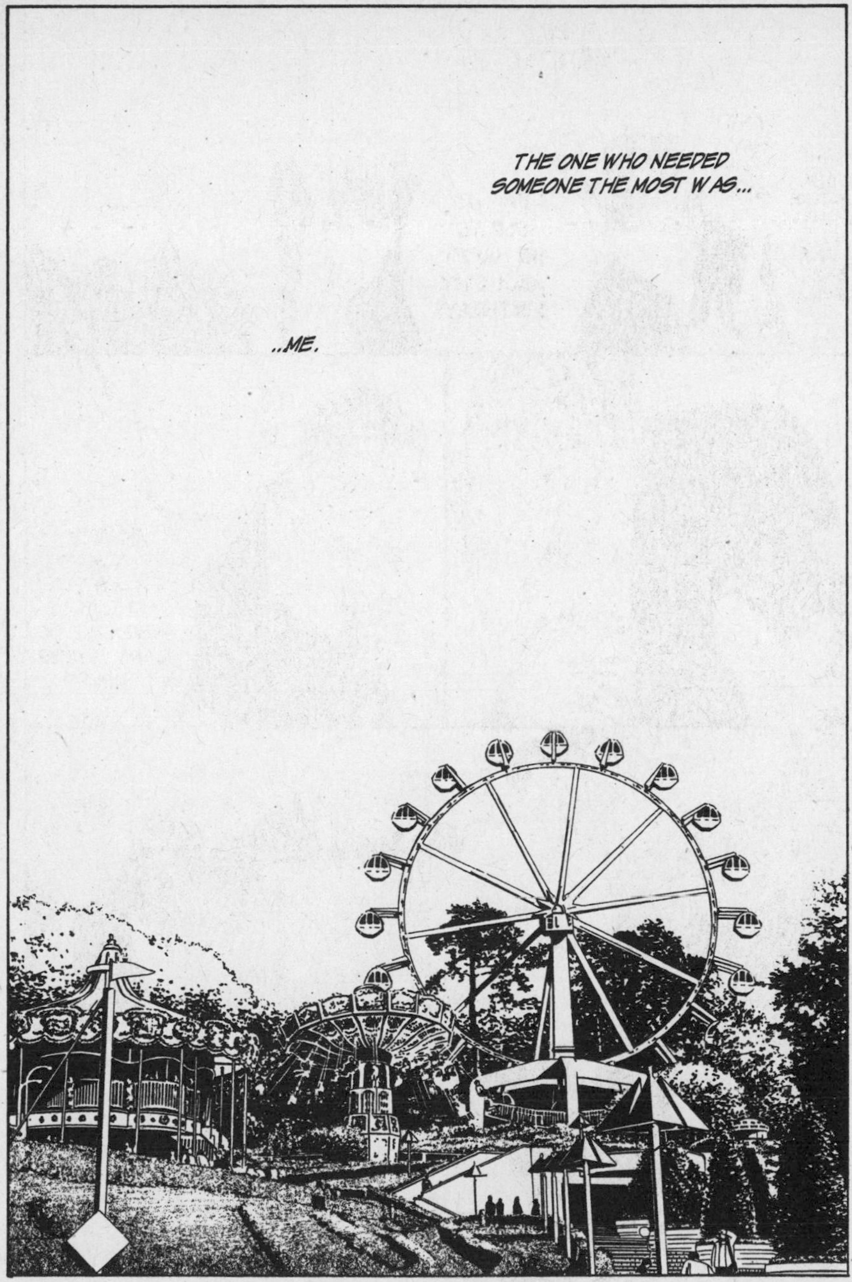
THE ONE WHO NEEDED SOMEONE THE MOST WAS...
..ME.

Secret 6 ⚜ End

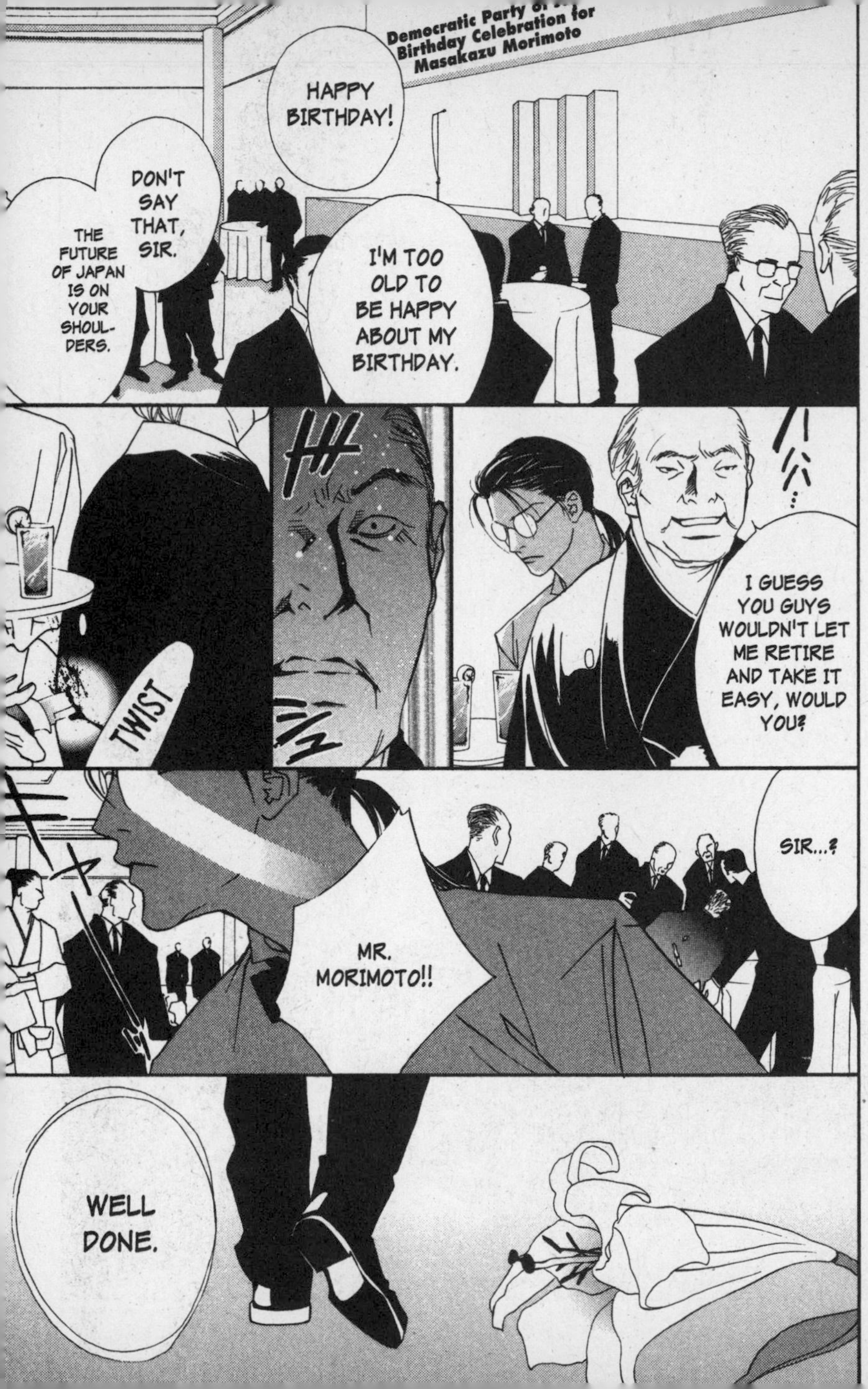
Democratic Party of
Birthday Celebration for Masakazu Morimoto
HAPPY BIRTHDAY!
I'M TOO OLD TO BE HAPPY ABOUT MY BIRTHDAY.
DON'T SAY THAT, SIR.
THE FUTURE OF JAPAN IS ON YOUR SHOULDERS.
I GUESS YOU GUYS WOULDN'T LET ME RETIRE AND TAKE IT EASY, WOULD YOU?
TWIST
SIR...?
MR. MORIMOTO!!
WELL DONE.

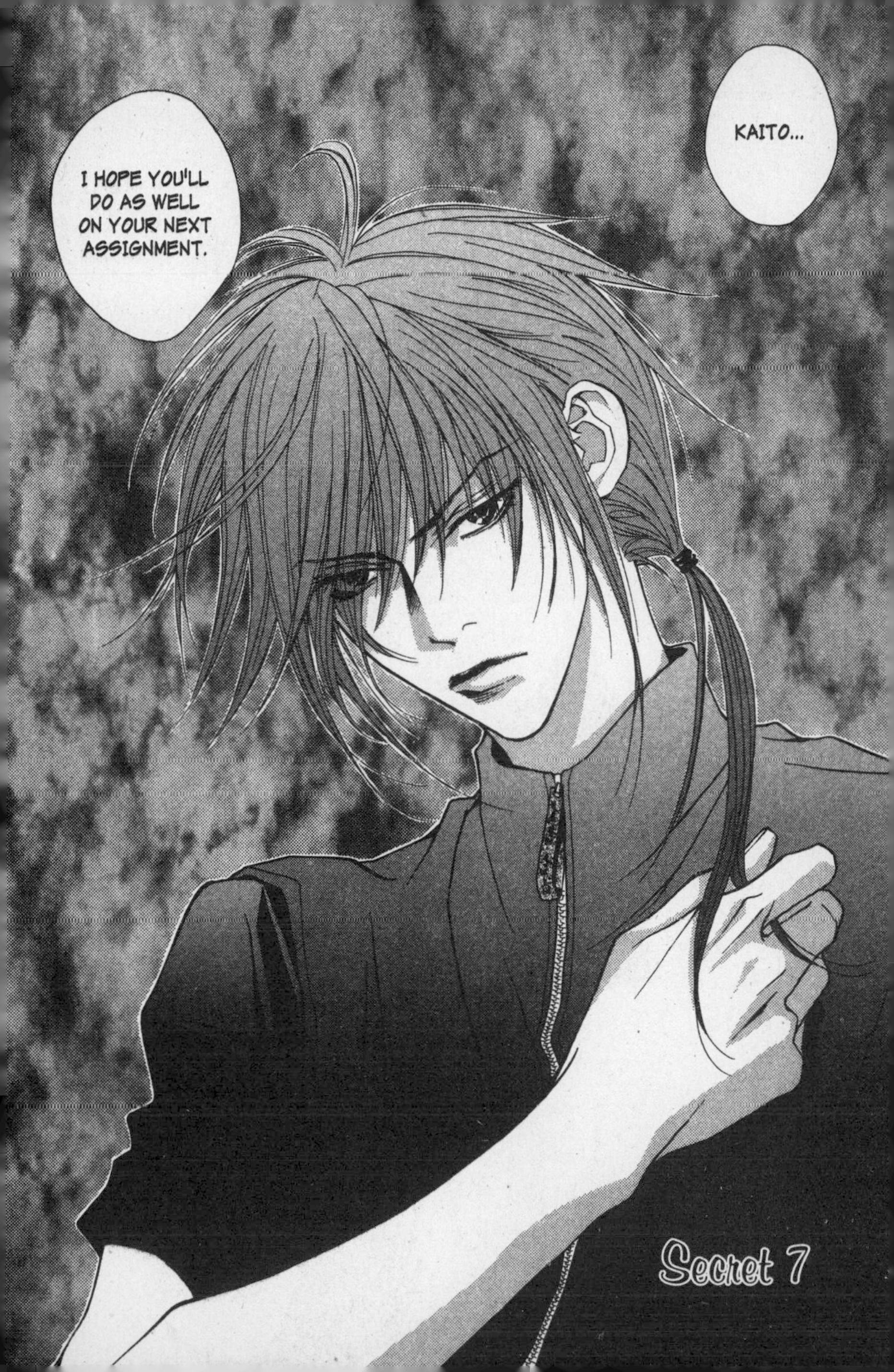
KAITO...
I HOPE YOU'LL DO AS WELL ON YOUR NEXT ASSIGNMENT.
Secret 7

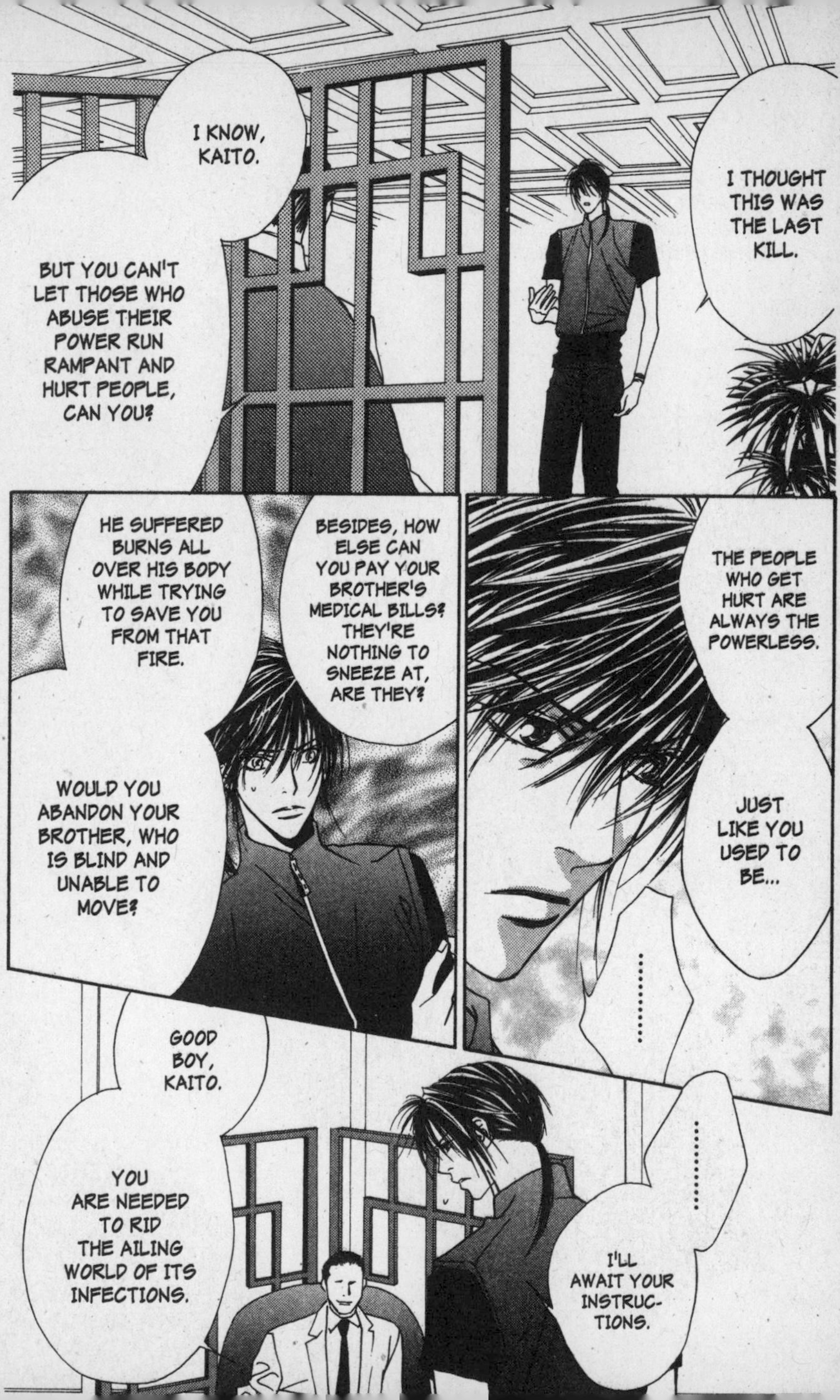
I THOUGHT THIS WAS THE LAST KILL.
I KNOW, KAITO.
BUT YOU CAN'T LET THOSE WHO ABUSE THEIR POWER RUN RAMPANT AND HURT PEOPLE, CAN YOU?
THE PEOPLE WHO GET HURT ARE ALWAYS THE POWERLESS.
JUST LIKE YOU USED TO BE...
BESIDES, HOW ELSE CAN YOU PAY YOUR BROTHER'S MEDICAL BILLS? THEY'RE NOTHING TO SNEEZE AT, ARE THEY?
HE SUFFERED BURNS ALL OVER HIS BODY WHILE TRYING TO SAVE YOU FROM THAT FIRE.
WOULD YOU ABANDON YOUR BROTHER, WHO IS BLIND AND UNABLE TO MOVE?
I'LL AWAIT YOUR INSTRUCTIONS.
GOOD BOY, KAITO.
YOU ARE NEEDED TO RID THE AILING WORLD OF ITS INFECTIONS.

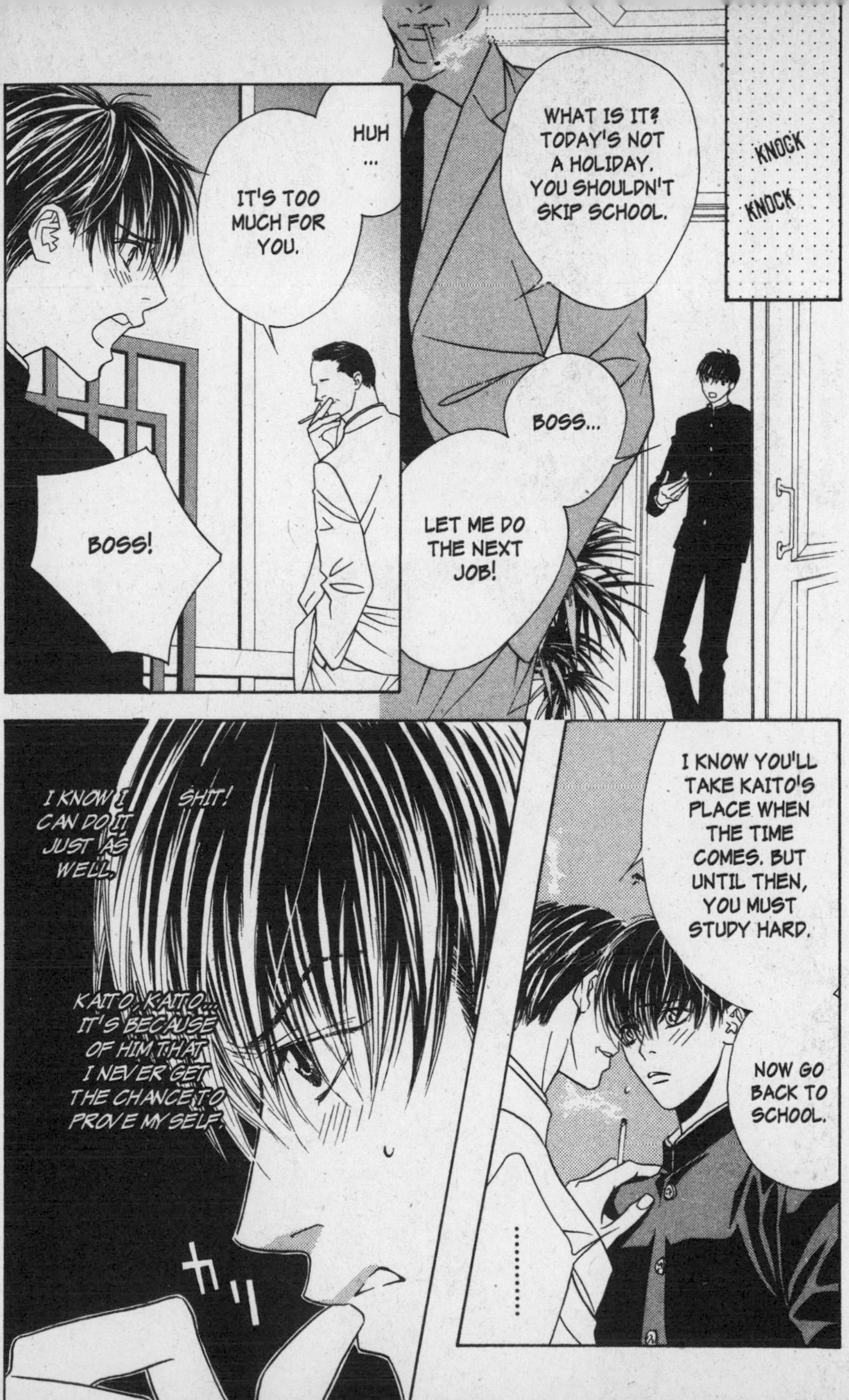
KNOCK
KNOCK
WHAT IS IT? TODAY'S NOT A HOLIDAY. YOU SHOULDN'T SKIP SCHOOL.
BOSS...
LET ME DO THE NEXT JOB!
HUH ... IT'S TOO MUCH FOR YOU.
BOSS!
I KNOW YOU'LL TAKE KAITO'S PLACE WHEN THE TIME COMES. BUT UNTIL THEN, YOU MUST STUDY HARD.
NOW GO BACK TO SCHOOL.
......
SHIT!
I KNOW I CAN DO IT JUST AS WELL.
KAITO, KAITO... IT'S BECAUSE OF HIM THAT I NEVER GET THE CHANCE TO PROVE MY SELF.
カリ

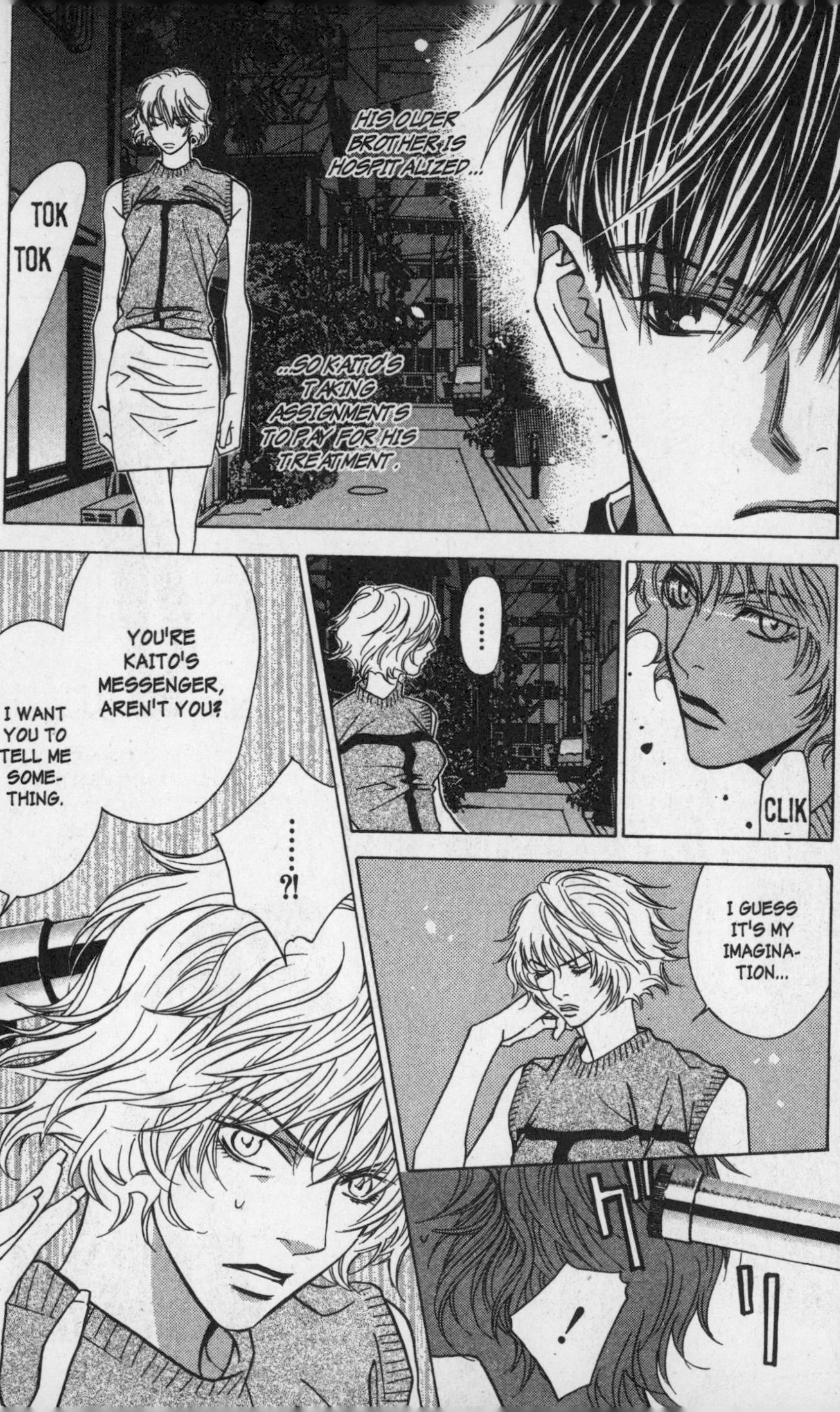
HIS OLDER BROTHER IS HOSPITALIZED...
...SO KAITO'S TAKING ASSIGNMENTS TO PAY FOR HIS TREATMENT.
TOK TOK
CLIK
......
I GUESS IT'S MY IMAGINATION...
!
YOU'RE KAITO'S MESSENGER, AREN'T YOU?
I WANT YOU TO TELL ME SOMETHING.
......?!

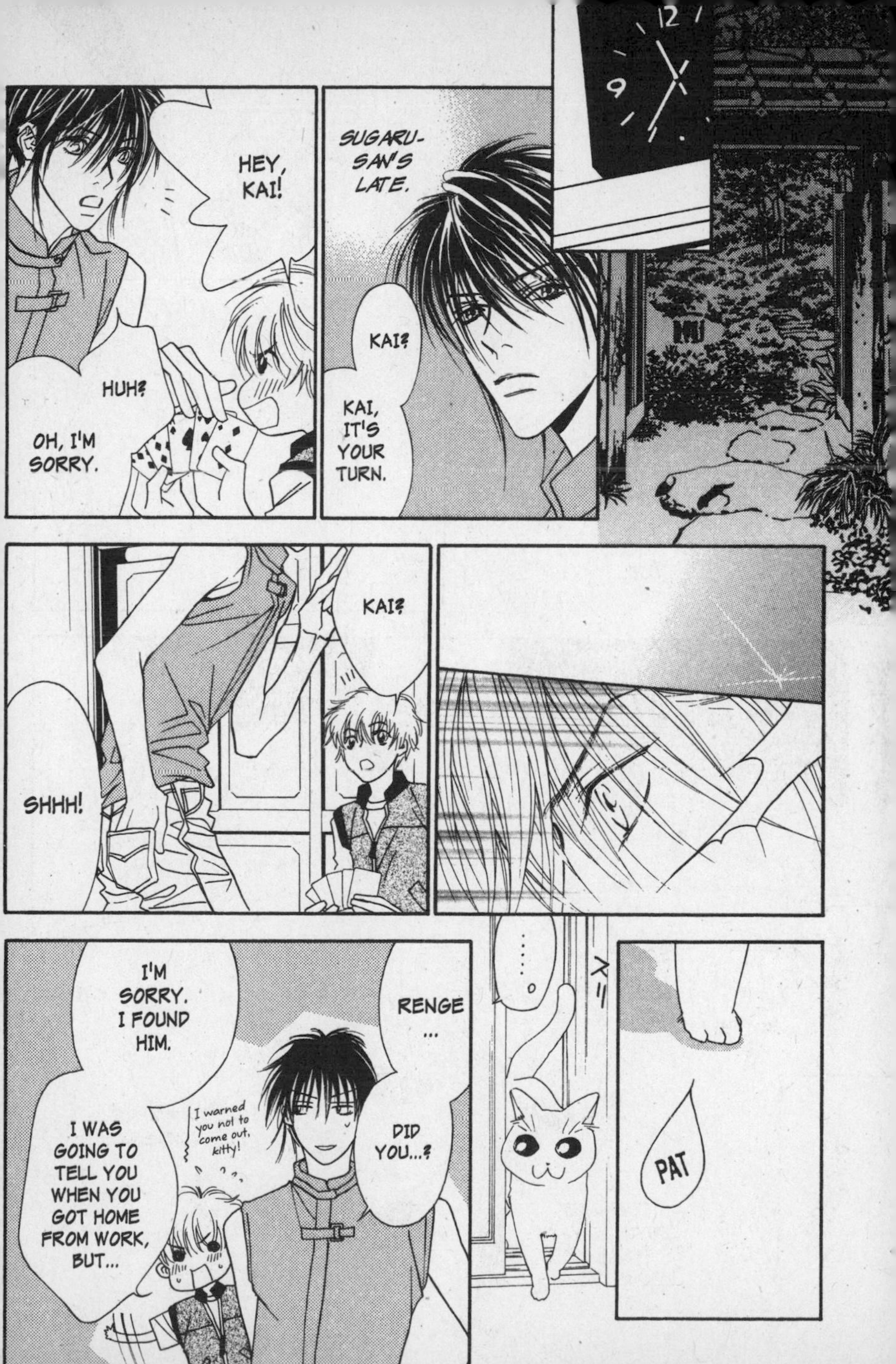

SUGARU-SAN'S LATE.
KAI?
KAI, IT'S YOUR TURN.
HEY, KAI!
HUH?
OH, I'M SORRY.
KAI?
SHHH!
PAT
.....
RENGE ...
DID YOU...?
I'M SORRY. I FOUND HIM.
I warned you not to come out, kitty!
I WAS GOING TO TELL YOU WHEN YOU GOT HOME FROM WORK, BUT...

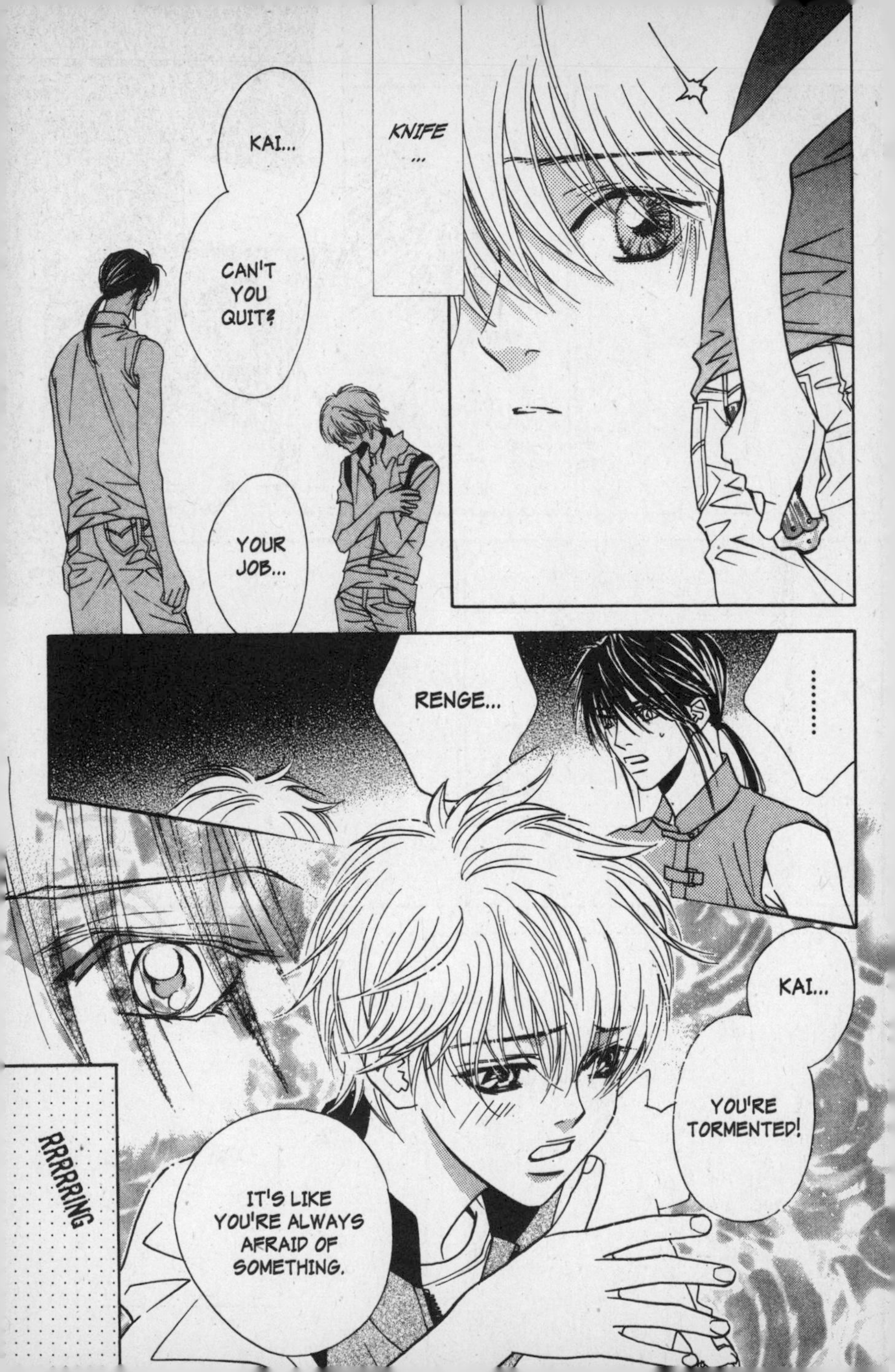
KNIFE ...
KAI...
CAN'T YOU QUIT?
YOUR JOB...
......
RENGE...
KAI...
YOU'RE TORMENTED!
IT'S LIKE YOU'RE ALWAYS AFRAID OF SOMETHING.
RRRRRING

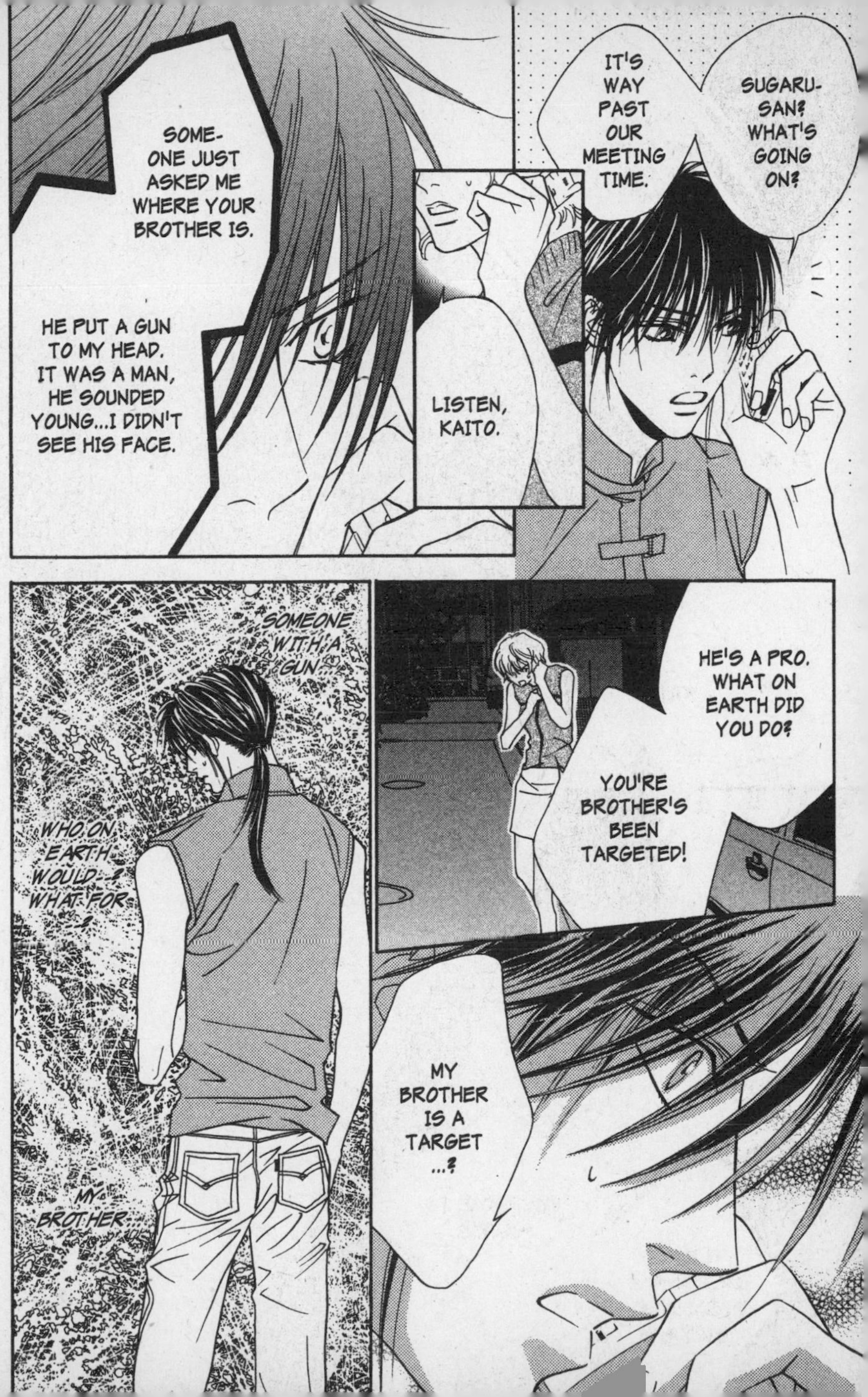
SUGARU-SAN? WHAT'S GOING ON?
IT'S WAY PAST OUR MEETING TIME.
LISTEN, KAITO.
SOME-ONE JUST ASKED ME WHERE YOUR BROTHER IS.
HE PUT A GUN TO MY HEAD. IT WAS A MAN, HE SOUNDED YOUNG...I DIDN'T SEE HIS FACE.
HE'S A PRO. WHAT ON EARTH DID YOU DO?
YOU'RE BROTHER'S BEEN TARGETED!
MY BROTHER IS A TARGET ...?
SOMEONE WITH A GUN
WHO ON EARTH WOULD--? WHAT FOR--?
MY BROTHER

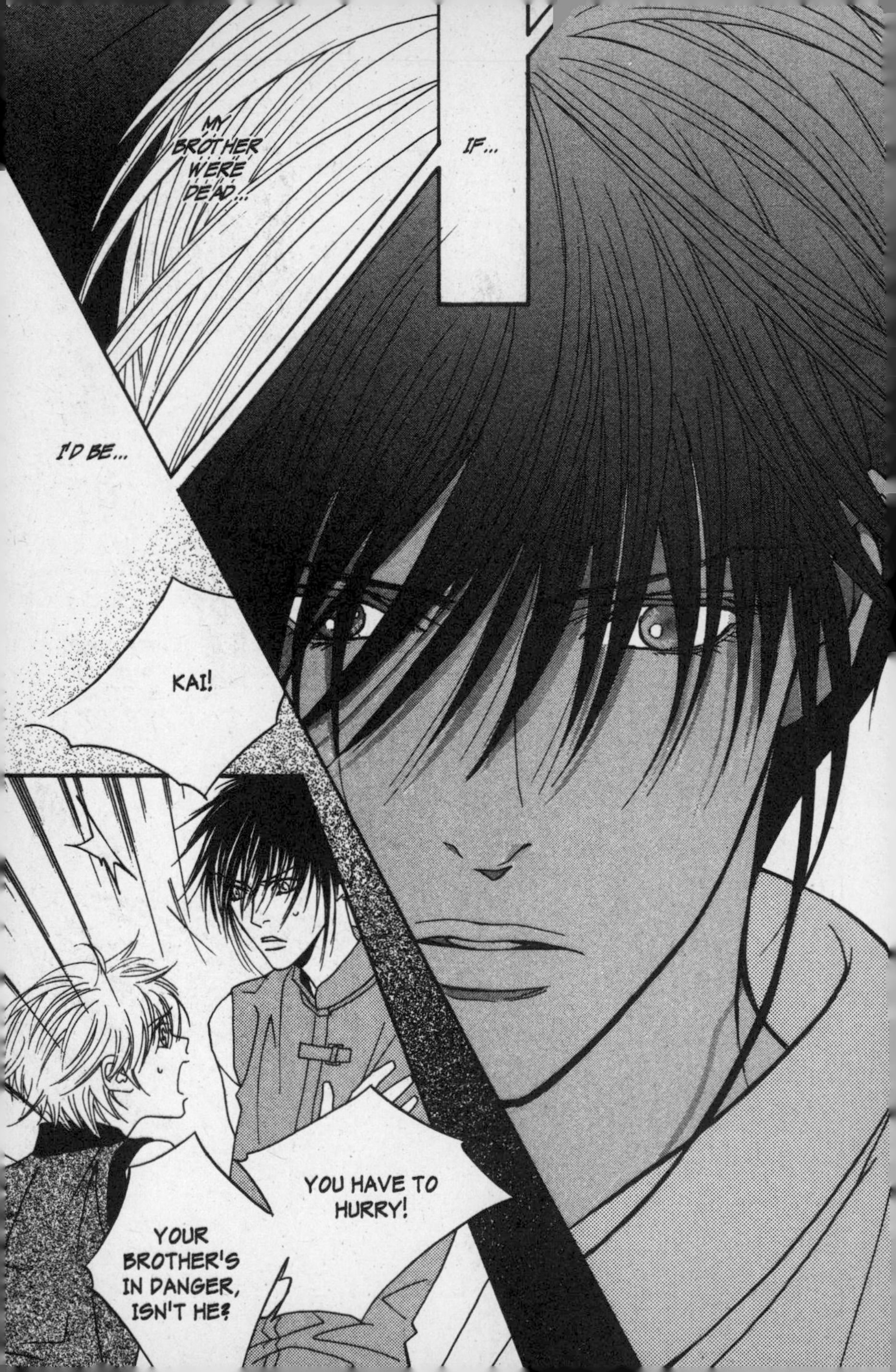
IF...
MY BROTHER WERE DEAD...
I'D BE...
KAI!
YOU HAVE TO HURRY!
YOUR BROTHER'S IN DANGER, ISN'T HE?

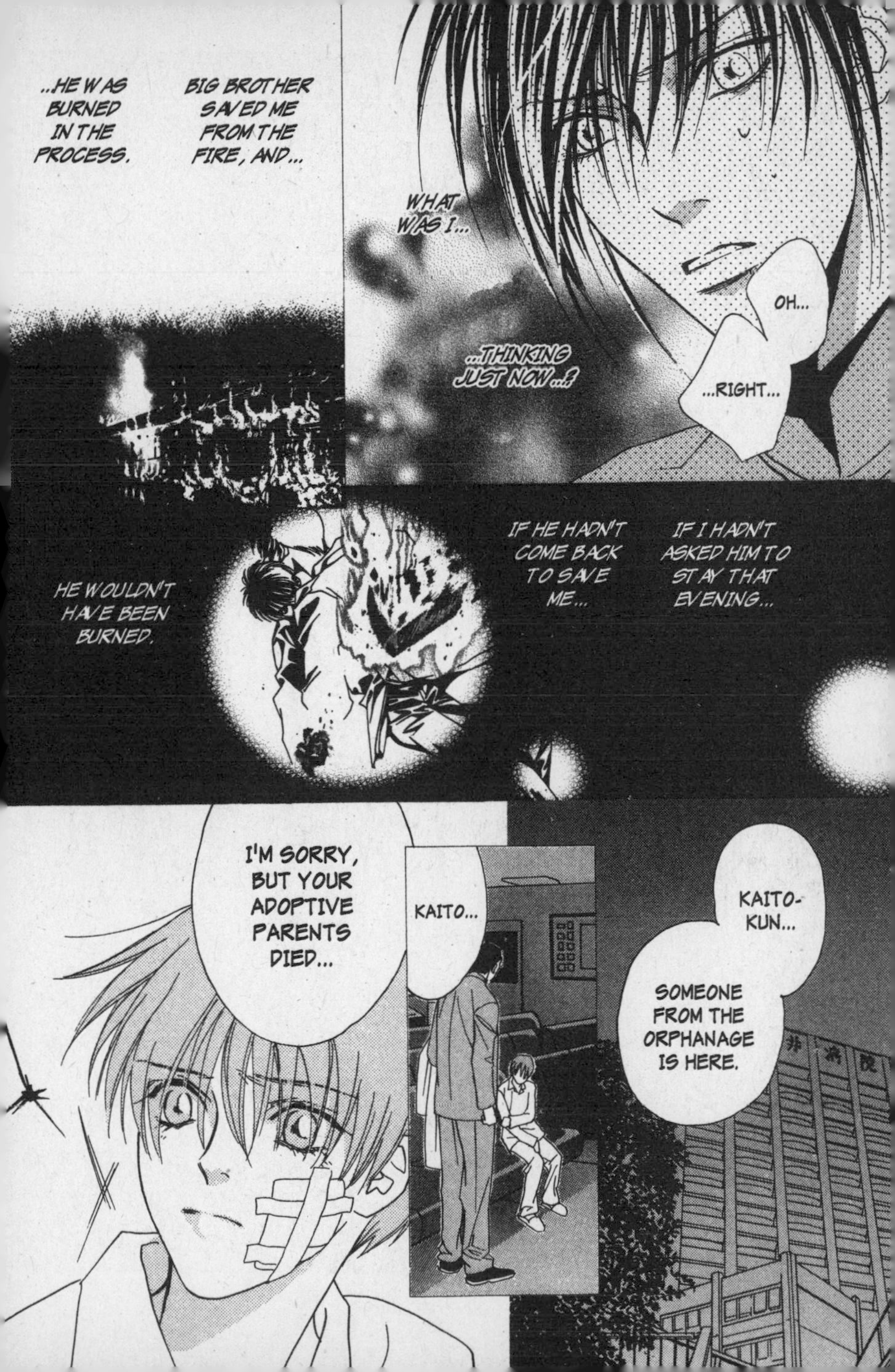
WHAT WAS I...
...THINKING JUST NOW...?
OH...
...RIGHT...
BIG BROTHER SAVED ME FROM THE FIRE, AND...
...HE WAS BURNED IN THE PROCESS.
IF I HADN'T ASKED HIM TO STAY THAT EVENING...
IF HE HADN'T COME BACK TO SAVE ME...
HE WOULDN'T HAVE BEEN BURNED.
KAITO-KUN...
SOMEONE FROM THE ORPHANAGE IS HERE.
KAITO...
I'M SORRY, BUT YOUR ADOPTIVE PARENTS DIED...

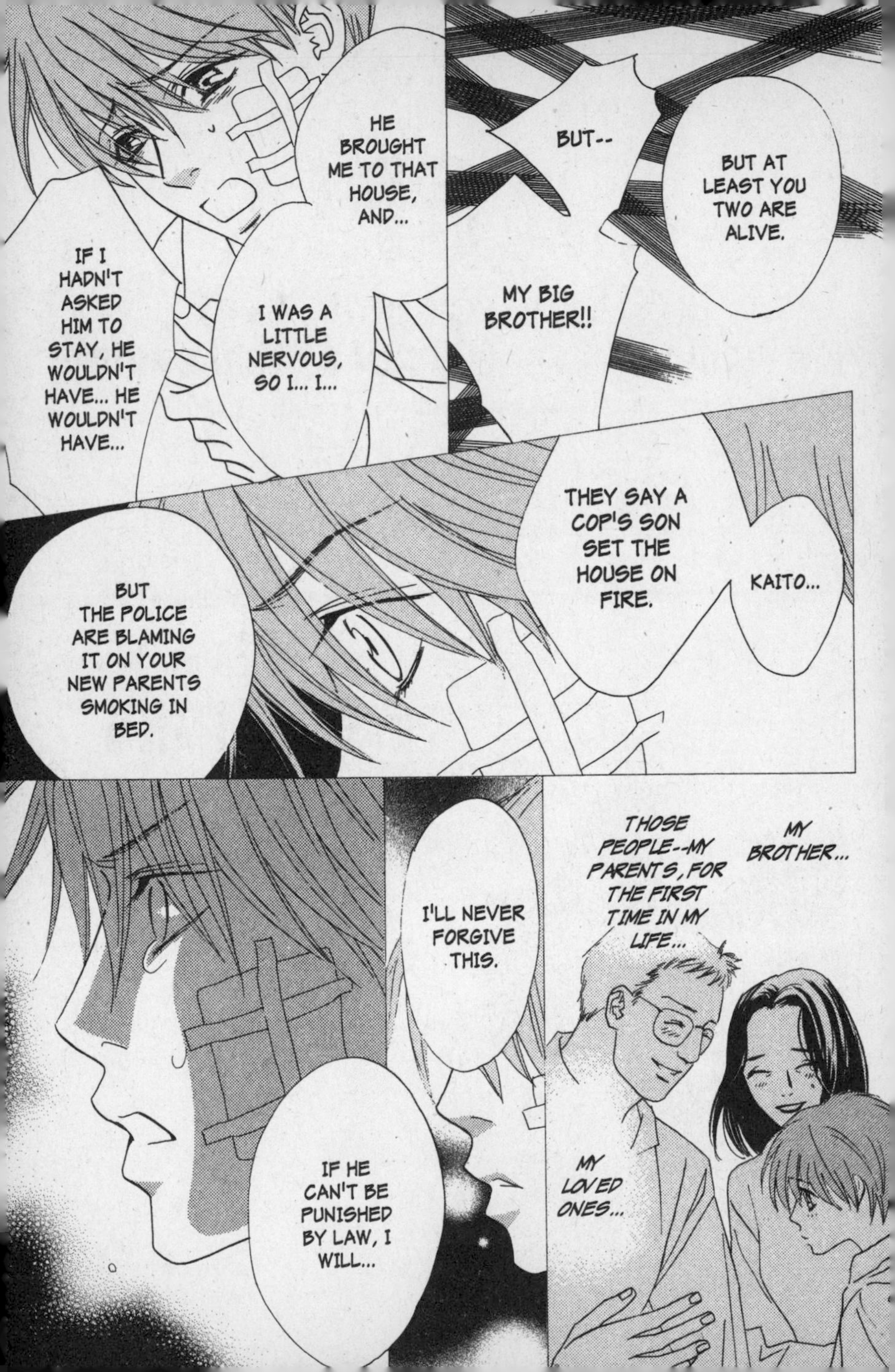
BUT AT LEAST YOU TWO ARE ALIVE.
BUT--
MY BIG BROTHER!!
HE BROUGHT ME TO THAT HOUSE, AND...
I WAS A LITTLE NERVOUS, SO I... I...
IF I HADN'T ASKED HIM TO STAY, HE WOULDN'T HAVE... HE WOULDN'T HAVE...
KAITO...
THEY SAY A COP'S SON SET THE HOUSE ON FIRE.
BUT THE POLICE ARE BLAMING IT ON YOUR NEW PARENTS SMOKING IN BED.
MY BROTHER...
THOSE PEOPLE--MY PARENTS, FOR THE FIRST TIME IN MY LIFE...
MY LOVED ONES...
I'LL NEVER FORGIVE THIS.
IF HE CAN'T BE PUNISHED BY LAW, I WILL...

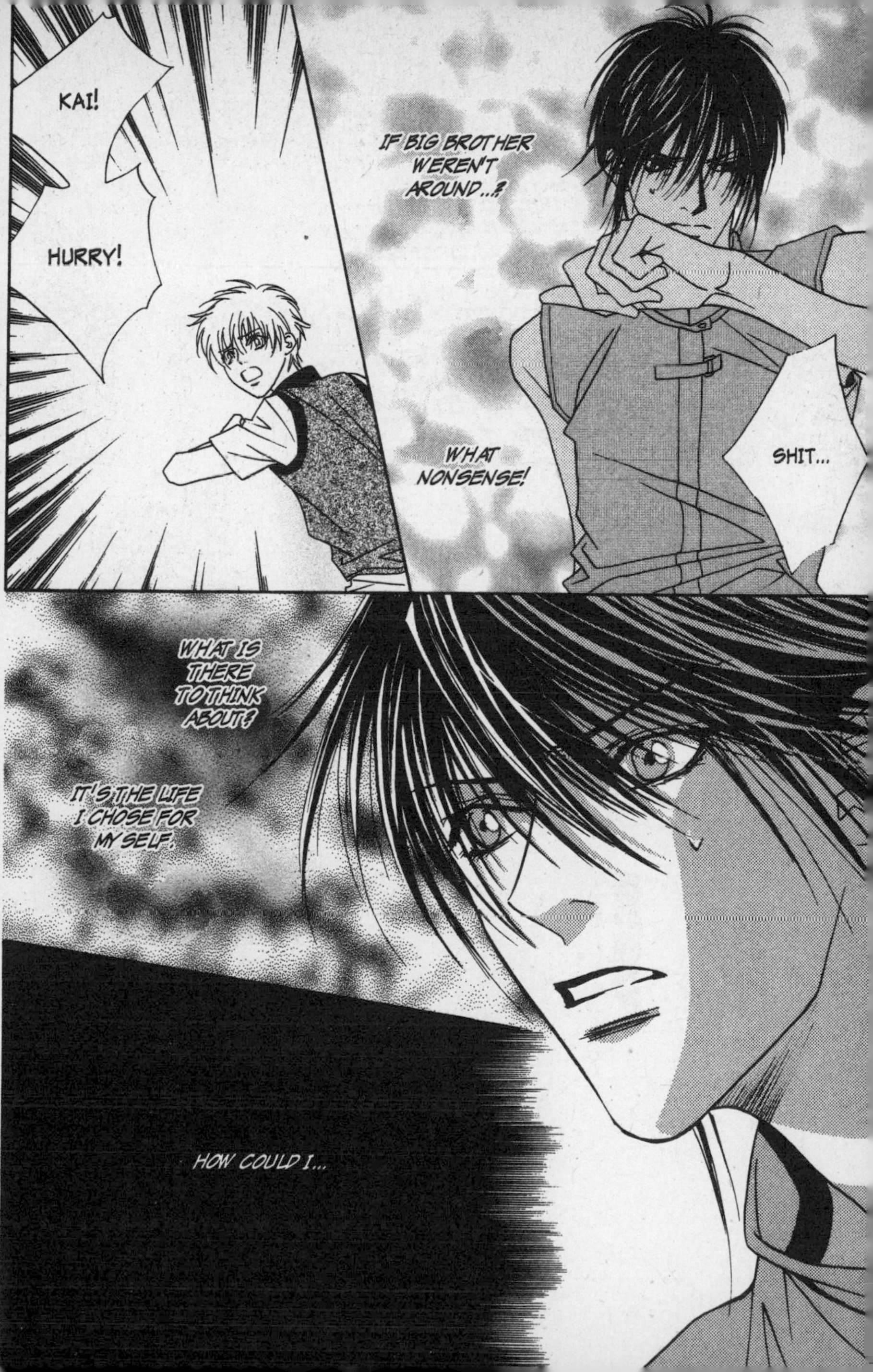
IF BIG BROTHER WEREN'T AROUND...?
SHIT...
WHAT NONSENSE!
KAI!
HURRY!
WHAT IS THERE TO THINK ABOUT?
IT'S THE LIFE I CHOSE FOR MYSELF.
HOW COULD I...

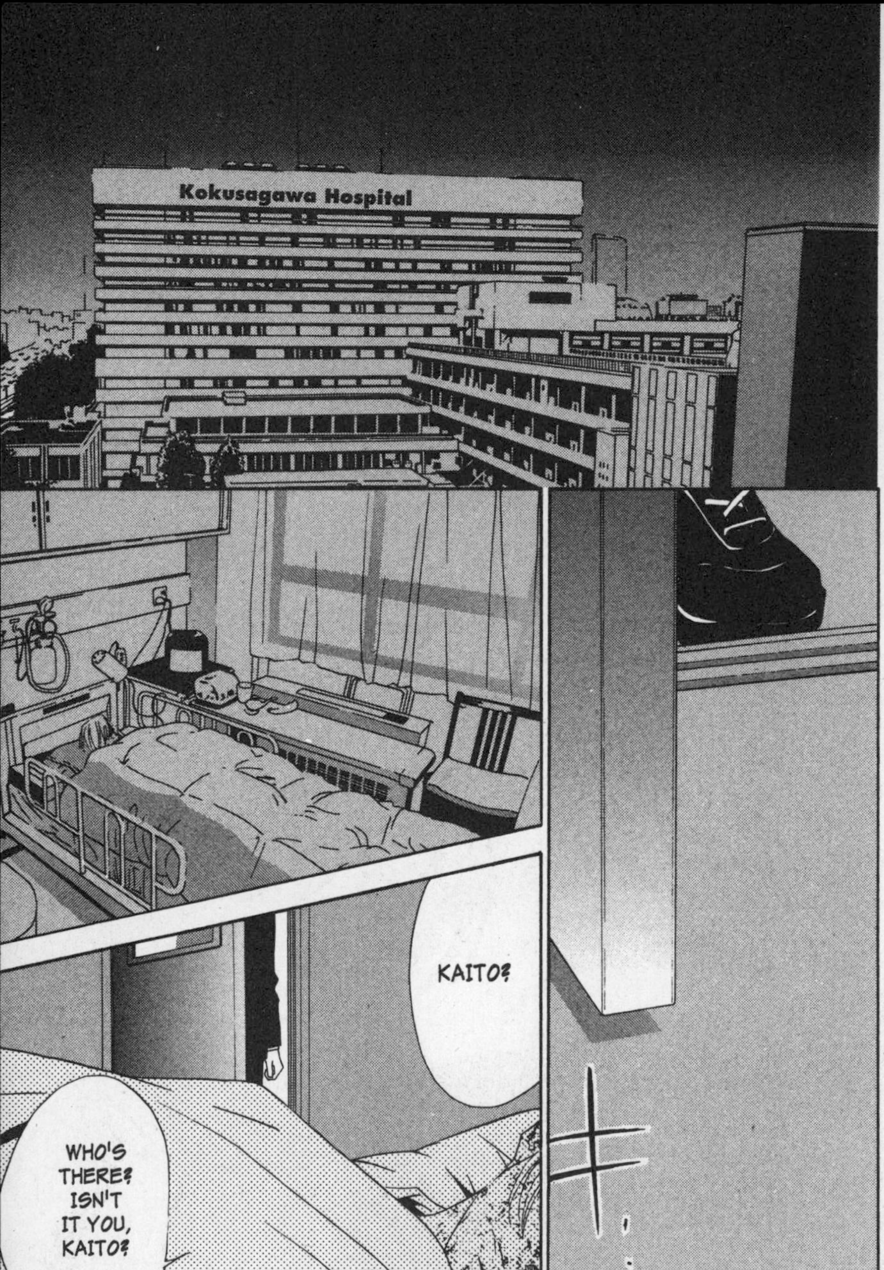
Kokusagawa Hospital
...
KAITO?
WHO'S THERE? ISN'T IT YOU, KAITO?

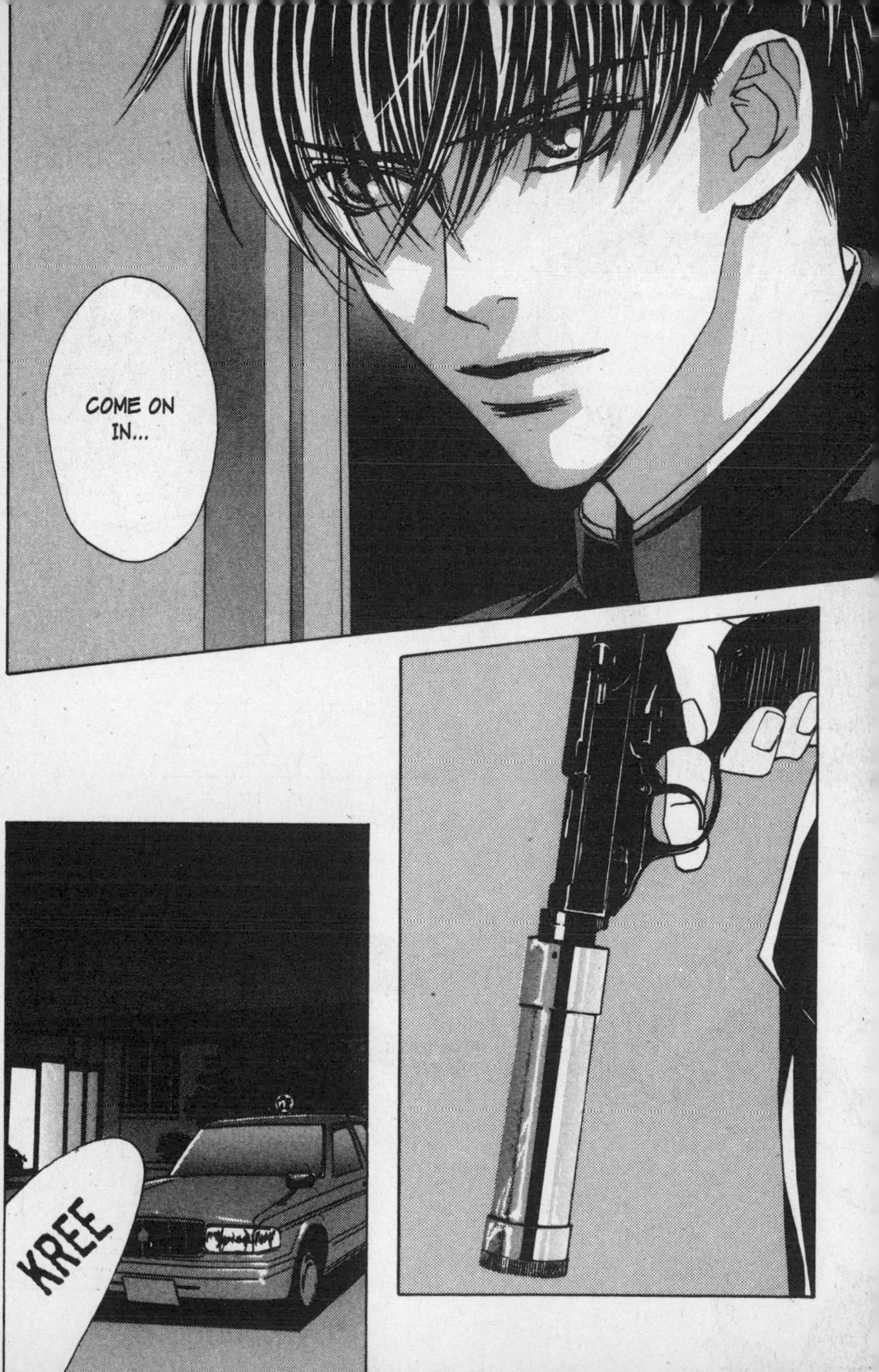
COME ON IN...
KREE

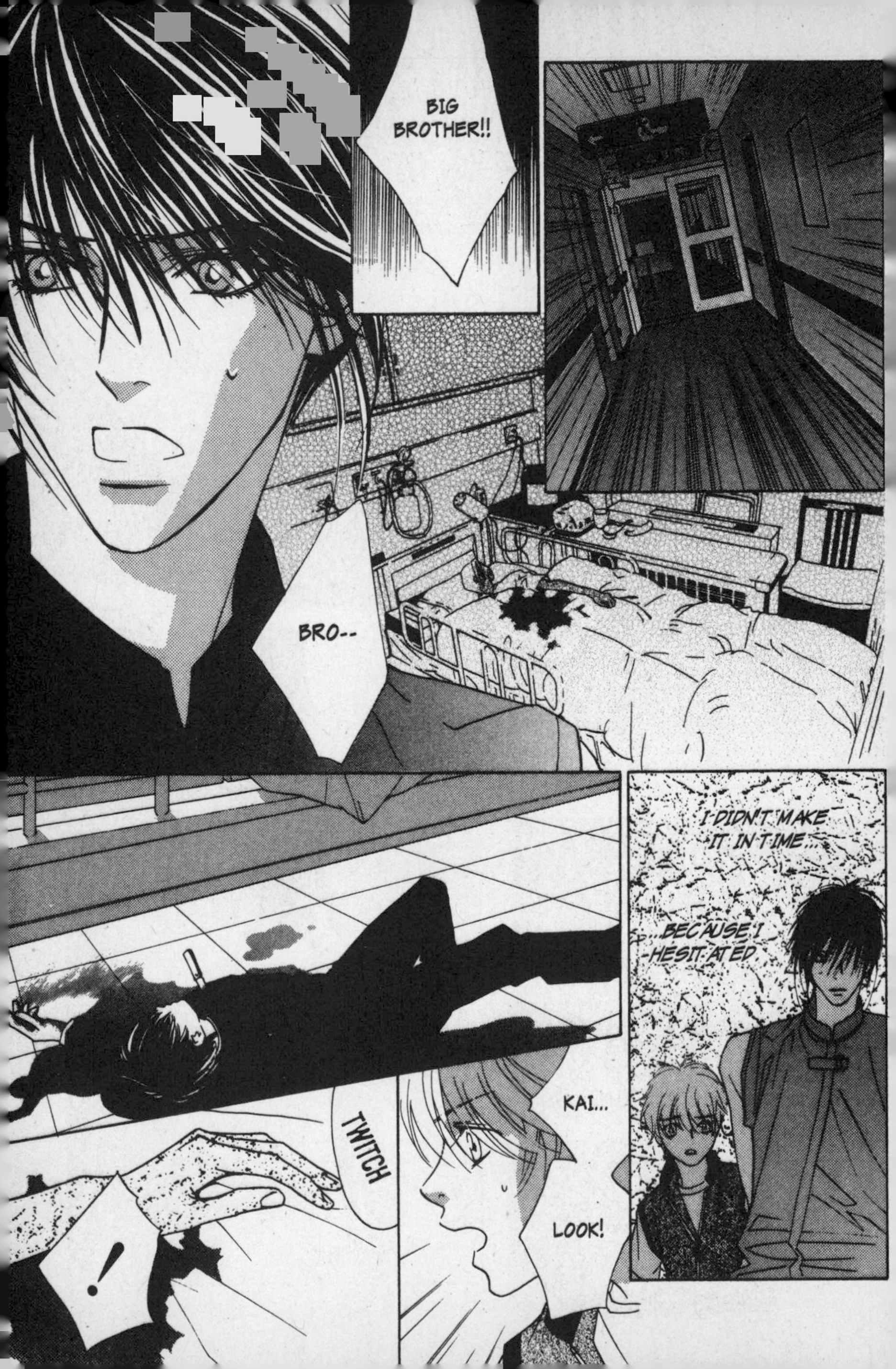
BIG BROTHER!!
BRO--
I DIDN'T MAKE IT IN TIME...
...BECAUSE I HESITATED
KAI...
LOOK!
TWITCH
!

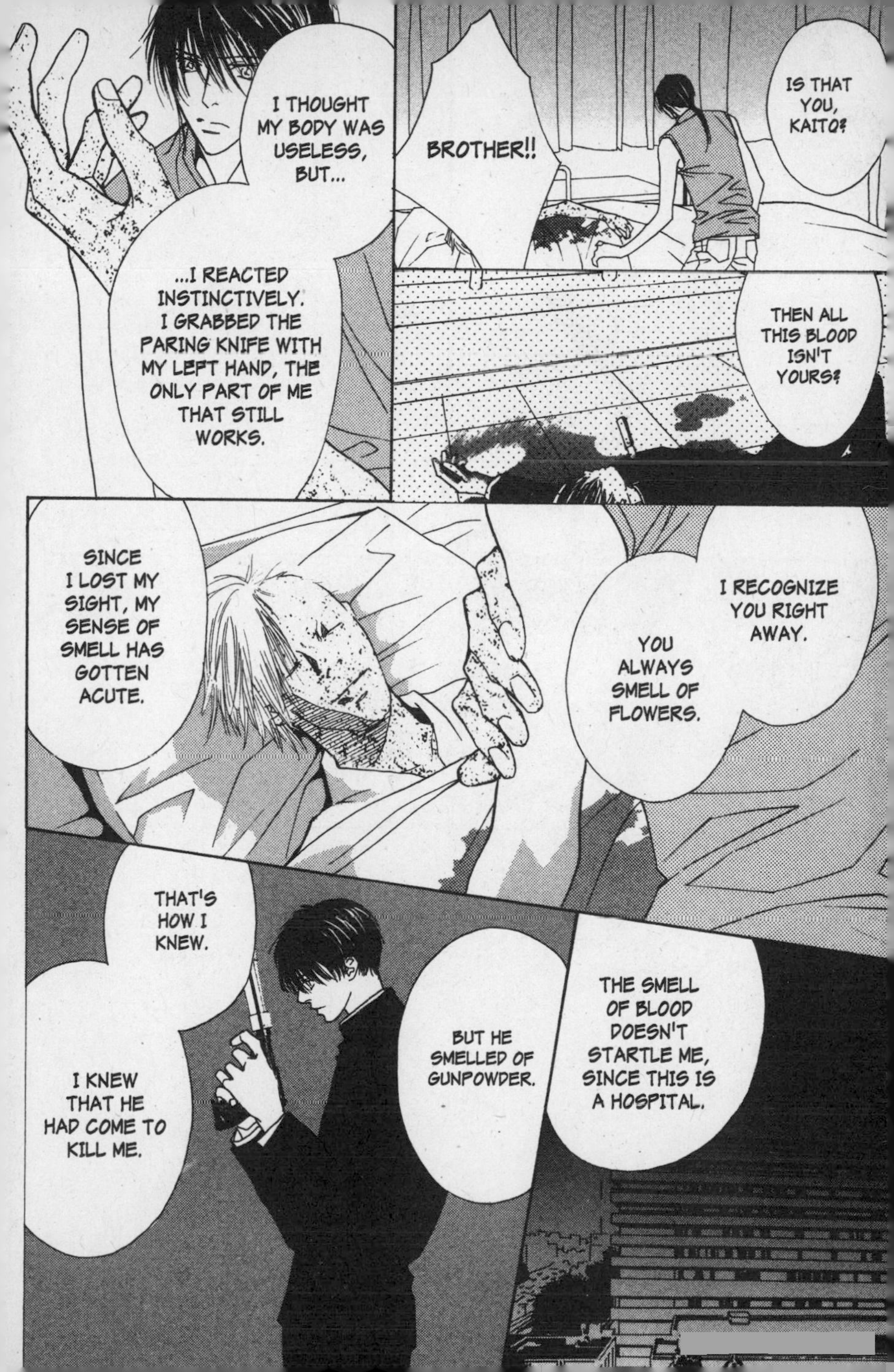
IS THAT YOU, KAITO?
BROTHER!!
THEN ALL THIS BLOOD ISN'T YOURS?
I THOUGHT MY BODY WAS USELESS, BUT...
...I REACTED INSTINCTIVELY. I GRABBED THE PARING KNIFE WITH MY LEFT HAND, THE ONLY PART OF ME THAT STILL WORKS.
I RECOGNIZE YOU RIGHT AWAY.
YOU ALWAYS SMELL OF FLOWERS.
SINCE I LOST MY SIGHT, MY SENSE OF SMELL HAS GOTTEN ACUTE.
THE SMELL OF BLOOD DOESN'T STARTLE ME, SINCE THIS IS A HOSPITAL.
BUT HE SMELLED OF GUNPOWDER.
THAT'S HOW I KNEW.
I KNEW THAT HE HAD COME TO KILL ME.

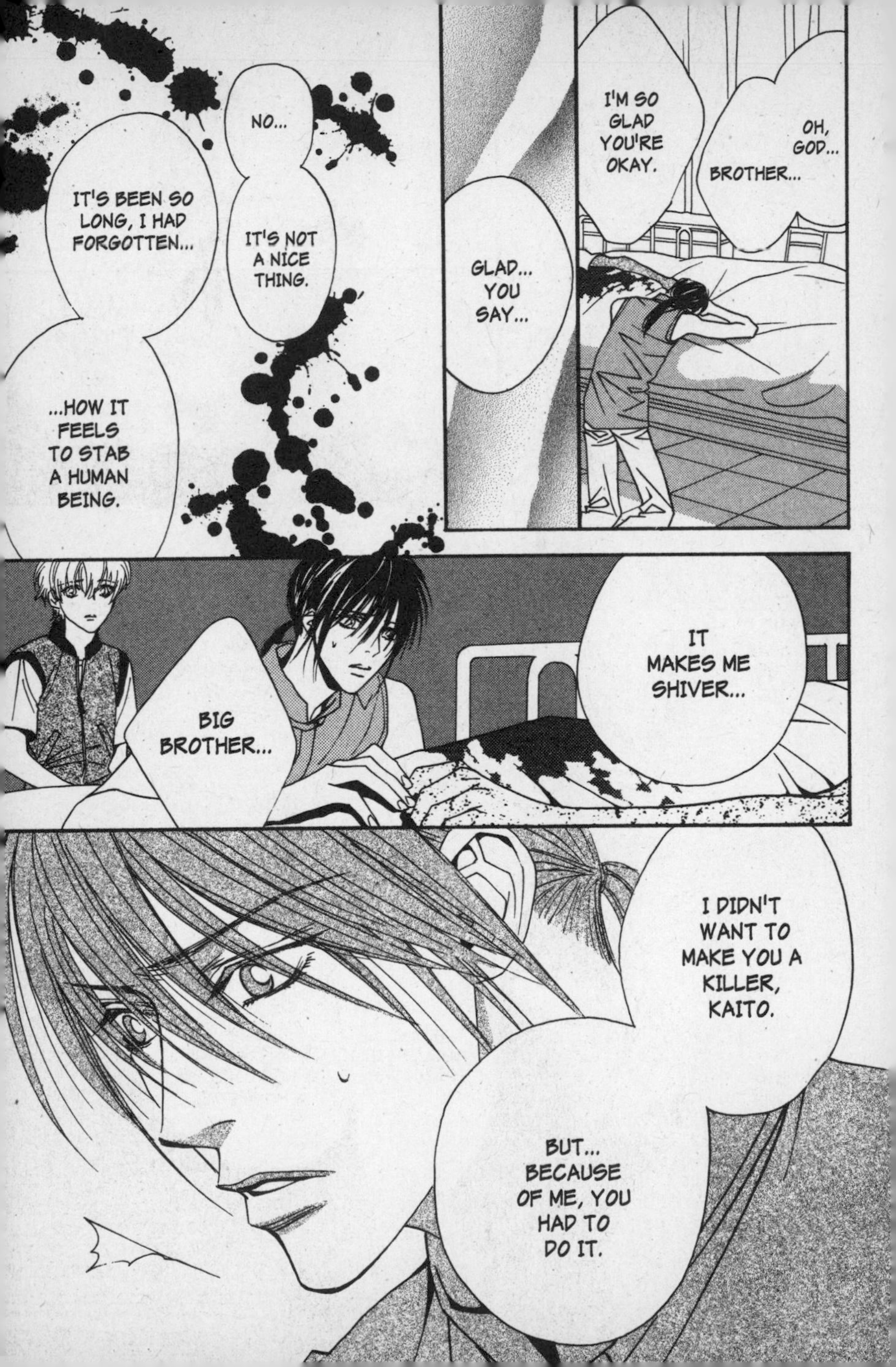
OH, GOD... BROTHER...
I'M SO GLAD YOU'RE OKAY.
GLAD... YOU SAY...
NO...
IT'S NOT A NICE THING.
IT'S BEEN SO LONG, I HAD FORGOTTEN...
...HOW IT FEELS TO STAB A HUMAN BEING.
IT MAKES ME SHIVER...
BIG BROTHER...
I DIDN'T WANT TO MAKE YOU A KILLER, KAITO.
BUT... BECAUSE OF ME, YOU HAD TO DO IT.

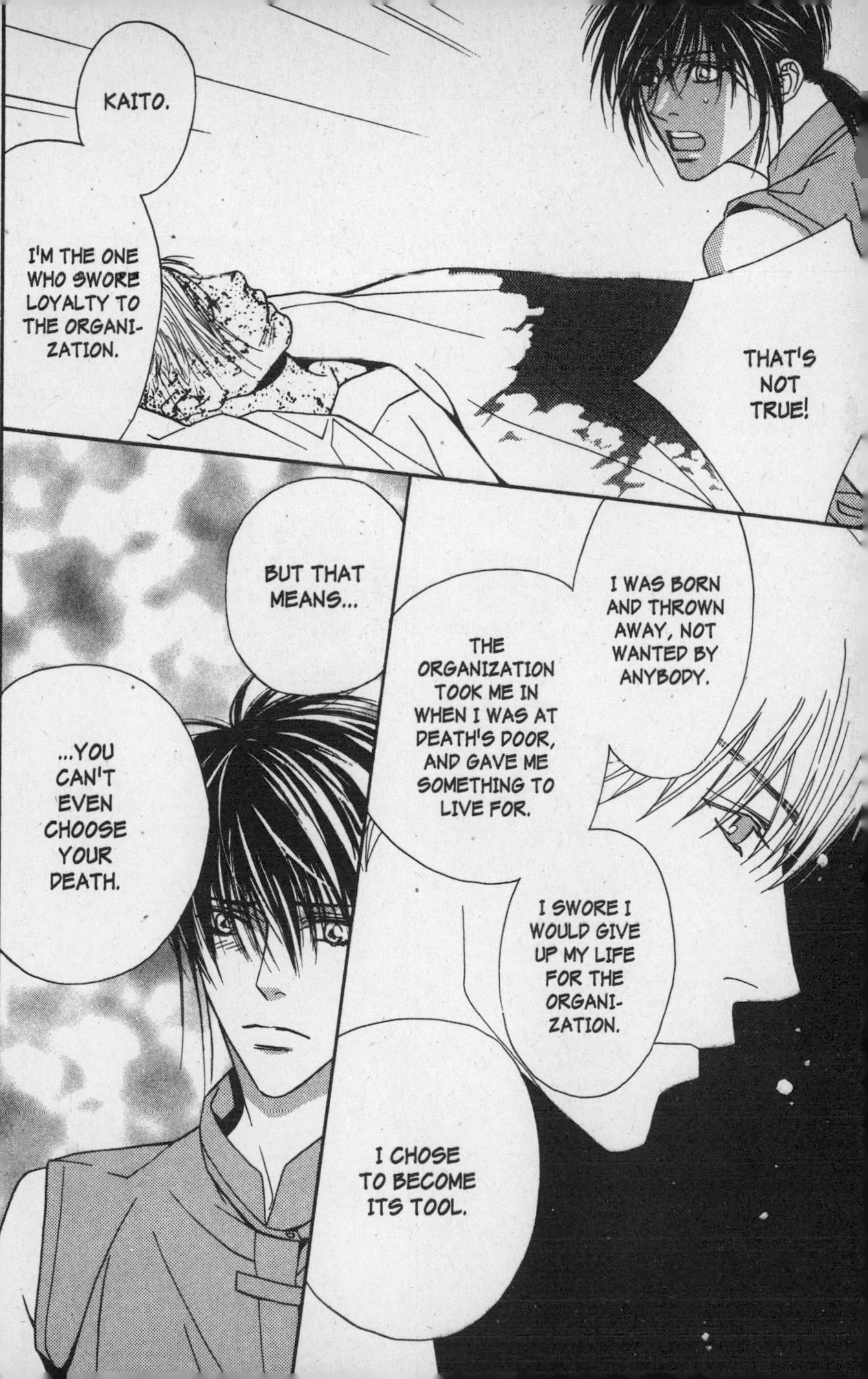
KAITO.
I'M THE ONE WHO SWORE LOYALTY TO THE ORGANI-ZATION.
THAT'S NOT TRUE!
I WAS BORN AND THROWN AWAY, NOT WANTED BY ANYBODY.
THE ORGANIZATION TOOK ME IN WHEN I WAS AT DEATH'S DOOR, AND GAVE ME SOMETHING TO LIVE FOR.
I SWORE I WOULD GIVE UP MY LIFE FOR THE ORGANI-ZATION.
I CHOSE TO BECOME ITS TOOL.
BUT THAT MEANS...
...YOU CAN'T EVEN CHOOSE YOUR DEATH.

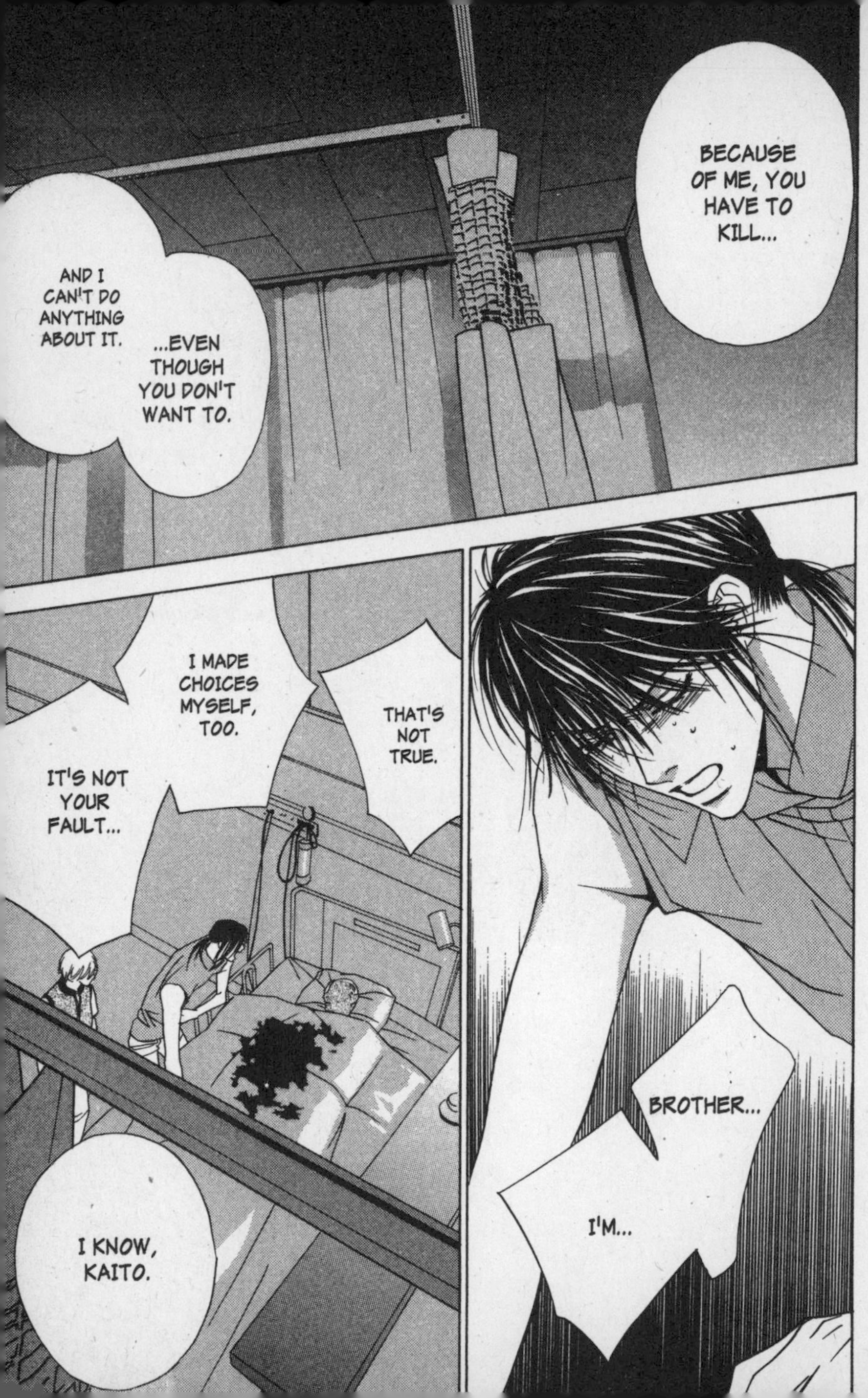
BECAUSE OF ME, YOU HAVE TO KILL...
...EVEN THOUGH YOU DON'T WANT TO.
AND I CAN'T DO ANYTHING ABOUT IT.
BROTHER...
I'M...
THAT'S NOT TRUE.
I MADE CHOICES MYSELF, TOO.
IT'S NOT YOUR FAULT...
I KNOW, KAITO.

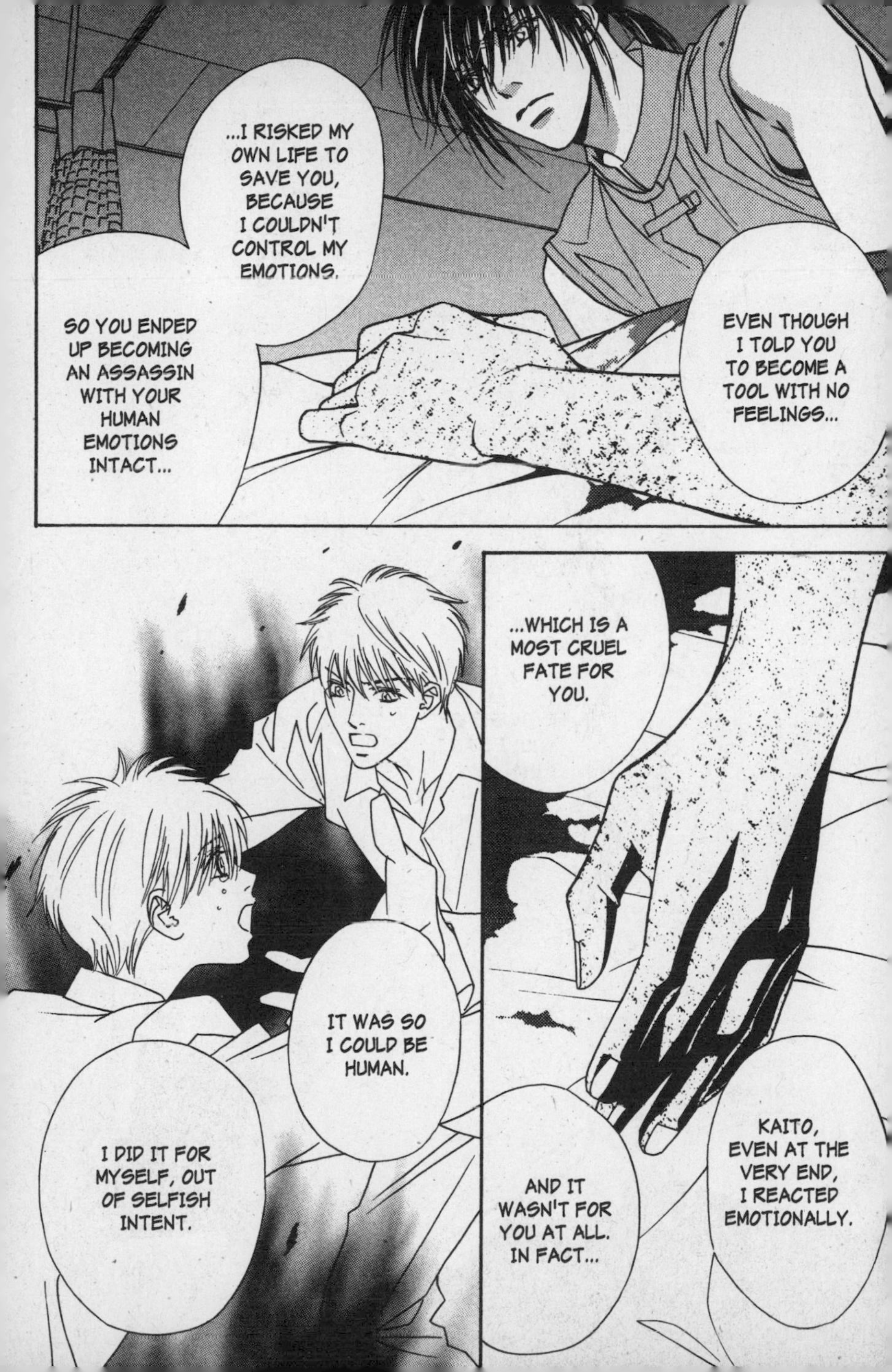
...I RISKED MY OWN LIFE TO SAVE YOU, BECAUSE I COULDN'T CONTROL MY EMOTIONS.
EVEN THOUGH I TOLD YOU TO BECOME A TOOL WITH NO FEELINGS...
SO YOU ENDED UP BECOMING AN ASSASSIN WITH YOUR HUMAN EMOTIONS INTACT...
...WHICH IS A MOST CRUEL FATE FOR YOU.
KAITO, EVEN AT THE VERY END, I REACTED EMOTIONALLY.
AND IT WASN'T FOR YOU AT ALL. IN FACT...
IT WAS SO I COULD BE HUMAN.
I DID IT FOR MYSELF, OUT OF SELFISH INTENT.

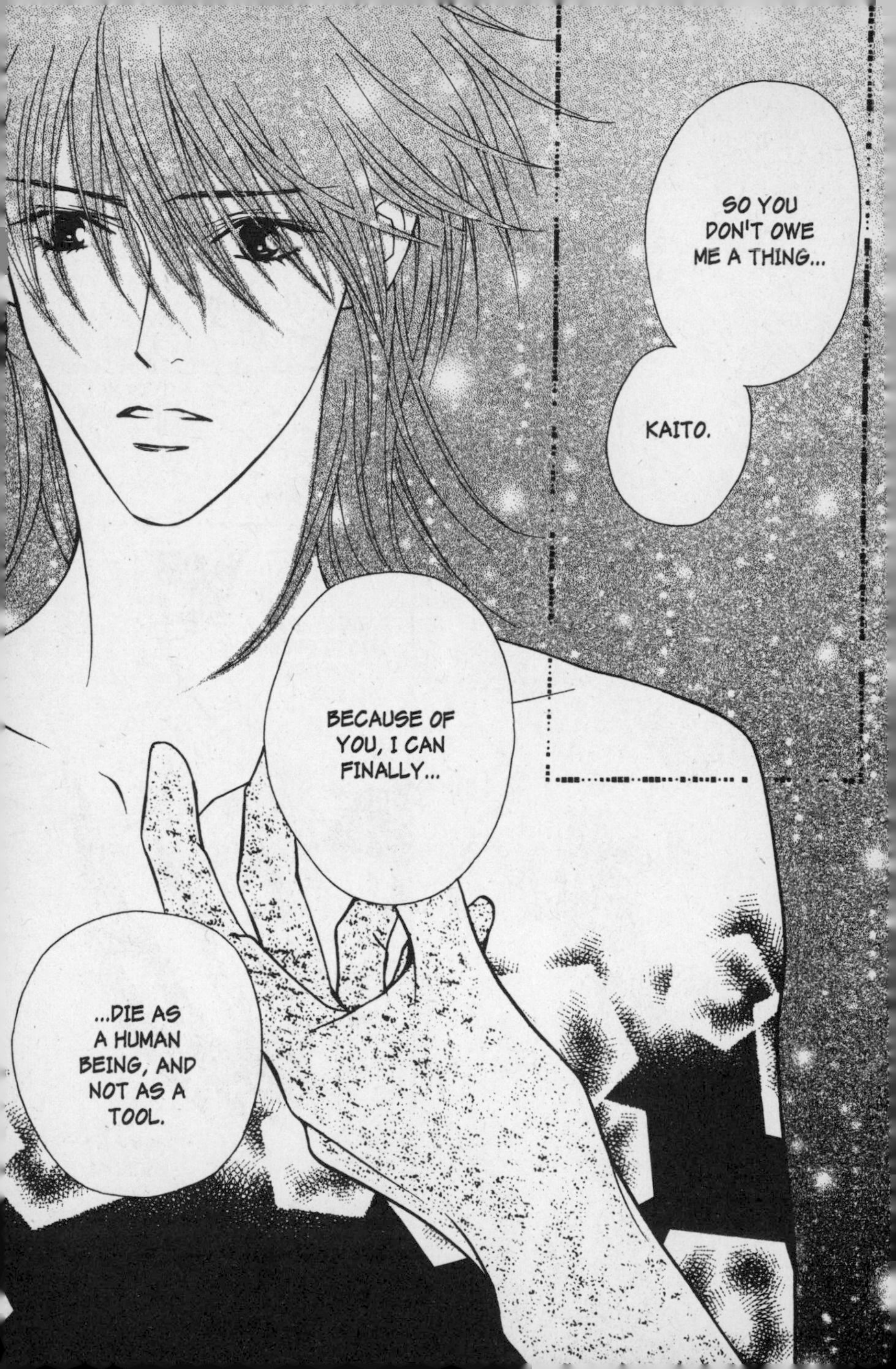
SO YOU DON'T OWE ME A THING...
KAITO.
BECAUSE OF YOU, I CAN FINALLY...
...DIE AS A HUMAN BEING, AND NOT AS A TOOL.

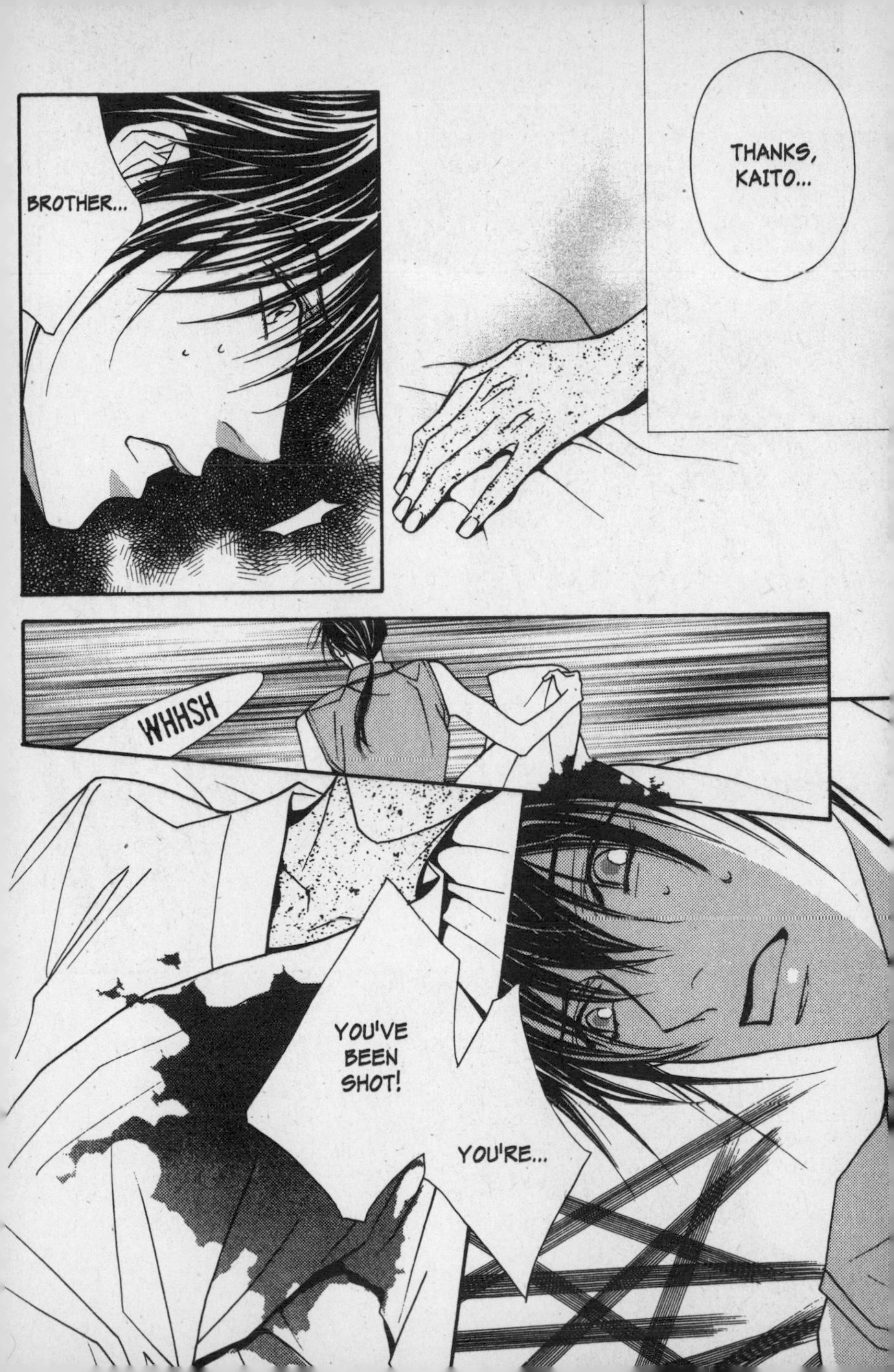
THANKS, KAITO...
BROTHER...
WHHSH
YOU'VE BEEN SHOT!
YOU'RE...

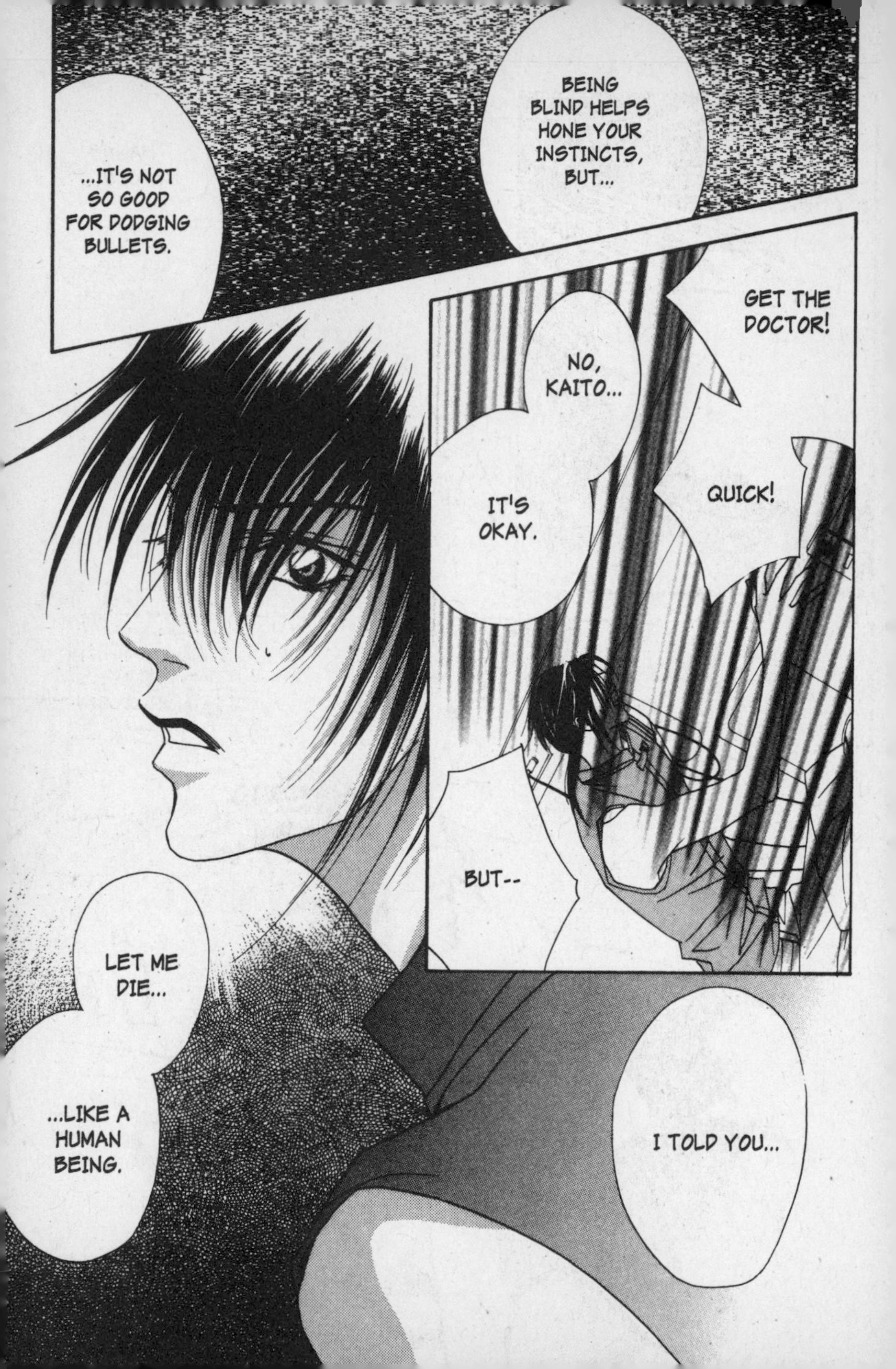
BEING BLIND HELPS HONE YOUR INSTINCTS, BUT...
...IT'S NOT SO GOOD FOR DODGING BULLETS.
GET THE DOCTOR!
NO, KAITO...
QUICK!
IT'S OKAY.
BUT--
I TOLD YOU...
LET ME DIE...
...LIKE A HUMAN BEING.

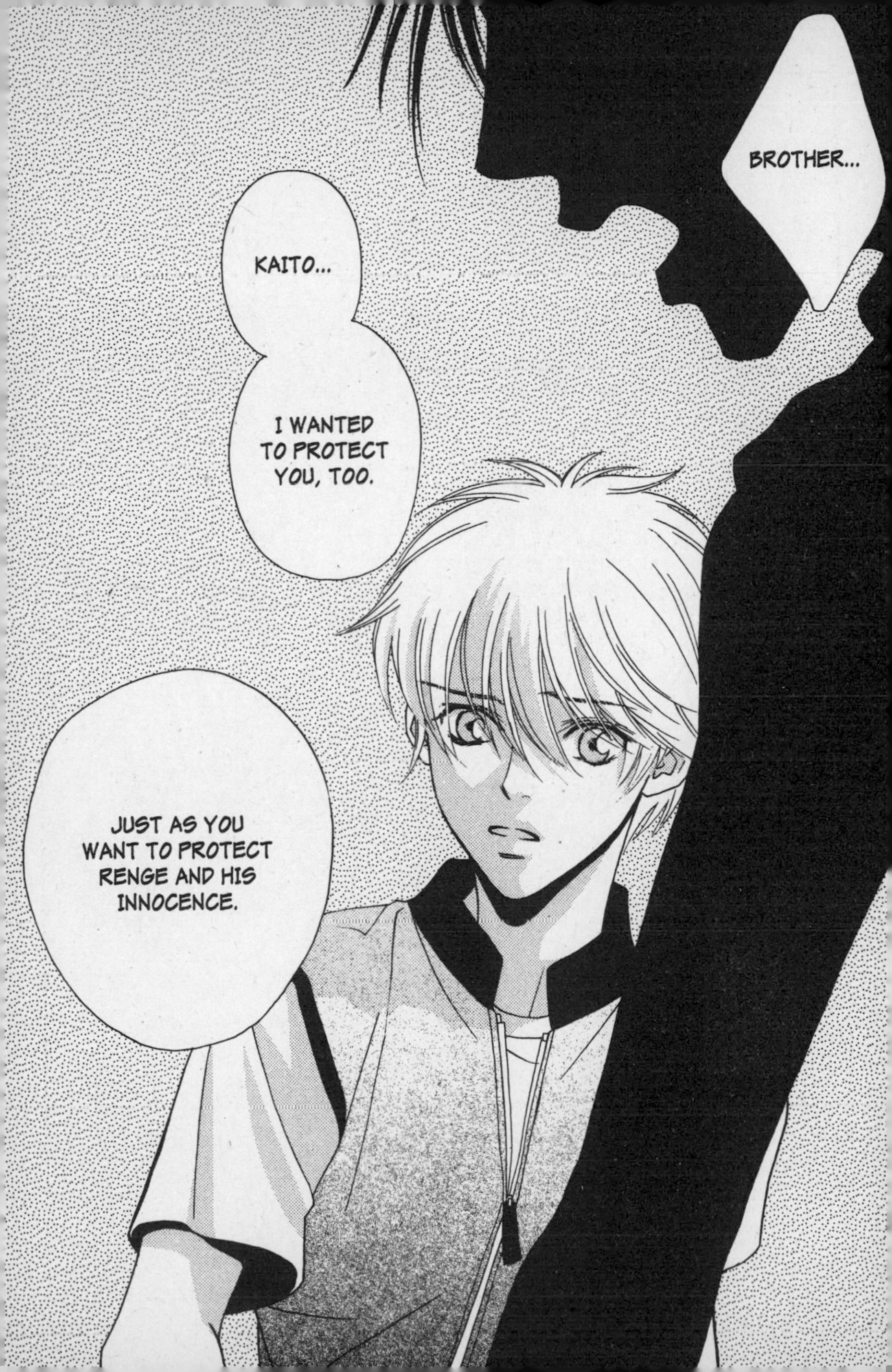
BROTHER...
KAITO...
I WANTED TO PROTECT YOU, TOO.
JUST AS YOU WANT TO PROTECT RENGE AND HIS INNOCENCE.

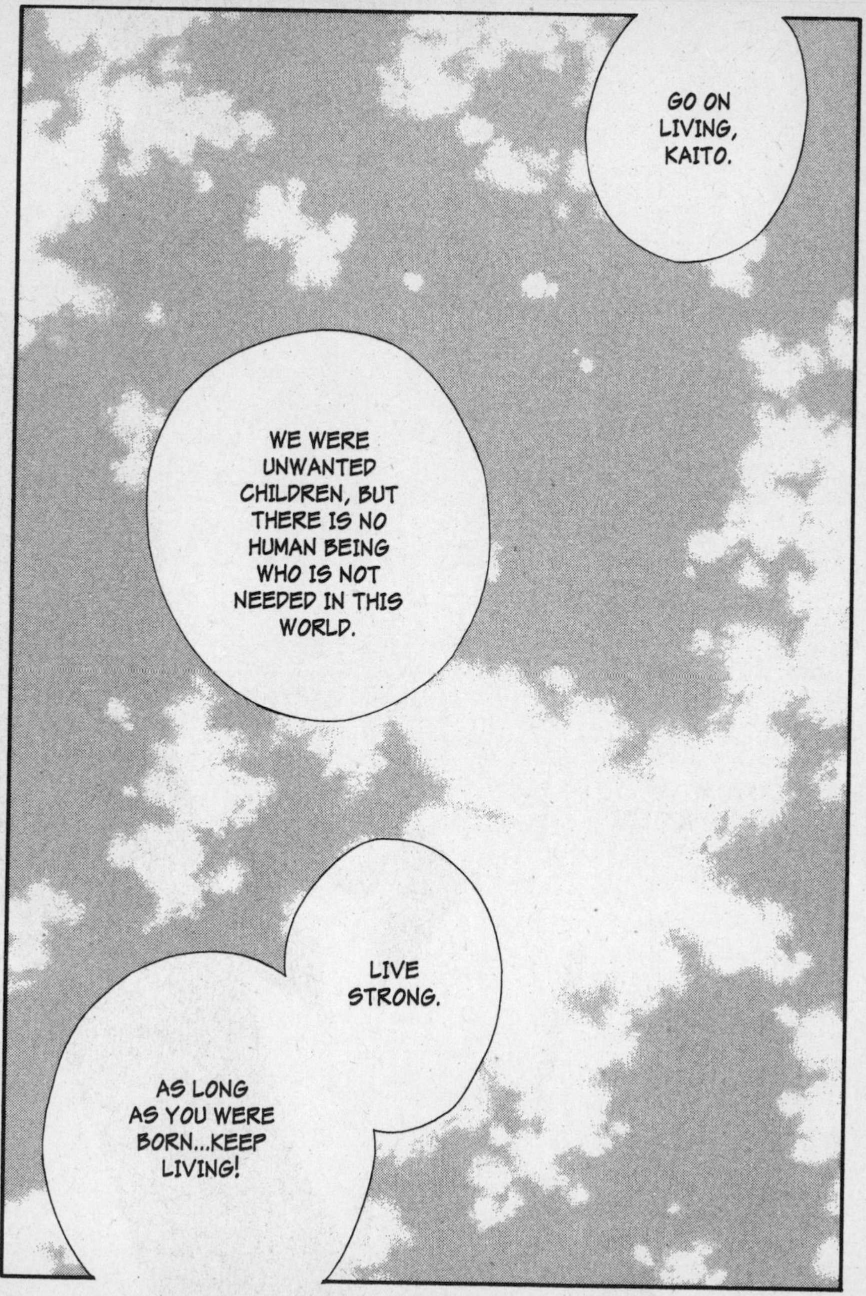
GO ON LIVING, KAITO.
WE WERE UNWANTED CHILDREN, BUT THERE IS NO HUMAN BEING WHO IS NOT NEEDED IN THIS WORLD.
LIVE STRONG.
AS LONG AS YOU WERE BORN...KEEP LIVING!

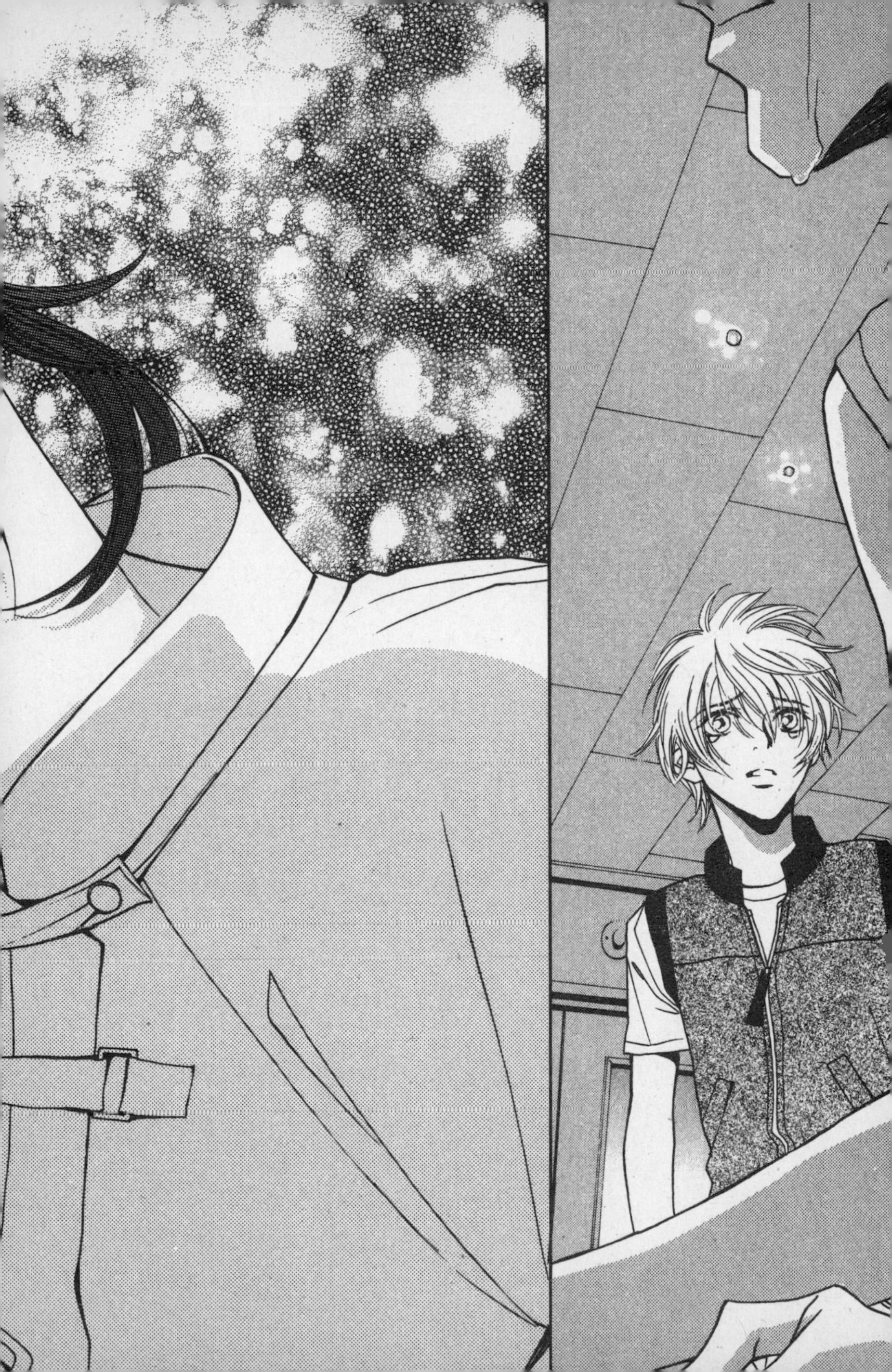

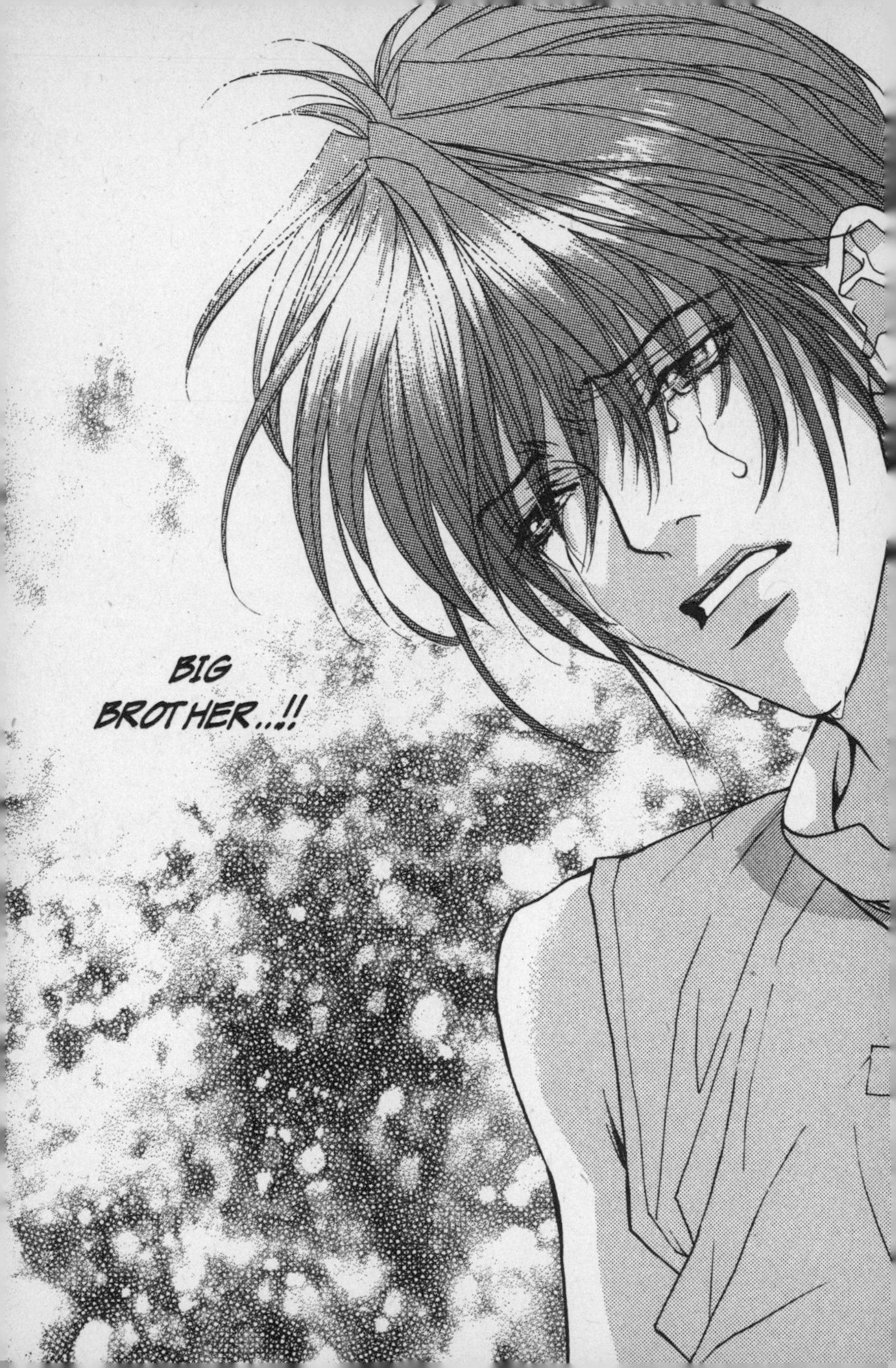
BIG BROTHER...!!

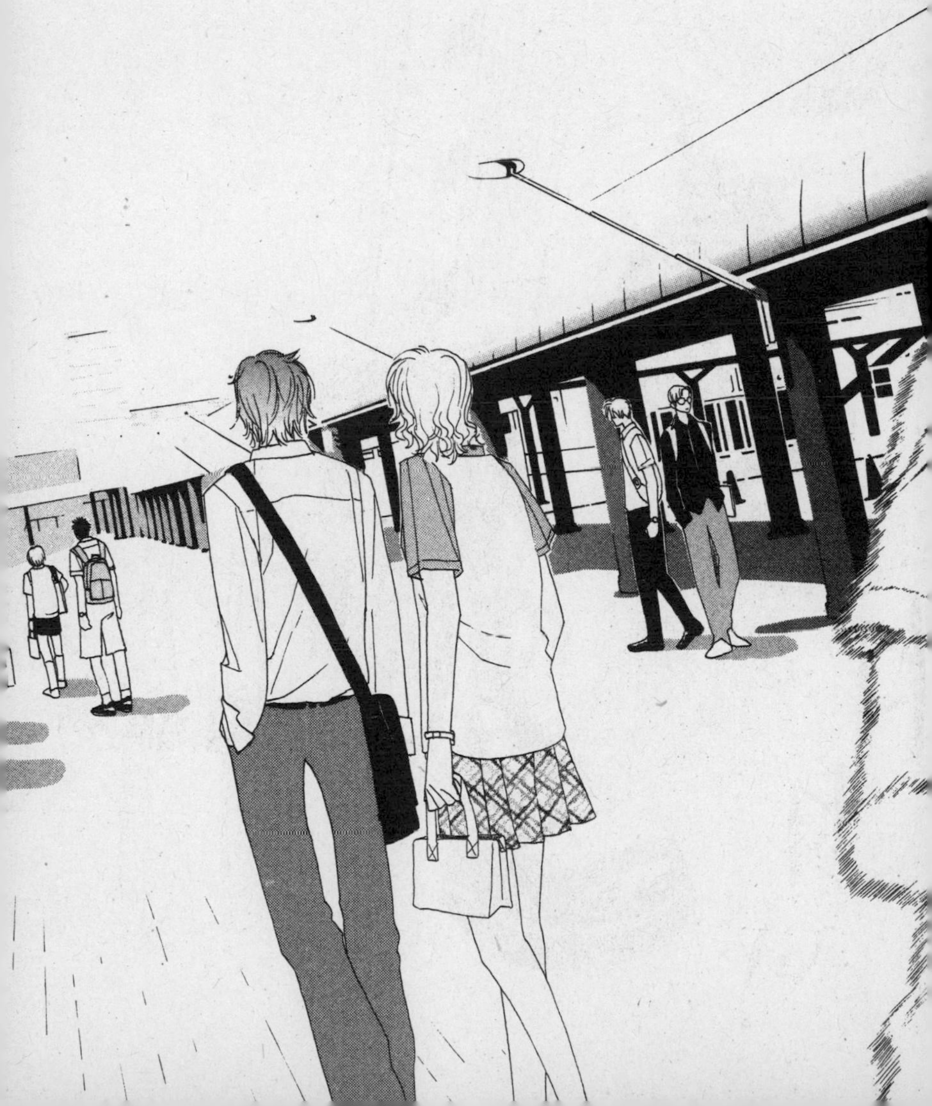

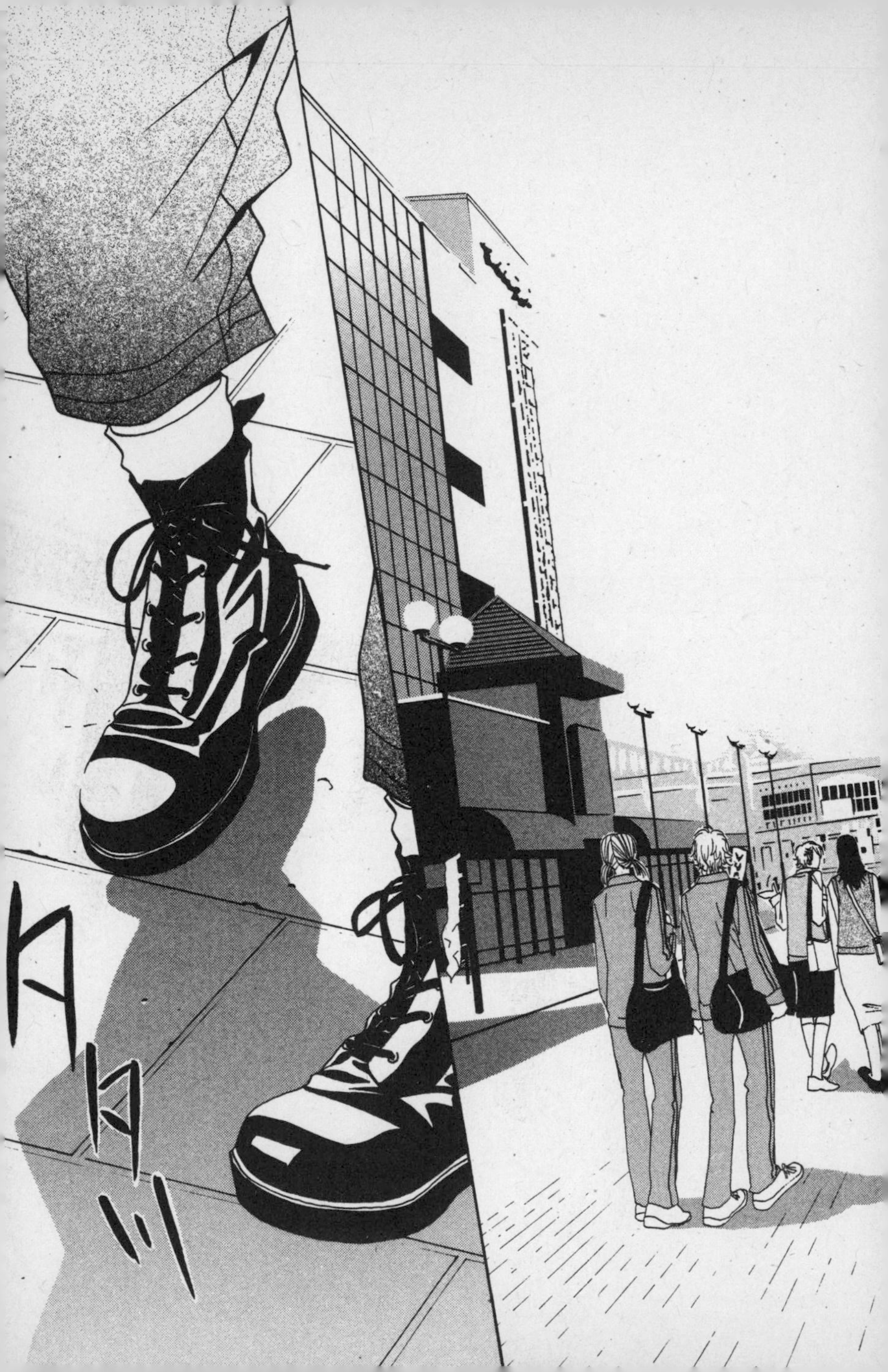
カカッ

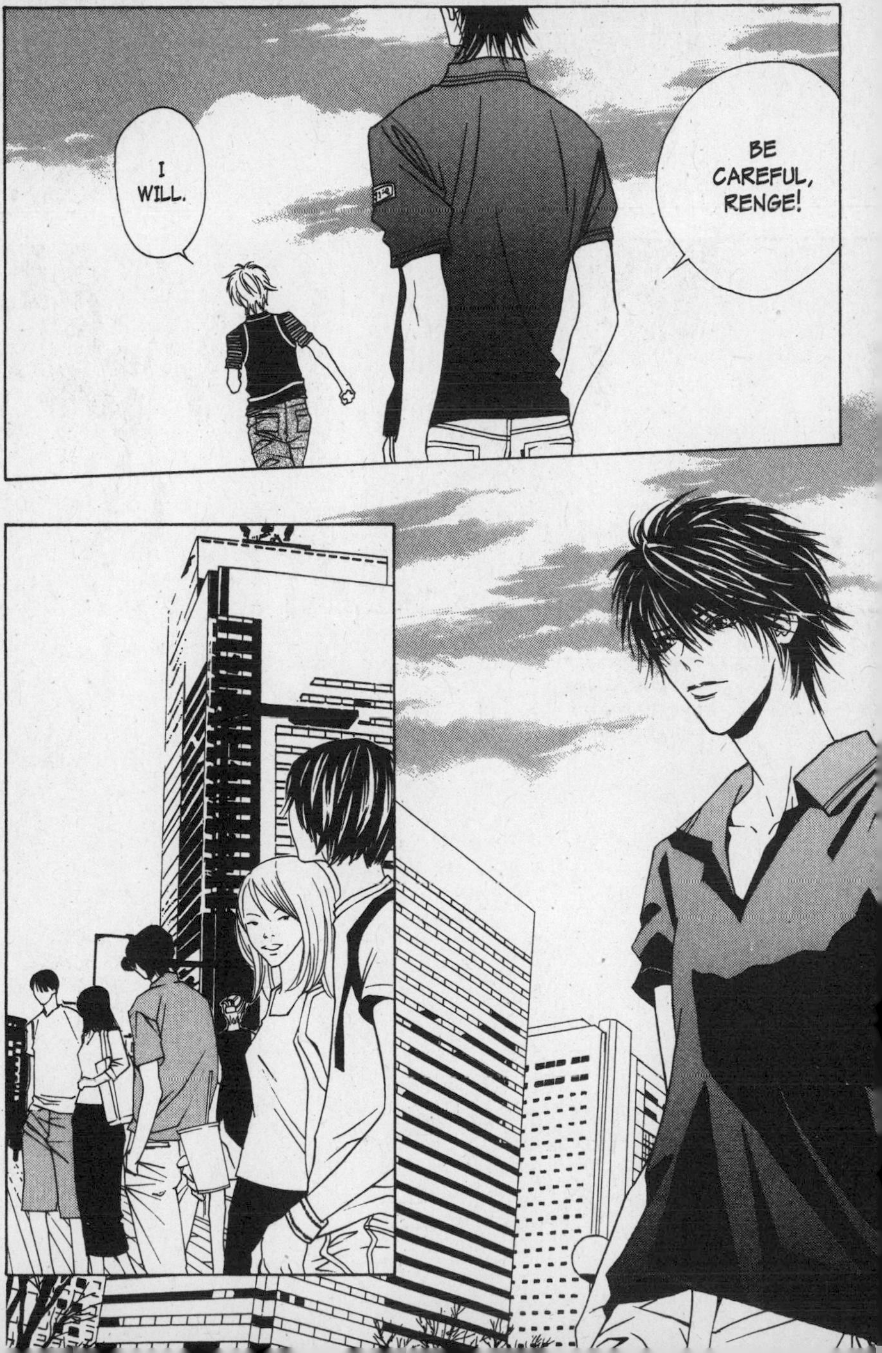
BE CAREFUL, RENGE!
I WILL.

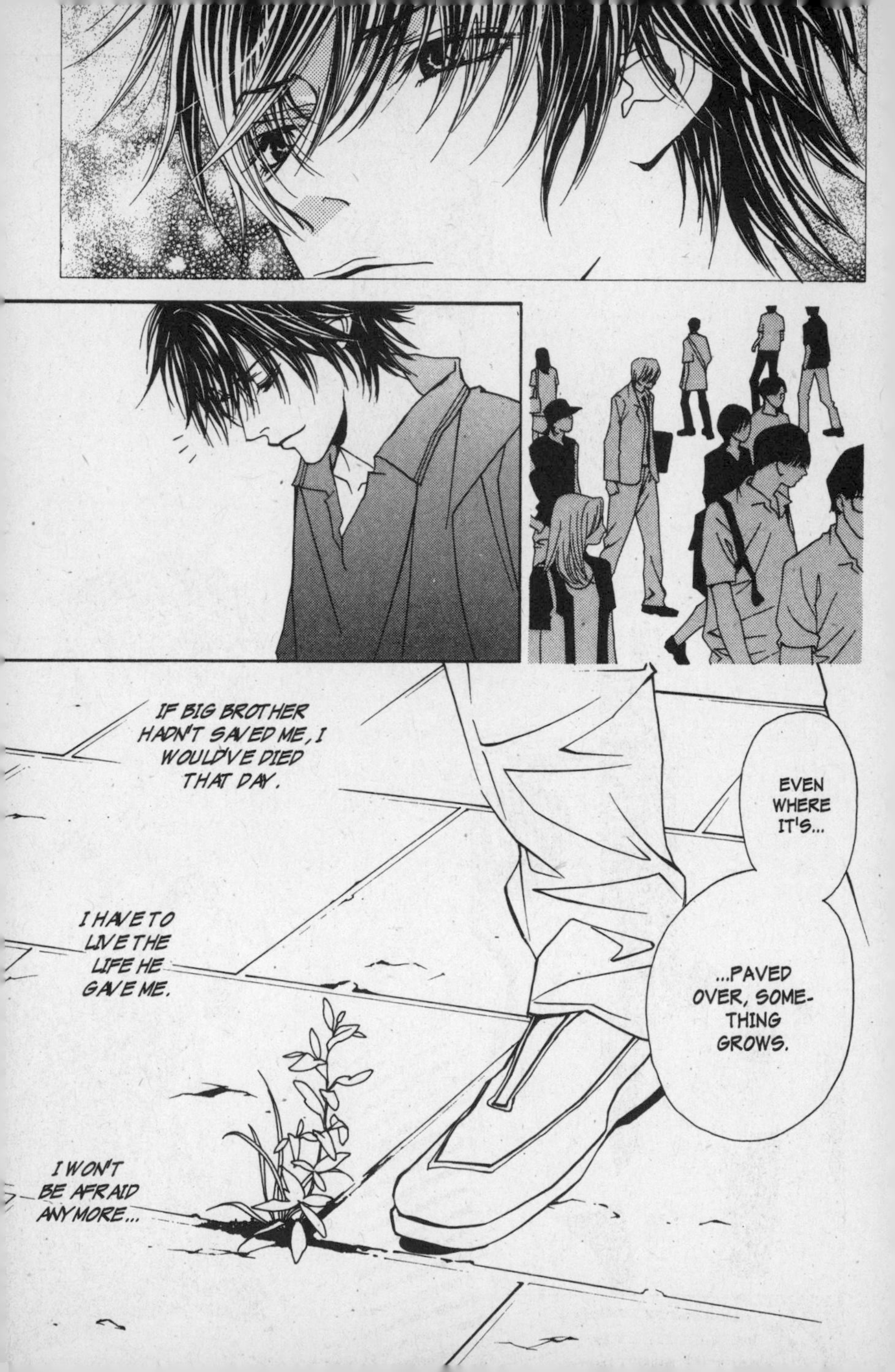
EVEN WHERE IT'S...
...PAVED OVER, SOME-THING GROWS.
IF BIG BROTHER HADN'T SAVED ME, I WOULD'VE DIED THAT DAY.
I HAVE TO LIVE THE LIFE HE GAVE ME.
I WON'T BE AFRAID ANYMORE...

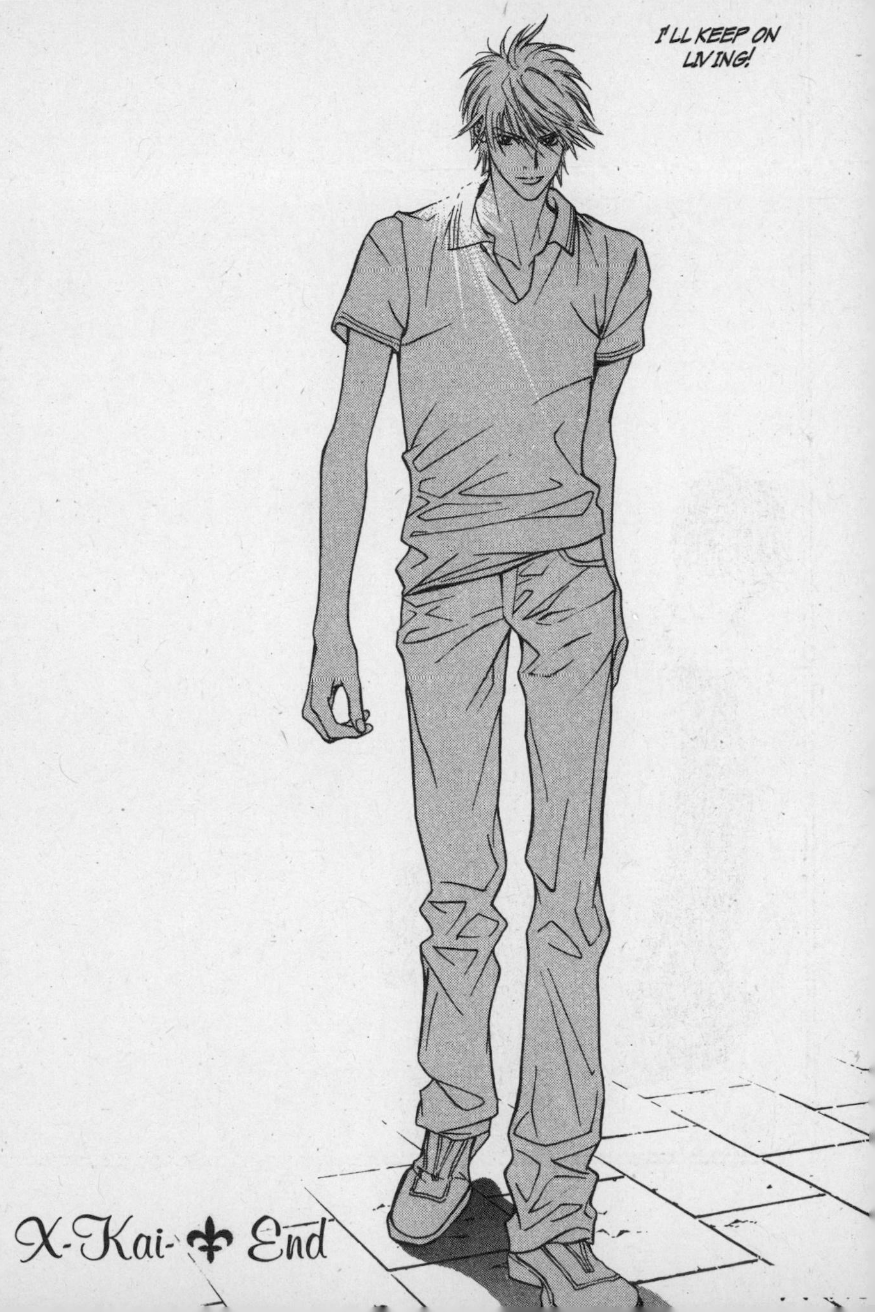
I'LL KEEP ON LIVING!
X-Kai- End

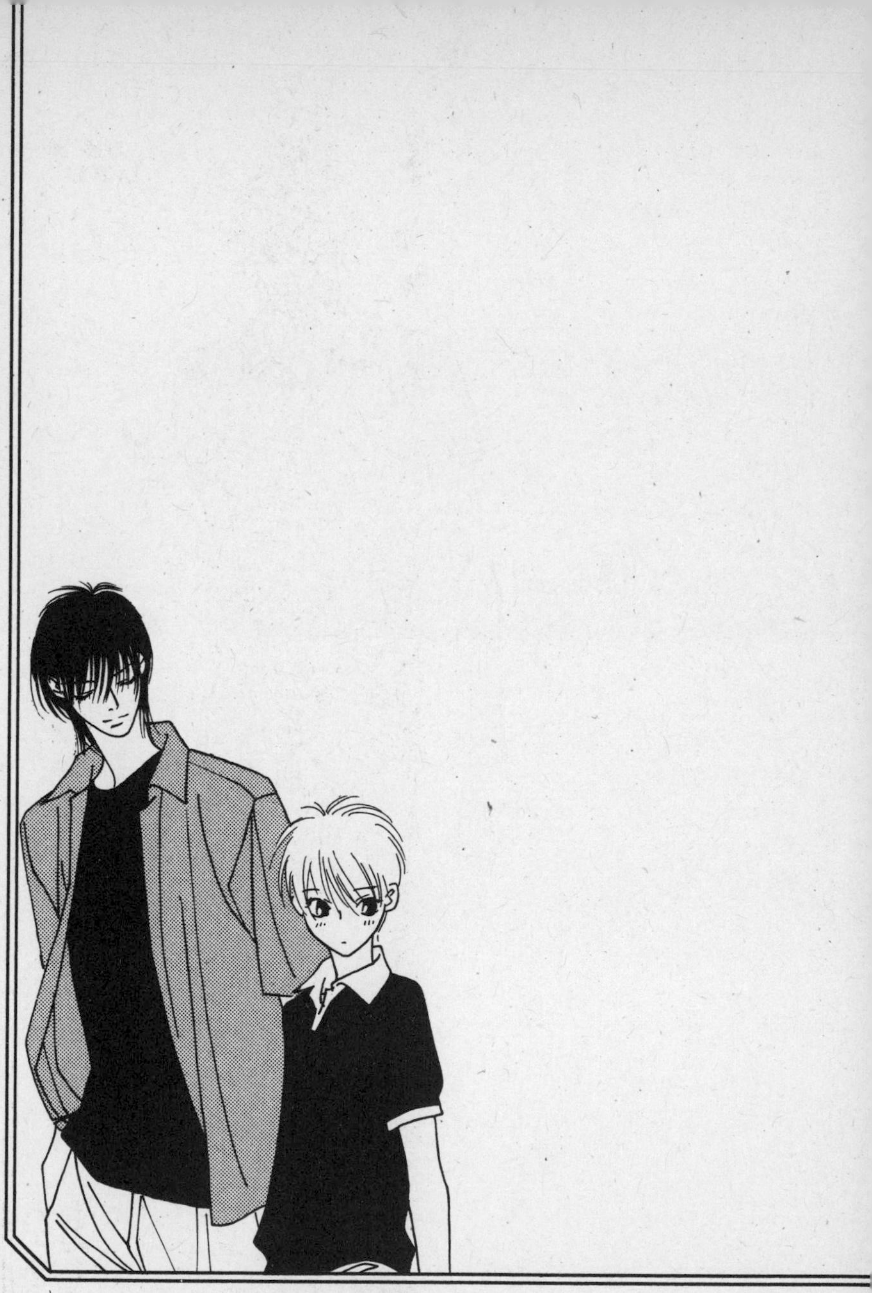

Postscript

Hello. Thank you for picking up this book. Since the story is rather bloody, I decided to introduce young Renge to lighten things up a little, and he ended up becoming the center of the story. Children...I love them! This story ends here, but I would have liked to have shown a few more warm exchanges between Kai and Renge.

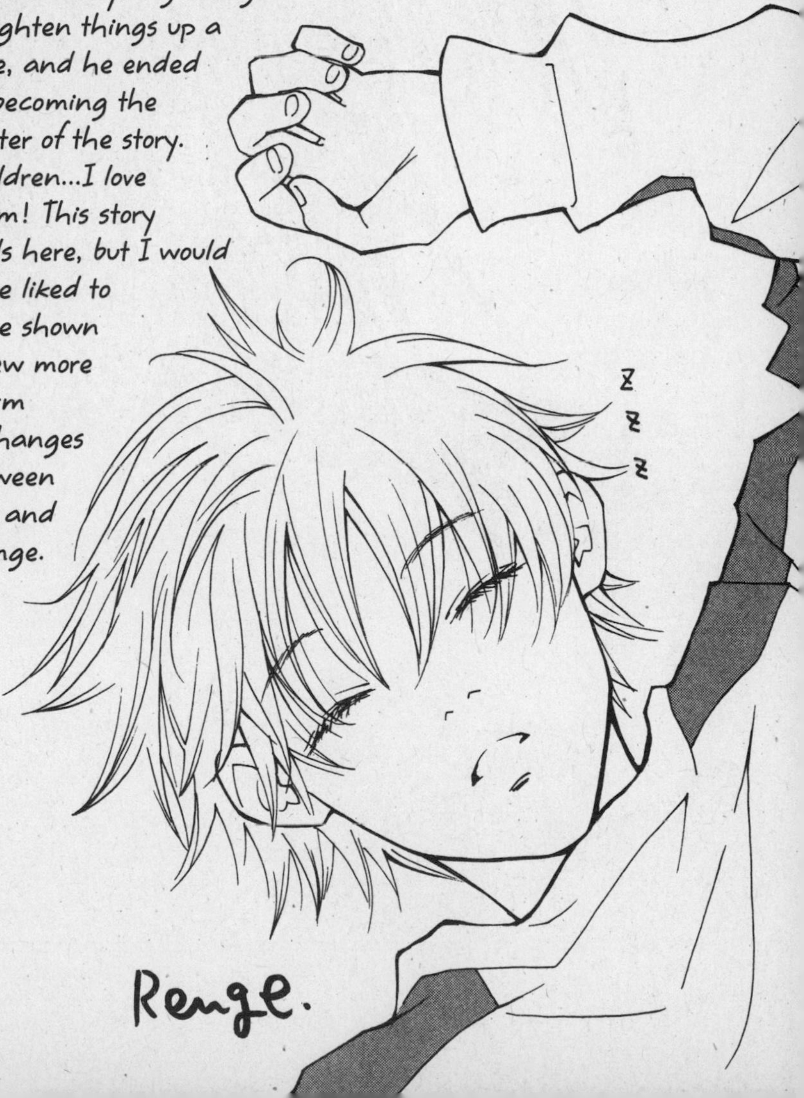
Z Z Z
Renge.

kaito.

"He's a bit nerdy," one fan wrote. But when he takes his glasses off, he's definitely eye candy! It's required in girl manga. (Hee hee!)

Taking today's social situation into consideration, I drew him to look older, but actually he's in his teens! He's an old-looking guy! Is it because he's been through a lot?

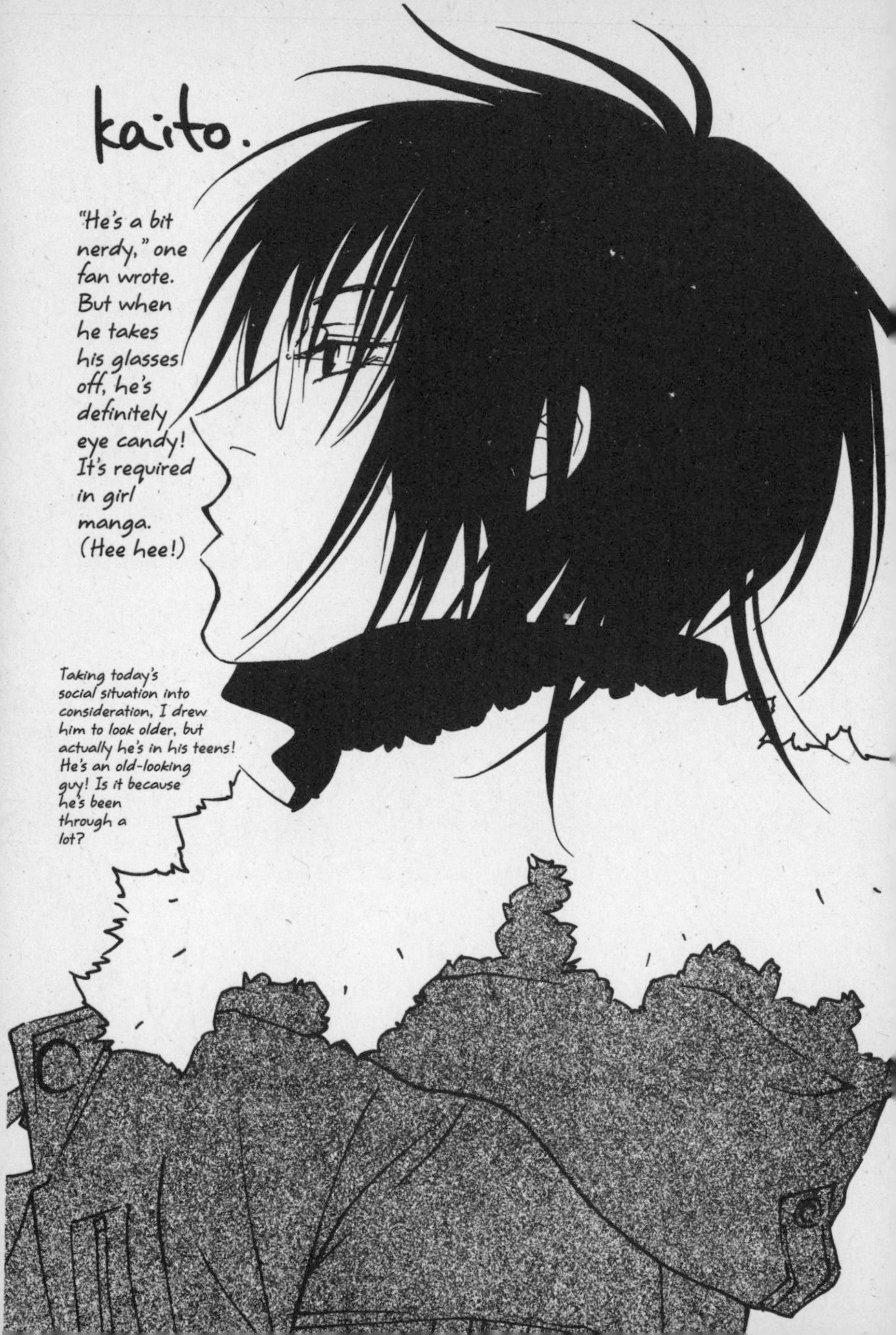

Editor

Nobumi Nohara

Thank you for hanging in there all the way to the end. Hope to see you again soon somewhere!

staff

Atsuko   Nishihara

Keiko   Takeda

Hisae   Fujii

Miki   Nishioka

Misaki   Iwamoto

Yuki   Ōmichi

and   Asami Tojo.

Postscript ✤ End

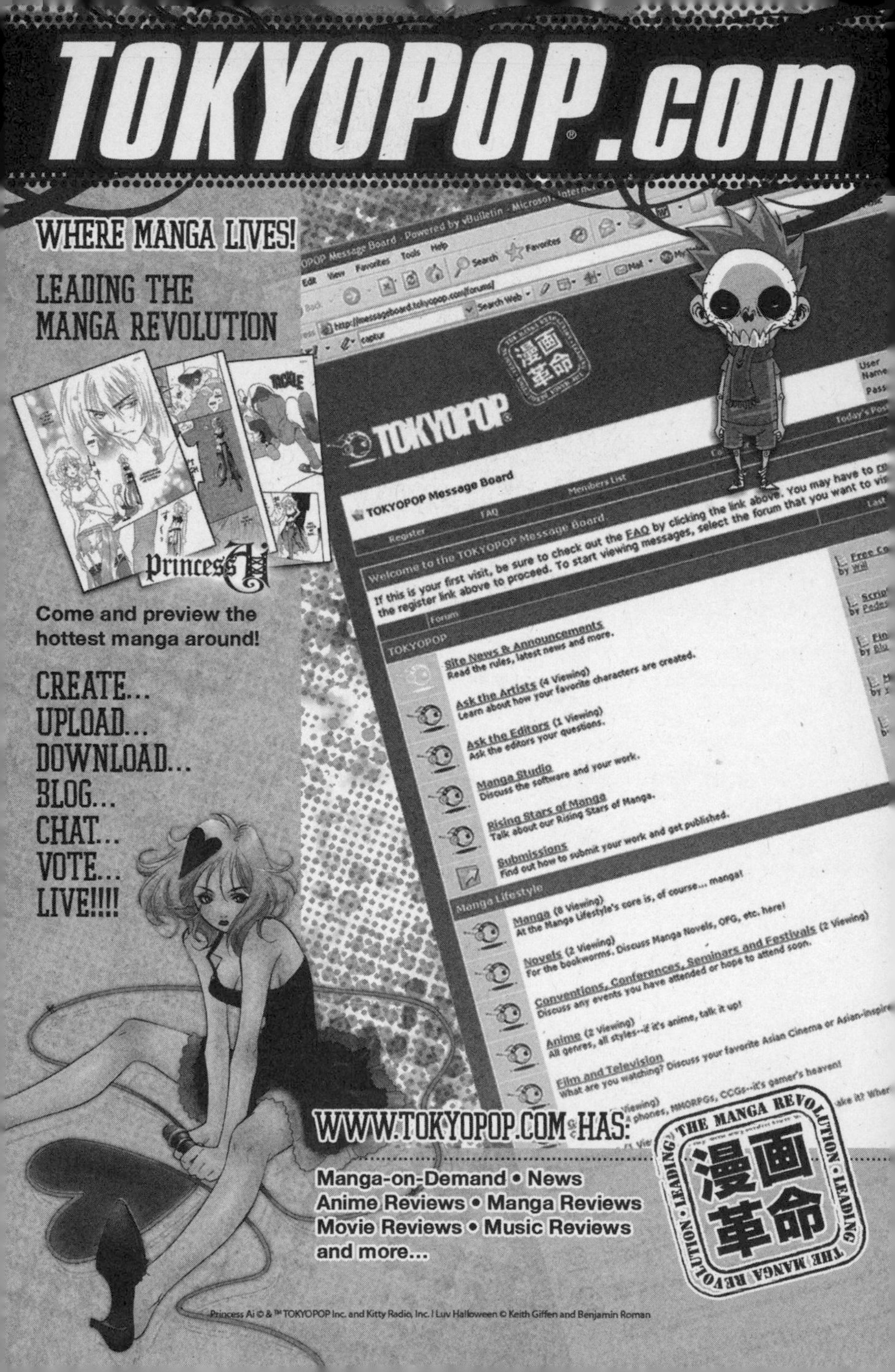

TOKYOPOP®.com
WHERE MANGA LIVES!
LEADING THE MANGA REVOLUTION
Princess Ai
Come and preview the hottest manga around!
CREATE... UPLOAD... DOWNLOAD... BLOG... CHAT... VOTE... LIVE!!!!
TOKYOPOP Message Board
Welcome to the TOKYOPOP Message Board
If this is your first visit, be sure to check out the FAQ by clicking the link above. You may have to register before you can post: click the register link above to proceed. To start viewing messages, select the forum that you want to visit
Site News & Announcements
Read the rules, latest news and more.
Ask the Artists (4 Viewing)
Learn about how your favorite characters are created.
Ask the Editors (1 Viewing)
Ask the editors your questions.
Manga Studio
Discuss the software and your work.
Rising Stars of Manga
Talk about our Rising Stars of Manga.
Submissions
Find out how to submit your work and get published.
Manga Lifestyle
Manga (8 Viewing)
At the Manga Lifestyle's core is, of course... manga!
Novels (2 Viewing)
For the bookworms. Discuss Manga Novels, OFG, etc. here!
Conventions, Conferences, Seminars and Festivals (2 Viewing)
Discuss any events you have attended or hope to attend soon.
Anime (2 Viewing)
All genres, all styles--if it's anime, talk it up!
Film and Television
What are you watching? Discuss your favorite Asian Cinema or Asian-inspired
WWW.TOKYOPOP.COM HAS:
Manga-on-Demand • News
Anime Reviews • Manga Reviews
Movie Reviews • Music Reviews
and more...
THE MANGA REVOLUTION • LEADING 漫画革命
Princess Ai © & ™ TOKYOPOP Inc. and Kitty Radio, Inc. I Luv Halloween © Keith Giffen and Benjamin Roman

Jim Henson's

RETURN TO LABYRINTH™

Jim Henson's classic continues...

The Goblin King has kept a watchful eye on Toby: His minions secretly guiding and protecting the child... Legions of goblins working behind the scenes to ensure that Toby has whatever his heart desires... Preparing him for the day when he will return to the Labyrinth and take his rightful place beside Jareth as the heir to the Goblin Kingdom.

That day has come...

...but no one has told Toby.

By Chris Lie
and Jake T. Forbes

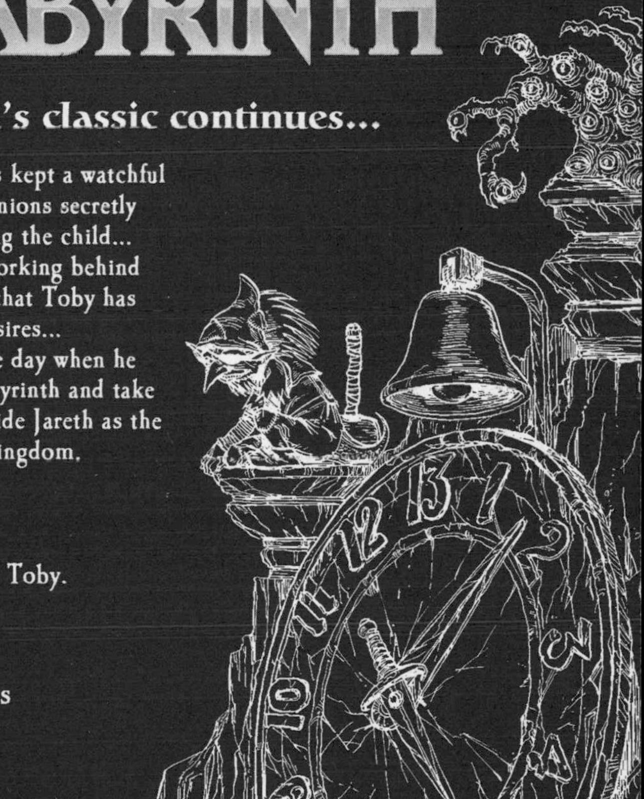

FANTASY

TEEN AGE 13+

FOR MORE INFORMATION VISIT: WWW.TOKYOPOP.COM

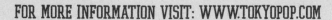

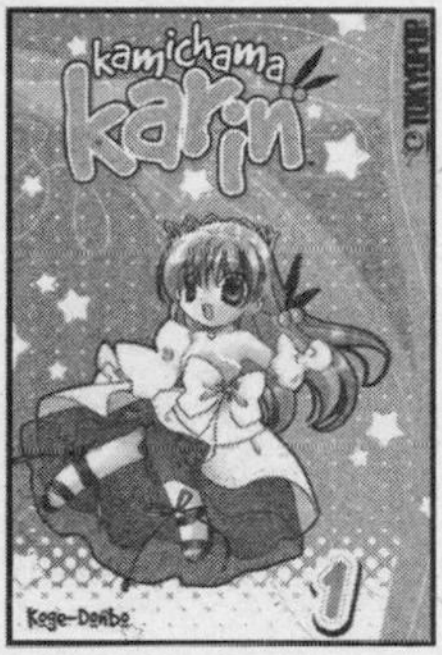
kamichama
karin
TOKYOPOP
1
Koge-Donbo

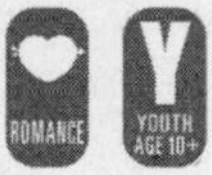
ROMANCE
Y
YOUTH AGE 10+

KAMICHAMA KARIN

BY KOGE-DONBO

This one was a surprise. I mean, I knew Koge-Donbo drew insanely cute characters, but I had no idea a magical girl story could be so darn clever. *Kamichama Karin* manages to lampoon everything about the genre, from plushie-like mascots to character archetypes to weapons that appear from the blue! And you gotta love Karin, the airheaded heroine who takes guff from no one and screams "I AM GOD!" as her battle cry. In short, if you are looking for a shiny new manga with a knack for hilarity and a penchant for accessories, I say look no further.

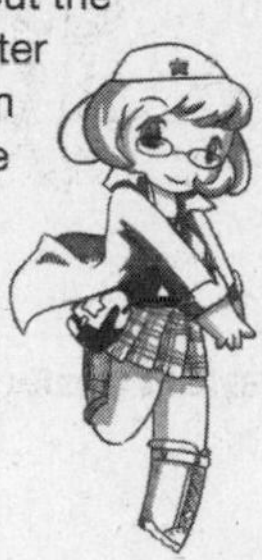

~Carol Fox, Editor

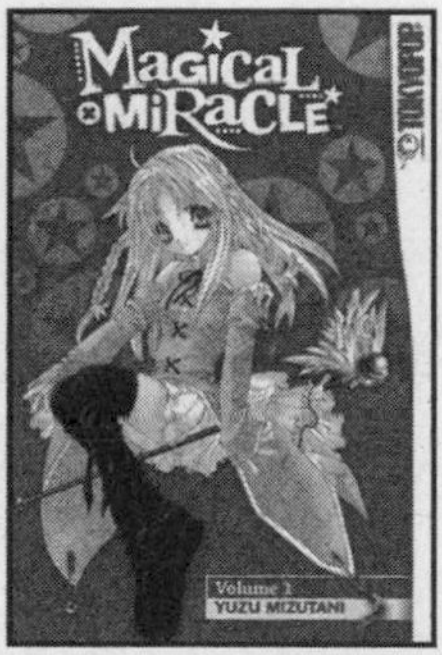
Magical
× Miracle
TOKYOPOP
Volume 1
YUZU MIZUTANI

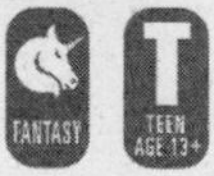
FANTASY
T
TEEN AGE 13+

MAGICAL X MIRACLE

BY YUZU MIZUTANI

Magical X Miracle is a quirky—yet uplifting—tale of gender-bending mistaken identity! When a young girl must masquerade as a great wizard, she not only finds the strength to save an entire kingdom...but, ironically, she just might just find herself, too. Yuzu Mizutani's art is remarkably adorable, but it also has a dark, sophisticated edge.

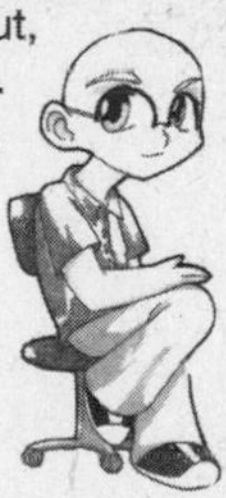

~Paul Morrissey, Editor

STOP!

This is the back of the book.
You wouldn't want to spoil a great ending!

This book is printed "manga-style," in the authentic Japanese right-to-left format. Since none of the artwork has been flipped or altered, readers get to experience the story just as the creator intended. You've been asking for it, so TOKYOPOP® delivered: authentic, hot-off-the-press, and far more fun!

DIRECTIONS

If this is your first time reading manga-style, here's a quick guide to help you understand how it works.

It's easy... just start in the top right panel and follow the numbers. Have fun, and look for more 100% authentic manga from TOKYOPOP®!

CONTENTS

X -Kai-

Volume 2

by
Asami Tohjoh

TOKYOPOP®

HAMBURG // LONDON // LOS ANGELES // TOKYO